PRAISE FOR *EMBODIED PERFORMANCE*

"Sarah Agnew's work is truly interdisciplinary. It engages with, and effectively introduces, traditional biblical scholarship on the Epistle to the Romans, narrative criticism of the Bible, and theatre studies on the relationship between the audience, the performer, and the text. The book weaves these themes, and many others, into a highly engaging and personal story of discovery of importance to anyone who takes the Bible seriously and wants to understand it better. Her perspective as performer-interpreter, and her development of 'Embodied Performance Analysis,' offers significant insights for biblical scholars and church people alike."

—*Alison Jack*, Senior Lecturer in Bible and Literature, Assistant Principal of New College, University of Edinburgh

"Embodiment is the key to this bold new approach to analyzing biblical texts. Relevant theoretical foundations for Embodied Performance Analysis are fleshed out by video recordings of a live performance interpretation of Paul's Letter to the Romans. Critical reflection elicits the embrace that is so central to the letter and allows it to speak afresh in our time. Sarah Agnew offers us a method that will transform both biblical scholarship and congregational audiences."

—*Jeanette Mathews*, author of *Performing Habakkuk* and *Prophets as Performers*

"Stop and think: when we interpret the body of texts that we claim as Scripture, we do it as embodied beings in the company of the bodies of people who make our communities of faith what they are: old bodies and young, women and men, Black bodies and others. Sarah Agnew offers us a mode of interpretation that takes all of these bodies seriously. This is a great gift."

—*Richard W. Swanson*, Director of the Provoking the Gospel Storytelling Project

"In this pioneering and multifaceted book, Sarah Agnew has developed an embodied performance methodology that builds on the foundations laid by biblical performance criticism in new and highly creative ways. As a published poet, biblical storyteller, and experienced performer, she has explored in detail the implications of the full employment of the body in interaction with audiences as a means of communicating the impact of biblical compositions. Her articulation of 'Biblical Performance Analysis' opens new doors into the world of critical engagement with biblical traditions then and now. The exposition of Romans as a test case reveals the passionate encounter that Paul seeks with the Roman community culminating in an invitation to mutual embrace. The embodied performance of Romans sets the theological arguments of the letter in the context of the emotional interactions within a highly diverse community who are invited to share the Holy One's love in their profound differences."

> —*Thomas E. Boomershine*, Founder of the Network of Biblical Storytellers, International, and author of *The Messiah of Peace: A Performance Criticism Commentary on Mark's Passion-Resurrection Narrative*

Embodied Performance

Embodied Performance

Mutuality, Embrace, and the Letter to Rome

SARAH AGNEW

foreword by Richard W. Swanson

☙PICKWICK *Publications* · Eugene, Oregon

EMBODIED PERFORMANCE
Mutuality, Embrace, and the Letter to Rome

Copyright © 2020 Sarah Agnew. All rights reserved. Except for brief quotations in critical publications or reviews, no part of this book may be reproduced in any manner without prior written permission from the publisher. Write: Permissions, Wipf and Stock Publishers, 199 W. 8th Ave., Suite 3, Eugene, OR 97401.

Pickwick Publications
An Imprint of Wipf and Stock Publishers
199 W. 8th Ave., Suite 3
Eugene, OR 97401

www.wipfandstock.com

PAPERBACK ISBN: 978-1-7252-5784-9
HARDCOVER ISBN: 978-1-7252-5785-6
EBOOK ISBN: 978-1-7252-5786-3

Cataloguing-in-Publication data:

Names: Agnew, Sarah, author. | Swanson, Richard W., foreword.

Title: Embodied performance : mutuality, embrace, and the letter to Rome / Sarah Agnew ; foreword by Richard W. Swanson.

Description: Eugene, OR: Pickwick Publications, 2020. | Includes bibliographical references.

Identifiers: ISBN 978-1-7252-5784-9 (paperback). | ISBN 978-1-7252-5785-6 (hardcover). | ISBN 978-1-7252-5786-3 (ebook).

Subjects: LCSH: Performance criticism. | Bible—Romans—Criticism, interpretation, etc. | Storytelling—Religious aspects—Christianity.

Classification: BS2665.52 A35 2020 (print). | BS2665.52 (ebook).

Manufactured in the U.S.A.   09/10/20

Unless otherwise noted, Scripture quotations are from the New Revised Standard Version Bible, copyright © 1989 National Council of the Churches of Christ in the United States of America. Used by permission. All rights reserved worldwide. Biblical quotations from the book of Romans are from the NRSV but are adapted by the author: these are found in Appendix A and are discussed in detail in Chapter 6 and Appendix B.

*This is for Holy One,
the people of Holy One,
and our mutual embrace*

Contents

Foreword by Richard W. Swanson	xi
Acknowledgments	xv
Prelude	xvii
Abbreviations	xix

PART 1. WHAT IS EMBODIED PERFORMANCE ANALYSIS?

1	Performance Interpretation *The Search for Method*	3
2	The Search Begins *Narrative and Performance*	35
3	The Search Continues *Recovering Historical Performance*	61
4	A New Beginning *Developing an Embodied Performance Method*	102

PART 2. IN PRACTICE: EMBODIED PERFORMANCE ANALYSIS OF ROMANS

5	Performance Interpretation of Romans	141
6	Critical Reflection	142
7	A Story of Mutual Indwelling	191

Appendix A: Script for Performance Interpretation	211
Appendix B: Preparation and Rehearsal Notes	239
Appendix C: Performance Examples	281
Video Credits	283
Bibliography	285

Foreword

You have in your hands a transformative book.

What might I mean by that?

First of all, I might be referring to the matter of performing biblical texts. Recent years have seen powerful work done by people who have learned to tell biblical stories by heart. They rightly report that this experience is life-changing, and their audiences report that the narratives they see performed come alive in surprising ways.

Predictably, perhaps, critical voices emerge that are suspicious of performance and its impact. Sometimes they recognize the power of this medium and distrust its ability to persuade an audience that loves just to have someone tell them stories. Such critics note that the whole enterprise of critical biblical study emerged out of a commitment to scientific study not swayed by social suasion, whether ecclesiastical or emotional. Other times, the critical voices applaud the performers tolerantly. Performance, they imply, is an interesting circus trick that some people have learned to do. These critics may even enjoy the interlude provided by the performer, but then they return to their libraries to continue the "real" work of technical biblical study.

Part of Agnew's transformative contribution lies in her ability to demonstrate that Biblical Performance Criticism is not a manipulative circus trick, not just something that "people who like doing that sort of thing" might find diverting. Sarah Agnew is up to something more remarkable than that.

Or, I might be saying something about the way these texts first came into being. Practitioners of performance critical work often point out that the texts of the Christian Testament, for instance, will first have been performed for an audience before they were studied in silent libraries or sanctuaries. In the case of the gospels, it is even likely that they were composed in performance, and thus were performed before they were written at all. This is also a transformative realization. Even the highest estimates of literacy rates in the ancient world leave us looking at a world in which most people did not experience narratives as a result of silent, private reading. Stories existed to be performed, and this was how they had their impact on the world. Given that the texts of the Christian Testament had a rather astonishing impact all around the Mediterranean basin, it changes things when you first sit down and realize that it was performers who brought that about.

Of course, critics will note that, even if you grant this, the stories and letters that were performed were finally committed to writing, and preserved as Scripture. To call something "Scripture" means several things. But at the bottom of it all, critics will tell you, Scripture is the body of *texts* that are studied by the faithful. Some of this study is done by all, since Scripture (especially since the Reformation among Christians) is available in vernacular languages precisely for this purpose. But communities of faith also nurture faithful individuals who devote their careers and their lives to the study of Scripture. Those devoted individuals include the biblical scholars who make critical comments about the impact of millennia of careful textual analysis done in libraries and other silent spaces.

Agnew's book is transformative especially because she takes these criticisms seriously. Biblical Performance Criticism as she understands it is not a circus trick or an intriguing way to present biblical messages to an audience. Biblical Performance Criticism is a powerful mode of analysis that can be applied to the body of texts that you hold as Scripture.

Notice what powerful resources this mode brings to the task. There is, of course, the performer who (like Agnew) may bring with her years of study of the original languages and a history as a published poet. And there is Scripture itself, with all of its quirks and complications. And there is the audience, with its own quirks and complications. Agnew pays exquisite attention to the way these partners interact with each other in performance. She brings to her work an insightful awareness of sensory-motor, emotional, and relational ways of making meaning. As a result, she uncovers a performance space filled with mutual interactions that can be studied using social scientific methods.

As Agnew shows, this mode of interpretive analysis reveals dimensions in the texts that other methods might well miss. Biblical Performance Criticism can confirm insights generated by other modes of analysis, or it can call them into question. This is transformative.

But Agnew goes even further. What is most exciting to me is that this mode of analysis can do the same for our understandings of faithfulness. I am one of the devoted readers who is fascinated by historical detail and philosophical implication. But those technical investigations have always finally aimed at making sense of how faithful people hope without being victimized. As I understand it, technical historical study aims at fostering reflection on what it meant, and what it might *ever* mean, to speak of a messiah in a world so clearly not turned right-side-up. And philosophically guided reading of scripture has among its goals the consideration of what it can mean to say the word "God" in a world in which God is achingly invisible.

These are the questions raised by faithfulness.

Agnew has not just laid out a new method of textual analysis. In this book, she argues for a mode of interpretation that understands what happens when you draw us all in, text and performers and audience, grandmothers and grandchildren, even insiders and outsiders to the community of faith. Biblical Performance Criticism creates a space within which we all are partners in making and exploring meaning.

This book can transform your understanding of that whole process. We are all in this together, and Sarah Agnew has handed us a powerfully insightful way of understanding our mutual work. For that, I am deeply thankful to her.

—Richard W. Swanson

Acknowledgments

This book began as the thesis for a PhD at The University of Edinburgh. With some minor adjustments for this new format, this work is in essence still that thesis. I am deeply grateful to Rev Dr Alison Jack and Prof Helen Bond and the New College School of Divinity. Throughout the project, my supervisors and peers were enthusiastic supporters, encouragers, and mutual learners with me throughout. Alison, in particular, went above and beyond her responsibilities as a supervisor in her support of me during those three years. Thank you.

The Network of Biblical Storytellers Scholars' Seminar has been a rich collegial community, for which I am also grateful. Thank you to Phil Ruge-Jones and the seminar members for your welcome. Thanks also to the Scottish Storytelling Centre, where I performed several times, in particular Donald Smith and Daniel Abercrombie. Thank you.

Feedback from Kathy Maxwell and Steve Chaffee was helpful for final polishing of the thesis. My thanks go to Ray Bown, Tim Lee, and Rowan Lee, for your technical support in the recording and editing of the Performance Interpretation. Also to Jason Chesnut, who recorded and edited the digital performance interpretation of Romans 1, Adam Jessup for recording the performance at Uniting College, and Lou Davis, who recorded the performance at the Scottish Storytelling Centre. Thanks also to Profs Richard Swanson and Timothy Lim for examining the thesis with generous wisdom, and to Richard for providing the foreword for the book.

My faith communities in Edinburgh and Adelaide offered prayerful, practical, and pastoral support for the project. In Scotland, Greyfriars Kirk, The Gathering (Edinburgh City Methodist), Augustine United Reformed Church, Upper Clyde Parish Church. In Adelaide, Belair Uniting Church, and Blackwood Uniting Church. Thank you. My current community at Wesley Uniting Church, Canberra, have been generous and supportive as I spent time preparing the book. Thank you.

I received funding for the PhD from New College, Uniting College for Leadership and Theology scholarship committee, Uniting Foundation, the Ken Leaver Fund, With Love to the World, the Loreto Sisters in Australia, private gifts and loans, and Patreon donors. This was truly a community effort, proving what I claim to be true: we are fully human only together.

I have a few close friends, and some mentors, in Australia, who cheered me on to and through the PhD, and without whom I would not have made it to the end with good health intact. There's no room to name you all, but please know I love you, and hope I can be there for you with such unwavering faith when you need me.

My sisters and brother-in-law did not want me to live so far away, but encouraged me and supported me as I followed my dream and my calling. Thank you for understanding, and for the sacrifices you made. I love you muchly.

My parents. I haven't the words. Mum told me long ago, when I dreamed of becoming a writer, not to have a fallback plan. Well, there wasn't a fallback plan for this adventure, even when we wished there was. When I stopped believing in myself, my mum and dad did not. Never did they tell me to come home, that I'd done enough. They knew it would only be enough when I had seen it through. You showed such generosity and courage and love. You are remarkable. I love you. More than I can say.

Prelude

Receiving the Bible Today

A woman is reading the Bible aloud in gathered worship. The portion is Romans 16, and she stumbles over the pronunciation of names unpracticed ("is it Try–phay–na or Tree–phan–na?"). The repetition of "greet" is unvaried in expression, meaningless to the receivers; she adopts a tone of stern rebuke for the warning of verses 17–20, because preachers have shown Paul to be a harsh teacher.

A scholar sits at his desk silently reading the Bible for an article he is writing. It is Romans 16, and with a socio-critical eye, he analyzes the names for their likely ethnicity ("Apelles could be a Jewish name"); employing textual criticism he redacts the interpolations of 17–20 and 25–27 out of the original letter, and is even uncertain as to the connection of the whole chapter to the rest of Romans. He deduces there is no more meaning to find in Rom 16 than fragmented remnants of a formal greeting to people long forgotten.

A storyteller performs the Bible for her community. She has spoken aloud the breadth of the letter to the Romans, and arrives now at Rom 16. She has translated ἀσπάσασθε (*aspasasthe*) as "embrace," speaks each name carefully, affectionately, looking towards her hand holding space for each one with a gesture of intimacy. The warning of verses 17–20 is spoken as a parent calls to a child to be careful, when sending them into the wonderful, but dangerous, world. The doxology *is* prayer; the audience sigh at the conclusion, for they have been caught up in the world of the letter brought to life in their midst; it has moved them, and they have understood the message to reach towards each other beyond difference, to their shared humanity with an embrace like the embrace Holy One offers to all.

I am the storyteller in this prelude; this is my story. It is the story of my search for a framework to support my embodied practice of interpretation. It develops into an examination of my practice as a biblical storyteller, from which I construct the method of biblical interpretation for which I was searching. It is a story of mutual embrace—performer and composition, performer and audience together.[1] It is both a personal story and a story of my communities of scholarship and church. I tell this story in the hope that it, and the Embodied Performance Method, will support and encourage the practice of other performers, scholars, and readers.

---

1. I might even say mutual *indwelling*, for the method invites the composition to dwell—make its home—within the performer, and the performer inhabits—makes her home—within the composition.

Abbreviations

BDAG	*Greek-English Lexicon*: Bauer, Danker, Arndt, & Gingrich
BPC	Biblical Performance Criticism
EPA	Embodied Performance Analysis
HB/OT	Hebrew Bible / Old Testament
JBL	*Journal of Biblical Literature*
JSNT	*Journal for the Study of the New Testament*
NT	New Testament
SBL	Society of Biblical Literature
ZNW	*Zeitschrift für die neutestamentliche Wissenschaft und die Kunde der älteren Kirche*

PART 1.

What Is Embodied Performance Analysis?

1

Performance Interpretation

The Search for Method

THE BEGINNING OF THE STORY

As I regularly performed compositions from the Bible for various gatherings in the church, I had noticed that by embodying and performing the Bible, I was discerning meaning intuitively, physically, emotionally. This felt to me a richer process than the biblical scholarship I encountered that attempted a disembodied rationality to claim enduring meaning in the text. Surely the field of biblical studies could benefit from such holistic meaning-making and interpretations of compositions which are again widely acknowledged to be intended for holistic reception and interpretation?

In order to bring such insights as I was discovering, from performance into scholarship, I felt I needed a methodology to ensure accountability, integrity, and repeatability between performance-interpreter practitioners. Biblical Performance Criticism (BPC) was becoming an established approach, so I initially looked there for a methodology. But I found something else; BPC described itself as a paradigm shift that sought to identify and understand the oral and performed origins of biblical writings, using performance today to help re-enact original performance situations.[1]

---

1. Rhoads, "Biblical Performance Criticism," 164; Seal and Partridge, *Performing Scripture*, 3; Boomershine, "All Scholarship Is Personal," 283.

In Chapters 2 and 3, I will describe what I found in BPC, and how I develop certain features and explore some of the questions raised by its practitioners, with the Embodied Performance method. For example, Rhoads asks how performance might "bring to the fore the emotive dimensions of meaning and persuasion? And how can we integrate critical thinking as a means to assess appropriate emotional responses?"[2] Embodied Performance Analysis (EPA) will directly engage with such questions. Another question from Rhoads is, "As scholars who are also critics of performance, what categories/criteria might we develop as a basis to reflect upon and to critique performance as interpretation?"[3] EPA may also reframe these emerging questions. For example, the Embodied Performance method will move beyond *critiquing* performance to instead use performance *to* "critique," or interpret, biblical compositions.

I observe in Narrative Criticism what I term the "storyteller's Biblical Performance Criticism." My own beginning in this scholarly project began with Narrative. After conducting a Narrative Analysis of Esther 4, I posed questions of the text in preparation for performance.[4] I noted the way movement helps establish proximity and identify voices as Hatach crosses the courtyard between Esther and Mordecai (Est 4:8–16), somewhat disappearing as a mediator as the narrator ceases to mention him and the performer represents only Esther and Mordecai, to give the audience the sense of the two speaking face to face, rather than through a third party.[5] Elsewhere, I have written on reception theory and audience studies in reflection on my practice as a storyteller, articulating the influence of audiences on my performance choices: children influencing the omission of the harsher lines in a story of slave trade, or a twentieth-century song shaping reception of a Psalm of exile for an audience for whom the song is cultural capital.[6] I also began to write reflections identifying choices I had made in particular performances of biblical portions for worship gatherings before or as a sermon.[7]

This self-reflection on my storytelling practice helped me to articulate my experience. My body was showing me meaning in a composition as I inhabited it. My emotions were showing me meaning as I chose songs to sing.

---

2. Rhoads, "Emerging Methodology Part 2," 177.

3. Rhoads, "Emerging Methodology Part 1," 127.

4. Agnew, "Mutuality of Esther and Mordecai."

5. Agnew, "Mutuality of Esther and Mordecai," 100–106.

6. Agnew, "Choice: Stories," 127–29. On cultural capital, see Chapter 4 and the discussion of Richard W. Swanson, "'This Is My . . .'"

7. For example, Agnew, "Telling Mark 10:13–16."

My audiences were showing me meaning as I sought to enable their reception of biblical compositions, the sacred writings of our community of faith. It was time to further examine my practice as a storyteller and more fully understand the way in which I was working as a "performer-interpreter," developing understanding of the meaning of biblical compositions as I mediated them for reception in live, embodied performance.

The Setting

In order to carry out this exploration of my practice as a storyteller or performer-interpreter (as I will now describe myself, bringing together the roles of storyteller and scholar), and to develop a methodology that would bring insights from performed interpretations for audiences today into scholarship, I identified Scotland as an ideal location. Scotland has a vibrant culture of appreciation for and encouragement of the art and craft of oral storytelling.[8] Developing a new methodology was one element of the overall development of my own professional art and craft as a performer, and being situated within such a storytelling environment would be conducive to deep reflection on my practice. My home town of Adelaide, Australia, would remain another important location for the development and demonstration of the Embodied Performance Analysis, as we will discover.

The Goal

I begin with the question, "is there a place for the intuitive insights of the physical body, emotions, and relationship in community in scholarly conversations about biblical compositions?" I aim to present a method that answers that question with a "yes"; a method through which performer-interpreters like myself may contribute embodied performance insights into scholarly discussion of biblical compositions, conversations long dominated by rational objectivity.[9] It will help if I tell the story of Biblical Performance Criticism, the scholarly context in which the method is situated. A diverse and to some extent still emerging field, BPC is practiced by performers and

---

8. Traditional Arts and Culture Scotland. "Scottish Storytelling Centre."

9. Iverson, "Biblical Performance Criticism." Ahmi Lee notes that modernity had bought into dualistic hierarchies that view oral as less than written, particular less than universal, and timely as less than timeless. Postmodernism embraces the spectrum in a both/and understanding of the need for fullness and diversity in our approaches, rather than an either/or dismissal of essential elements of our meaning-making endeavors: *Preaching God's Grand Drama*, 64.

critics, integrates scholarly methods from within biblical scholarship and beyond, and overall is interested in identifying and understanding the performed or oral context of biblical compositions in their origins. I found in BPC a foundation on which to build the Embodied Performance method. Within the field of BPC are practitioners who may employ the EPA themselves, as this approach seeks to engage with and begin to answer questions raised through their endeavors.

I build a further foundation for the new method by examining the ways in which scholars in various fields have understood the meaning-making processes of humans as involving more than a disembodied rational intellect. Insights from an interdisciplinary study of scholarship on human epistemology provide rationale for the three tools in the Embodied Performance method: body, emotion, and audience.

After introducing the method, its process of preparation, performance, and reflection, and its outcome of an Analysis comprised of Performance Interpretation and Critical Reflection, I demonstrate the method with a test case Embodied Performance Analysis of Romans. Through Performance Interpretation and Critical Reflection, I present a fully embodied encounter with, and interpretation of the letter for reception by an audience in Adelaide, Australia, in 2016. Following the test case and analysis of its strengths and limitations, I make some adaptations to the method as initially presented, and am able to present an innovative method for biblical interpretation that has been rigorously tested.

In this book, then, you will find a methodology by which performer-interpreters can bring their intuitive interpretations to the scholarly conversations about biblical compositions. It may not be comfortable, for scholarship is out of practice in listening to emotion and intuition. It may not be the only way to bring the fullness of human meaning making into scholarly discussions; indeed, elements of this method may be employed without a full application of the whole (see Chapter 7). It is a beginning, with areas that warrant further exploration of the embodied interpretation of biblical compositions through performance.

THE STORY OF THE STORYTELLER

I said in the beginning that this is my story, so who am I? I am a storyteller, poet, and minister (Uniting Church in Australia); a scholar, liturgist, and performer. I bring to this project more than ten years' experience as a storyteller. I have qualifications in creative writing, am a published poet and liturgist, have experience as a leader of Christian communities, both traditional and alternative in form, and both as embedded (Australia) and itinerant (Australia and Scotland). As a storyteller, I have performed in large and small gatherings within and beyond the church, facilitated workshops, and am a member of the Network of Biblical Storytellers' Scholars Seminar.[10] I have presented at conferences on storytelling, theology, and biblical studies, published articles on storytelling and biblical interpretation,[11] and have taught and/or tutored biblical studies at Flinders University and Adelaide College of Divinity (South Australia), and the University of Edinburgh (Scotland).

Storytelling shapes my approach to pastoral care by employing tools of narrative therapy.[12] Workshops I run help people to identify their own story and tell them, as a way of nurturing their own and others' wellbeing.

I have a relatively small, but dedicated, audience for my work (many drawn from my communities of faith), including blogs that tell my own story or offer poetic prayers based on biblical portions for use in worship. Particularly evident in my writing in these contexts are themes of relationship and the dignity and mutuality of all humans together.

Story and mutuality are two dominant lenses through which I see the world. That my audiences, my communities, know this of me through my work is significant motivation for decisions I make in the Performance Interpretation (Chapter 5); decisions in pursuit of maintaining integrity and trust between performer, composition, and audience.

Telling the Story: Auto-ethnographic Reflection

As is already evident, this book is written in a self-reflective style. The Embodied Performance Analysis itself is also auto-ethnographic in approach, with the interpretation explicitly discerned through the experience of the performer.[13] I take this approach not only because "people have always used

---

10. Network of Biblical Storytellers "NBS Seminar."

11. See entries in the bibliography.

12. "Narrative therapy seeks to be a respectful, non-blaming approach to counselling and community work, which centers people as the experts in their own lives. It views problems as separate from people and assumes people have many skills, competencies, beliefs, values, commitments and abilities that will assist them to reduce the influence of problems in their lives": Dulwich Centre, "What Is Narrative Therapy?"; Morgan, *What Is Narrative Therapy?*

13. Similar to the theatrical approach to biblical interpretation of Shimon Levy, in which his group participants practiced "intentional subjective-personal" engagement with the text, asking, "how do I interpret myself through the . . . text; how does the text interpret itself through me?" (*Bible as Theatre*, ix).

their experiences, whether these be in the natural world, in familiar human relationships, or amid challenging historical events, as a vivid source of theological understanding."[14]

The method I introduce here, moreover, is itself mutual, integrated, and interdisciplinary in nature.[15] Although located within biblical studies, this study's instigation and implications are to some extent shared with practical theology. "Practical theology is particularly concerned with worship,"[16] and this is the usual context of the performance practice under examination in this project. The greater authenticity given to experience is a vital element in the Embodied Performance Analysis: as with practical theology, Embodied Performance Analysis is therefore "well placed to engage in the imaginative labors that call into question 'common understanding' and contribute to social change."[17] We may view "hermeneutical processes themselves as forms of imaginative play";[18] EPA is a methodology that embraces the imaginative, playful nature of bringing biblical compositions to life for meaningful reception by audiences today.[19] Finally, the drama of performance is an appropriate mode of reception and reflection in a "cultural context where moral absolutes are increasingly challenged."[20]

While I do not seek to develop new metaphors, as a theologian might,[21] I do seek to develop new, or renewed, language for biblical scholarship, which incorporates the "language" of the body, emotions, and relationship. I will seek to describe my experience as a scholar looking to the field of BPC to find language and form for my practice. I will describe what I found,

---

14. Walton, *Writing Methods*, xiii. One need not look further than the Bible itself, especially the Psalms.

15. Iverson notes that BPC is also mutual, or interdisciplinary, by nature: "Biblical Performance Criticism."

16. Iverson, "Biblical Performance Criticism," 147.

17. Iverson, "Biblical Performance Criticism," 147.

18. Iverson, "Biblical Performance Criticism," 143.

19. In this work, when using language of "meaningful," "meaning-making," and "making meaning" I evoke the social science notion of a human making sense of—or *interpreting*—an experience. For example, a person approaches you in the street and says something you do not understand: you interpret, or seek to make sense of, the encounter. What did they say? Were they even trying to communicate, or is there another agenda at play? (Henricks, *Selves, Societies and Emotions*, 13). In general, I use such language to refer to the interpretive action of performer and audience. A "meaningful" encounter is one that holds meaning, or presents interpretive potential; it has the potential to impact and transform a person's understanding.

20. Walton, *Writing Methods*, 143.

21. Walton, *Writing Methods*, xvii: "New metaphors can be forged through reflective writing that seeks to employ literary conventions."

and how my expectations were met, and not met. I will show the reader the encouragement I found in this field to develop EPA as a way of exploring, and perhaps answering, questions posed by and through the work of BPC scholars.

In this approach, as for the "autobiographical biblical critic," an embodied performance interpreter "makes himself or herself vulnerable and takes considerable risks, but on the other hand, biblical criticism was never really without a personal autobiographical dimension. It is always about what I make of the biblical text."[22] Therefore, in this approach, I do not disguise my "person and life with the third person pronoun [or] constructions in the passive voice."[23] I am present, my interpretation visibly contextualized, and the critique all the more rigorous for including self-criticism.[24]

It may feel to the reader that the more "crafted" literary style of writing undermines the authenticity of the scholarship herein,[25] or the authority of the research. But Walton observes of ministers engaged in professional development exercises, that storytelling empowers learning and the development of "more critical, but also appreciative, understanding."[26] One may describe me as a "mythopoetic" scholar: one who "believes in the centrality of stories, poetry, and narrative, offers an alternative to a privileging of literal and rational knowledge . . . values mystery, the unconscious and the indefinable."[27] I am seeking through this study to articulate what is "not easily articulated":[28] my deeply sensed intuition that my embodiment of biblical compositions for performance *is* interpretation of those compositions. I seek to establish what my intuition shows me: that the body's fuller ways of making meaning enrich the conversation about biblical compositions, and that this enrichment is appropriate and helpful for the field of biblical scholarship.

As literary works engage the imagination, a more literary form may help to bring embodied interpretation into scholarly conversations about biblical compositions. The approach of "reflective writing that seeks to

---

22. Schutte, "When *They, We,* and the Passive Become *I*," 414–15.

23. Schutte, "When *They, We,* and the Passive Become *I*," 403.

24. Schutte, "When *They, We,* and the Passive Become *I*," 403.

25. Schutte, "When *They, We,* and the Passive Become *I*," xii: it may be that "the requirements of craft and authenticity often appear irreconcilable."

26. Schutte, "When *They, We,* and the Passive Become *I*," xix.

27. Shann and Cunneen, "Mythopoetics and the English Classroom," 49. Also Shann, "Mating with the World," 26.

28. Walton, *Writing Methods*, 12.

employ literary conventions"[29] will aid in expanding exegesis into the realm of affect, imagination, and intuition.

What Do I Mean by "Story" and "Storytelling"?

Story and storytelling are foundational concepts for this work, as for the development of Biblical Performance Criticism. It is to some extent "fundamental to speak of the human being as the storytelling being: without the story we do not have human identity or human society."[30] However, storytelling and oral performance are still often dismissed within the scholarly world as "light fare."[31] Perhaps because "storytelling is so commonplace that we live in it rather than with it," we "fail to notice it . . . or at least we do not give it the attention it deserves."[32] But "storytelling needs a sharper hearing"[33] than it has received, for humans do "communicate through our stories, whether across back-fences or eras, and when we hear stories, we recognize our own kind."[34]

Understanding "Story" in Context

"Story is constitutive of what it means to be human."[35] Stories build a person's sense of identity and wellbeing, with a power that both teller and listener experience; storytelling helps us "make sense of what it means to be human."[36] "Poets, mystics, contemporary truth-tellers like Gandhi, Martin Luther King, Oscar Romero," as well as Jewish prophets and Jesus of Nazareth,[37] tell stories in order to challenge oppression, so that injustice will not be forgotten. Many such storytellers have lost their lives because of the stories they have told; it is impossible to measure the number of lives their stories have transformed, or even saved.[38]

---

29. Walton, *Writing Methods*, xvii.

30. Wire, *Holy Lives, Holy Deaths*, 1. Also McKenna, *Keepers of the Story*, 195: "Storytelling is an art. It is basic to communication. Some say it is essential to our survival as human beings."

31. Wire, *Holy Lives*, 19.

32. Wire, *Holy Lives*, 1.

33. Wire, *Holy Lives*, 19.

34. Wire, *Holy Lives*, 1.

35. Rhoads, Dewey, and Michie, "Reflections," 274.

36. Ahumada, Möller, and Brown, "Introduction," xi.

37. McKenna, *Keepers of the Story*, 198.

38. McKenna, *Keepers of the Story*, 199.

To tell stories is a fundamental feature of human being, communication, and identity formation; and performance (as generally uncrafted "doing")[39] or oral storytelling is the most common way we share stories with one another.[40] Story and performance-based methods of biblical interpretation are therefore appropriate ways in which to engage stories told by and for humans seeking to communicate something about being human and our encounters with creation and its Creator. Those in communities of faith "listen to stories to remember who we are and to be urged once again to divine service in our human encounters, to holiness, obedience and awe of what is divine, to love, to devotion, to compassionate justice."[41] Stories evoke senses and emotion.[42]

Narrative Criticism identifies elements of a story as setting, plot, narrator, and character.[43] Biblical Performance Criticism, as we will see in the review of that literature, is often employed in partnership with Narrative Criticism, particularly for scholars who employ BPC with the Gospels. Indeed, some even suggest that performance criticism of the Bible ought to be *based on* Narrative Criticism.[44] However, while in my practice I conceive of the Bible as the "Sacred Story" of the Jewish and Christian traditions, the writings that comprise the "Story" are, individually, not all "stories." The stories of creation are told in narrative in Gen 1–3, but creation's story is also told elsewhere in poetry (for example, Pss 8; 19; 104; 139). Stories of prophets are told in narrative alongside the oracles and speeches they uttered. The Gospels are the story of Jesus, told four ways, and Acts tells the stories of some of the earliest gatherings of Jesus' followers and their leaders. But the letters are not stories, although they do point to the stories of churches, relationships, characters, and conflicts in various settings in the ancient world.

The art form I practice is named "oral storytelling," but I do not only tell stories. I will employ a stance as priest, poet, prophet, or orator in delivery

---

39. I discuss performance as "doing" further in Chapter 4, with reference, for example, to Freshwater, *Theatre and Audience*, 7.

40. "Our lives are made up of stories," as we make sense of our lives and learn about each other through the stories we tell and hear: Fairbairn and Fairbairn, "Why Use Storytelling as a Research Approach?," 5–6.

41. McKenna, *Keepers of the Story*, 205.

42. Ahumada, "Introduction," ix.

43. See, for example, Hearon, "From Narrative to Performance." *Mark as Story* identifies rhetoric or narrator, setting, plot, and character, and in the third edition adds audience: Rhoads, Dewey, and Michie, *Mark as Story*. Adele Berlin's analysis of Ruth focuses on characterization, narrator, and structure: *Poetics and Interpretation*, 83–110. For Gunn the elements of Narrative Criticism are structure, plot, characterization, point of view, and theme: Gunn, "Narrative Criticism," 201.

44. Van Oyen, "No Performance Criticism," 107.

(rather than always narrator), adapting the art form to fit the composition rather than forcing a composition into the form of a "story" or narrative, when in fact it is a poem or oracle or letter. Baniceru's observation of the basis of oral storytelling in the practice of rhetoric is pertinent here, for the practice of rhetoric is also a strong influence on the composition of New Testament letters and their intended oral delivery in community.[45] We will see in Chapter 3 that I differ in practice from Rhoads' treatment of letters as stories,[46] instead adapting my presentation and persona to be more in the style of oratory than the telling of a story.

I have chosen to present this project using the language of "story," using a first-person narrative voice in which to reflect on my experience; I, the main character, the subject and object upon which this study is carried out. However, it is not a "story" in the sense of which I have spoken here. It is reflective writing, as noted, which employs some literary techniques, and the language of "story" for effect. "Stories, regardless of the media used to portray them, seem to share some basic characteristics: they represent our interaction with the world in which we live."[47] In this way, the work is a representation of my interaction with the worlds of performance and biblical scholarship, BPC in particular, and in response to that experience, developing a new method of biblical interpretation. EPA itself may be understood as a representation of the performer-interpreter's interaction with the world of the biblical composition.

The Art Form of Oral Storytelling

Not only is story an underlying idea and ideology for this work, it is at the core of my practice as a performer. When I say that storytelling is the art form I practice, what I mean is that I internalize stories (or poetry, or letters), to present them by heart in live embodied performance for a live embodied audience. In this art form an "at-onement is created between poem, performer, and audience," as the performer inhabits a composition and mediates it for others.[48]

Storytelling is relational: "storytellers experience companionship and proximity as hallmarks of the storytelling event."[49] Utilized in human rights advocacy, storytelling seeks to build understanding, evoke empathy, and

---

45. See Baniceru, "Telling Academic Stories," 11.
46. Rhoads, "New Testament as Oral Performance."
47. Ahumada, "Introduction," ix.
48. Bozarth, *The Word's Body*, 114.
49. Iverson, "The Present Tense of Performance," 141.

inspire a response of care—of relationship—between the listeners and the subjects of the stories.[50] In Chapter 2 we will encounter further reflections on storytelling and the role of the storyteller, when I discuss the work of Philip Ruge-Jones and Thomas Boomershine.

Stories also connect "our most rational self with our most emotional one," as holistic artefacts that "allow us to be in touch with what makes us human."[51] Further, they "can help us make sense of what seemed uncertain."[52] Thus, when seeking a composition for a test case, I looked for one about which I was uncertain, for my art form seemed well suited for an exploration of doubts, concerns, unfathomable passages, a problematic history of reception. As we will see in Chapter 6, there is much about the letter to the Romans that I found did not hold meaning for me, but I have told the letter anyway.

For a biblical storyteller, or at least for the storyteller under the microscope in this project, this conviction to tell stories that hold meaning for me applies to the Sacred Story (the Bible) as a whole. Within the Story will be passages with which I have difficulty, for their theology, or language, or the contextual mismatch between the time of composition and this time now of reception. But still I tell the Story, and its constituent letters, psalms, and stories. Moreover, as a minister, one of the order within my tradition who hold the stories and interpret them for our generation, I am expected to engage with all the compositions of the Bible, problematic as they may be. I am, however, allowed to engage with them *as I am*, as this particular individual introduced to you above. Indeed, this is necessary, in order to effectively communicate meaning from within them. So I chose a letter for this study that is problematic. I omitted some of the portions I felt I could not interpret on stage in performance alone. I left some of those problematic portions in, to allow my voice to speak the tensions, to sound aloud in my shaky, uncertain voice, the discomfort we—my community and I together—feel with some of Paul's words and theology, and with his interpreters. Embodiment would allow this uncertainty, the vulnerability of composition, mediator, and receivers, to be experienced, as part of the experience of the letter. We will see the particular ways in which storytelling as an art form offers a medium for reception and interpretation that utilizes experience, for interpretive beings who *do* make meaning through experience.

---

50. Ahumada, "Introduction," x.
51. Ahumada, "Introduction," x–xi.
52. Ahumada, "Introduction," xi.

Each telling or retelling of a story is a creative (re)generation; each performance is its own "original" version of the story.[53] Indeed, "all stories that persist, continuing to be cherished, reread and recited, undergo change."[54] Therefore, as Gregg notes, a community of faith will carry out the "simultaneous tasks of safeguarding its sacred stories *and* of sustaining their vitality through the necessary art of revising and updating their meaning."[55]

For Wire, this renders the search for an—or "the"—"original" of any story or composition futile, unless one looks to the present performance of a story as it carries forward all its past performances. The present story is the leading edge of the story, or the visible peak of the proverbial iceberg, with depth below speaking of the story's "tenacious past."[56]

In this study, the particular performance of the composition is such a "leading edge of the [letter]." We will note in the Analysis of Romans the need for the performer-interpreter to acknowledge and attend to the "tenacious past" of the letter if this present audience is to receive this work meaningfully and faithfully today. Further, the Embodied Performance Analysis takes seriously what Biblical Performance Critics have observed, that "a contemporary memorized performance of a biblical text . . . is an interpretation, just as a commentary or a monograph is an interpretation. It is an embodied interpretation."[57] In this study, the practice of storytelling is both the means and the end of the research.[58]

STARTING SOMETHING NEW

On not Finding What I Was Looking For

I have mentioned the Network of Biblical Storytellers, and that I belong to the associated Scholars Seminar. As I considered the question that arose from reflecting on my performance practice, I was aware that there were scholars who engaged in something called "Biblical Performance Criticism." My first thought when embarking on the quest to find a methodology for interpretation-by-performance was that BPC would provide what I was looking for.

---

53. Wire, *Holy Lives*, 8.
54. Gregg, *Shared Stories, Rival Tellings*, xv.
55. Gregg, *Shared Stories, Rival Tellings*, xv.
56. Wire, *Holy Lives*, 9.
57. Rhoads, "Emerging Methodology Part 1," 127.
58. As it has been for others in the field, for example, A. Boomershine, "Breath of Fresh Air," 72–73.

BPC is a scholarly approach that examines biblical compositions for their performance history. For many scholars in this field, the level of literacy among first century audiences is a key focus, in order to establish the oral origins for reception and/or composition of the Gospels and other biblical works. The level of literacy in the first century is not at issue here, however, nor is the extent to which orality is the origin of a particular composition. I proceed on the general assumption that the first century communication culture was complex and integrated,[59] although the mode of reception for most biblical works was assumed by their composers to be in oral performance, for either cultural or practical reasons.[60] It has been necessary to re-establish this point, for in the aftermath of the printing press, mass production of Bibles, and growing literacy rates in the Western World at least (the dominating context for biblical scholarship also), the assumption of a Bible's reception as read, silently and by the individual alone, has been projected back onto the compositions in their origins, and has distorted our picture of their nature.[61] Rather, the nature of biblical compositions is that they are intended for reception in performance, in community.[62] If this is the primary reception mode expected by its composer for a composition, the fullest experience and understanding of it will come through performance in community.[63]

BPC has recovered this picture of the biblical works, long hidden under the assumptions of the post-printing press approach to biblical scholarship. Biblical Performance scholars have also raised questions from the performance of biblical compositions today, as noted. Interpreter-performers are observing the interpretive decisions that are shaped by the context of the audience for whom a composition is presented in performance.[64] Interpreter-performers have not been maximizing such insights in the presentation of exegesis or comment on biblical works, however; Rhoads claims his

---

59. Hurtado, "Oral Fixation and New Testament Studies?," 187; Hearon, "Interplay between Written and Spoken Word."

60. For example, Hearon, "Interplay of Written and Spoken Word," 67, 71; Levy, *Bible as Theatre*, ix.

61. Maxwell, "From Performance to Text to Performance," 160, 79.

62. Maxwell, "From Performance to Text to Performance," 176. These assumptions are by no means unanimous within the field. Van Oyen states that analysis begins with the written text, because that, and not oral tradition, is what we have, and we cannot tell whether, or how, performance in the earliest Christian communities took place ("No Performance Criticism," 114).

63. Seal and Partridge, *Performing Scripture*, 9.

64. As we will note, for example, through Hearon's study of the differences in performance of the same text in different contexts by David Rhoads and Philip Ruge-Jones: "From Narrative to Performance."

movements and expressions in performance are "integral and indispensable means by which the meaning of the words is determined and the impact of the rhetoric is conveyed,"[65] but does not articulate *how*, or explicitly, *what* meaning particular gestures or expressions determine. Although Perry and Cousins both discuss their audiences, and to some extent their own emotional engagement with their performed compositions,[66] I have not discovered a comprehensive discussion of *how* it was that a performer-interpreter's audience shaped meaning, or body or emotion showed new or nuanced understanding of the composition in performance. BPC largely still seeks, furthermore, to understand meaning in a composition's *origins*, and it is largely an approach to exegesis of the performed history, with contemporary performance a demonstration or test of that exegesis. Embodied Performance Analysis, in contrast, is an approach to exegesis *by*, or *through*, performance.

EPA begins with embodiment and notes embodied responses; it begins with reception today and observes the way a work is nuanced by the audience's particular context. EPA is interpretation in both the performance and reflection on the performance. It is a new step for "storyteller" BPC that listens first and foremost to the experience of the performer from inside, from having internalized, the composition.

Building a Method from My Practice: Embodied and Performed

I seek to attend to a way of making meaning, then, that is constantly engaged for humans, yet rarely heeded within biblical scholarship.[67] This project is an attempt to bring the whole human person to the task of biblical interpretation—not only our rational, objective, cognition. For the arts restore the integrity of mind and body,[68] so that by perceiving—which is a whole body exercise—we understand; for "imagining and understanding are the same thing."[69] Lorraine Helms claims that "feminist Shakespeareans may

---

65. Rhoads, "Emerging Methodology Part 2," 177.
66. Perry, *Insights from Performance Criticism*; Cousins, "Pilgrim Theology."
67. Ward and Trobisch, *Bringing the Word to Life*, viii–xii.
68. Wilson, *Psychology for Performing Artists*, 19.
69. Cook, "Interplay," 589. In fact, Cook suggests that difficult plays such as those of Shakespeare may continue to be performed precisely *because* they require more imaginative work from the audience, engaging more of the brain in order to make meaning (587). Shakespeare demands much of the actor, too, who in the embodied acts of speaking the dialogue and enacting the play onstage more fully discover the meaning in the words, and in the spaces between them: Brown, "Learning Shakespeare's Secret Language," 217.

begin to create a theatre where patriarchal representations of femininity can be transformed into roles for living women";[70] my hope is that Embodied Performance Analysis might create a forum in which objective rational representations of the Bible can be transformed into a story for living humans. Further, as Hristic sees in Aeschylus (*Agamemnon*): "A connection . . . must exist between what is happening to us and what we think, between experience and the idea, between the body and the philosophy."[71]

An Embodied Approach: Personal and Particular

Rosemary Radford Ruether observes that "all theology reflects the experience of the theologian."[72] Most often, however, the physical, emotional and relational experience of a theologian is relegated to the background, with a cursory acknowledgment of "bias" before a supposedly disembodied, rational and objective discussion. Humans *are* embodied, however, by the very fact of being organisms with bodies that engage with the world.[73] The proposed Embodied Performance method foregrounds the embodied situatedness of the biblical interpreter as more than mere bias: for in complex, integrated, and mysterious ways (which I will attempt to describe), "the body knows."[74]

The tools of the method distinguish three elements of "embodiment": physicality, emotionality, and relationality, tools that I am naming "body," "emotion," and "audience." Emotions are *embodied* and will be described and employed as such; the audience is utilized as an interpretive tool through the live *embodied* relationship an audience has with a performer; and most obviously, perhaps, the body is the site of the performer's *embodiment* of the text, with breath and a physical voice, posture and movement. We will hold in view at several stages through the development and test case of the method, the body of the performer, the emotions of the performer, and the performer's audience.

Further, the Critical Reflection will refer to *my* body, *my* emotions, and *my* audiences, as the performer in focus. This particularity of a person's embodied experience, rather than *dividing* "my" experience from another's and making it inaccessible to another, actually "may be the sign and substance

70. Helms, "Playing the Woman's Part," 200.
71. Hristic, "On the Interpretation of Drama," 352.
72. Ruether, *Sexism and God-Talk*, 12–13. Also May, "'Body Knows,'" 346.
73. Gallagher, "How the Body Shapes the Mind," 3. Further, all exegesis, its methods and approaches, is situated in particular locations and times: Porter, *Linguistic Analysis*, 95.
74. Wiebe, "Body Knows as Much as the Soul," 200.

of the promised abundance of life together."[75] For the goal of particularity is not to enable "abstract generalizations," but to provide clear and accessible points of connection and identification for the receiver, through which they are able to feel emotion, use imagination, and themselves become immersed in the world of the "story" so as to make, or discover, meaning. Furthermore, literature (and we might confidently include the Bible in such a category) "engages the emotions in processes of wise discernment through which we strongly identify with others whose lives are different from our own."[76] As noted, the Critical Reflection, while within the broad genre of academic writing and biblical commentary, will be presented in a more narrative style. This element of the analysis tells the story of my encounter with Romans in performance, preparation, and reflection, and features me as the main character along with my audiences and even the letter, our characterization developing through the narrative, and changing in response to the encounter. In this way (as does the discussion in the book overall), it resembles theological reflective writing. Heather Walton describes reflexivity as "an important concept within current debates about epistemology (ways of knowing), where it is used to highlight the role that the self plays in the generation of all forms of knowledge about the world."[77]

The complex and mutually transformative interplay between the self and the other that Walton further describes[78] will be observed between not only performer and audience, but also between performer and the biblical composition. For "the text is also a body, one that shows itself to (and hides itself from) its readers. Those readers are *also* living bodies entering into dialogue and struggling with that other body, the text."[79]

In order to understand the contribution performance can make in biblical studies, it is vital to acknowledge that this particularity of experience an interpreter brings to her encounter with a composition is a strength, a positive element of the experience.[80] As Sadia Zoubir-Shaw notes from her study

---

75. May, "'Body Knows,'" 347: "To claim my body as knower is to claim epistemological physicality and possibility."

76. Walton, *Writing Methods*, 144. Following philosopher Martha Nussbaum. See, for example, Nussbaum's examination of emotions through various creative works in *Uphevals of Thought*.

77. Walton, *Writing Methods*, xvi.

78. Walton, *Writing Methods*, xvi.

79. Pereira, "Body as Hermeneutical Category," 236. Rhoads makes a similar observation: "the texts take on different meanings spoken to different people in different social locations" ("Emerging Methodology Part 2," 179).

80. As we noted above that Shimon Levy and his theatrical interpreters do (*Bible as Theatre*, ix).

of students engaged in a performance learning project: "theatre pedagogy gives access to participants' own ideas and impulses, expanding the avenues of communication and interaction with the self and one's socio-cultural environment."[81] If it is in the constrained situatedness of an embodied organism that experience leads to knowing, then whatever state "I" am in as an embodied organism will shape how I perceive the world, respond to the world, and make meaning of the world.[82] This *is* how humans understand, and this current project seeks to attend to that knowing in the context of encounters with biblical texts.

It may well be noted that any scholarly interpretation is a weighing of possible meanings, by a particular scholar, discerning the most plausible option in their particular temporal and cultural (and everything else) context. Traditional Bible commentaries do not "speak" from the first person perspective, however ("I" think this, "I" observe that), but from a rational objectivity that seeks to create distance between scholar and text.[83] To the detriment of the field, in my estimation, the kinship between imagination and theology is "often forgotten in our time, especially in theological circles."[84] For, again, "people have always used their experiences . . . as a vivid source of theological understanding."[85]

An Embodied Approach: Immersive and Intuitive

As embodied beings, immersed in particular contexts, experiences, and relationships, humans learn what they know with all their being, intuitive and conscious. A striking example of such immersion and intuition comes from the life and death world of the armed services. Studies have shown that a soldier can intuitively predict an ambush, and that this intuition is based on experience. A lieutenant is described as having the following stored in her memory when she makes that intuitive deduction:

---

81. Zoubir-Shaw, "Staging History." I return to this study below.

82. Gallagher, *How the Body Shapes the Mind*, 2–3. From feminist theory we learn that "the world looks different according to the place from which it is viewed": Walton, *Writing Methods*, xvii.

83. Boomershine, *Messiah of Peace*, 9.

84. Kreglinger, *Storied Revelations*, 5. See also Walton's discussion of poetics (crafted creative writing) and practical theology: *Writing Methods*, 137ff.

85. Walton, *Writing Methods*, xiii. Further, Boomershine identifies that contemporary audiences "will be interested in the experience of the literature as well as its analysis," advocating for renewal in the format of biblical commentary: "All Scholarship Is Personal," 287. Also, Hefner, Pederson, and Barreto, *Our Bodies Are Selves*, 182: "When we remember and share our life stories with one another, we encounter the sacred."

> She has a list of the dimensions detailing what constitutes an ambush site versus a nonambush [sic] site. She has values along each of these dimensions for each of the ambush and nonambush sites that she has experienced or learned about. She has a mental model that assigns weights to each of these basic dimensions or features (and to higher order features, such as the interaction between two dimensions). On the basis of past experiences with similar sets of features, she determines whether the present features more closely resemble those associated with ambushes or nonambushes.[86]

Another example is the experienced chess player who can recreate the moves that led to a mid-game scenario presented to them, and do so in five seconds; they are immersed in chess-playing, and so understand intuitively the story of the game.[87] Seligman and Kahana also observed intuition learned by immersion, noting that "simple repeated experience with forced choice seems to build intuition."[88] They observed that "professional Japanese chicken-sexers can tell male from female chicks at a glance, and they cannot explain how they do it."[89] That embodied, intuitive knowing is often difficult to articulate, is one of the significant challenges for this study.

An example more closely related to this present study is the theater-pedagogy study mentioned earlier. One can observe the efficacy of immersion in the experience of students learning about an event in French history as a part of their French language studies.[90] The students reconstructed the historical events of the "wrongful 1895 conviction of French-Jewish army captain Alfred Dreyfus as a German spy"[91] for an interactive, mixed-media theater performance. Immersed in the researching, composing, producing, and presenting of this historical event for an audience, students were seen to engage more thoroughly and positively in their studies, to direct their own learning, and to demonstrate successful learning outcomes. "Aspects of the

---

86. Seligman and Kahana, "Unpacking Intuition," 400.

87. Schwerdtfeger, "Learned Intuition."

88. Seligman, "Unpacking Intuition," 401. See also Jorgen Weidemann Erikson's application of Dreyfus and Dreyfus' theories of learned intuition in the military context. "Dreyfus and Dreyfus understand moral behavior as a skill, and as such they claim that it is possible to develop this capability through practice. They even claim that intuitive behavior is the hallmark of the way experts respond to situations. The article seeks to investigate if the prerequisites for development of experience-based intuition are fulfilled inside the frames of military operations": "Should Soldiers Think before They Shoot?," 195.

89. "Unpacking Intuition," 401.

90. Zoubir-Shaw, "Staging History."

91. Zoubir-Shaw, "Staging History," 21 (n. 1).

actor-character relationship that ensued revealed multiple layers of interpretive knowledge and discourse that students drew from their research and collaborative work, and shed light on the non-linguistic cultural elements of the course: costumes, music, props, illustration, conception, staging, conceptualization, characterization, and class mates' and protagonists' interacting."[92]

In Chapter 3, I will discuss the work of educators using performance in the Biblical Studies classroom.[93] The emphasis in that discussion will be the scholars' observation of their and their students' performance choices and the influence of those choices on interpretation. Here, it is worth noting that these students immersed in biblical compositions, embodying them for a performance as part of their studies, experienced a profound depth of engagement and understanding unlike more traditional learning. Students may have previously "discussed the humanity of Jesus in Mark's portrayal, but they did not really understand what this *meant* until they played Jesus themselves in flesh and blood."[94] Students described feeling and thereby understanding Jesus' human emotions, the challenges he faced, and his challenge to the traditions and customs of his time and their own.[95]

If biblical scholars immerse themselves in the biblical compositions, physically, emotionally, and in community,[96] they will experience a level of familiarity with those compositions that will enable intuitive understanding. Such immersion in the biblical compositions activates and stimulates the unconscious, embodied, multi-layered knowing of these texts, knowledge unavailable through traditional interpretive methods.

The challenge for this project, then, is how to engage with and communicate from that knowing? For Zoubir-Shaw's French students, "performance, as a didactic tool, provides an opportunity to close the distance between the static account of a factual textbook and the comprehension and cognitive immersion needed to transcend the remoteness inherent to past and historical events."[97]

---

92. Zoubir-Shaw, "Staging History," 20.
93. For example, Swanson, "'This Is My . . .'"; Ruge-Jones, "The Word Heard."
94. Ruge-Jones, "The Word Heard," 106 (emphasis added).
95. Ruge-Jones, "The Word Heard," 106–7.
96. Ruge-Jones, "The Word Heard," 106. Also, Boomershine, *Story Journey*, 18: "Storytelling creates community."
97. Zoubir-Shaw, "Staging History," 12.

A Performance Approach: Personal and Particular

The live performance moment creates a relationship between performer and audience. The biblical compositions that a performer-interpreter embodies also possess a personal, relational quality, for their writers "were enmeshed participants" in community, "not at all objective" in their composing of these works.[98] We are enmeshed participants in our world, too, so that we cannot "listen to the prophet's cry for justice without seeing the need for justice for exploited workers at garment factories in Sri Lanka," for example.[99]

The live, embodied performance moment brings people, whole, physical, emotional, and relational beings, into a space in which they encounter each other and themselves, performer and composition, none of them leaving the encounter unchanged.[100] Renowned theater practitioner Stanislavski observes: "in the theatre with a packed audience, with a thousand hearts beating in unison with the actor's heart a wonderful resonant acoustic is created for our feelings. For every moment genuinely experienced onstage we get back a response from the audience, participation, empathy, invisible currents from a thousand living, emotionally stimulated people who create the performance with us."[101] It need not be a thousand hearts. I have performed in my home for one person, been the single audience member for them in return, and it is the same personal, relational connection of those hearts beating in unison, within the world of the composition in performance that Stanislavski describes. Again, this is true for the performer of poetry: "live poetry entails a direct encounter and physical co-presence of poet-performer and audience in a specific spatio-temporal situation."[102] Novak's observation here speaks not only to the personal, but also to the particular nature of performance. The particularity of each performance of a biblical composition brings about a different approach to biblical interpretation. Performance Criticism of the Bible is thus "no longer objective."[103] The language for discussing insights and meaning discerned must also change tone from a more pejorative declamation of meaning that might be expected to remain true across time and place, or a claim for a supposed original meaning of a composition, to more careful, nuanced, qualified

---

98. Perry, *Insights*, 151.
99. Perry, *Insights*, 156.
100. See, for example, Fischer-Lichte, *Ästhetik des Performativen*.
101. Stanislavski, *An Actor's Work*, 294.
102. Novak, "Performing the Poet," 358.
103. Perry, *Insights*, 156.

observations of meaning in this time and place, for this audience.[104] Embodied Performance Analysis acknowledges that in each reception, a biblical composition is somewhat changed by its encounter with this receiver, this context, this lived experience into which it has been proclaimed.[105] That is not to say other approaches are somehow invalid or not useful; it is to say, however, that in a time in which our culture is reclaiming more positive and holistic perspectives of the human person,[106] new ways of engaging with sacred compositions will emerge that reflect and speak to and with that changing perspective.

This personal, and therefore subjective, nature of EPA may be subject to the same sort of critique sometimes made of audience studies. Such an approach "can open itself to accusations that it fails to situate the performance within a broader social context, that it replaces rigorous research with self-indulgent soul-searching, and that it ultimately tells us more about the writer than about the work being commented upon."[107]

Taking a more reflective and narrative approach to the Critical Reflection I will explicitly tell the story of my encounter with the composition, as its mediator, and seek to utilize the particularities of my personal encounter with the letter to describe the meaning I found through that encounter. I do not claim to offer an interpretation that stands outside time or place, but intentionally to analyze what the biblical composition means when received in a particular location, community, time. For this *is* the interpretive work of communities of faith, their readers and preachers, week upon week.[108] It is time, I contest, to attend to that interpretive work and allow it to contribute to broader conversations about the meaning of biblical compositions, as a legitimate interpretive process that foregrounds the human meaning-making tools of body, emotion, and relationship. It is time to let go of the scholarly fear of subjective knowledge that comes from experience, and

---

104. Wire, *Holy Lives*, 11–12. As Frederick Buechner observes: "Once upon a time is this time, now" (*Telling the Truth*, 90–91), as cited in Lee, *Preaching*, 122.

105. In post-modern understanding, meaning is "a product of communal interpretation and intersubjectivity": it is contextual, timely, subjective, and fluid (Lee, *Preaching*, 60, 65).

106. See Hefner, *Our Bodies Are Selves*. See also discussion in Lee, *Preaching*, 60–65.

107. Freshwater, *Theatre and Audience*, 25.

108. Hunt, "Be Ye Speakers," 152. Richard Ward finds meaning in the Gospel through performance in community, noting that "the 'action' of Mark's gospel is performed—that is, 'carried through to completion'—in the *actions of the community* to which it is given": "The End Is Performance: Performance Criticism and the Gospel of Mark," in *Preaching Mark's Unsettling Messiah*, 88–101.

embrace the first-hand knowledge of one who has encountered a composition through mutual embrace (or indwelling).[109]

Caution will need to continue in the performer-interpreter's approach, however, for the personal nature of performance can also lead an audience to conflate the performer's identity with the character/ author / poet / persona.[110] A poet in residence may lose his position if the listeners conflate the distinct voices of author / performer / fictive speaker in the poem, to misinterpret the poem and the poet's intentions and meaning and take offence where none was meant.[111] "On a perceptual level the spoken word still appears to listeners as 'entirely tied up with the person.'"[112]

The experience of the performer and a particular performance will continue to shape one's interpretation of a play or biblical composition beyond the moment. If performer and audience approach the encounter with humility and an openness to the ongoing conversation in which any work participates in reception, the of-the-moment particularities may add richness to the composition's evolving meaning. For the "meaning of the text [does come] to bear at the point where it is performed,"[113] as an audience's responses, or the context of the moment, shape, and enhance meaning. For example, actual tricks in the sky augmented the impact of a moment in an open-air performance of *Measure for Measure*. There is a scene in which the character describes human ignorance, and then the actress said: "'Play such fantastic tricks before high heaven, as makes the angels weep,' and just as I said 'Play such fantastic tricks before high heaven,' this big helicopter came over, and I just indicated it, because a helicopter is a pretty fantastic trick!"[114] In the moment, the "fantastic trick in heaven" was interpreted to be a helicopter. And I imagine that actors and audience experiencing that moment will recall it in future encounters with *Measure for Measure*'s discussion of human ignorance, or, indeed, with helicopters. The merit in an interpretation in the moment is the meaning for that encounter of a work, unique

---

109. Novak observes the trust in a poet from an audience who assume the poet performing her own work has "first-hand knowledge" of the meaning of the poem: "Performing the Poet," 365. In the context of the performance of the sacred works of a community of faith, there is some implicit trust placed in the performer-interpreter from the audience, that she will speak from first-hand experience of encounter with the composition and the Holy One these works are expected to reveal (see Buckley, *Dancing with Words*, 54–56).

110. Novak, "Performing the Poet," 372.

111. Novak, "Performing the Poet," 372.

112. Novak, "Performing the Poet," 372.

113. Rhoads, "Biblical Performance Criticism," 163.

114. Gale, "Isabella Played by Mariah Gale. Performance 1."

and original in that performance, and also the texture that interpretation adds to the continuing conversation of the composition in future reception scenarios.

A Performance Approach: Immersive and Intuitive

This example also provides insight into the immersive nature of performance: that Gale could in the moment respond to the helicopter to see it as a "fantastic trick before high heaven" shows that she understood the language and meaning of that phrase from within the world of the play. From my experience, I suggest that Gale had some image in her mind of a "fantastic trick before heaven," with which the helicopter resonated, so that in that iteration of the play, she could point to a physical representation of what she would have otherwise imagined.

Performances are immersive experiences most profoundly for the performer, but also meaningfully for the receivers: "Story spoken aloud, poetry seen and silently read from a page or recited aloud from a podium, drama acted out and/or spoken by actors on a stage or on a television or movie screen—these are creative acts imbibed by our very bodies, felt and experienced there,"[115] and "the more fully experienced the more fully embodied."[116] Such immersion in the text will encourage non-verbal communication and integrated whole person understanding, utilizing both embodied, intuitive knowing, as well as conscious understanding. Thus EPA presents a way to know and understand the Bible experientially as embodied interpreters; to communicate our learning with embodied receivers; to learn again in those embodied relationships; and to communicate again the embodied process as interpretation.

Biblical texts as "creative acts" are whole body experiences: "Performance criticism helps readers of the Bible reconnect the body (including emotions) with the mind in experiencing the text."[117] Performance criticism engages in participatory epistemology, as meaning is made through experience of the composition in community,[118] the experience of the mutual indwelling of performer, composition, and audience.

---

115. Wiebe, "The Body Knows as Much as the Soul," 190.

116. Wiebe, "The Body Knows as Much as the Soul," 190.

117. Perry, *Insights*, 147.

118. Perry, *Insights*, 147. This does not negate the value of propositional knowledge, however; for a full meaning-making process, both propositional and participatory knowledge are required: Mathews, *Performing Habakkuk. Faithful Re-Enactment in the Midst of Crisis*, 31. See also Conquergood, "Performance Studies."

MUTUALITY: UNREALIZED PURPOSE?

Mutuality has a quality of mutual obligation born of mutual need; of other-regard that seeks the good of the other first, *and also* good of self. For people of faith, "God is the basis of mutual relation."[119] This goal of good for the other is not entirely selfless, however. The give and take of relationships of true mutuality *is* intrinsically beneficial to both parties to the relationship. Mutuality is paradoxical: its outcome of good for the self is a consequence of the objective of seeking good for the other. Even so, for this project at least, mutuality is not understood to be synonymous with reciprocity, particularly the formal reciprocity that was a guiding principle for first century relationships in Roman culture.[120] Indeed, "mutuality would be perverted if it would seek for reciprocity."[121] The distinction is in the *intent* of participants in a relationship: reciprocity being characterized by self-regard, mutuality by other-regard.[122] Mutuality is a theme identified in the letter to the Romans, a feature some scholars have observed in Biblical Performance Criticism, and a focus for my broader work as a storyteller-poet-minister, as I have already noted. The context for my practice therefore brings together BPC and the letter to explore the further potential of mutuality within the scholarly field and our understanding of the composition.

Mutual Indwelling

I have described the experience of embodying a biblical composition for performance as an experience of mutual embrace, or perhaps better, indwelling: the words reside within the performer, the performer inhabits the "text" and both are changed. With this phrase of "mutual indwelling" one might think of Thomas Aquinas: "Mutual indwelling in the love of friendship can be understood in regard to reciprocal love: inasmuch as friends return love for love, and both desire and do good things for one another."[123]

---

119. Ehrensperger, *Mutually Encouraged*, 118.

120. See Osiek for a study of reciprocity in first century Roman culture: "Politics of Patronage."

121. Ehrensperger, *Mutually Encouraged*, 118.

122. In Paul's letters, such verses as Philippians 2:3–4, Gal 6:10, 1 Cor 12:25, and Rom 14:19 are examples of such "other-regard." As I will mention below, David Horrell notes Paul's deliberate use of kinship language "as part of an appeal for mutual regarding; for an 'other-regarding' morality, and specifically [in Rom 14 and 1 Cor 8] a concern for the weaker sibling": Horrell, *Solidarity and Difference*, 115.

123. Aquinas, "Summa Theologicae," QQ26–28. According to a recent study, mutual indwelling is arguably the "most proper" effect of love: Burns, "St Thomas

Such a relationship of love "involves what Tillich describes as mystical, ethical, and ontological faith."[124] It is a feature of the earliest Jesus-communities, which we understand through Paul's letters to be groups "of people who mutually committed themselves to act in concert."[125] One and another simultaneously give and receive, for the benefit of each.[126]

In the context of performance and interpretation, this kind of love means "that the interpreter enters into a relationship with the text and longs for union with it, but through surrender of self to the text, is committed to the preservation of its integrity and identity as a subject apart."[127] It is important to remember that mutuality requires that the two participants in the relationship *are* distinct, discrete, subjects apart. If they become one entity, unable to be discerned one from the other, this is something other than mutuality, and not the aim of a performer-interpreter's relationship with composition or audience, nor the aim of Paul's vision of community.

The inherent mutuality of performance art is not a new topic of study or discussion, as we will see in the theater and audience studies that inform the development of the Embodied Performance methodology. In particular, the feedback from audience to performer that influences the performer's returning gift to the audience is a profound experience of the mutual acts of creation and meaning-making of a live performance event.

The mutuality of the strands of human being, with physical and affective, cognitive and soulful, rational and imaginative, individual and communal elements distinct and yet vitally linked in a whole is perhaps more often discussed in terms of holistic approaches to human being and well-being, rather than in internal mutuality of a person as environment.[128] And again, the integrative ethos of BPC as it draws on a range of approaches to biblical analysis is rarely described in terms of "mutuality" as such, but it is indeed such a giving and receiving of one to another in life-giving relationship.

In his letter to the Romans, Paul seeks to encourage mutuality as a feature of the Christ-following communities in Rome.[129] Their relationships

---

Aquinas's Philosophy of Love."

124. Bozarth, *The Word's Body*, 38.

125. Ehrensperger, *Paul and the Dynamics of Power*, 55.

126. For "love, as an act of charity, includes goodwill, but adds to it a union of the affections": Davies, *Thomas Aquinas's Summa Theologicae*, 243.

127. Bozarth, *The Word's Body*, 38.

128. Person as environment is an idea in Hefner, *Our Bodies Are Selves*, 88.

129. A feature identified by Ehrensperger, as discussed. See also Gaventa, "Cosmic Power of Sin," 236. Oestreich's interpretation of the impact of Paul's rhetoric in Rom 14 to move the audience from division to unity may also be an understanding of Paul's affirmation of mutuality: *Performance Criticism of the Pauline Letters*, 174–75.

are to be those of mutual encouragement, accommodating one another as Christ accommodates God's beloved, welcoming, loving, embracing, and thereby inhabiting one another's space. But they are to maintain their own identity, subjects apart, Jew *and* Gentile; not assimilate one group's identity into the other's. Difference is not to be overcome, but is rather a "presupposition for real unity."[130]

This feature of Paul's letter (his letters broadly) drew me to a biblical composition to which I had not previously been naturally drawn because of its internal complexities and its problematic history of reception. If mutuality, mutual indwelling, is a particular feature of the art of storytelling, and if letter writing is "the only written form of communication which allows for dialogue and mutuality"[131] (at least within the first century media culture), then storytelling is an ideal medium through which to further explore the mutuality one may find in Romans. The letter to the Romans may in turn be an ideal medium for exploring the potential for performance interpretation of the Bible.

Mutual indwelling is, then, the theme in both the test case and the proposed methodology alike. Mutuality needs both the individual and the communal, distinctness and difference along with unity and togetherness. We will see that Paul's vision of Christian community is one that celebrates difference, indeed welcomes it, for the opportunity it provides for mutual embrace of one another. We will see that Embodied Performance Analysis is an approach that celebrates the fullness of human being and ways of understanding—not only the rational, cognitive and objective, but also the intuitive, affective, relational, and physical ways of making meaning. As we consider this central focus of the project, it will be helpful to further reflect on mutuality as a theme across Paul's letters generally.

Mutuality in Paul's Letters

Mutuality emerged as a key feature of feminist theology and approaches to biblical scholarship. It is a feature that has been identified as shared with the letters of Paul, in a meeting that seeks to read those letters anew.[132] Identifying mutuality as a key ethic for Paul, Ehrensperger also suggests that it is a key for ethics and theology today, in the endeavor to encourage healthy relationships across difference.[133]

130. Ehrensperger, *Mutually Encouraged*, 199.
131. Ehrensperger, *Paul and the Dynamics of Power*, 56.
132. Ehrensperger, *Mutually Encouraged*, 194.
133. Ehrensperger, *Mutually Encouraged*, 193.

The mutuality between individuals and between individual and community is the overarching concern of Paul in his writing to emerging Christian communities.[134] Paul's letters build a picture of one whose "emphasis is on being an apostle among other apostles, that is, on the mutual recognition of each other's work in a community of equals."[135] Named variously by interpreters as solidarity,[136] benefaction, friendship,[137] kinship[138] and mutuality,[139] the letters speak of brothers and sisters[140] (Phlm 1:16; Rom 16:1), partnership (Phlm 1:17), loving each other (Gal 5:6b; 1 Cor 12:31; Phlm 1:8; Rom 12:8–10; Phil 2:1–2), "mutual upbuilding" (Rom 14:19) and, most profoundly perhaps, of the many members becoming one body in Christ (1 Cor 12:14; Rom 12:4–5). Paul himself "appears as one of many engaged in the work of the gospel and his primary concern seems to be that this work be done."[141] Note the multiple examples I have cited from Philemon; Rhoads sees the original performance of this letter as a teaching opportunity in which the whole community are reminded to participate in counter-cultural relationships of mutual respect and care.[142]

Of particular interest to this study, mutual obligation in a legalistic sense has been observed between Paul and Phoebe; in 16:1–2 Paul is seen to introduce Phoebe to his networks as a reciprocal requirement in return for the benefaction Phoebe has given to Paul.[143] Here we encounter the debate over the interpretation of προστάτης (*prostates*).[144] Paul names Phoebe προστάτης—which may be translated as *patron*. But are we to see here the formal patron–client reciprocity of expectation and hierarchy? Or is this,

---

134. Particularly evident in the letter to the Romans, in which the theme of mutuality is present throughout, with more concentrated discussion in 12–15, and reflected particularly in the greetings in Rom 16: Mathew, "Women in the Greetings of Romans 16:1–16, 42. See also Ehrensperger, *Mutually Encouraged*, 193.

135. Ehrensperger, *Paul and the Dynamics of Power*, 45.

136. Seeing solidarity as a "corporate bound-togetherness": Horrell, *Solidarity and Difference* 99.

137. MacGillivray offers an interpretation of the relationship between Paul and Phoebe as a kind of benefaction between friends: MacGillivray, "Romans 16:2," 198–99.

138. Horrell, *Solidarity and Difference* 119.

139. Mathew, "Women in the Greetings," 37.

140. "Sibling language is preferred by Paul when speaking directly to his communities, indicating that although in an asymmetrical relationship with them, he sees himself as one within a group of siblings": Ehrensperger, *Paul and the Dynamics of Power*, 126 n. 43.

141. Ehrensperger, *Paul and the Dynamics of Power*, 53.

142. Rhoads, "The New Testament as Oral Performance."

143. Mathew, "Women in the Greetings," 22.

144. I return to this issue in Chapter 6.

as MacGillivray describes, a "reciprocity between friends" more akin to the mutuality I describe above?[145]

Ehrensperger poses the question of hierarchy, wondering if Phoebe is Paul's equal, superior, or subordinate.[146] The possibility that she could be all three, whether simultaneously or at different times, is a feature of the fluid and flexible power dynamics of the networks of mutual responsibility and solidarity Ehrensperger observes through Paul's letters.[147]

Carolyn Osiek would see the relationship between Paul and Phoebe as exhibiting a kind of mutuality that completes, or makes whole, each person in the relationship.[148] As an artist may have once depended on a patron for financial resources not otherwise available, the artist would have taught, guided, provided art and beauty the patron could not do for him/herself.[149] In such mutual relationships, each has something to give, and each has something to receive. As noted, humans need each other, in our difference, for our wholeness. I will discuss this further in Chapter 6, and my intuitive sense that Paul acknowledges and affirms such mutual care and respect, not only with his words, but also in his relationships, indicated by those words. I will also discuss in the Critical Reflection (Chapter 6) the way that, in Performance Interpretation (Chapter 5) of Romans a community-ethos of true mutuality between humans became evident through the repeated gesture accompanying words describing mutual relationship. Feeling this rhetorical and emotional movement towards the climax in Rom 16, with Paul's repeated exhortation to embrace one another, I sought out the ways in which others have interpreted this ethos.

David Horrell, for example, argues that "other-regard" and "corporate solidarity" form central tenets in this community-ethos of Paul's letters.[150] By mutuality I mean such "other-regard" as Horrell describes,[151] or even the ability of individuals "to relate to each other and form a community because

---

145. MacGillivray, "Romans 16:2," 198. Osiek ("Politics of Patronage," 147) suggests that Paul's choice of language of kinship rather than language of friendship supports his encouragement of unity and harmony.

146. Ehrensperger, *Paul and the Dynamics of Power*, 53.

147. Ehrensperger, *Paul and the Dynamics of Power*, 54.

148. Osiek, "Politics of Patronage," 150: describing the relationship as "complementary."

149. Osiek, "Politics of Patronage," 150

150. Horrell, *Solidarity and Difference*, 204.

151. This other-regard has its foundation in the self-giving of Christ: "Self-giving out of regard for others is no minor virtue in Paul's ethics, but rather a metanorm, a key moral value which fundamentally determines the shape of Christian relating" (Horrell, *Solidarity and Difference*, 242).

they share a common consciousness, or because they can empathetically understand the distinctiveness of the other and react to the other's needs and capacities so that the other feels recognized."[152] The Embodied Performance Analysis discerned in Paul's introduction of Phoebe his presentation of her to the church as representative of not only himself, but also of this very mutuality, as *our sister, one who leads the church by giving of herself.*

This is a relation-focused letter,[153] and Phoebe's introduction is given in relational terms with its sibling language, and her community roles. For Paul, baptism into Christ is a transformative act, creating "a new kind of social reality," as can be seen in Romans 6.[154] He may have struggled with full immersion in such practice himself, as traces do remain in his letters of the distinctions he elsewhere claims have been rendered irrelevant by God in Christ.[155] He does not speak against the slavery one might argue is a diminishing of humanity, for example, and in places he allows the gendered hierarchy of the culture to override the gender equality he demonstrates in his own relationships of mutuality with women such as Phoebe.[156] On occasion, in order that the message of the gospel may be clearly shared, the maintenance of cultural practice is privileged above the radically transformed way of being of Christian community.[157] Paul's affirmation and appreciation of the leadership of women in Romans 16 is, however, offered "without any reservation."[158]

We can thus say, these diversions notwithstanding, Paul's theology of mutuality in community does appear in what evidence we can glean from the letters to be supported in his own practice of mutual partnerships that draw on the strengths of each in humility for the sake of the fullness of all, through God in Christ. Indeed, what power is exercised within the leadership structures is fluid, negotiated in service of the gospel, and even designed

---

152. Horrell, *Solidarity and Difference*, 204–05.

153. Ehrensperger, *Mutually Encouraged*, 108. Further, it is through ἀδελφός language that Paul exhorts the community to engage in the practice of "other-regard" that Horrell identifies: *Solidarity and Difference* 115.

154. Ehrensperger, *Mutually Encouraged*, 193. Ehrensperger notes that Paul is especially concerned with the mutuality of members of the Jesus-community who are different, who occupy different positions vis-à-vis power dynamics in the Roman church. Paul exhorts welcome of one another as equals, in their differences.

155. Horrell, *Solidarity and Difference* 104.

156. Thurston, *Women in the New Testament*, 158; Osiek, "Politics of Patronage," 31.

157. For example, see Khiok-Khng's discussion of 1 Cor 11: "Differentiation and Mutuality."

158. Ehrensperger, *Paul and the Dynamics of Power*, 55.

to "render itself obsolete."[159] Examples of Paul's mutual relationships with others can be found in the commendations of Phil 2:25–30; 4:2–3; 1 Cor 16:15–18; and 1 Thess 5:12–13. Ehrensperger highlights the corporate task of communication, with greetings offered from others in the letters suggesting a group with whom Paul is in conversation over issues concerning life in the way of the gospel.[160] These conversations are easily imagined to have shaped and contributed to the content of his letters (as I have done in the Phoebe narrative presented at Uniting College in 2016).[161] The list of people in Rom 16 is the most comprehensive picture of Paul's own commitment to the goal of mutual encouragement.[162]

OUTLINE: PLOTTING THE STORY

Now that I have introduced the project, and myself as storyteller seeking to examine my process and the scholarly field of Biblical Performance Criticism and the Embodied Performance Analysis as a new methodology, let us consider how the story will unfold from here.

The next step is a fuller discussion of BPC, the first foundation on which my new method stands. Chapter 2 describes the narrative beginnings of what I am naming the "storyteller's" stream of BPC. I will discuss the approach that began to treat Gospels as stories, integrated and whole, and we will see that this approach elicited the question, "How, then, were those stories told and received?" *Mark as Story*[163] in its three editions, and *Mark as Story: Retrospect and Prospect*,[164] will frame the discussion of Narrative and Performance approaches to biblical interpretation as we uncover the central aim of BPC I had not anticipated when I embarked on this journey: to identify and understand the oral and performed *history* of biblical compositions.

---

159. Ehrensperger, *Paul and the Dynamics of Power*, 61–62. Further, Ehrensperger suggests a temporal aspect may be observed, in that those who were in Christ first have responsibility to help those who come after to learn the way of the gospel. The aim is to become equal siblings together.

160. Ehrensperger, *Paul and the Dynamics of Power*, 57.

161. See track 24 in the video material online at https://sarahagnew.com.au/embodied-performance.

162. Agosto, "Patronage and Commendation," 109–19. These commendations are not discussed by Agosto for the theme of mutuality, but that Paul commends folk with whom he shares in ministry is itself testament to his practice of what he "preaches" concerning a community ethos of other-regard modelled on Christ.

163. Rhoads and Michie, *Mark as Story*; Rhoads, *Mark as Story* 3rd ed.

164. Iverson and Skinner, ed. *Retrospect and Prospect*.

Chapter 3 will further explore this feature of BPC as historical re-enactment, and fill out the picture of the two streams of "insider" and "outsider" practitioners that I identify.[165] I have mentioned already that EPA is aligned with the insider, or storyteller's stream of BPC, so while we will encounter some examples of scholarship that take an outsider, or "critic's" approach to BPC, my focus is on the storytellers. I will discuss in particular the application of Performance Criticism to Pauline epistles, to provide some context for the test case Embodied Performance Analysis of Romans. Finally, I will discuss the work of Peter Perry and Melinda Cousins, both of whom I have noted in this introduction, as their applications of BPC take further, and helpful, steps towards the approach of Embodied Performance Analysis.

Having sought and not found, it will then be my task to establish and introduce the method for EPA. To set the second foundation for the method, I engage in an inter-disciplinary discussion of the ways in which humans "know" or make meaning of the world beyond "intellect" or "cognition" that is often separated from the body and emotions in a privileging of rational objectivity in many fields of scholarship, including biblical studies. Scholarship from psychology, philosophy, and sociology is joined by insights from the theater, and in particular, actors and directors who present the works of William Shakespeare. As well as discussion of how the body knows, how emotion helps to understand, and how audiences shape performance, I will describe the ways in which these three tools will function within the Embodied Performance method. The method includes three stages of Preparation, Performance, and Reflection, and the Embodied Performance Analysis consists of two components, Performance Interpretation, and Critical Reflection. I will introduce Romans as the test case for the method, to conclude Part 1.

Part 2, Chapters 5 and 6 comprise the test case Embodied Performance Analysis of Romans. The first component of the Analysis is a recording of the live Performance Interpretation of Romans presented in Adelaide in April 2016. I encourage the reader to watch the performance without reference to the written script or biblical text, for it is an interpretation as it is, embodied, and to be watched, heard, and experienced. The Critical Reflection component discusses certain features of the Performance Interpretation that demonstrate the ways in which I interpreted the letter through my body, emotion, and with my audience. I identify the audience's influence on translation choices, and the way my audience helped to clarify an understanding of Paul's audience as both Jew *and* Gentile, together, which Paul

---

165. See Cousins, "Pilgrim Theology," 78.

seeks to encourage them to become once again. I will describe the way gesture highlighted the anticipated theme of mutuality, movement clarified the distinct voices Paul employs in the letter, and the influence of the method itself, as an approach valuing the body, along with the audience context, shaped my interpretation of Paul's "sin versus body" argument. The voice will be discussed at various points throughout the Critical Reflection, as it features in the application of all three tools of this method. In the discussion of emotion, I will particularly attend to what the voice says beyond words, the impact of inhabiting the rhythm of the letter, and the way that silence also speaks. I will identify particular emotions such as love, joy, disappointment, and compassion as significant in discerning meaning in the letter.

I finish the Critical Reflection with a more integrated discussion of Rom 16 and its call to enacted mutual embrace as the climax, the impact, and the meaning for today that emerged in the letter in performance. I describe the introduction of Phoebe as a key element in this climactic nature of the final chapter; narrate the significant interpretive decision away from the NRSV's "greet" to "embrace," influenced by, and with profound impact on, my audiences. Love is the emotion that weaves throughout the letter, and it makes sense of a point of disjunction for many as Paul warns the Romans to "take care." We experience Paul as a participant in relationships of mutuality in this chapter, asking nothing of the church in Rome that he himself does not practice. In the final doxology, as we will experience throughout the letter in performance, EPA is shown to be an interpretive approach that is confessional, unapologetically and necessarily so, in the embodiment of a letter, of any composition, whose purpose is to transform its receivers.[166]

Drawing this story to a close, and looking towards the work it has begun, Chapter 7 will review what we have learned from observing my practice as a storyteller. As we review the Embodied Performance methodology and its application in the test case, I will suggest some revisions to the method in light of this auto-ethnographic study. I will consider the contribution this study makes to biblical scholarship, situating EPA within the field of BPC. I will then suggest ways in which Embodied Performance may transform the work of scholars beyond BPC or even EPA, and the practice of readers and preachers in gathered worship, by attending to their physical, emotional, and relational responses to biblical compositions. In these primary contexts in which biblical interpretation occurs Embodied Performance methods may transform encounters with biblical compositions in scholarship and worship gatherings as the Bible is received in Jesus-communities of mutual embrace today.

---

166. Cousins, "Pilgrim Theology," 69. "The ultimate goal of such performance is audience or community transformation, a goal that corresponds with the ultimate goal of theological interpretation of Scripture."

2

The Search Begins

Narrative and Performance

Performing parts of the Bible showed me through my embodiment, new meaning in these compositions. How could I discuss those interpretive moves with other scholars and performers? Would Biblical Performance Criticism provide method and means? My search began.

NEW WAYS WITH GOSPEL STORIES

Having grown disillusioned with Redaction Criticism's deconstruction of the Gospels in the dominant approach to Gospel scholarship in the 20th century, some scholars looked to the techniques of narrative analysis that had long been applied in the field of literary studies.[1] David Rhoads, first with Donald Michie, then with Michie and Joanna Dewey, has authored one of the most important works in Gospel Narrative Criticism, now in its third edition. *Mark as Story*[2] will provide the basis for the ensuing discussion of Narrative Criticism, and BPC as one of a number of further new approaches to biblical interpretation to develop in its wake.

---

1. Rhoads, "Narrative Criticism," 412. Also Gunn, "Narrative Criticism," 201. Although by no means the first time the Bible had been approached through the lens of narrative: for example, the homiletical illustrations of Jacox, in *Traits of Character*.

2. Rhoads, *Mark as Story*; and Rhoads, *Mark as Story*, 3rd ed.

In a tribute to Rhoads on finishing his role at Lutheran School of Theology at Chicago, Thomas Boomershine describes the way both he and Rhoads became immersed in the new approach to criticism that is Narrative methodology.[3] Boomershine goes on to describe dissatisfaction even with this narrative approach they both helped to shape; a dissatisfaction created by their experiences of telling the stories as oral performance. The narrative methodology being employed, which had been developed for analyzing novels, was appropriate for a genre that emerged in the seventeenth century and grew through to the present. But the first century development of narrative was different, and through their impulse to discover the historical understanding of the original context of New Testament compositions, Rhoads and Boomershine had begun to imagine the oral communication prevalent, and perhaps dominant, in the first century.[4] Rhoads asked before the publication of *Mark as Story*, "was Mark's Gospel written to be read aloud? Should we not speak of 'hearers' (Boomershine, 1974) rather than readers? What would it suggest about the way we do scholarship on Mark if we began to relate to the text aurally as well as visually?"[5] To the aim of historical re-enactments of early performances of the Gospels and other biblical compositions, I return in Chapter 3. First, however, and although the historical and narrative questions overlap to a certain extent, I specifically address in this chapter the narrative origins of BPC. The discussion here will focus on the first and third editions of *Mark as Story*, with little reference to the second edition, then engage with selected chapters in the 2011 volume *Mark as Story: Retrospect and Prospect*.[6] Along the way, further scholarship on narrative and performance will add depth to the discussion.

MARK AS STORY

That *Mark as Story* is a foundation for BPC is acknowledged in the retrospective[7] that celebrates the first two editions and the fruit of its authors' work. The year following the retrospective, a third edition was published, which more explicitly incorporated the understanding of Mark as an oral composition.[8]

   3. Boomershine, "All Scholarship Is Personal," 280.

   4. Boomershine, "All Scholarship Is Personal," 280–81.

   5. Rhoads, "Narrative Criticism," 425. Note his reference to Boomershine's earlier doctoral dissertation, which provokes the question for Rhoads: Boomershine, "Mark, the Storyteller."

   6. Iverson, *Retrospect and Prospect*.

   7. Iverson, *Retrospect and Prospect*.

   8. Rhoads, *Mark as Story*, 3rd ed., xi–xii. It is interesting to note that in the

The aim of *Mark as Story* is to read the Gospel of Mark *as* a story: "this work was one of the early fruits of a movement within biblical scholarship that focused on Mark and other works of the New Testament as unified narratives rather than as a product of a tradition history process that could be traced by the methods of form, source, and redaction criticism."[9] By its third edition, *Mark as Story* helped to establish Mark as an oral, performative composition, after its first edition "helped to establish narrative criticism as a viable methodology for the study of biblical narratives."[10] The appendices of *Mark as Story* (third edition) include a set of steps for a narrative analysis of a biblical text.[11] Also included in the appendices are guidelines for learning and telling (performing) episodes of a Gospel.[12] These guidelines for performance take as their foundation the narrative analysis described in the appendix and demonstrated in the book. Even in its third edition, the analysis of Mark in *Mark as Story* is clearly a work of Narrative Criticism, although this work does describe the origins of the story as within an oral culture, and makes strong claims for it as orally composed and received. By this stage, *Mark as Story* encourages performance as well as narrative interpretation of the gospel.[13]

Mark as Story presents a translation of the Gospel that is set out like a short story, rather than with conventional biblical chapter and verse markers. This supports and demonstrates the central claim, that the Gospel of Mark is a story and is best treated as such.[14] The authors present four features of narrative analysis: rhetoric, setting, plot, and character.[15] The narrative analysis then proceeds as a reading of the story through the lenses of each of those features. The interpretation is not

---

retrospective, the authors were not anticipating this further revision of their work: "since there will be no third edition of *Mark as Story*, we are indeed grateful to have this chance to add a few of our recent insights and shifts in thinking" (Rhoads, "Reflections," 274).

9. Boomershine, "All Scholarship Is Personal," 280.
10. Boomershine, "All Scholarship Is Personal," 280.
11. Rhoads, *Mark as Story*, 3rd ed., 163–65.
12. Rhoads, *Mark as Story*, 3rd ed., 173–77.
13. Rhoads, *Mark as Story*, 3rd ed., xi–xii.
14. Rhoads, *Mark as Story*, 3rd ed., 1–8.
15. Rhoads, *Mark as Story*. In the third edition, rhetoric is analyzed in terms of the narrator, and audience is added to the analysis as the authors foreground the oral reception origins of the gospel: Rhoads, *Mark as Story*, 3rd ed. Neither approach is by any means indicative of a unified approach across the field of Narrative Criticism in biblical scholarship: Gunn lists features of structure, plot, characterization, point of view, language, and theme as integral to a narrative analysis ("Narrative Criticism," 201).

> an abstract substitute for the story itself. We do not want to reduce the story to a moral or a message or a summary, for then it is no longer a story. A story is not just a vehicle for an idea, such that the story can be discarded once one has the idea. Rather, our goal is to enhance the experience of the story as a story . . . For it is only in the reading and the hearing of the story itself that we experience its magic and its capacity to change us.[16]

It is not clear to what extent, if any, this analysis has drawn on performances by the authors themselves, although by the time of the third edition, Rhoads at least was regularly performing the Gospel and other NT writings.[17] *Mark as Story* imagines examples of ancient presentations of the Gospel, although the authors "think Mark's story was composed for performances before many different audiences."[18] However, they do imagine an ideal audience,[19] which Mark creates through the rhetoric of the story.

The central claim, that Mark is a story, is a feature of Narrative Criticism that has greatly influenced the field of Markan studies, as well as wider scholarship in the study of both the New Testament and the Old Testament/Hebrew Bible.

Strengths and Limitations

As noted, narrative critics such as Rhoads soon began to ask how the story was received in its origins and to use performance or oral storytelling to reconstruct possible ancient reception scenarios. By the third edition, *Mark as Story* foregrounds first-century orality as a feature of the Gospels to be taken seriously, with its concluding chapter's discussion of the audience presenting a picture of the ideal audience for a possible ancient performance scenario.[20] Although I was disappointed to find such a dominant historical focus within BPC, considering it to limit the potential contribution of the act of performance to interpretation today, this is indeed one of the strengths of the early period of BPC. Reimagining not only the nature of the Gospels *as* story, but also *how* these stories were composed and received, has ignited a rich debate about first century literacy and oral communication, challenging the accepted view of the Gospels (the whole Bible) as

---

16. Rhoads, *Mark as Story*, 3rd ed., 8.
17. As Boomershine notes in "All Scholarship Is Personal."
18. Rhoads, *Mark as Story*, 3rd ed., 146ff.
19. A particular feature of Narrative Criticism: for example, see Malbon, "Characters in Mark's Story."
20. Rhoads, *Mark as Story*, 3rd ed., 137–52.

static, book-bound pages of written text alone.[21] Experienced as a story, the Gospel of Mark is more dynamic and fluid in its content and meaning. This enriches our reimagining of the first century church and the transmission of the Gospels, as a gift to historical-critical research and study of the New Testament. It also pre-empts the contemporary performance focus I was seeking from BPC—for, "having experienced this story world [of Mark], contemporary readers may be able to think anew about the meaning of life, its purpose, its possibilities, and its outcome—to see and struggle with the real world in new ways and perhaps be better prepared to live more faithful and humane lives."[22]

The authors of *Mark as Story*, studying the Gospel *as* a story, then began to wonder how the story was initially received, and look for the evidence of performance and orality within the written text. *Mark as Story* is not BPC itself, nor does it claim to be so, even in its most recent edition, but it does represent a significant step on the path towards performance analysis of biblical compositions.

From the earliest edition of *Mark as Story* the authors acknowledge the first century context for receiving the Gospel: "Mark's Gospel was probably written to be heard rather than read. It would therefore be appropriate to refer to the hearers of the drama."[23] However, *Mark as Story* seems remarkably focused on the "reader"[24] rather than "audience." While addressing "readers" in first and second editions, because their own audience were understood to *be* readers (not hearers) of the Gospel in their scholarly pursuits, the authors nevertheless "encourage the reader to listen to the story read aloud, for hearing the story may help to broaden and deepen the experience of it."[25]

In the third edition, the authors have made progress in their own treatment of the Gospels towards what they would define as Biblical Performance Criticism. The purpose has not changed, however, as it is still written as a resource for (by now) twenty-first-century *readers* of the Bible, offering an approach to reading and interpretation that treats the Gospel as a unified,

---

21. Boomershine, "All Scholarship Is Personal," 283–86. See also Dewey, *Oral Ethos*; and Hurtado, "Oral Fixation."

22. Rhoads, *Mark as Story*, 3rd ed., 152.

23. Rhoads, *Mark as Story*, 143.

24. According to Boomershine, this was a deliberate choice for the original edition, as the target audience was seminary students who would likely predominantly engage with the biblical texts by silent reading: "All Scholarship Is Personal," 280.

25. Rhoads, *Mark as Story*, 7. And to hear it in full, although they do not describe *how* the experience of hearing the Gospel will enrich the experience of it.

autonomous whole.²⁶ By the third edition, Rhoads, Dewey, and Michie allow the continuing work in orality and performance studies to more directly shape their approach to Mark as a story. Now fully committed to an understanding of the original reception context as predominantly oral/aural, through storytellers, the authors treat the Gospel as a "composition," and its author as a "composer."²⁷ This reflects treatment of biblical writings as scripts, historical artefacts, or remnants of performances with embedded clues for its later performance.²⁸ As well as exercises for narrative analysis, the third edition includes exercises for learning and performing the Gospel.²⁹ Performance of Mark today in this approach arises from the narrative engagement with the Gospel, a practical application of the approach to the Gospel that treats it as a story, employing the craft of "storytelling."³⁰

The development of this stream of Biblical Performance Criticism thus begins with treating the Gospel as a story, and engaging with it as such, to observe what nuanced experiences and new interpretations that yields. We will see examples of this approach in selected chapters from *Mark as Story: Retrospect and Prospect,* below. Over the course of its revisions, *Mark as Story* plots the development of BPC from an acknowledgment-in-passing of the oral/aural reception context of the first century, with simultaneous acknowledgment of the reception today predominantly by silent individual reading; to overt change in language, foregrounding the oral/aural origins of the Gospel with strong encouragement for twenty-first-century readers to become performers and hearers of the Gospels.

The guidelines for telling the story move towards what I was seeking from a biblical performance method, including a preparation phase, performance, and reflection stages, and attention to the body's speaking and moving, and emotion.³¹ However, in this early method "the goal is to gain an understanding of the passage and its potential impact, and *then* seek

---

26. Rhoads, *Mark as Story*, 3rd ed., xii.

27. Rhoads, *Mark as Story*, 3rd ed., xii. See Dewey's collected essays for more on the oral origins of Mark: *Oral Ethos* (especially Part 2).

28. Rhoads, *Mark as Story*, 3rd ed., xii. Such treatment has influenced the perspective and approach of scholars and storytellers alike to view the biblical writings as "fossil" records "of a lively storytelling tradition": Dewey, "Performing the Living Word," 148. When I speak of my "script" for performance of Romans (included at Appendix A), this is the reformatting of the letter into a script that enables rehearsal, and to which I add performance notes as I discern my physical and emotional interpretation for presentation.

29. Rhoads, *Mark as Story*, 3rd ed., 173–77.

30. As described in Chapter 1.

31. Rhoads, *Mark as Story*, 3rd ed., 173–77.

to find ways to present it that are faithful to that interpretation."[32] In this method, performance is the medium for telling the story, not the tools by which the story is interpreted. Meaning found through a narrative analysis informs the decisions made for gesture and expression that the performer will employ in communicating the story to an audience. Any insights gained through performance itself (if they are explicitly articulated at all) are presented by interpreters-as-performers in terms of Narrative Criticism, using language of character, setting, plot, and narrator.

Furthermore, this early BPC methodology begins with *narrative* analysis, and is thus a method that is only applicable to *narrative* texts.[33] I had been seeking a method for inhabiting the Bible and asking questions as they arise from felt emotion, movement, and expression, and my experience as a storytelling performer suggested that such analysis would be applicable beyond narrative texts. I was still in search of a methodology that begins with performance, rather than narrative, analysis.

As Romans is to be the test case for the EPA, it is interesting to note that Rhoads applies a narrative-based BPC to the Pauline epistles, treating them as story or narrative, as we will see in Chapter 3.[34] Other scholars also treat the letters as narrative, to varying extents,[35] but I do not. Rhoads and others claim performance as appropriate for use with biblical compositions because of the performed origins of these works: "If the biblical writings were composed for performance, then we certainly should use performances to interpret these writings."[36] Following that argument to a different conclusion, I suggest it is more appropriate to perform letters *as* letters according to their origins; letters that were composed with tools of rhetoric, expected to be completed as compositions through oral letter delivery.[37]

NARRATIVE AND PERFORMANCE:
MARK AS STORY: RETROSPECT AND PROSPECT

In this story of the narrative origins of BPC, I turn now to the commemorative volume of essays celebrating the contribution of *Mark as Story* and its

32. Rhoads, *Mark as Story*, 3rd ed., 175, emphasis added.
33. An approach taken emphatically by Van Oyen, who insists that Performance Criticism *must* begin with Narrative analysis: "No Performance Criticism," 107.
34. Rhoads, "The New Testament as Oral Performance."
35. For example, the perspectives in Longenecker, ed. *Narrative Dynamics in Paul*.
36. Rhoads, "Emerging Methodology Part 2," 173.
37. See, for example, Lee Johnson's discussion on letters as a distinct genre and reliant on oral delivery for fulfilment: "Paul's Letters Reheard," 61.

authors, noting the ways in which the field has grown and made way for other innovative approaches to biblical interpretation, and pointing to the future. Through discussion of selected chapters, *Mark as Story: Retrospect and Prospect* will help us to chart the further development of BPC from its beginnings in Narrative Criticism.

Telling the Story

Christopher Skinner claims the publication of *Mark as Story* as a "turning point in Gospel studies, both for the contribution it made to Markan scholarship and for the methodological insights that it advanced."[38] Techniques once employed without being stated as a method now form a distinct approach that permeates much biblical scholarship: "Narrative criticism and its assumptions have become an organic part of biblical exegesis in the new millennium, and some (if not much) of this is due to the seminal contributions of *Mark as Story*."[39]

Skinner notes the origins of Narrative Criticism within study of the OT/HB.[40] However, while NT applications of BPC emerged from narrative and the question of how a story was received in its original context, other questions led OT/HB scholars to apply Performance Criticism with those works.[41] Skinner also notes the work of Robert C. Tannehill in the same period as Rhoads and Michie were developing *Mark as Story*, and his identification of Mark's narrative Christology.[42] According to Skinner, Tannehill's scholarship on the Gospel of Mark recognizes that its author "uses the story form to explain the significance of Jesus' life and vocation [which is] foundational for the literary study of the Second Gospel as well as the other New Testament narratives."[43]

---

38. Skinner, "Telling the Story," 11.

39. Skinner, "Telling the Story," 11.

40. Gunn sees the development of narrative approaches in OT/HB and NT as progressing in parallel, and also notes that although the techniques are employed in scholars of both Testaments, the term "narrative criticism" is more prevalent within the NT field: "Narrative Criticism," 201, 02.

41. Although with works such as Niditch's *Oral and Written Word* in 1996, the application of performance and orality studies to Hebrew Bible compositions coincides somewhat with these moves in New Testament studies, the momentum of Biblical Performance Criticism has largely been with New Testament compositions: Mathews, *Performing Habakkuk*, 54.

42. Skinner, "Telling the Story," 5–6.

43. Skinner, "Telling the Story," 6.

Further, Skinner draws attention to earlier writing from Rhoads, which notes the way that historical-critical scholarship would fragment the text, so that scholars hardly read it as a whole.[44] By the late 1970s, Redaction Criticism was dominating Gospel scholarship. In contrast to this approach, which begins with what we *do not* have—the gaps in the history of the textual tradition—Rhoads and Michie, with Narrative Criticism, started with what we *do* have, "the text itself, assuming that the final form of Mark should be treated as an autonomous and unified narrative."[45] This is the most significant shift that Narrative Criticism brought about in scholarship of the Gospels, emphasizing not the world behind the text, but "the story world of the text."[46] Skinner notes Holly Hearon's claim in her chapter that "where narrative criticism calls attention to the world created within the text, performance criticism explores this same textual world mediated by a performer in the presence of an audience."[47] Again, I was somewhat disappointed to find that Narrative and Performance Criticism is interested in the story world of the text *in its origins*, when I was looking for a method of analysis using reception of the story world of a composition through performance *today*. The starting point in my practice is with the story world of the composition that is regenerated[48] for each original performance that is each embodied encounter. As we will see, a biblical composition spoken aloud in community today will simultaneously bring to life not only the story world of its origins, but also the various incarnations of the story told since it began.

Characters and Narrator

Elizabeth Struthers Malbon's chapter claims that Narrative Criticism "is best understood as active appreciation of the narrative *process,* from implied author to implied audience, rather than as simple analysis of a straightforward *product* or a real author passively read by a real reader."[49] In this statement, several further points are evident; for example, Malbon's focus on the narrative approach's creations of implied and real author and audience,

---

44. Skinner, "Telling the Story," 7. For example, Rhoads, "Narrative Criticism," discussed above.

45. Skinner, "Telling the Story," 3.

46. Skinner, "Telling the Story," 4.

47. Skinner, "Telling the Story," 15. Also, Hearon, "From Narrative to Performance" (discussed below).

48. See Wire, *Holy Lives*, 8.

49. Malbon, "Characters in Mark's Story," 47.

distinguished further from the narrator. I find such conversations easily become convoluted, and more so when the shift to performance analysis from narrative tries to employ such terms or find equivalents. Malbon, in analyzing the role of the storyteller or oral performer of the gospel *vis à vis* the narrator in the text, claims that "the storyteller *frames* the literary narrator (and the implied author, characters, narratee, and implied audience as well) for a new implied and real audience."[50] This contrasts with the position held by many storytellers, including Phil Ruge-Jones[51] and myself, that the oral storyteller / performer takes on the role of the narrator.[52] It will be helpful to discuss this further, and to do so we will briefly move beyond the *Mark as Story* volumes.

Narrator and Storyteller

Philip Ruge-Jones is another who views Mark as composed and experienced in the performance of first century oral storytellers.[53] He seeks to "formulate an . . . understanding of narrating based on live performance of the story before a living and breathing audience."[54] While these insights are gained by performing the Gospel of Mark, in its entirety, for audiences today,[55] again, it is important to note that the focus of Ruge-Jones' inquiry is the original reception context: "We, after a long silencing of the story, must reconstruct as best we are able possible ways the story might have sounded to its original hearers."[56] Ruge-Jones acknowledges the fluidity of first-century performance, allowing that the "storytelling had a life of its own prior to and beyond the transcribing moment. It was not frozen forever once it was transcribed."[57]

But where he is interested in the opening sound of the repeated "ou"-sounding endings in the Greek "as drawing the audience into ritual space,"[58]

50. Malbon, "Characters in Mark's Story," 66.

51. To whom Malbon refers. See Ruge-Jones, "Omnipresent, not Omniscient."

52. This is particularly helpful when distinguishing the storytelling craft from the craft of acting, in which an actor assumes a particular character and speaks and acts as that character throughout. The storyteller remains herself and speaks in her voice to tell the story, taking on the voice and position of all the characters as she does so, as if changing hats.

53. Ruge-Jones, "Omnipresent, not Omniscient," 30.

54. Ruge-Jones, "Omnipresent, not Omniscient," 30.

55. Digital version: Chesnut (dir.), "The Gospel of Mark."

56. Ruge-Jones, "Omnipresent, not Omniscient," 31.

57. Ruge-Jones, "Omnipresent, not Omniscient," 31.

58. Ruge-Jones, "Omnipresent, not Omniscient," 33.

my question would be to observe the actual embodiment of the performer today, and note the way the story's opening shapes the space and the experience for this performer and this audience. However, in his attention to sound, Ruge-Jones' performance interpretation highlights an evangelistic quality to the Gospel, which he sees "is meant to turn the hearers around."[59] "The storyteller is not informing the audience, but rather impacting, forming, reforming, and transforming them by the announced word."[60] The transformative nature of these compositions will give to Embodied Performance Analysis a confessional nature, particularly in the Performance Interpretation the storyteller offers in speaking those compositions aloud.[61]

As far as the narrator is concerned, Ruge-Jones draws on his experience of performing Mark with comments on gestures, what the storyteller does, and what that communicates to an audience. In this, Ruge-Jones' reflection remains on the performance moment; I was looking for more. I sought a method that articulated insight from behind the curtain, to examine the impact on the performer in the process of interpretation during preparation, as much as on the audience in the reception of the interpretation.

Among his observations, Ruge-Jones notes that the narration of Mark includes transitions into the speech and action of key characters, which in performance indicates to the audience in advance that the storyteller will now represent that character and speak with her or his voice.[62] This, for Ruge-Jones, situates the audience in the role of the addressees of that character's speech—for example, when the narrator speaks as John the Baptizer in Mark 1, the audience become the crowd whom John addresses.[63] This is a depiction of the way the "storyteller and audience are enveloped in the story,"[64] the world of the story that Narrative Criticism has helped scholars to identify, and treat seriously.

Ruge-Jones thus challenges the idea of an "unlimited omniscient narrator," as proposed by Rhoads, Dewey, and Michie in "their exquisite

---

59. Ruge-Jones, "Omnipresent, not Omniscient," 35.

60. Ruge-Jones, "Omnipresent, not Omniscient," 34.

61. We can observe the confessional nature of biblical storytelling or performance in the work of many scholars, for example, Boomershine: "telling the story is the calling of every follower of Jesus in daily life," *Story Journey*, 194. Also, the emotional interaction of the live performance forms a relationship that carries "the audience toward the desired outcome of an intimate relationship with Jesus," "Audience Address and Purpose," 134. I discuss this feature of EPA in Chapter 6 in particular.

62. Ruge-Jones, "Omnipresent, Not Omniscient," 35–36.

63. Ruge-Jones, "Omnipresent, Not Omniscient," 36.

64. Ruge-Jones, "Omnipresent, Not Omniscient," 36.

book, *Mark as Story*."[65] He claims that this may work on the page for a literary narrator, but in the live enfleshed storyteller is the potential for more complex and nuanced presentation of characters and their motivations.[66] For example, in recounting a story, a person can simultaneously convey a character's expression whilst also demonstrating in expression or gesture one's own disagreement or disapproval.[67] Humans make meaning from others' expressions, and in retrospect gain insight into the feelings and motivations seemingly interior to other "characters" in the story. In performance an audience experiences not an omniscient, created narrator, but a real live human teller of the story who is thus present inside the story.[68]

A live storyteller "is always present before the audience," and it is in this visibility and presence that her authority and authenticity are found.[69] The written narrator is celebrated for being invisible, for receding into the background when characters speak. This is impossible in live storytelling, in which the whole event is direct address, so difficult to convey in written narration.[70] Speaking to the audience in this direct address, the storyteller shows her care and concern for the audience; and in allowing the words to meet the audience where *they* are, invites those words to transform those who have ears to hear. Again, we note the confessional nature of performed interpretation, in the performing of the story of Jesus, daring to make him present again in response to the audience's troubling questions.[71] I could use these words to describe my experience as a storyteller today; but Ruge-Jones speaks with a view to understanding the first century reception context of the Gospel. Even so, I will return to these insights of a fellow storyteller and scholar in the discussion of the relationship between audience and performer in Chapter 4. For now, I return to Malbon's discussion of narrator and characters.

Characterization

As she compares narrator and performer, Narrative Criticism and Performance Criticism, Malbon notes the birth of Biblical Performance Criticism within the narrative approach: "as biblical scholars have come not only to

---

65. Ruge-Jones, "Omnipresent, Not Omniscient," 37.
66. Ruge-Jones, "Omnipresent, Not Omniscient," 37.
67. Ruge-Jones, "Omnipresent, Not Omniscient," 40.
68. Ruge-Jones, "Omnipresent, Not Omniscient," 37.
69. Ruge-Jones, "Omnipresent, Not Omniscient," 39–40.
70. Ruge-Jones, "Omnipresent, Not Omniscient," 40–41.
71. Ruge-Jones, "Omnipresent, Not Omniscient," 41, 42.

realize but to appreciate that Mark's first century audiences were hearing and seeing performances of the narrative made to groups, not reading it silently and individually, performance criticism has emerged out of narrative criticism and orality studies."[72]

Malbon suggests that the performer is "most analogous to the 'real author' because the performance is a new creation; the performance is *not* the Gospel of Mark but a performance of the Gospel of Mark."[73] However, if Performance Criticism is to stand alone as a distinct approach to interpretation, why make the analogy between performer and any one of the roles assigned by a narrative critic at all? If BPC is a new methodology, surely new tools would be most appropriate, especially as Performance Criticism is not, nor should it be, restricted to narrative compositions.

The key focus of Malbon's chapter is, however, characterization in Mark. On this point, she notes the progression within Narrative Criticism from the early 1980s to the late 1990s when "characters are seen not only in relation to other characters but also—and especially—in relation to the implied audience and often to various real audiences as well."[74]

The shift of focus in scholarship to the audience is an observable trend in Narrative and Performance Criticism, and in such other perspectives emerging from Narrative as Reader-Response Criticism. Rhoads, Dewey, and Michie note that while they were unaware of it at the time of the second edition's development, their work in Narrative Criticism had by then helped to inspire a reader-response approach to be employed in biblical studies.[75] The consequence of thinking more about the audience, as narrative critics were doing, was that the role of the audience in meaning-making began to be emphasized more. As narrative and performance scholars looked for the audience in front of the text at its origins,[76] reader-response began to attend to the reader in front of the text in the present encounter.

---

72. Malbon, "Characters in Mark's Story," 65.

73. Malbon, "Characters in Mark's Story," 66. She adds in parentheses, "just as every reading is a reading of the Gospel of Mark."

74. Malbon, "Characters in Mark's Story," 65. Kelly Iverson's chapter *Retrospect and Prospect* further explores the role of the audience in interpretation, analyzing the composition for its potential impact on its original audience/s: "'Wherever the Gospel Is Preached.'" Van Oyen claims that the interest in a "real" audience is a feature distinguishing performance from narrative criticism and the latter's focus on implied audience: "No Performance Criticism," 112. I agree, but BPC, even in its use of performance for real audiences today, is still interested more in recreating and understanding ancient real audiences than attending to the impact on contemporary real audiences.

75. Rhoads, "Reflections," 271.

76. This is particularly evident in the chapters from Boomershine and Iverson.

At this stage in the development of BPC, narrative and performance critics were not using the contemporary audience as a tool for interpretation, and not articulating the influence of the audience on their interpretation. We will see in Chapter 3, however, that interpreter-performers are now beginning to comment and reflect on performance of the Gospels and other compositions, implying an interpretive influence on the part of their contemporary audience. The Embodied Performance approach will build on such beginnings in BPC to foreground the influence of the audience on interpretation for reception today.

One of the issues for audience members is that the performer mediates the composition, and fills in gaps a reader would fill for himself. Watching video recordings of biblical storytellers, Malbon's students would occasionally express disappointment that the performers had made the interpretive decisions they, the audience, would like to have made for themselves.[77] However, when the narrative mentions that Jesus got into a boat, a film-maker must make decisions regarding what sort of boat, what size, how many are in the boat, when telling the story in the new medium.[78] Similarly, when a storyteller presents the story, she will make decisions about how the words are spoken, what emotions to elicit from the story, whether a child is a toddler or a teenager or somewhere in between. Would Malbon's students lament the interpretive decisions made by the film-maker on behalf of the audience when transposing a biblical story to the medium of film? Their comments in the classroom might betray a lack of understanding of the craft of storytelling and oral performance. If we are to engage in performance interpretation of the biblical compositions, we may need to re-introduce the art form of oral performance / storytelling to audiences and scholars today.[79]

The Authors—Rhoads, Dewey, and Michie Respond

Rhoads, Dewey, and Michie reiterate in their reflections on *Mark as Story* the need "for narrative criticism to affirm the narrative as a historical artefact of the first century."[80] They note Boomershine's observation in his chapter, "when the Gospel of Mark is interpreted in the context of the media world

---

77. Malbon, "Characters in Mark's Story," 66.

78. Rhoads, "Reflections," 270. The authors are referring to Fowler, "In the Boat with Jesus."

79. McKenna, *Keepers of the Story*: on the distinct art form, see p. 175.

80. Rhoads, "Reflections," 270.

of the first century CE, the medium of Mark has to be reconceived."[81] To this end, "the Markan narrative is to be studied as a first-century narrative composed and heard in a particular historical, political, and cultural context of the first century."[82]

I acknowledge that reconceiving the medium of Mark gives rise to the impetus to perform the texts today as part of the interpretive process. As they were composed for the ear and the eye, obviously one more fully appreciates the composition in its intended medium. But can we *only* study the Markan narrative as a first-century narrative for its particular first-century context? Or does the continuing practice of the church to re-read and re-hear such compositions demand that they also be studied as products of each time and place in which they are read and heard?[83] For we have noted Malbon's recognition that every performance is a "performance of the Gospel of Mark," rather than simply "the Gospel of Mark."[84]

Furthermore, "criticism" may be the inevitable outcome of silent reading: reading culture shapes the way we read and the way we interpret, and "scholars are trained as critics who read Mark from a psychological distance."[85] Alternatively, to embody is to inhabit and to understand each character so as to represent them; and to understand is not to agree, but to know, to feel their motivations and emotions—you cannot hold them at a distance and "other" them for objective critique.[86] I will describe the way that immersion leads to intuitive knowing and interpretation in Chapter 4, laying the foundations for the Embodied Performance methodology. Rhoads, Dewey, and Michie themselves observe that "the performer inevitably inserts another layer of interpretation between the story and the hearers," so that when "the performer embodies the story . . . [t]hat *is* the story."[87] They see exemplified in Hearon's analysis (discussed below) the way that "every performance is different and every performance is an interpretation."[88]

While Rhoads, Dewey, and Michie note in these reflections that performance criticism opens up the "many possibilities of interpretation"

---

81. Boomershine, "Audience Address," 121.

82. Rhoads, "Reflections," 270.

83. As we noted from Wire's observations, in Chapter 1: "Perhaps the most productive discovery of 20th century research in oral tradition has been that a storytelling is not saying certain words, but recreating a story in a new context": *Holy Lives*, 16. See also, Gregg, *Shared Stories, Rival Tellings*, xv.

84. Malbon, "Characters in Mark's Story," 66.

85. Boomershine, "Audience Address."

86. Boomershine, "Audience Address," 119.

87. Rhoads, "Reflections," 273.

88. Rhoads, "Reflections," 273; Hearon, "From Narrative to Performance."

evident in the narrative approach, as I will discuss below performance commentaries are yet to fully embrace this polyvalent nature of interpretation that employs a performance approach. Boomershine's "Performance Criticism" of Mark's crucifixion-resurrection narrative, for example, presents its notes for performance as if there is but one interpretation and but one way of performing.[89] The language of performance commentary has yet to embrace fluidity, liminality, uncertainty; it is still shaped by the present culture of biblical "criticism."[90] Many, if not all, of the scholars in the field of BPC are converts, if you will, from other fields and approaches, historical-critical, redaction, even narrative, approaches that are text-based and employ a particular style of academic discourse. What would happen if a scholar positioned herself first as a performer, in order to translate what meaning she discovers through an artistic process into an accessible form for scholars? In this study I seek to determine if such a re-positioning will indeed prove a more effective approach in finding the language for presenting the insights of performed interpretations of biblical compositions.

Rhoads, Dewey, and Michie's acknowledgment of the polyvalent nature of Narrative Criticism, with its potential to elicit "multiple and creative interpretations"[91] of the one story, still only attends to one performance context, its original reception, even as these scholars themselves perform the biblical compositions with audiences today.[92] Likewise the natural shift of attention "from the story world to a focus on the reader—on the hearers, or audience "'in front of the text' rather than on the history behind the text"[93] is still, in practice, a focus on history. The primary interest of these scholars is in the first century audience (real or implied, following the narrative approach) before the text, even as a twenty-first-century audience is in mind, when the performer prepares to address them as if they were first century listeners.

Biblical Performance and Narrative critics explicitly state their purposes in searching for real and implied audiences of the first century performance of these stories.[94] They meet their aim, and have enlivened

---

89. Boomershine, *Messiah of Peace*. Discussed in detail in Chapter 3. This is also a feature of the much earlier *Story Journey*.

90. The EPA seeks to represent the fluidity of performance regenerations of compositions in its Critical Reflection on a particular Performance Interpretation by explicitly claiming it as *one* iteration and interpretation of the composition among the *potential* iterations and interpretations made possible by the work.

91. Rhoads, "Reflections," 271.

92. Rhoads, "Reflections," 272.

93. Rhoads, "Reflections," 271.

94. Rhoads claims for performance criticism its aim of informing "in fresh ways our understanding of the meaning and rhetoric of the Second Testament writings and

understanding of the original reception context of these compositions. In my practice, however, my gaze is first towards my audience today. As a storyteller and minister bringing the biblical compositions to life in gathered communities today, "audiences" comprising people of Christian faith for whom these writings are a spiritual inheritance, I ask first, what does this composition mean for these people, here, now? This difference in gaze and purpose necessitated the development of a new methodology for interpretation *by* performance, as will become evident in Chapter 3.

Biblical Performance Criticism shows promise when its scholars write of the way that "performance creates an intimacy with the audience in relation to the characters in the narrative world . . . restores the affective dimensions to the story, makes the story a 'visceral' experience."[95] However, the interest of Biblical Performance Critics is in what this means for the first recipients of these stories; the responses of their own audiences in performance today are primarily viewed as intimations of what might have been the responses of first century audiences. We are observing a new field emerging, in this discussion. Its practitioners acknowledge the need for further development.[96] This field emerged when scholars wondered how a story was received when the story began. This question has elicited lively debate around the nature of the Gospels in particular, their composition, and their earliest reception. Rhoads' question about what we could learn from performers today (in the previous note) is yet to be explicitly or adequately addressed. Interpreter-performers are beginning to discuss the influence of performance on interpretation, but their methodology begins with an analysis of the text in writing. This study engages Rhoads' question, and asks, "can we learn from performer-interpreters who analyze a composition in embodied performance?" Rhoads identifies the process of immersion in a text, the world of the text, and growing to thus understand the "emotive and kinetic dimensions of the text in ways I would not otherwise have been aware."[97] But he does not articulate those dimensions and the particular understanding they illuminate, speaking rather in more general terms. I wish

---

our re-constructions of early Christianity": "Emerging Methodology Part 1," 118. Ruge-Jones looks back to the first century performance context of Mark, noting that if the Gospel was performed at Easter, on the occasion of baptisms, the opening words speak especially of the beginning of the story in these new members of the community: Ruge-Jones, "Omnipresent, Not Omniscient," 33.

95. Rhoads, "Reflections," 272.

96. For example, "How could we benefit from dramatists who use their experience of performance as a basis for their understanding of the meaning and impact of a play?" Rhoads, "Emerging Methodology Part 2," 173. See also Perry, *Insights*, 157–62.

97. Rhoads, "Emerging Methodology Part 1," 120.

to understand the process of embodiment itself, the ways in which physical instinct, emotive response, and audience context illuminate meaning in a biblical composition as I prepare, perform, and reflect on performance reception of these compositions today.

Critiquing Performance

The title of Holly Hearon's chapter, "From narrative to performance," might suggest a progressive development leaving Narrative behind for a new Performance approach. There is much comparison and contrast in the article, between the narrator and the performer, the reader and the audience, and this may indeed be the intended meaning of the title.

In her chapter, Hearon identifies Narrative Criticism as a foundation for Performance Analysis. Is performance thus treated as an addition to narrative, in a combined narrative-performance approach?[98] In Chapter 3 we will observe the methodological trend of the storyteller's BPC, which begins with narrative exegesis as preparation for a performance to re-enact the historical performance situation. Such methodology thus does move internally "from narrative to performance." Hearon's approach here is somewhat different, however, beginning with the performance, from the perspective of the audience. Hearon conducts her analysis using the method, tools, and terminology of Narrative Criticism. This is, then, an approach from a narrative perspective looking at performance. I take the time to make this point because I am telling here the story of my search for a methodology that gleans the insights of performers as interpreters. My expectations for Hearon's approach were not met; but neither were they entirely *un*met. Hearon presents an approach that begins with performance, and contemporary performance at that. My starting point is also contemporary performance, although beginning with the embodiment of the composition in rehearsal from the perspective of the performer. Hearon's approach, as we will see, demonstrates a rich dynamic of Narrative and Performance Criticism together, which enlivens the study of the Gospels in particular. She also offers the perspective of the audience for contemporary performance, and insight into the meaning-making in which audiences engage, experiencing the performance. I will note again that the perspective of the audience is an area for further research through which to develop the application of performance analysis with biblical compositions in contemporary reception. It may be that Hearon's work will assist such study.

---

98. Such an approach is employed by Iverson: "'Wherever the Gospel Is Preached.'"

So, to Hearon's chapter, and the analysis of the composition-in-performance,[99] using narrative tools of character, setting, plot (or conflict), and narrator. As audience member, Hearon notes the experience of physical proximity of characters in performance, in contrast to the experience of a reader.[100] In the way that Rhoads and Ruge-Jones "place a beat" in their vocalizing of the story of the woman who is healed, the crowd is made present as the performer recreates the story world in their midst. By pausing "between Jesus' departure with Jairus and the mention of the crowd," Hearon observes Rhoads creating a separate context for the crowd and the woman.[101] Ruge-Jones, however, pausing *after* he mentions the crowd, makes "it clear that the crowd is following Jesus with Jairus" to witness what will happen at Jairus' home.[102] An audience will "see and hear more than is revealed in the words of the story"[103] physically realized before them, the gaps in narration concerning emotion, motivation, gesture, interaction with other characters, all interpreted and mediated by a living, embodied person.

Considering setting in a performance approach, according to Hearon, involves attention to the audience as much as the story. Performer and audience must negotiate a performance space, which "creates an interpretive lens through which the performance is interpreted."[104] A performance in a prison will frame the interpretation of liberation (for an audience whose freedom has been removed) in a very different way to performance in the context of a church during gathered worship (for an audience perhaps with considerable personal freedom). Hearon notes that the conflict of a story will be altered in each presentation, with tone, gesture, expression, and translation all nuancing the meaning in the story, though the structure remains the same.[105]

Hearon poses a new set of interpretive questions that she sees being raised by Performance Criticism, which rely significantly on narrative methodology.[106] It is helpful for those employing a narrative-performance approach, with narrative compositions, but again, there are more genres in the Bible than narrative. Can performance analysis begin elsewhere, use a different methodology, different terminology, to narrative?

99. "The composition-as-performance is not a written text but an oral presentation. It is a living word, with a life of its own": "Emerging Methodology Part 1," 127. See also Wire, *Holy Lives*, 16; Malbon, "Characters in Mark's Story," 66.
100. Hearon, "From Narrative to Performance," 216.
101. Hearon, "From Narrative to Performance," 216.
102. Hearon, "From Narrative to Performance," 216.
103. Hearon, "From Narrative to Performance," 224.
104. Hearon, "From Narrative to Performance," 217.
105. Hearon, "From Narrative to Performance," 219.
106. Hearon, "From Narrative to Performance," 231–32. So for ensuing discussion.

Furthermore, Hearon's list of questions is too long to present a workable methodology, and many of the questions feel to me—a performer-interpreter—to be not the right questions to ask. Questions about character and narrator are appropriate for the Gospel compositions, but limit Performance Criticism's applicability to narrative compositions only. Concerning the "narrator," it would be helpful to name the performer as "performer" or "storyteller," to distinguish from the text-bound "narrator" of Narrative Criticism; as noted in Ruge-Jones' work above, narrator and storyteller function in distinct ways.[107]

Some of Hearon's multiple questions concerning the audience-performer relationship could perhaps have been phrased as one question: "what is the relationship between performer and audience?"[108] Hearon does provoke reflection on the context of the audience of the performance, and that question *is* key. The question concerning "in what ways . . . you want the audience to be moved," however, seems rather closed and tending towards proscription, when story and storytelling (since Hearon is in the narrative world of the Gospels) is inherently open and invitational. The suggestion regarding "playing the audience" seems out of place, and perhaps best left implied within the questions of relationship between audience and performer, and audience context.

Hearon identifies "two distinctive contributions that Performance Criticism makes to the interpretive task": "character and narrator," and "time and space." Implicitly, Hearon points here to the embodiment at the heart of the performance moment, and interpretive moves that are made in the live, mutually embodied encounter between performer, composition, and audience. The distinctive contribution of performance, as I see it, is not "character and narrator," nor is it "time and space"; these are features of embodiment. I suggest "embodiment" itself more accurately describes the distinctive difference between Narrative and Performance approaches.

Narrative Criticism, carried out by a reader, involves the reader encountering the text on the page and using their own imagination to fill the gaps left by the narrator. Performance Criticism is carried out by the performer-interpreter who mediates the text in her body, filling in gaps so as to open a live, embodied encounter between themselves and the audience, and the composition. While Hearon acknowledges relationship as a consequence of performance and the trust developed between performer

---

107. Ruge-Jones adopts narrator/he for the written narrator, and storyteller/she for the live performer, which provides clarity in his discussion: "Omnipresent, Not Omniscient," 30.

108. Such a question would resemble the audience tool in the EPA method, as I will discuss in Chapter 4.

and audience, and the impact of the story on performer and audience experiencing it that moment, she does not consider that impact further for its influence on interpretation.

Hearon notes the different perspective gained when experiencing the text performed, and especially when observing multiple performers.[109] For example, Rhoads depicts the woman who has had long years of bleeding look at Jesus when she says, "If I just touch his clothes"; in this telling we are shown the woman's faith in a spotlight.[110] "Ruge-Jones has her looking in the direction of the audience with her eyes almost closed"; his telling thus depicts the interior hope and prayer of the woman, and with a sharp intake of breath as he gestures her reaching out and touching the clothes of Jesus, he signals "that something has happened."[111]

Characters in performance are seen by Hearon to take on life, springing from the mind and body of the performer and "burnished in response to an audience."[112] Hearon thus observes the interpretive role of the performer, in filling narrative gaps, very nearly naming performance *as* interpretation. But even though she describes the emotion-laden performances of Rhoads and Ruge-Jones, Hearon almost entirely overlooks emotion itself as a vital element of performance. Emotion is key in my performance practice. Indeed, from the times of ancient orators, writers on oratory practice have understood that it is emotion that moves an audience, thus transforming ideas and behavior.[113] The contribution of emotion to the work of biblical interpretation has been neglected for too long; with EPA I present a method by which to attend to the insights of emotion.

In her identification of the performer as mediator, Hearon contrasts the imbuing of trust from reader to narrator and audience to performer. This trust is implied for a narrator, but must be earned by the performer.[114] "How is this trust to be earned? It is earned in part by the quality of the performance. Is the performer able to create an imaginative space in which the audience is willing to participate?"[115] Hearon claims that the mediation of characters by the performer creates distance between audience and

---

109. Hearon, "From Narrative to Performance," 221.

110. Hearon, "From Narrative to Performance," 219, 20.

111. Hearon, "From Narrative to Performance," 220.

112. Hearon, "From Narrative to Performance," 226. We will hear echoes of this observation in the words of twenty-first-century Shakespearean actors discussing their relationship with the audience, in Chapter 4.

113. Shiner, *Proclaiming the Gospel*, 57–76.

114. Hearon, "From Narrative to Performance," 229.

115. Hearon, "From Narrative to Performance," 230. Hearon says more on this point elsewhere, as will be discussed in Chapter 3: "Characters in Text and Performance."

character not experienced by the reader.[116] I disagree, for in the live embodied presentation of the character before them, and in the collaboration between imaginations of performer and audience, the characters are made "real," are present in the "story" world between them. Hearon herself notes the dynamic of performance and the physical proximity of characters to each other, realized off the page:[117] it seems somewhat contradictory, along with its diminishing of the audience's imaginative work, to claim performance also creates distance from the characters. There is in Hearon's chapter here, and in BPC elsewhere, a tendency towards oversimplification of the difference between reader and audience, and a downplaying of the role of imagination, at times for a reader, and at other times for an audience. For example, to claim that an audience "sees" more of the character before them, while the reader imagines the character for themselves, diminishes the role of the imagination on the part of the audience.

To Whom the Story Speaks

On the question of audience, Thomas Boomershine claims that the performance of the Gospel of Mark changes our understanding of Mark's original audience from believers to outsiders. Searching for the impact of the Gospel on a *reader*, Boomershine contends, a commentator "implies a picture of the reception of Mark as that of a single person sitting alone reading the manuscript, generally in silence as in modern reading, but perhaps aloud," possibly to a small group.[118] The consequence of this picture is that the addressees must be understood to be disciples of Christ already. Boomershine argues instead that in a performance of the Gospel, the listening audience are drawn into the performance to identify at first with those opposed to Jesus, before gradually coming to identify with the ideal follower of Jesus.[119] The implication of this understanding is that the intended audience are understood as non-believers, and the Gospel as a story for evangelism.[120] In part, it is emotion in performance that carries the audience thus from non-believer to follower of Jesus;[121] and emotion is deemed by Boomershine to have a different effect on a listening audience to a silent reader.[122] It is also

---

116. Hearon, "From Narrative to Performance," 224.
117. Hearon, "From Narrative to Performance," 216.
118. Boomershine, "Audience Address," 117.
119. Boomershine, "Audience Address," 132, 34.
120. Boomershine, "Audience Address," 132.
121. Boomershine, "Audience Address," 134.
122. Boomershine, "Audience Address," 141. Kelly Iverson, in the same volume,

the rhetorical implication that leads the hearers of this story to become followers of Jesus; rhetorical implication that sees the audience addressed as the characters in the story so that when the storyteller poses questions to the characters she thereby demands of the audience that they also wrestle with those questions.[123]

I do not agree with Boomershine's claims that the addressees of the narrative so clearly indicate the ethnicity of the audience.[124] For Boomershine, Mark is addressed to non Jesus-following Jews, and therefore the audience must be understood to be majority Jewish rather than Gentile. However, he also acknowledges the likelihood of varying audiences, noting that for each different context the asides the storyteller may have added would differ for a Jewish or Gentile majority, as different cultural details would need explanation.[125]

In practice, Boomershine's rhetoric of implication understands that the storyteller or performer addresses the audience as various characters in the story, a practice of Ruge-Jones also, as mentioned above. Rhoads, on the other hand, takes the stage in a manner more akin to acting.[126] Actors take the part of a character and address other actors as the characters they inhabit on stage, behind an invisible "fourth wall" that separates them from the audience.[127] Storytellers are usually understood to differ in their practice from acting through the removal of this fourth wall, directly addressing their audience, acknowledging their presence explicitly by telling *them* a story.[128]

In my practice, when stepping as "narrator" into the position and voice of a character, I also employ a technique of addressing other characters as actors would on stage, turning away from the audience towards, in my imagination, that other character.[129] Placing the audience in the position of a

---

observes that reading does also evoke emotion, and is perhaps more generous in his estimation than Boomershine ("Wherever the Gospel Is Preached," 203).

123. Boomershine, "Audience Address," 129. Boomershine says more about the rhetoric of implication in *The Messiah of Peace*, discussed in Chapter 3.

124. With Rhoads, "Reflections," 272; Boomershine, "Audience Address," 129.

125. Boomershine, "Audience Address," 129.

126. Boomershine, "All Scholarship Is Personal," 282.

127. Boomershine, "All Scholarship Is Personal," 282. For more on the difference between storytelling and drama, see Buckley, *Dancing with Words*, 41–42. In their practical guide to storytelling, Sloane and Partridge advise consideration of when to direct your gaze to the audience, to other "characters," or to God: *Performing Scripture*, 22–23.

128. For instance, as noted, Ruge-Jones claims that storytelling is "always direct address": "Omnipresent, Not Omniscient," 69.

129. As storyteller Ray Buckley describes: "In simple dialogue, a storyteller may turn toward the right for one character, and turn slightly to the left for another" (*Dancing with Words*, 76).

character is not the only approach to storytelling. I will often speak as Jesus in a Gospel story looking to my left or right at the woman to be healed, or the disciples to be taught, as often as I speak to the audience "as a character." The particular circumstances of each performance will affect these decisions in performance, and nuance the interpretation in the changes. It is *this* feature of performance, fluid and of the moment, that has not been fully exploited for its interpretive insights by Biblical Performance scholars thus far.

Boomershine's approach is to "evaluate the data of the text as essentially a script for storytelling performances."[130] His aim in this task is to "reconstruct the meaning of Mark for its original audiences."[131] Boomershine asks "how can we as modern readers study ancient narratives in a manner that is appropriate to their original media culture? . . . how can we *hear* in contrast to *read* Mark's stories?"[132] Boomershine's language in writing about the storytelling craft presents as though there is one way the script suggests it must be performed. For example: "The tone of the storyteller's voice as Jesus [8:1–21] is *best described* as exasperation mixed with anger."[133]

Boomershine sees that Rhoads, with and following *Mark as Story*, takes steps towards some answers to the historical questions with Performance Criticism. But I wonder if the question is not so much "how can we hear, because *they heard* in origins these compositions," but "how can *we* (how *do* we) hear these texts intended for a live, embodied experience"? As a movement still evolving, BPC is yet to fully embrace the authority of the performer's experience, the experience of embodying the texts and *thus* interpreting them for reception today.

CONCLUSION

In its earliest stages, Biblical Performance Criticism, emerging as it did out of the still new Narrative approach to the Gospels, became an oral-narrative approach to interpretation. For scholars immersed in the narrative world

---

130. Boomershine, "Audience Address," 122. My practice is to turn a biblical composition into a script, adding my own performance "directions" as I inhabit the composition and reflect on intuitive and instinctive responses, as we will see in Chapters 4 and 6.

131. Boomershine, "Audience Address," 122.

132. Boomershine, "Audience Address," 122.

133. Boomershine, "Audience Address," 131, my emphasis; further, his note that at 7:17 when Jesus leaves the crowd and enter the house, the storyteller sits down. By contrast, we will see a shift in language in the EPA reflection, as I describe what I did in performance, and what my choice (and the options from rehearsal I did not choose) showed me of the meaning in the composition.

of the Gospels, beginning to treat these stories *as* stories, Performance Criticism emerged "organically" from Narrative Criticism.[134] *Mark as Story* established a firm foundation for the development not only of narrative approaches to the Gospels, but for this progression into oral-narrative interpretation of New Testament compositions. In the following chapter, we will observe the application of this narrative-shaped Performance Criticism approach to the letters, with a performed interpretation of Philemon that seeks to recreate the first-century performance situation.

As Rhoads, with his co-workers, sought to treat the Gospel of Mark *as* a story rather than as repository of an idea dispensable once the idea is discovered, he became aware of the anachronism it is to treat biblical compositions as fixed, written, "texts." Rhoads, Boomershine, and others began to recover the oral dynamic to original reception of biblical compositions, forgotten, buried under all those manuscripts mined for evidence of the original. But the "original" is a false idea, as we will note in the continuing discussion, and the fluidity and constant re-generation of biblical compositions is once more beginning to be identified and celebrated.

Alongside the question of what is a story, the questions of who were the storytellers, where were the stories told, and how were they performed or read aloud became the questions of interest in an oral-narrative approach to interpretation. BPC in these early stages of development acknowledged the world of the story, the impact of the storyteller, and the influence of the audience. Hearon observed performances today in a critique of performance using the language of Narrative Criticism. Malbon also heavily relies on the language and method of Narrative, incorporating an awareness of oral or performed origins into her discussion of character in the Gospel. Ruge-Jones makes a helpful distinction between narrator and performer or storyteller, offering some insight into the dynamic of oral performance and the presentation of characters. The understanding of the character comes from analysis of the "text," which determines the manner of performance. Ruge-Jones shows that audience and performer are involved together in the world of the story, but his gaze is in the direction of the first century.

It was becoming apparent as I engaged with BPC that new language would be necessary to achieve my aim; simply adding a performance lens to existing literary methodology did not describe the embodied manner of interpretation I experienced in my practice. What would happen if I, as performer and scholar, positioned myself *first* as performer, and then as scholar reflected on the process of mediating a composition for a live audience to articulate the meaning thereby illuminated?

---

134. Rhoads, "Reflections," 272.

Rhoads, Dewey, and Michie herald Narrative Criticism's polyvalent nature, its potential to elicit multiple, creative interpretations of a story. But Rhoads seems to treat every text as a story, even when it is a letter; and they attend to the first century reception context alone. The biblical compositions are received today along with their history of interpretation, and contemporary performance must negotiate that whole conversation and its consequences.

In Chapter 3 I will discuss the Provoking the Gospel project, whose director does seek to learn from his actors.[135] However, the question of how BPC can learn from performers today is yet to be more broadly addressed. What can the scholarly conversation receive from the performers who bring to life the biblical compositions in community today, who every time they speak, interpret these works through voice and movement, emotion, and interaction with their listeners?

While BPC does seem to attend to the influence of an audience, acknowledge the role of the emotions, and consider the particularity of performance moment and performer, this attention is focused on the first century, not reception today. As noted in discussion of Boomershine's chapter in the commemoration of *Mark as Story*, it is the influence of imagined first century audiences on the meaning of these works in their origins that is of concern when a performance lens is invoked in a study of a Gospel.

Narrative continues to significantly influence the way performance is employed in biblical interpretation for many scholars. These scholars, employing an oral-narrative approach, are moving towards a more distinct "performance" criticism approach to biblical interpretation. In the following chapter we will observe some of the directions[136] that these and other scholars have taken, both from these beginnings in Narrative/Performance Criticism, and from the broader discipline of Performance Criticism. Narrative tools of character, plot, setting, and narrator often still shape the interpretive methodologies being employed; but the goal is no longer simply to understand the autonomous, unified story. The goal of Biblical Performance Criticism has explicitly become historical, as scholars seek to understand how the biblical compositions were received in their origins.

---

135. Swanson, *Provoking the Gospel*.

136. Boomershine himself notes the diverse evolution of Biblical Performance Criticism: "Audience Address," 141.

3

The Search Continues

Recovering Historical Performance

As I discussed the narrative origins if Biblical Performance Criticism, we have seen its development to a focus on reconstructing and understanding the performance context of the original reception of biblical compositions. In the Performance Critical approaches influenced by narrative, a strong focus on Gospel material is evident; Performance Criticism as historical inquiry, however, has been applied across the range of biblical compositions from both Testaments. We will now turn our attention to the varying approaches to the study of biblical compositions as oral performance in their origins.

I begin with David Rhoads, as his articles outlining an "emerging methodology" for BPC give grounding to the work of many in the field following what I name the "storyteller's BPC." As we consider the methodologies employed by scholars in both the storyteller's and the performance critic's BPC, we will note the consistent aim throughout to reconstruct the performance situations of these compositions in their origins. Boomershine's Performance Criticism commentary presents much in the way of innovation for the field, with linked video of his performances in Greek and English in accompaniment on-line. Giles and Doan lead the performance critic's BPC approach, operating from a performance mode of thought to identify performative elements of a composition in order to imagine its performed history.

From there I will return to Rhoads for a discussion of his interpretation and performance of Philemon in a 2016 lecture.[1] Bernhard Oestreich's approach to BPC will be discussed here also, as he applies it with Pauline literature. These two examples of BPC with the letters will provide helpful context for the test case Embodied Performance Analysis of Romans in later chapters.

Finally in this chapter, I turn my attention to several scholars who begin to articulate more clearly and explicitly the influence of performance on their interpretation. Whereas Giles and Doan seek to identify historical performative elements in a text, Rhoads and Boomershine present examples of interpretation undertaken *for* performance. Hearon, Ruge-Jones, Swanson, and Cousins primarily follow this latter approach, but also observe decisions made *in* performance that shape their interpretation. Further again, Peter Perry articulates a methodology that incorporates performance and reflection on performance, with some similarities to my Embodied Performance approach.

The key difference I will note between these methods and my own is that of the starting point for interpretation. My Embodied Performance approach begins with embodiment and integrates literary, historical, and ideological tools as the rehearsal process illuminates insight and raises questions of the composition. Biblical Performance Criticism in these various approaches either does not incorporate performance today at all, or begins with an analysis utilizing established methodologies with a view to performing the composition as thus interpreted and understood.

AN EMERGING METHODOLOGY

For professional storyteller Dennis Dewey, "The written/printed text, as we have it in the Bible, is a transcript of a performance, the fossil record of a lively storytelling tradition."[2] The challenge that BPC scholars then identify is to "form a coherent discipline that is able to give a comprehensive account of [these] oral dynamics of performance events in the early church."[3]

---

1. A later article from Adam White takes a similar approach, though without reference to performance by the author today, nor, interestingly, to Rhoads' performance interpretation of Philemon ("Visualising Paul's Appeal"). I focus my attention on Rhoads' interpretation, as his use of performance provides pertinent contrast to the use of performance in the EPA.

2. Dewey, "Performing the Living Word," 148. Kathy Maxwell sees the written text we have today as "a compilation of 'caught' or inscribed performance": "From Performance to Text to Performance," 174.

3. Rhoads, "Emerging Methodology Part 1," 121.

It is to David Rhoads that most scholars interpreting for performance refer when describing what BPC is, and how it works. As a methodology from still early in the development of this field, building on the work of the Bible in Ancient and Modern Media seminar at the Society of Biblical Literature,[4] it is certainly "emerging," holding much breadth and potential, and posing many questions.

Historical Reconstruction

A dominant view held by Biblical Performance scholars is of biblical compositions as remnants of oral performance. In particular, New Testament scholars view its writings as transcriptions or transpositions of "oral utterances into writing, sometimes a written accounting of one of many performances given over time."[5] The purpose of writing in the ancient world is seen to enhance, not replace, orality. Supplemented with insights from a range of scholars, our discussion begins with David Rhoads, whose articles on an emerging methodology of BPC are cited in a majority of subsequent scholarship in the field.

This aim for historical re-enactment underscores the kind of questions Biblical Performance scholars ask. For example, of scholarship, Rhoads asks, "Why have we not given greater attention to the performance dimension of the ancient world and to the experience of biblical performances by ancient Christian audiences?"[6] The aim of understanding the original reception context leads to an emphasis on reconstructing the first century audience scenarios "as a basis for interpretation."[7] This has led to bold claims concerning the oral media culture of the first century; for example, that 95% of the earliest Jesus-followers "experienced their traditions . . . only in some form of oral performance."[8] Perhaps even bolder is the claim for the oral composition of biblical writings, most notably, the Gospel of Mark.[9] Kathy

---

   4. Rhoads, "Emerging Methodology Part 1," 120.
   5. Rhoads, "Emerging Methodology Part 1," 123.
   6. Rhoads, "Emerging Methodology Part 1," 118.
   7. Rhoads, "Emerging Methodology Part 1," 131.
   8. Rhoads, "Emerging Methodology Part 1," 118.
   9. Beginning with Kelber, *The Oral and the Written Gospel*. More recently, Wire, *The Case for Mark*, and Dewey, *Oral Ethos*. Already noted is Hurtado's contestation of such claims, with a view of the dynamic relationship between written and oral communication: "Oral Fixation." Not all BPC scholars are interested in the orality debate: Van Oyen, "No Performance Criticism," 112. Furthermore, Perry acknowledges that the time may have come to step back from hyperbole, now that reaffirmation of the orality in biblical compositions is established: *Insights*, 158.

Maxwell outlines the need for a renewal of the scholarly approach that will acknowledge the differences between print culture and rhetorical culture: drawing on tradition, creating new compositions, those responsible for the New Testament we now have did all this "from memory—from the memory of a text that existed with dynamic form, in flux between oral and written form."[10] Ultimately, the point is that "oral performances were an integral and formative part of the oral cultures of early Christianity and the primary medium through which early Christianity received and passed on the compositions now comprising the Second Testament."[11]

Whatever claims one might make for the orality and literacy of the first century media culture, BPC has again made clear that the biblical compositions were created with the expectation of being heard and read aloud, of being received in performance and in community, as discussed earlier. A noteworthy implication for scholarship is that "studying these texts in an exclusively written medium has shaped, limited, and perhaps even distorted our understanding of them."[12]

In summary, the aims and outcomes for BPC identified by Rhoads (and for the significant number of scholars in the field who follow his approach) are to:

- explain oral culture and manuscripts and the interface between them
- describe a historical picture of performance
- assess the oral context of New Testament writings at their origins
- model the performance event
- map the oral features in Greek and implications for aural impact
- interpret New Testament writings and rhetoric in the original oral medium
- conduct performances
- translate for performance to a live audience
- develop theories and practices to glean the insights of performers
- attend to the power dynamics present in performance
- renew the broad field of biblical scholarship with shift of medium.[13]

---

10. Maxwell, "From Performance to Text to Performance," 171.
11. Rhoads, "Emerging Methodology Part 1," 126.
12. Rhoads, "Emerging Methodology Part 1," 126.
13. Rhoads, "Emerging Methodology Part 2," 180. This list of key features summarizes the content of Rhoads' discussion.

The important feature to note in these aims and outcomes, the key feature of BPC, is the heavy emphasis on reconstructing and interpreting *first-century* performances, "insofar as we are able to (re-)construct them or re-enliven them."[14] "The challenge of performance criticism is to learn everything we can about performances of early Christian traditions and to interpret, as best we can, the texts before us as 'performance literature.'"[15]

Whitney Shiner is regarded as having established much of the foundation for such scholarly inquiry, at least in relation to Mark.[16] Shiner presents a picture of ancient literacy that meant that the "meaning of the Gospel in its original setting would not be found in the text. It would be found in its performance within a community."[17] Shiner's work is thus "an attempt to recover the experience of a Gospel performance in its first-century setting."[18]

Helpful in illuminating the first-century context, I do, however, find Shiner's dualistic approach to silent reading as compared with oral performance unsatisfactory: "silent reading involves eye and brain. An oral performance involves the ear, the eye, and whole body."[19] I suggest that silent reading is an embodied experience because of the simple fact that an embodied being is doing the reading.[20] There is no doubt that there is a marked difference between silent reading and performance, and that the live, mutually embodied nature of the performance moment is at the heart of this difference. Dualistic presentations of either silent reading or performance, either orality or literacy, have perhaps been necessary in the re-establishing of the inherent oral quality of biblical compositions.[21] As Perry notes, however, it is now time to recover the nuances of the first century context.[22] I suggest it is also time to move to more nuanced understandings

---

14. Rhoads, " Emerging Methodology Part 2," 165.

15. Rhoads, " Emerging Methodology Part 2," 165.

16. Shiner, *Proclaiming the Gospel*. "Shiner has set out a way for exploring the performance of early Christian narrative texts": Oestreich, *Performance Criticism of the Pauline Letters*, 44. William Shiell has written a similar study of Acts: *Reading Acts*.

17. Shiner, *Proclaiming the Gospel*, 1.

18. Shiner, *Proclaiming the Gospel*, 1.

19. Shiner, *Proclaiming the Gospel*, 1.

20. To repeat an earlier observation: "The text is also a body, one that shows itself to (and hides itself from) its readers. Those readers are *also* living bodies entering into dialogue and struggling with that other body, the text": Pereira, "Body as Hermeneutical Category," 236.

21. Perry, *Insights*, 158. Lee notes the unsatisfactory nature of modernist dualisms in her examination of modes of preaching, and the consequent diminishing and dismissal of integral elements of human knowing, experience, and meaning-making: *Preaching*, 64.

22 "Performance critics need to be more careful and specific about performance

of the way humans understand and interpret by means beyond detached, rational, cognition. BPC has taken steps toward such understanding with the recovered appreciation for the inherent orality of biblical compositions, and incorporation of performance into interpretive activity. The step that I had hoped BPC would have taken, not merely anticipated, is to recover through these inherently performative compositions the embodied ways of interpreting that must have been the experience of original audiences, but which have been ignored and overlooked in the interpretive work of generations of scholars. Understanding the first century practice of oration and performance builds the picture of the context in which biblical compositions were formed. Understanding the ways in which humans make meaning, through recent scholarship, will bring ancient world and our own together for the enrichment of our understanding of both.

Shiner draws on the writings of ancient orators, or observers of oratory, to describe the context of an oral media culture in which the Gospel of Mark was composed. Following Quintillian, Shiner observes, for example, that the

> delivery of the speaker . . . is itself an actual event. We experience a living person before us, one who has something at stake in the performance. We are affected by the speaker's presence. We are affected by his emotions. We have an opinion of the speaker. That affects how we receive the performance. We are surrounded by other people in the audience. They make their opinion clear. Their expressions of opinion affect our experience of the performance.[23]

He acknowledges both the uniqueness of any given performance, and that ultimately there is no way to recover a clear picture of the oratory style of performers of Mark in the first century.[24] Shiner is able to identify five likely features of that style. "Texts were generally memorized for performance, and the text was recited rather than read"; the performance did not have to be verbatim, but the general structure would have remained stable; the dramatic style of oral performance would have used character, inflection for emotion, gesture for expression; "the performer was expected to feel the emotions of the characters and convey those emotions to the audience"; and

---

scenarios in the ancient world": Lee, *Preaching*, 64.

23. Quintillian was "a famous orator and teacher of rhetoric in the first century CE": Shiner, *Proclaiming the Gospel*, 3.

24. Shiner, *Proclaiming the Gospel*, 2. Kelly Wilson observes: "the obvious problem is that we simply lack the data necessary to analyze ancient performances": "Performance-critical Analysis," 32.

finally, a bombastic presentation with yelling, almost singing, was prized by audiences, and bombastic audiences, using different types of applause, were physically active, and vocally noisy in signifying what did and did not please them.[25]

Further to these key features, Shiner places a particular emphasis on emotion in performance in the first century, and suggests that "we are not hearing the Gospel through first-century eyes if we do not hear the emotions."[26] For Shiner, the ancient "church's apparent preference for narrative Gospels over sayings collections for use in the church probably reflects their interest in the emotional impact of the narrative."[27]

Shiner is another who views the text we have as a script for performance of Mark, and looks for clues in the text such as stereotyped characters, or indicators of pace (e.g. "and immediately" suggests a faster pace) for original performance possibilities.[28] He does also look for clues for performance today: inspired by his research, Shiner has used sound effects in his performances, such as storm noises to contrast with silence when Jesus and the disciples are in the boat.[29] However, even though he did perform for audiences in his own time, Shiner's concern for the impact on an audience is largely in order to understand the impact on a first century audience of the Gospel of Mark in performance.[30]

> The rhetoricians of the Greek and Roman world understood the intense power that could be generated by the embodied word. They studied carefully how to create the desired effects. They practiced constantly to perfect the power of their presence. They also understood how to use the power of the embodied word to bring into the present the events that happened, or that might have happened, in another time and place. The performed word creates events right before your very eyes and makes you feel them as if you were there.[31]

---

25. Shiner, *Proclaiming the Gospel*, 3.
26. Shiner, *Proclaiming the Gospel*, 4–5.
27. Shiner, *Proclaiming the Gospel*, 5. Further, "Delivery is the art of filling the lifeless words on a scroll with fire and life and emotion" (79).
28. Shiner, *Proclaiming the Gospel*, 57. As does Levy, *Bible as Theatre*, 5.
29. Shiner, *Proclaiming the Gospel*, 89, 92–94.
30. Shiner, *Proclaiming the Gospel*, 96.
31. Shiner, *Proclaiming the Gospel*, 143.

Dynamics of Performance

Rhoads outlines the features of the performance event, to which the performance critic will attend, for "meaning is in the whole event at the site of performance."[32] These features are: the act of performing; the composition-in-performance (unique on each occasion); the performer, audience, and their social location/s; the material context and cultural/historical situation; and the rhetorical impact on the audience. BPC then must ask, as one of its tasks, how "these factors combine to suggest a range of meanings and potential rhetorical impacts?"[33]

Rather than an explicit methodology, Rhoads presents the performance "dynamics . . . that are helpful in the effort to comprehend the meaning and rhetoric of Second Testament writings."[34] These dynamics are:

- acting
- presenting the world of the text
- personification
- onstage/offstage focus
- non-verbal communication
- emotions
- states of consciousness
- humor
- temporal experience
- rhetoric.

We will observe in other methodologies the features of emotion, rhetoric, non-verbal communication, and personification (named as character or characterization). Rhoads includes audience considerations throughout and in the features of the performance event,[35] while others consider the audience as a discrete element in the methodological process.

Rhoads encourages and demonstrates the importance of an integrated approach to interpretation that BPC can offer. It is important that this approach be eclectic, "and that it partner with many other fields of biblical

---

32. Rhoads, "Emerging Methodology Part 1," 126.
33. Rhoads, "Emerging Methodology Part 1," 126.
34. Rhoads, "Emerging Methodology Part 2," 174.
35. Rhoads, "Emerging Methodology Part 1," 126.

study."[36] Rhoads comprehensively describes the mutual contributions BPC makes and receives to and from other approaches to biblical scholarship, from literary and historical, to more recent "ideological" approaches. He even anticipates a new kind of commentary that will bring "together the insights of many disciplines."[37] For Rhoads, performance is the final step in the process, the culmination of the (text-based) analysis, perhaps acknowledging the stage of embodiment or internalization,[38] with the interpretation communicated or tested in the performance event. What is still needed in and for BPC is a method by which performer-interpreters can describe how they arrive at their conclusions through the process of performance.[39]

A BIBLICAL PERFORMANCE COMMENTARY

Boomershine's performance commentary on the passion-resurrection narrative in Mark is innovative in many ways. Not least of the innovations is the accompanying website with video of Boomershine performing the composition in Greek and English.[40] Boomershine's method is based on the practice of "sound mapping," introduced by Lee and Scott.[41] His analysis is, as it is in much of his work, focused on the impact of the composition-in-performance on the ideal or real original audience. Audience impact is discussed in terms of rhetoric, specifically the "rhetoric of alienation and condemnation" (the feeling of identification or distance an audience establishes with a character),[42] and the "rhetoric of involvement and implication" (in which good characters, with whom the audience has been led to identify, do something wrong, thereby also implicating the audience in their transgression).[43] In the passion-resurrection narrative of Mark, the rhetoric of alienation and condemnation is established through the flat characterization of the chief priests, for example.[44] The audience is invited to distance themselves from, and to condemn, those characters and their actions. The more complex characterizations of Peter, the women and even the crowd

---

36. Rhoads, "Emerging Methodology Part 2," 173.
37. Rhoads, "Emerging Methodology Part 2," 173.
38. This is more explicit in Perry's methodology, as we will see below.
39. A development anticipated by Rhoads: "Emerging Methodology Part 2," 180.
40. Boomershine, "Messiah of Peace," http://messiahofpeace.com. An innovation this book has also embraced.
41. Lee and Scott, *Sound Mapping the New Testament*.
42. Boomershine, *Messiah of Peace*, 23–25.
43. Boomershine, *Messiah of Peace*, 25–27.
44. Boomershine, *Messiah of Peace*, 29.

invite the audience to "sympathize and identify with these characters . . . prior to a climactic action or response that is unambiguously wrong."[45] The identification with the crowd through this rhetoric of implication differs from more common interpretations that assume the audience must distance themselves from and condemn the crowd.[46]

Direct address also functions to implicate the audience in the role of various characters. For example, at 14:1–2, Jesus' listeners, the disciples, are required to "rethink their assumptions about the Messiah"; so, too, are the audience, who (for Boomershine) are addressed as the disciples by the storyteller in performance.[47]

In *The Messiah of Peace*, Boomershine has committed to the technique of sound mapping. In this approach, one analyzes the Greek for breath units—how many words can be spoken in one breath.[48] The claim is that variations in breath unit length will indicate variations in pace, and thereby also emotion and meaning. A longer unit will need to be said faster, and so conveys urgency, or a succession of relatively unimportant actions before a shorter unit that can be spoken aloud slowly to highlight something important, such as the words of Jesus to a recipient of healing.

Boomershine's sound map of Mark 14:1–2 renders the "periods" (breath units) as short, which he takes as an indication of a slow pace.[49] However, he also understands the tone of this portion to be one of urgency, the authorities running out of time to implement their plan against Jesus.[50] If I were performing these verses, with their sense of urgency, I would take my cue from that feeling, the emotions, and probably *not* employ a slow pace. My expression might be deliberate, and certainly tense, and perhaps not necessarily "quick," but slow seems to me not a choice I would make in performing these verses.

The sound mapping approach seems to suggest that one can look at the Greek words and see in their structure an indication of phrasing that conveys *the* intended tone, pace, emotion, and expression. However, as I have demonstrated, each performer will put those words onto their voice differently, as is appropriate for them, for their audience, as well as for the story. Lee and Scott do acknowledge the potential for variability between

---

45. Boomershine, *Messiah of Peace*, 29.
46. Boomershine, *Messiah of Peace*, 30.
47. Boomershine, *Messiah of Peace*, 43. See Chapter 2 for more on direct address in relation to Ruge-Jones, "Omnipresent, Not Omniscient."
48. Lee, *Sound Mapping*, 169.
49. Boomershine, *Messiah of Peace*, 44.
50. Boomershine, *Messiah of Peace*, 40.

readers in the way they "declaim a passage";[51] a range of ways in which to faithfully receive each composition,[52] which will be influenced by performer, audience, and location.

When viewing the text as a script, a fossil remnant of an ancient performance, scholars such as Boomershine seek clues for how the ancient storyteller of this captured performance would have delivered these words. As there is no way of knowing for sure, and as even these scholars readily acknowledge the fluidity of first century performance, I do not find this approach in general or sound mapping in particular convincing. I may go as far as to agree with Burke Long and say that "reconstructions are fundamentally and inherently misleading simply because too many of the necessary data are unavailable."[53]

Boomershine also acknowledges the fluid nature of performance, and that differences between either his sound map or his translation, and his performance will be noticeable.[54] However, his performance comments can appear to suggest that he observes a fixed intent for performance held within the text. In the earlier example of Mark 14:1–2, he claims the "periods are short and should, therefore, be told slowly."[55] In performance comments for Judas' arrival in the garden, and the aside reminding the audience exactly who this is, Boomershine states, "there is no sympathy in the storyteller's voice for Judas and his gang."[56] Likewise, "the description of Judas' identification of Jesus with a kiss is to be told with a tone of disbelief and scandal."[57] As a storyteller, I ask, "but *could there* be sympathy for Judas? Is it entirely beyond the limits of this story to give the storyteller a tone of compassion for Judas?" For if one did, interesting questions would arise as to the influence of the other Gospel accounts on the storyteller, the history of reception of this story, the context of the audience and their lived experience at the time of the (contemporary) performance. These questions would all, in critical reflection on the embodied response of the storyteller, lead the performer-interpreter to discern meaning in this portion for her audience today; and likely highlight in new ways meaning for the story in its origins and intent.

51. Lee, *Sound Mapping*, 70.

52. Lee, *Sound Mapping*, 71.

53. Long "Recent field studies," 188, cited in Wilson, "Performance-Critical Analysis," 32.

54. Boomershine acknowledges the inability to ignore the "inspiration of the moment": *Messiah of Peace*, xi.

55. Boomershine, *Messiah of Peace*, 44.

56. Boomershine, *Messiah of Peace*, 152.

57. Boomershine, *Messiah of Peace*, 152.

For one who does acknowledge the fluidity inherent in performance, that no two performances will be the same, this more fixed quality of Boomershine's directorial notes seems incongruent. Further, the inclusion of the innovative feature of a commentary is prevented from realizing its fullest potential. That potential, as I see it, would be to discuss what the performer-interpreter actually *did* in a particular performance (or has done over a range of performances), informed by the interpretation, the sound map, or in contrast to it, the body and intuition finding something unexpected perhaps in the composition that the literary, text-based analysis that a sound map ultimately represents, did not discover.

The layout of the commentary follows a conventional written commentary in general, with portions distinguished for focused discussion. For each portion Boomershine offers his title, a brief synopsis or précis, the sound map and translation, notes on details and translation,[58] comments on meaning and impact[59] and the performance of the story. Occasionally an additional section is inserted after the sound map and translation, "ancient associations and connections," in which Boomershine notes the possible content of the original audiences' collective memories; for example, the stories of the garden in Genesis, and of David and Nathan, when hearing the story of Jesus in the garden before his arrest.[60]

Boomershine also considers to some extent the stories held in collective memory for contemporary audiences, or in the memory of the performer. At 14:26–52, Boomershine notes the possible connections with the stories of Gandhi or Martin Luther King Jr., when engaging with the story of Jesus in the garden through performance.[61] Though not explicitly attending to those stories as they emerge in response to embodying the story, or experiencing it in performance, Boomershine nevertheless acknowledges that memory and experience will provide points of connection for receivers of the story (and implicitly suggests this will be part of the meaning-making process).

---

58. An emerging theme in the literature is that translation matters—translation for performance. Whether from a position of capturing the sound of the source language, or translating the essence of the experience of the composition, or some other rationale, storyteller BPC scholars seem to agree that translation for performance is a vital element in the process.

59. Another emerging theme in the literature is the notion of the "impact" of the composition-in-performance on the audience. This acknowledges that the "meaning" of the composition, the meaning it holds in potential for each audience, will sometimes be felt as "impact" rather than coherent thoughts or ideas easily able to be articulated. An audience will often respond, "I felt . . . ," and somewhere in those feelings is the meaning of the composition, which will unfold over time.

60. Boomershine, *Messiah of Peace*, 188.

61. Boomershine, *Messiah of Peace*, 153.

In this structure we see an approach common in the storyteller's BPC, in which Biblical Performance scholars conduct an analysis of the composition in preparation for performance. Such analysis places a historical performance lens or filter over a methodology such as Narrative Criticism, in order to re-enact the performance events of the first century. Boomershine's comments for each portion culminate in notes for performance, which are undoubtedly shaped by his experiences performing the Gospel of Mark, but which are presented in the manner of a director instructing a performer in the desired manner of performance.

Boomershine's focus on the rhetoric of implication leads to an understanding of direct address of the storyteller to the audience as the dominant posture throughout. "As we will see throughout the story, the audience is always addressed as Israelites, who share Israelite norms, experience, and tradition."[62] This in turn leads Boomershine to conclude that Mark's Gospel is "in no sense an anti-Jewish story," but rather a story told by Jesus-following Judeans for a mixed audience of Gentiles and other Judeans.[63]

While decades of performance and interpretation have informed his commentary, rarely does Boomershine explicitly articulate the choices *he* made as choices he made, for, or in, any given performance, or discuss what bearing those choices had on his interpretation, which is what I had sought. The step I therefore take from an approach to BPC that is quite innovative in a number of ways, is to more directly comment on a particular performance or series of performances and what the storyteller / performer did in those particular performance events that interpreted the composition in specific ways.

PERFORMANCE MODE OF THOUGHT

Digging for Clues to Performance of the Composition

Giles and Doan claim that a performance mode of thought and "manner of communicating that is common in theatre and performance resides just beneath the surface of much of the Hebrew Bible text."[64] This leads them to employ such a performative mode of thought as a method for reading biblical texts: "a way of thinking that engages both the cognitive and imaginative aspects of thought to conceive of reality not in propositions, but in actions and being."[65] They define the kind of text with which Performance

62. Boomershine, *Messiah of Peace*, 44.
63. Boomershine, *Messiah of Peace*, 44.
64. Giles and Doan, "Performance Criticism of the Hebrew Bible," 278.
65. Giles, "Performance Criticism of the Hebrew Bible," 274.

Criticism is particularly applicable as "those texts with oral presentations at their origin."[66] This leads them to look for remnants of orality held within the written text, analyzing through those remnants an ancient performance event that used formal patterns "in order to create a shared reality between actor and spectator."[67] This is the approach I am naming the critic's BPC.

Giles and Doan outline the central concepts that build their framework,[68] beginning with the transferability of medium for a text, from oral or performance to written, with the echo of a performance event discernible in the written text.

Act-schemes are identified as "the building blocks of performance events."[69] "Opening up valuable new lines of inquiry is a cognitive and literary cultural theory concerning how embodied action shapes both thought and language . . . [seeing] cognition as 'embodied action.'"[70]

Giles and Doan understand Performance Criticism to represent "what we perceive through . . . embodied enactment,"[71] making performance a mode of communication, with meaning determined by other methods. Is this approach, rather than being a discrete, new, "Performance Criticism" approach, in fact a literary approach, which employs "performance" as a tool within an already established methodology?

The "audience—act—actor" dynamic is another key concept; however, in *Twice Used Songs,* the terminology has changed to "actor—character—audience," in a relationship that is "characterized by direct presentation, that is, presentation where the performer acknowledges the presence of the audience and makes that presentation explicit."[72] The creation and formation of the audience is a "major component of performance and performance criticism," with a "dynamic exchange [that] occurs between the act and the spectators."[73] This exchange occurs in a space in which "the spectator unites with the performance through identification of shared or conflicting values, and belief";[74] a connection "brought about by the actor/presenter whose human presence makes the event possible."[75]

---

66. Giles, "Performance Criticism of the Hebrew Bible," 274.
67. Giles, "Performance Criticism of the Hebrew Bible," 274.
68. Giles, "Performance Criticism of the Hebrew Bible," 279–81.
69. Giles, "Performance Criticism of the Hebrew Bible," 276.
70. Giles, "Performance Criticism of the Hebrew Bible," 277.
71. Giles, "Performance Criticism of the Hebrew Bible," 277.
72. Giles and Doan, *Twice Used Songs,* 21–22.
73. Giles, "Performance Criticism of the Hebrew Bible," 280.
74. Giles, "Performance Criticism of the Hebrew Bible," 280.
75. Giles, "Performance Criticism of the Hebrew Bible," 280.

Iconic and dialectic modes of presentation are further concepts of performance in Giles and Doan's framework. "Simply put, iconic modes of presentation stress being while dialectic modes of presentation stress becoming. Iconic modes of presentation tend to present, celebrate, and reify who we are, while dialectic modes of presentation stress conflict, tension, and change."[76]

Giles and Doan also examine different kinds of action in their performance analysis. "Wherever some explicit activity (such as prophesying or singing) is present, a series of implicit questions may be asked."[77] Such questions concern, for example, how, when, and where they prophesied, and how they used their voice and body. These questions cannot be answered with much certainty, but they "provide a way into the oral and performed world of the Bible, which can impact our understanding of the text . . . seek to draw out the nature of the activity . . . embedded in the text."[78]

Giles and Doan look for the performed history of a text, "detecting the clues of orality that remain in the literary text."[79] They claim that "performance events . . . have left their mark on portions of the biblical text," and see Performance Criticism as a "methodology that seeks to identify, describe, and analyze those communicative structures and conventions"—their echoes, left in the text.[80] This method is particularly applicable for "those texts with oral presentations at their origins" or dramatic features. They name Song of Songs as an "obvious" candidate for Performance Criticism; likewise, the "grand, sweeping story of Genesis 1–11," for its iconic and dialectical elements that tell the story of human being as it is, and of human transformation.[81] Giles and Doan also claim Performance Criticism as an approach applied with prophetic books, and that the books of Jonah, Ruth, Esther, and Hosea "construct intricate dramatic tensions through the constructs of act-schemes and character formation, [coming] to life in a whole new way" when analyzed through the Performance Critical approach.[82] In a more recent work, Giles and Doan undertake something of

---

76. Giles, "Performance Criticism of the Hebrew Bible," 281.
77. Giles, "Performance Criticism of the Hebrew Bible," 281.
78. Giles, "Performance Criticism of the Hebrew Bible," 282.
79. Hearon and Ruge-Jones, "Preface," xi.
80. Giles, "Performance Criticism of the Hebrew Bible," 274.
81. Giles, "Performance Criticism of the Hebrew Bible," 274.
82. Giles, *Twice Used Songs*, 136. Marvin Lloyd Miller sees ancient Jewish letters as appropriate for performance criticism, as he seeks to overcome misconceptions resulting from reading back onto these compositions assumptions of a post-printing press culture, and understand the letter as actualized in performance: Miller, *Performances of Ancient Jewish Letters*, 19, 27.

an archaeological dig with the book of Ruth.[83] Their aim is to uncover an earlier, orally composed and transmitted story focused on Naomi, behind the revised and adapted story now found in the OT/HB.

As well as composing a script for the Naomi Story, the authors have written a script for a play, which envisages a performance by four actors.[84] It is unclear, however, to what extent the experience of performance (either as performer or audience) has shaped the interpretation of the book of Ruth for these authors, for it is not explicitly stated. The approach to Performance Criticism of the biblical compositions is dry, not the paradigm shifting approach of even BPC, which I argue is yet to achieve its paradigm shifting potential. This is a Historical-Critical approach, looking for the performed history of the text; a Form-Critical analysis seeking to identify an oral tradition within the bounds of the written short story. This approach employs techniques of Performance Criticism to observe repetition, grammatical problems that are resolved in performance, humor, a small number of actors. The analysis of semantic structure concludes that there is an identifiable progressive development of the book of Ruth from an earlier Story of Naomi,[85] "performed by women for women."[86] This approach may "listen" for verbal constructions "used to create visualization as a part of a definition," to see in the naming of Naomi and Bethlehem a question from the women, "has pleasantness returned to the House of Bread?" when she returns.[87] However, beginning thus with linguistics, is this a performance interpretation, or a linguistic, or even historical-literary interpretation? Giles and Doan see that the historical performance of the Naomi Story "involves not only the voice but the body of the performer, [so that] everything about the physical presence, including the gender of the creator/performer of the Naomi Story are important factors in determining the manner in which the story is presented."[88]

Here, the integration of feminist type questions is not as foregrounded as the linguistic analysis of names; therefore when, as here, the performance question is foregrounded, the method is more clearly a "Performance Critical" approach. It is a question about ancient, rather than contemporary, performance. Questions of performance and cultural memory and community

---

83. Giles and Doan, *The Naomi Story*.

84. "Everywoman," mentioned, Giles, *Naomi Story*, Chapter 3. The Script for the Naomi Story is outlined in structure and contrasts with the book of Ruth, and presented in full in Chapter 6.

85. Giles, *Naomi Story*, Chapter 3.

86. Giles, *Naomi Story*, Chapter 1.

87. Giles, *Naomi Story*, Chapter 1.

88. Giles, *Naomi Story*, Chapter 2.

identity formation demonstrate the integration of socio-cultural criticism and memory studies into this approach to BPC. As we have seen, integration of various methods, of scholarship within and beyond biblical studies, is also a vital feature of storyteller's BPC.[89]

Finding Performance in the Composition

Jeanette Mathews is another employing a performance mode of thought to examine "the performative structures resident within biblical texts."[90] Mathews' "approach moves beyond the application of a performance 'concept' to a biblical book and rather asks whether it is valid to view an ancient text such as the book of Habakkuk in its entirety from the perspective of performance theory."[91]

In particular, she looks for features of performance that might impact the interpretation of the composition in its present form as a written text. Further, Mathews not only seeks to reconstruct the performed history of the text, but also asks, "is it a text open for re-enactment by communities of faith, not necessarily as a staged drama . . . but as a 'script' that continues to be acted out in the life of today's faithful communities?"[92] Ahmi Lee's discussion of a theatrical approach to preaching resonates with this view that the Bible is to be enacted. She celebrates the ability of such an approach to facilitate the community's performance of Scripture through their participation in "God's grand drama," as the Bible's composers intend.[93]

In her Performance Critical reading of Habakkuk, Mathews presents the script in translation, with introductory literary-critical comments "divided into acts and scenes that will be established on the basis of changes in genre, actors, and content."[94] She then analyzes each scene for features identified by Performance Criticism and similar to those identified by Giles and Doan: "author and script, actor, audience, setting, and improvisation."[95] Themes found in other disciplines employing Performance Criticism—such as

---

89. Giles, *Naomi Story*, Chapter 2.

90. Mathews, *Performing Habakkuk*, 68; following Giles and Doan. As mentioned above, Miller's study of ancient Jewish letters as performance events is a further example of this method of performance criticism: *Performances of Ancient Jewish Letters*, 19–27.

91. Mathews, *Performing Habakkuk*, 69.

92. Mathews, *Performing Habakkuk*, 69.

93. Lee, *Preaching*, 114.

94. Mathews, *Performing Habakkuk*, 70.

95. Mathews, *Performing Habakkuk*, 70–72.

self-reflexivity, universality, embodiment, process, and re-enactment—are discussed as observed in, and "helpful in analyzing the message of Habakkuk."[96]

In this way, Mathews reads "the text from a performance perspective,"[97] looking for performance themes and features in the script of Habakkuk. Taking an example of her analysis at 2:1, we note that this is an analysis of performance *within* the text, as evident in the observation of the setting and the script as a public performance in a public place.[98] From 2:2 and God's response there, Mathews can extrapolate that the actor in 2:1 is Habakkuk.[99] Considering the audience, Mathews notes the mocking tone of the language in 2:1, which would "begin to raise the emotional level of a crowd."[100] An element of Mathews' analysis of particular note is that of improvisation, where the author has employed traditions in new ways for effect.[101] At 2:1, Mathews notes that the customary intermediary role of a prophet has been improvised, or adapted, into a more proactive challenger to YHWH.[102]

Further, Mathews engages in an analysis that demonstrates the potential for this script's re-enactment in communities of faith today, going so far as to claim "that Scripture cannot remain relevant *unless* it is performed, re-enacted, and improvised continually," and that it is "in 'performing' Habakkuk (or any other Biblical script) that Scripture remains relevant and alive in today's world."[103] She presents examples of re-enactment in different times and places, arguing that "a new setting has influenced the way the ancient text has been understood and re-presented" in each performance.[104] One example of this re-enactment of Habakkuk is a Max Ernst sculpture in the permanent collection of the Australian National Gallery. Titled "Habakkuk," this sculpture, for Mathews, "reflects performance themes of . . . self-reflexivity . . . and process," its form suggesting movement, and providing comment on idolatry and prophetic vision as in Habakkuk.[105]

---

96. Mathews, *Performing Habakkuk*, 72.

97. Mathews, *Performing Habakkuk*, 165.

98. Mathews, *Performing Habakkuk*, 118. Recall that for BPC scholars in both streams, the biblical composition is already a "script"; for EPA, the composition becomes a "script" when formatted for the particular performance moment.

99. Mathews, *Performing Habakkuk*, 119.

100. Mathews, *Performing Habakkuk*, 123.

101. Mathews, *Performing Habakkuk*, 72. Again, Lee affirms performance as the goal of Scripture, and that in their performance (behavior), Christians are to speak and act "with both innovation and consistency": *Preaching*, 98–99.

102. Mathews, *Performing Habakkuk*, 120–21.

103. Mathews, *Performing Habakkuk*, 200.

104. Mathews, *Performing Habakkuk*, 189.

105. Mathews, *Performing Habakkuk*, 194.

As Mathews reads Habakkuk "through the lens of performance studies," she hopes it will ensure "these ancient texts are not locked away as historical artefacts but instead continue to have an impact on communities of faith and the surrounding world."[106] Typically for the performance critic's BPC, and despite Mathews' discussion of various re-enactments, this is not an analysis that employs performance itself, either as communication or interpretation.

PAUL'S LETTERS AS PERFORMANCE EVENTS

Applying Performance Criticism to the Pauline corpus, scholars employ a range of approaches. I will discuss two examples; one performing the letter as a reconstruction of a first-century occasion, and the other considering cultural anthropology, rhetorical practice, and the oral media culture of the time in order to construct a possible, theoretical, scenario. These are undoubtedly not the only ways performance is employed in the analysis of Paul's letters. Contributions to *Orality and Textuality in Early Christian Literature* attest to that. In that volume, Richard Ward explores the impact of the bodily presence and voice of the presenter of Paul's letters, with reference to the letter speaking to Corinthian divisions (2 Cor 10–13).[107] Arthur Dewey discusses Paul's use of Deut 30 in Rom 10:1–15 as an orally delivered subversive message to the non-elite.[108] Other BPC studies of the letters include the sound-mapping approaches of Nina Livesey with a portion of Romans, and Lee and Scott themselves with Philemon, and the more general discussion of the importance and role of letter bearers in the performed delivery of Paul's letters to the church, by Lee Johnson.[109]

Letter as Story

Our first example of Performance Criticism with Pauline letters is David Rhoads' performance of Philemon as part of a lecture event at the Moravian Seminary in 2016.[110] As anticipated in Chapter 2, this performance is an

---

106. Mathews, *Performing Habakkuk*, 200.
107. Ward, "Pauline Voice."
108. Dewey, "A Re-Hearing of Romans 10:1–15." Wire then responds to these chapters: "Performance, Politics, and Power: A Response."
109. Livesey, "Sounding Out"; Lee, *Sound Mapping*, 225–46; Johnson, "Paul's Letters Reheard." I will also make some reference to White's Performance-criticism of Philemon ("Visualising Paul's Appeal").
110. Rhoads, "The New Testament as Oral Performance."

80 PART 1. WHAT IS EMBODIED PERFORMANCE ANALYSIS?

excellent example both of the narrative shape to BPC, and its focus on historical re-enactment. Rhoads' introduction includes an invitation to "think about letters as story."[111] He then lays out an analysis of Philemon using "story categories" of setting, characters, plot, and purpose, before a performance that recreates the first-century performance event.

Rhoads describes settings of the time (late 50s to early 60s CE), the city (Philippi), the house church in Philemon's home and Paul's prison in Ephesus, and the socio-cultural setting of patron-client relationships, slavery, an honor-shame society, and customs of hospitality. The characters are Paul, Timothy and other "co-workers," Philemon, Apphia "our sister," "Archippus our fellow soldier," the community, and, of course, Onesimus. God—described by Rhoads as the only "patron" in this story—and Christ—the only "lord"—(i.e., not humans) are also considered "characters."

To construct the plot of a letter as story, one takes "every specific event in the letter . . . and puts it in chronological order."[112] Rhoads begins with what happens before the letter: Paul founded the church, converted Philemon, left, and found himself in prison; Onesimus ran away and found Paul; and Philemon continued as host to the church. The story continues with the event of the letter's reception (Paul writes a letter to Philemon, "and sends it with someone who will perform it *as if* he were Paul, in the community"), and ends with "what Paul wants to happen after that."[113] The latter being, in particular, the welcome of Onesimus as a brother, his liberation from slavery, and return to Paul as a help to him in Philemon's name, until Paul can return to receive Philemon's hospitality again.

Rhoads identifies the purpose of the letter as persuasion. His analysis notes the ways the language and structure of the letter, with its conventions of letter organization and rhetorical features, and choice of words using sound and plays on words, all work together to achieve this purpose. Of particular importance is the public performance of the letter in the task of persuasion. Rhoads' interpretation of Philemon is thus carried out according to narrative method with attention to the performed reception of the letter in antiquity.[114]

---

111. In contrast, when I performed the letter for students in Adelaide, I told the story of Phoebe, constructed from historical and socio-critical research, and with a lot of imagination. The second half of the performance was Rom 12–16, a Performance Interpretation according to my Embodied Performance approach. The letter was introduced by narrative, but was not analyzed *as* a narrative. See this performance in track 24 of the videos online at https://sarahagnew.com.au/embodied-performance/.

112. Rhoads, "The New Testament as Oral Performance."

113. Rhoads, "The New Testament as Oral Performance."

114. Adam White arrives at a similar conclusion through his "outsider's" historical

Demonstrating this method in the lecture, Rhoads then performs the letter, with four other people (volunteers from the audience) on stage, seated around him. To his right is Apphia, and his left, Archippus and Onesimus (closest to Rhoads); Philemon sits facing Rhoads, with his back to the audience. Rhoads introduces his role as that of the letter bearer and performer, speaking with Paul's voice. In other words, Rhoads speaks in character as the letter bearer, not as himself the storyteller. In the greeting with his gesture out towards the audience, Rhoads indicates that they take on the role of the community. To be sure, it is a complex layering of voices and personas as one performs the letter today. By acting, Rhoads seeks to reenact the first century reception context of a reader reanimating the words to evoke "a sense of Paul's presence in the room," as White puts it.[115] As a storyteller, I do not take on the letter bearer's persona who takes on Paul's voice, but rather, I assume the role of *a* letter bearer myself, in a way, and in performance will evoke the presence of Paul and his community of senders and receivers.

Throughout, Rhoads directs his gaze mostly towards "Philemon,"[116] although as he greets Apphia and Archippus, he looks at the people on stage representing them, and up to the audience when speaking the greeting and the closing "the grace of the Lord Jesus Christ be with your spirit" as to the community. Further, when Rhoads gives voice to words about Onesimus, such as, "he is so important to me," he steps to stand beside him, and places a hand on his shoulder, urging his welcome as a brother. With posture, expression, and comedic timing, Rhoads invests Paul's "not to mention you do owe me your life" with effective humor that is well appreciated by the audience. As noted above, Rhoads highlights humor as a feature of his Performance Critical method.

After the performance, by way of critical reflection, and after allowing people a chance to talk to each other about their experience of the performance, Rhoads mostly discusses the purpose of the letter in its origins and what Paul did to achieve that purpose. This is a discussion mostly pertaining to language choice, the word-plays and connections, such as "refresh my heart in Christ" after having earlier described Onesimus as "my

---

and rhetorical performance-critical analysis of the letter, somewhat paradoxically for me reminding us that the intent of these letters was to be fully realised *in performance* ("Visualising Paul's Appeal," 5). White draws on the writings of orators and rhetorical theoreticians and practitioners from the ancient world to imagine the scenario Rhoads presents in performance.

115. White, "Visualising Paul's Appeal," 2.

116. Although it may be understood, as White suggests, that in such a performance context in first century reception of a letter, when one is addressed, others may feel themselves addressed also: "Visualising Paul's Address," 5.

heart."[117] Rhoads also acknowledges the role of social pressure created by the public performance of a letter. The use of many *sun-* prefixes, such as for co-worker, fellow soldier, and fellow prisoner, are seen to evoke Paul's vision of mutuality in the community of Christ-followers. Further, his own claiming of "prisoner," rather than "apostle" as a designation in this letter, for Rhoads, places Paul in a position of vulnerability, as he makes an appeal from a basis of love, rather than from a position of authority. This is demonstrated in Rhoads' performance: the movement towards Onesimus on stage, a reminder that Paul sent Onesimus with the letter bearer back to Philemon, physically and dynamically represents the love of Paul for "his child." In his emotions of affection, compassion, and love for Onesimus and Philemon, and the whole community, Rhoads conveys the tone of mutual encouragement of brothers and sisters in Christ, perhaps the central image, theme, and purpose, of the letter.

In this performance analysis we see Rhoads' method of story-based performance criticism, overtly employing the tools of a narrative methodology in an analysis of the composition in preparation for performance. In the performance itself, the goal of historical recreation of first-century performance situations is clear in the presence of the letter's three addressees and its subject on stage with the performer, and the implication of the audience into the role of the first century community. Interestingly, the "characters" of Philemon and Onesimus spontaneously embraced at the close of the performance—a testament to the impact of performance, an embodying of the letter's meaning and purpose.

Again, I have only mentioned White's performance-critical treatment of Philemon in passing. He arrives at very similar conclusions, though without performing the letter himself. White follows a similar approach to Shiner[118] in gaining insight into ancient performance practice from the likes of Quintillian and his contemporaries; or, indeed, like that of Oestreich in imagining the original reception scenario, whose work I will introduce to you now.

---

117. Rhoads' discussion of word choices pertains to *Paul's* choices, which in the manner of historical inquiry may lead an interpreter to want to identify the original version, for Paul's authentic words. In Chapter 6, I discuss word choice as pertains to *my* choices, in an approach that treats the tradition with respect, but seeks to enable reception of the letter as it is presented in the Bible, in language appropriate for my listeners. This approach acknowledges that each iteration of the composition is "original," removing the need to identify "the" original, in many instances a difficult, if not impossible, task.

118. Shiner, *Proclaiming the Gospel*.

Rhetoric, Oral Media Culture, and Cultural Anthropology

Bernhard Oestreich's analysis of Rom 14:1—15:13 comes from within his broader work applying Performance Criticism in analysis of Pauline letters.[119] Oestreich begins with a statement of the context and limits of the pericope, and continues with an analysis of the structure, with particular attention given to linguistic and rhetorical features of the text. He argues for the unity and cohesion of the unit, and does not see that the argument claiming that the doxology of 16:25–27 belongs at 14:23 has been well enough established to challenge this unity.[120]

His focus on linguistic and rhetorical technique, and in the verse by verse comments, is on parallelism, which he sees as "a 'performative text strategy' indicating that the text was designed to be read out before a disunited audience."[121] He thus not only makes the claim for its performative purpose, but for the nature of the original audience/s. However, understanding the audience as disunited "does not mean that the diversity must be abandoned, as the final parallelism in Rom 15:8–9 reminds us: despite the different reasons for praising God, the hymn can be sung in unity."[122]

The integrated nature of BPC is a feature of Oestreich's approach, in the use of socio-cultural and linguistic analysis of the term "weak," and its function here. The linguistic analysis includes the intertextual critique of Paul's use of the term in his letters more broadly.[123] He concludes that the effect of Paul's language on the hearers of the letter is to emotionally influence, and thereby involve listeners in judgment and compassion: "the words of blessing for the one who has found certainty awakens the eaters' sympathy for those with deep-seated doubts."[124] Again, when the audience hears "For the kingdom of God is not food and drink, but righteousness, peace, and joy in the Holy Spirit" (14:17), they "feel involved in the judgment because the traditional wisdom is also their own wisdom."[125] Oestreich believes of this latter maxim that listeners were "invited to adopt the poetically expressed wisdom for themselves by repeating" it aloud during the performance.[126]

---

119. Oestreich, *Performance Criticism of the Pauline Letters*.
120. Oestreich, *Performance Criticism of the Pauline Letters*, 153.
121. Oestreich, *Performance Criticism of the Pauline Letters*, 156.
122. Oestreich, *Performance Criticism of the Pauline Letters*, 156. On this point, see also Jewett, *Romans*, 885.
123. Oestreich, *Performance Criticism of the Pauline Letters*, 158–60.
124. Oestreich, *Performance Criticism of the Pauline Letters*, 183.
125. Oestreich, *Performance Criticism of the Pauline Letters*, 180–81.
126. Oestreich, *Performance Criticism of the Pauline Letters*, 181.

Oestreich's analysis considers the impact of the performance setting on the original audience, with the "symbolic character of the performance space ... during the meeting of the believers" given particular attention.[127] Such a meeting would have been held in the home over a common meal, with the connotations of family and hospitality; "this means that during the performance, the surroundings would have given the listeners a vivid illustration of what was expected of them."[128] "The symbolism of the performative space would reinforce what was said in the performance,"[129] and may even have "initiated interaction between the groups" who were divided on these lines of food practices.[130] This embodying of the message resembles insights uncovered through my Embodied Performance Analysis of Rom 16.

For Oestreich, the speaker and listeners are all involved in the performance event, and in "collectively ... generating the meaning of the text."[131] Here he draws on the work of contemporary scholars such as Erika Fischer-Lichte, who "has established that the *human body* is the precondition that constitutes a performance, specifically the co-presence of performer and audience."[132] Further, Oestreich notes, "an important characteristic of performance is that it depends on the physical participation of the performers and of those experiencing the performance."[133] The effect is mimetic; mimesis sees the physical action of the performer triggering a physical, emotional, and/or cognitive response in the audience.[134]

Based on conclusions about the closeness of written and spoken language, with spoken word being seen to have a *binding* nature in first century media culture, and writing to give the word an *enduring* nature, Oestreich pays particular attention to rhetoric in his analysis of the letters.[135] Paul's use of rhetorical technique and strategy is seen "to establish and shape not

---

127. Oestreich, *Performance Criticism of the Pauline Letters*, 161.

128. Oestreich, *Performance Criticism of the Pauline Letters*, 162.

129. Oestreich, *Performance Criticism of the Pauline Letters*, 162.

130. Oestreich, *Performance Criticism of the Pauline Letters*, 167.

131. Oestreich, *Performance Criticism of the Pauline Letters*, 4.

132. Oestreich, *Performance Criticism of the Pauline Letters*, 54, italics original. See, for example, Fischer-Lichte, *Ästhetik des Performativen*.

133. Oestreich, *Performance Criticism of the Pauline Letters*, 55.

134. Oestreich, *Performance Criticism of the Pauline Letters*, 56. In Chapters 4 and 6 I discuss the various ways in which performer and audience give to and receive from each other in the mutually embodied performance moment, and how this is meaning-making activity. We may also recall Ruge-Jones' perspective of the impact and transformation experienced through the "announced word," which I noted in Chapter 2: "Omnipresent, Not Omniscient," 34.

135. Oestreich, *Performance Criticism of the Pauline Letters*, 4. Rhetoric is understood to be "the basis of any communication, oral or written" (18).

only the relationship between the one presenting the letter and the audience but also the relationships between the different parts of the audience."[136] Rhetoric is one of three strands of scholarship Oestrich identifies as coming together to form a Performance Criticism approach to the letters, along with epistolography and oral tradition studies.[137]

Although not aiming to present an exact description of the scenario in first century Rome, Oestrich does strive to present a "possible and probable performance" situation.[138] In so doing he suggests, for example, the use of hand gestures back and forth between two extremes of life and death in 14:7–9 as the performer delivers the parallel lines. He also suggests an intensifying of volume and expression of these words that have "a pulsating rhythm."[139] Oestrich's method for arriving at such conclusions is introduced in terms of characteristics of performance drawn from cultural anthropology and theatrical studies.[140] The particular focus of his cultural anthropology is to look at the broader context of performance in Greco-Roman times, so again the integrated nature of BPC with multiple modes of inquiry is evident.

While Oestrich acknowledges the uniqueness of performance and the particular embodiment of a particular performer in a particular performance,[141] and also the referential nature of a performance to what has gone before,[142] the focus is, as we have seen many times already, on what these features of performance tell us about the letters as performance events *in their origins*. Specifically and explicitly for Oestrich, "performance criticism is a historical analysis."[143] His is a study focused on reception of the letters in their first century contexts, helping "today's readers gain access, at least in part, to this wealth of meaning and impact inherent in the oral events to which the texts of the New Testament bear witness."[144]

Oestrich appears not to engage in performance himself, which, although he is strongly influenced by Rhoads and much of the storyteller's BPC approach, would place him, according to my definitions, in the

---

136. Oestrich, *Performance Criticism of the Pauline Letters*, 6.
137. Oestrich, *Performance Criticism of the Pauline Letters*, 7.
138. Oestrich, *Performance Criticism of the Pauline Letters*, 175.
139. Oestrich, *Performance Criticism of the Pauline Letters*, 174. I return to these observations again in the Critical Reflection, Chapter 6.
140. Oestrich, *Performance Criticism of the Pauline Letters*, 5.
141. Oestrich, *Performance Criticism of the Pauline Letters*, 62, 63, 67.
142. Oestrich, *Performance Criticism of the Pauline Letters*, 65–66.
143. Oestrich, *Performance Criticism of the Pauline Letters*, 275.
144. Oestrich, *Performance Criticism of the Pauline Letters*, 282, 83.

performance critic's BPC stream. While the imagination is a vital interpretive tool to recover for biblical scholarship, as Oestreich does imagine the early performance contexts, BPC is ostensibly a method reliant on the premise of embodiment, not only of performer, but more particularly of performer and audience together. Rhoads claims that a performance critic *must* perform, or experience performance as audience.[145] However, the *experience* of performance is absent from the approach of many scholars analyzing biblical compositions through the lens of performance (or at least, from their discussions). For those who do engage with contemporary performance, it is the end point of the process. In my Embodied Performance approach, the entire method relies upon the embodied performance of the interpreter today.

PREPARING FOR CONTEMPORARY PERFORMANCE

Translating the Ancient Performance Experience

As noted in Chapter 1, educators have been using performance in teaching the Gospel of Mark in seminaries and universities.[146] For Ruge-Jones, this primarily "has to do with its original media setting."[147] The rationale for these educators is also, then, grounded in seeking to understand, and help their students understand, the performance contexts of these compositions at their origins.

> Performance criticism takes the character of New Testament texts as Hellenistic literature seriously. As a historical method, it recreates the situation for which these texts were designed and encourages the interpreting performer to experiment and explore multiple possibilities of authorial intention, structure, argument, and audience reactions through the act of performing the text before an audience.[148]

Further, as they work with students to prepare performances for contemporary audiences, some scholars observe performance choices made in rehearsal, in the embodying of the Gospel in order to perform it, and the way these choices shape interpretation. These observations have not been

---

145. Rhoads, "Emerging Methodology Part 2," 173.
146. See also essays in Part Two of Shively and Van Oyen, ed. *Communication, Pedagogy*.
147. Ruge-Jones, "The Word Heard," 102.
148. Ward, *Bringing the Word to Life*, 60.

articulated in any methodological outline, but are made in critical reflections on the process of preparing and performing biblical compositions.

So, for example, Ruge-Jones, as he performs or prepares, discovers that the structure of the story leaves a lot to the audience to imagine. He notes, "I suspect the original audience unfortunately knew well Roman violence and probably even this particular form of Roman violence in the wake of the recent Jewish-Roman war so that imagining someone crucified was painfully easy for them."[149]

Although his interpretive aim is historical inquiry, the aim of performance for Ruge-Jones is to communicate the story for an audience today in appropriate ways for them, as much as it is in light of the understanding of its performance for a first century audience. "Make the recorded storyteller's story your story, a gift to offer to a living audience."[150] On the rendering of Jesus' words in Aramaic at Mark 15:34, and having the original storyteller translate them, Ruge-Jones observes that "in the wake of the Jewish-Roman war, you ask this question on behalf of the audience. Jesus' question, becomes your question, which voices that question asked by the whole community. In a very experiential way, Jesus voices the lamentation as he hangs in the place of the grieving people."[151]

He notes further that the challenge for the storyteller *today* is to make clear again, new again, the scandal in the story of Jesus' crucifixion.[152] Sheila Rosenthal observes that readers today respond to the Bible with "casual familiarity." Reimagined performances, storytelling as in this project or theater as Rosenthal discusses, enable listeners to hear again and be astonished, amazed, saddened, challenged. Rosenthal makes this observation within her study of *Measure for Measure* as Shakespearean Performance Interpretation of the story of Jesus raising Lazarus. Though we do no know how Jesus felt, she suggests that by observing the Duke bringing Claudio "back to life," we may "see something similar."[153]

Thus we begin to see in questions posed for the *communication* of the story, the influence of their audiences on their *interpretation* of the story for today. So that Ruge-Jones can state, "I am not suggesting that I have figured out the definitive stances that early storytellers used for these characters or the ones we must use today. I am claiming that in both the first and the twenty-first century, a storyteller found and will find ways to use the body to

---

149. Ruge-Jones, "Those Sitting around Jesus," 51.
150. Ruge-Jones, "Those Sitting around Jesus," 48.
151. Ruge-Jones, "Those Sitting around Jesus," 49.
152. Ruge-Jones, "Those Sitting around Jesus," 50.
153. Rosenthal, "Shakespeare as Biblical Performance Critic."

indicate character distinctions in order to communicate the narrative flow clearly to the audience."[154]

Richard Swanson uses performance in an educational setting with his Provoking the Gospel project, which involves a series of workshops in which the actors experiment with various ways to perform the text.[155] With his troupe of actors, Swanson produced a "St Mark's Passion," for which he wrote the script, and commissioned new music for a choir.[156] Swanson's aim was to translate not only the words, not only the meaning, of the Passion in Mark, but to translate the first century reception experience.[157] His historical focus thus also keeps a keen eye on the reception of the composition by a contemporary audience.

Layers of meaning became apparent when considering the various possibilities for performance. At Mark 9, Swanson identifies a link with the scenes of John the Baptist and considers ways to represent this link on stage for the audience. Having had John wear clothing and use gestures that link him to Elijah and the prophetic tradition, putting the character of Elijah in the same clothing for this scene not only explicitly echoes John the Baptist, but creates a "reverse echo, since John's clothing recalled Elijah for ancient audiences."[158] Further, if the same actor plays both characters, the link is even clearer: translating into embodied performance the "vigorous" hint Swanson hears from the storyteller "that John is Elijah, and Elijah is John."[159]

Swanson's challenge was to evoke something in a contemporary audience akin to the layers of meaning that would be evoked for a first century audience possessing the cultural memory the composition assumes: translating a story laced with memory "for a current audience that lacks a memory."[160] Swanson is keenly aware of the distance an audience today must travel in their imagination, to connect with the generative origins of the Gospels. Audiences today come to the story from a great distance, "a distance made greater by our millennia-long encounter with the story as a vehicle for Christian theology, as a part of a Christian lectionary, all in service of Christian dogmatics and apologetics. We could decide that the story *is* what the story has *become*, but that defeats the key strategy deployed by

---

154. Rosenthal, "Shakespeare as Biblical Performance Critic," 43.
155. Swanson, *Provoking the Gospel*.
156. Swanson, "'This Is My . . .'"
157. Swanson, "'This Is My . . .,'" 209.
158. Swanson, "'This Is My . . .,'" 197.
159. Swanson, "'This Is My . . .,'" 197.
160. Swanson, "'This Is My . . .,'" 197.

the ancient storyteller, who wrapped every bit of the performance in deep, ancient memory."[161]

Here a nuanced contrast with my own approach may be evident: I *do* take the story to be what the story has become. Embodied Performance Analysis is an interpretation of the story in reception today, as it *is* in this iteration or re-generation. That will always be a story that has been told through generations, bringing with it all those re-tellings,[162] thickening the story in a way that ancient audiences did not and could not experience.

Swanson uses appropriate communication media, a "thickness" of performance that employs acting and music, as an appropriate form for reception today. He does so in order to represent a thickness of reception original audiences may have experienced, so that the ancient performance event, as much as the text itself, is part of the composition that is received and interpreted in the contemporary performance event. In his own words, the production, "with an ensemble of actors and a choir of singers, surely does not replicate ancient practice, but it does arguably reproduce ancient audience competence and experience."[163] As noted earlier, the lack of sufficient data for accurate replication or reenactment may suggest this way of enabling a current audience to access competence and experience more appropriately translates the whole composition (written and performed), not only from language to language, but from bodies to bodies.

Preparation, Internalization, Performance

Peter Perry's method comprises three stages in a circular multi-directional process, which nevertheless begins with preparation.[164]

During the preparation stage, translation for sound and embodiment is highly encouraged; inquiry into the world behind the text, incorporating historical-critical interpretive methods, takes place, "especially focusing on the media culture" that is presumed by the text.[165] Considering the world in front of the text, Perry's method focuses on the first century world, but also takes into consideration the twenty-first-century world in front of the text, the context of the audience to whom the contemporary performer presents the composition. Gesture, voice, and expression are all informed by what

---

161. Swanson, "'This Is My...,'" 194.
162. As Swanson notes, Swanson, "'This Is My...,'" 183.
163. Swanson, "'This Is My...,'" 209.
164. Perry, *Insights*, 40.
165. Perry, *Insights*, 39; cf. 44–53.

clues can be identified in the text.¹⁶⁶ Although this method gives attention to coherence and to the impact of a performance on the audience, such attention seems, again, to be primarily focused on first century performance situations.

Internalization is a discrete step in Perry's method, following the interpretive decisions of the preparation stage.¹⁶⁷ In this stage, the interpreter-as-performer learns and rehearses the script for performance,¹⁶⁸ with that performance shaped by the interpretive work of the first stage of the process.

Perry's third stage is performance, in which "communication happens: a performer embodies a text for an audience in a given situation and all are transformed in some way by the experience."¹⁶⁹ Perry integrates responses from the audience and critical reflection on the part of the performer-interpreter into this performance stage. We will examine Perry's approach in practice with a return to the book of Habakkuk.

He begins with preparation, which includes three phases of inquiry—into the world behind, of, and in front of the text. Perry employs techniques and applies insights from Historical and Socio-cultural Criticism, as well as from anthropology, to build the world behind the text as the Chaldean period of the late seventh century BCE.¹⁷⁰ He identifies from this inquiry themes of "the excesses of property and increasing violence,"¹⁷¹ and literary features of five "woes" of the prophet in response to this situation.¹⁷² A further literary feature is the psalm that the prophet invites the people to sing (Hab 3); "because of the psalm, the performance of Chapter three becomes explicitly interactive with the audience. The psalm form suggests the audience may have sung together with the performer in a familiar way that the psalms were often used."¹⁷³

Perry's inquiry into the world of the text focuses on actors, named as "characters" in narrative analysis.¹⁷⁴ Identifying the three "actors" of

166. We will see that my method differs in that I am not looking for the clues before I embody it, but let my body respond to the text as it will, and pay attention to that, as it is incarnated and mediated through me at this time in this place.

167. Perry, *Insights*, 70–71.

168. Here, "script" is used in a manner akin to that of the EPA, the form of the composition adapted for a particular, contemporary performance.

169. Perry, *Insights*, 72.

170. Perry, *Insights*, 74.

171. Perry, *Insights*, 74.

172. Perry, *Insights*, 76.

173. Perry, *Insights*, 78.

174. Perry, *Insights*, 79. Perry points to the fuller discussion of this feature of performance criticism found in Mathews, *Performing Habakkuk*, 177–82.

Habakkuk, God, and the Babylonian king (who he calls the Man), Perry pays particular attention to speech.[175] In performance, Perry does not speak "as himself," but understands himself to be taking on a persona, perhaps in this instance particularly appropriate as it is the story of the prophet.[176] "In performance, the performer takes the place of the prophet through [a] movement from sarcastic accusation to perseverant questioning to praise to trust in the midst of fear."[177]

In this inquiry phase, Perry's discussion is for the most part somewhat distant, removed, and general. As noted, he begins to incorporate insights from his own performing experience with Habakkuk, but still I was prompted to ask, "what difference would it make to foreground the performer-interpreter's embodiment of the composition *before* engaging with historical and literary analysis?"

The king is "described and addressed" in Habakkuk, but does not speak directly.[178] From his experience in performance, Perry notes his decision to address both the king and the audience to reflect this implication of the people along with the king. He does this "by looking at the audience for the general 'woes,'" and after an initial look then gestures towards "the king" for the second person address of "you."[179] In performance, the "audience becomes a character ... implicated in the lack of justice in the land."[180] Further audience address is discerned in the passages that speak of God in the third person, for which Perry uses direct address to the audience. In these direct addresses, Perry senses a yielding of power from performer to audience, a vulnerability in joining the fear of the audience at impending attack, while still inviting the people to praise God.[181]

Perry's inquiry into the world in front of the text begins with reception of Habakkuk from its origins, through different times in the third century BCE, the mid first century CE at Qumran and in Paul's writing, a ninth-century epic poem that places the song of Habakkuk beside Moses' song, to finally noting the context of his own 2009 performance in Arizona.[182] He notes the way the terrorist attack in Paris not long before this performance

---

175. Perry, *Insights*, 79, 80.
176. Perry, *Insights*, 89.
177. Perry, *Insights*, 79–80.
178. Perry, *Insights*, 80.
179. Perry, *Insights*, 82.
180. Perry, *Insights*, 81.
181. Perry, *Insights*, 82–83.

182. As noted, Mathews presents a fuller history of "re-enacted" performances of Habakkuk: Mathews, *Performing Habakkuk*, 189–96.

shaped the interpretation of both the composition and the particular performance event for his audience, seeing Paris as Judah.[183]

The next phase of Perry's performance analysis is Imagination: internalization.[184] In this process, although he describes listening for connections between the different parts of the composition, "trying out different intonations, gestures, and facial expressions," and retranslating for effect for this particular audience, Perry seems more focused on how to communicate the meaning found through inquiry than further interpreting the text through his embodied responses, which are not mentioned here.

The final phase is Intervention: performance.[185] This phase begins before the performance event, "with the relationship between the performer, audience, and situation."[186] This is also evident in the consideration given to the audience during earlier stages, as noted.

For Perry, both introduction and audience feedback are included in the intervention or performance phase, and his critical reflection considers the impact on both audience and performer. Perry provided guided questions for his audiences in the 2015 performances. I see this as on the one hand, giving Perry the opportunity to gauge the extent of his audience's comprehension of the content he has performed.[187] On the other, I wonder if such guidance for audience responses is too proscriptive? Again, I note that audience response in the contemporary performance event as interpretation deserves further scholarly attention.

Of particular note in this study are the key things Perry learned by performing Habakkuk, including the importance of translating for the audience (he gives an example of revising translation from "deer" to "mountain goat" after audience members admitted their associations with Bambi);[188] clarification of character voice, finding coherence through performance;[189] and the sympathy between performer and audience as they in the twenty-first century, with the ancient prophet and his community, "waited on God" for a response.[190] Perry notes the importance of multiple performances for a particular audience, to settle beyond the initial newness of form, and grow

---

183. Perry, *Insights*, 85.

184. Perry, *Insights*, 86–88.

185. Perry provides links to video recordings of selected performances online: *Insights*, 88 n. 12.

186. Perry, *Insights*, 88.

187. Perry, *Insights*, 90.

188. Perry, *Insights*, 93.

189. Perry, *Insights*, 96–97.

190. Perry, *Insights*, 98–99.

in familiarity with content so as to notice details.[191] Within the composition he noticed the tension between confidence and fear, praise and resignation that is created by Habakkuk as a helpful response to crisis.[192] This is noticeable in particular in the prophet's expression of dissatisfaction after the singing of the psalm in Hab 3: that "the psalm does not eliminate fear or create a false sense of 'everything will be OK'" is an important nuanced interpretation of this key feature of the composition.[193]

Perry begins to move towards an articulation of the learning of interpreter-as-performer through the process of performance. While his method begins with Literary and Historical Analysis, and does not appear to attend explicitly to the embodied responses and meaning-making of the internalization phase, he does reflect on the performance event, and the choices made for performance. In that critical reflection, Perry does articulate the impact of speaking the words with his own voice—he discerns the voice of the prophet, where others see (probably *not* "hear") the voice of God in a problematic interpretation. He articulates the impact of his movement and gesture and engagement with the audience in the understanding of the importance of waiting for a response from God. With the live, embodied, actual pausing and uncomfortable waiting, this performer-interpreter gained deeper appreciation for the ancient community's waiting for the word of God, and to some extent, the waiting on God of his own community.

Perry's work more closely approaches what I had sought from BPC: the articulation of the meaning that is found when one internalizes the biblical compositions, inhabits them, and looks and speaks towards a contemporary audience from within the world of the "text."

Observing Interpretive Decisions in a Performance

To Holly Hearon's work again, and this time her analysis of characters in John which also begins with analysis of the text in order to determine how to perform it.[194] Even so, it does seem less focused on uncovering the original performance context than the methodologies discussed so far. It is interesting to note, however, the extent to which she draws on the work of such ancient orators as Quintillian for insight into elements of performance. For example: "exhortations or statements of fact are effectively accompanied by a gesture in which the middle finger is placed against the thumb and the

---

191. Perry, *Insights*, 99.
192. Perry, *Insights*, 100.
193. Perry, *Insights*, 100.
194. Hearon, "Characters in Text and Performance," 67.

remaining fingers as the hand is moved forward firmly."[195] It is unclear from these references to ancient oratory practice whether Hearon intends to suggest that a contemporary performer would use this gesture, or whether it is simply a point of interest.

As we saw earlier in her work analyzing the performances of Rhoads and Ruge-Jones,[196] Hearon is significantly influenced by Narrative Criticism in her application of performance analysis (with her interest "in what the implied author shows and tells about the character,"[197] and the "filling of the gaps" required in a performance-critical analysis[198]). As she is commenting on Gospel compositions, this seems a reasonable approach, and demonstrates well what Hearon sees as the complementary nature of Narrative and Performance approaches, contending that an interpreter could fold either into the other, "and both would be enriched."[199]

The components of Hearon's process are to pay attention to: time, space, character interaction, tension, dialogue, cues in the narrative, implications for a solo performer, and coherence and credibility in characterization across the narrative. For Hearon, these are the distinct questions Performance Criticism poses "in an effort to make the character three-dimensional."[200]

Among the comparisons she draws between Narrative and Performance approaches to the story of Nicodemus in the Gospel of John, Hearon's observations regarding the performance interpretation of his role in the burial of Jesus are particularly insightful. Having noted that the "storyteller says that *together* they take the body, wrap it in linen with the spices and lay it in the tomb (19:38–42),"[201] Hearon observes that the narrative critic, as a reader, can hold in their imagination both Nicodemus and Joseph of Arimathea and their separate bodies and actions, though working together. "A solo storyteller, however, enacting the story as narrated, embodies the unity of their joint action."[202] Hearon notes various interpretive trends that have sought to imbue Nicodemus with guilt for complicity in the crucifixion: in the embodied performer, there is no room for such an interpretation to be played out as Nicodemus is unified with the faithful Joseph of Arimathea. Performing the story addresses interpretations of Nicodemus

---

195. Hearon, "Characters in Text and Performance," 74–75.
196. Hearon, "From Narrative to Performance." Discussed in Chapter 2.
197. Hearon, "Characters in Text and Performance," 67.
198. Hearon, "Characters in Text and Performance," 68.
199. Hearon, "Characters in Text and Performance," 76.
200. Hearon, "Characters in Text and Performance," 76.
201. Hearon, "Characters in Text and Performance," 75.
202. Hearon, "Characters in Text and Performance," 75.

and his role in the story that have been problematic in the past, and offers an embodied presentation of the characters that might more accurately portray the intentions of the story.

Hearon does note that it is not entirely beyond the bounds of possibility for a performer to embody two distinct characters here, but this would require some rather convoluted miming. The most effective performance choice is to move in such a way as to represent something of the laying out of the body and anointing it, in unison, as Hearon observes. The body of the performer thus defines limits for its own interpretation of the story at this point; further examination may explore how performance interpretation may define limits to the interpretation of the story more generally, if it is indeed understood as a story written for performance. Hearon demonstrates that performance-criticism both features fluidity, with no two performances being the same, and sets "interpretive limits" to that fluidity.[203]

Hearon notes the key difference between Narrative and Performance Criticism, the disappearance of the textual world to be "replaced by a person, a storyteller, who embodies the world of the story, translating it into real time and space."[204] She thereby arrives at a vital observation for performance interpretation: the integrity of the performer-interpreter, embodied and embedded in time and place, as mediator of the text.

> The ethical obligation that accompanies every act of biblical interpretation is increased in performance criticism. Performance in real time and space cannot help but engage issues in our own particular time and space . . . this is precisely what makes performance criticism so important and so necessary. It holds us to a level of accountability that is easily sidestepped in other forms of biblical criticism and reminds us of the tremendous power of stories to transform lives.[205]

Hearon's aim with this chapter was to give a "sense of how a performance critic undertakes an analysis of character with a view to performance before a live audience."[206] She thus takes a further step towards the kind of methodology that I develop, one that takes seriously the work and the interpretive decisions of a performer bringing a composition to life.

---

203. Hearon, "Characters in Text and Performance," 76. As does the Bible itself, perhaps, offering a script with multiple possible ways to play it, within limited bounds of authenticity, integrity, faithfulness (Lee, *Preaching*, 110).
204. Hearon, "Characters in Text and Performance," 77.
205. Hearon, "Characters in Text and Performance," 77.
206. Hearon, "Characters in Text and Performance," 76.

Integrating Performance Decisions into Interpretive Comments

We have one last step to take towards that development I make with Embodied Performance Analysis. Melinda Cousins adopts an approach in her PhD thesis that brings "a canonical-theological perspective to bear on a close reading of the Psalms of Ascents and then [uses] a performance-critical methodology to enhance theological interpretation of the text."[207]

Cousins' theological interpretation of these Psalms in text and performance demonstrates once again the integrated nature of BPC. Beginning with a close reading of the Psalms, which results in a translation for performance, Cousins then proceeds to multiple performances of the Psalms as a collection, for different audiences in Australia.[208] The translation and performances then proceed in a "hermeneutical circle," as Cousins' rehearsal and performance of the Psalms instigates nuances in her translation; she discusses making "alterations to the translation after hearing and performing the text out loud," alterations that highlighted for the audience the poetic nature of the text.[209] For example, a "more literal translation of 'ask for the peace' was changed to 'pray for the peace' to provide alliteration."[210] Translating for specific Australian audiences, she notes:

> I had translated נפשׁ (*nephesh*) as "life" throughout the collection so as to avoid contemporaryy connotations evoked by the word "soul" that are foreign to the text. This presented a challenge when the word הי (*hy*), "life," is used in Ps 133:3. The distinction was conveyed by changing my tone of voice: life (נפשׁ) was spoken conversationally and accompanied by a simple gesture toward my heart, whereas life (הי) was pronounced emphatically and exuberantly with both hands open toward the audience.[211]

Following performance, Cousins invited audiences to engage in small group discussion, then to complete a questionnaire.[212] Cousins' engagement with the audience responses, searching for themes and trends, is the most comprehensive study of audiences in BPC I encountered.[213]

207. Cousins, "Pilgrim Theology," 96.
208. Cousins, "Pilgrim Theology," 181.
209. Cousins, "Pilgrim Theology," 185.
210. Cousins, "Pilgrim Theology," 186.
211. Cousins, "Pilgrim Theology," 195.
212. Cousins, "Pilgrim Theology," 204.
213. Cousins, "Pilgrim Theology," 97. Recalling observations made earlier in discussing, for example, the approach of Peter Perry, who also employs audience questionnaires, but who suggests this area is a fertile ground for further research in this field: cf.

> My initial analysis of the responses sought to discover the most frequent words and phrases used by audience members in relation to their experience in order to evaluate how the interpretation was seen, heard, and felt by the audience. By far the most frequent comments were about emotions, with 57% of respondents noting that the emotions they saw or felt were what would primarily stay with them from the performance.[214]

For Cousins as interpreter-performer,

> performance confirmed insights from the close reading of the text that these psalms provide an exploration through the lens of pilgrimage of the experience of humanity, the world, and God. Performance also allowed me to experience the worldmaking dynamic: learning and enacting these psalms has reframed the way they influence not only my thinking but also my engagement with the world.[215]

As she "draws from the audience research and [her] own experience as performer," Cousins' theological interpretation highlights key effects of the text that were observable by "using performance as a research methodology and might otherwise be overlooked: in particular its affective, kinesthetic (spatial + movement), and relational dimensions."[216] Cousins' discussion over four chapters, in which she integrates insights from close reading and performance in a "dialogical rhythm,"[217] begins at each point with the textual comments. While her performance insights do, to some extent, resemble my Embodied Performance approach, with a more explicit discussion of the influence of audience and performance on translation and re-translation than we see elsewhere, for example, this approach nevertheless *begins with the text* beyond the interpreter, where Embodied Performance Analysis *begins with embodiment,* bringing the text within.

The key shift from BPC as practiced by performers and critics to EPA is this starting point. As interpreter-performers are beginning to integrate their insights from performance in their writing, as they embody the compositions, feel their emotions, and encounter them in live imaginative spaces with their audiences, it will be helpful to analyze that process in more depth. To support the work of both interpreter-performers and performer-interpreters, I present a methodology that articulates the ways in

---

Insights, 90–92; 159.

214. Cousins, "Pilgrim Theology," 207.
215. Cousins, "Pilgrim Theology," 203.
216. Cousins, "Pilgrim Theology," 221.
217. Cousins, "Pilgrim Theology," 223.

which sensory-motor responses, emotional responses, and envisaging and experiencing audiences, all illuminate meaning in a biblical composition as it is received today. Embodied Performance Analysis will also further clarify these insights in order to invite more embodied, intuitive and affective, and relational interpretation to make their valuable contributions to the field of biblical scholarship. BPC has shifted the gaze of biblical scholarship from the page to the ancient performative origins of the compositions. It has begun to shift the experience of these compositions from page-oriented, silent, individual reading, to contemporary, live, mutually embodied performance events. Now is the time to turn the BPC gaze a little further around, and begin with the embodied immersion in the text that Cousins notes is a unique experience for the performer,[218] and which will yet further deepen and broaden understanding of the meaning and transformative impact of the biblical compositions.

SHIFTING THE GAZE

> *A scholar performs biblical compositions and observes her body, emotion, and audience shaping the meaning she discerns in that composition. The scholar seeks to understand this interpretive action, and to contribute the wisdom gained from embodying the biblical writings in scholarly conversations. Will the emerging field of Biblical Performance Criticism provide the means for understanding and communicating her performed interpretations?*

So, then, what I found in BPC was not what I was looking for. It is nevertheless a rich and enriching recovery of the inherent orality of biblical compositions. I did not find an established methodology, but emerging trends and approaches, which, in some cases, begin to attend to the movements, emotions, and audiences of contemporary performers as interpretive activity in and of themselves.

When Rhoads states that performing 1 Peter has impacted his understanding of the letter, this is a general statement pointing in the direction of performance as interpretation, but not articulating *what* in the performance process or experience, not describing a methodology or showing how he arrives at that conclusion.[219] BPC methodology has brought us as far as acknowledging that performance at least influences, and perhaps even *is* interpretation, but has not yet, to my satisfaction, outlined a methodology

---

218. Cousins, "Pilgrim Theology," 226.
219. Rhoads, "Emerging Methodology Part 2," 174.

that describes the process by which that interpretation is derived for the performer-interpreter, and through which such embodied insights may be communicated as scholarship.

Swanson also demonstrates a kind of approach that engages in analysis of the text first, then determines the way the text says it should be performed (and was performed in its origins because the text is a record of a performance), before making decisions for a performance today that carries the essence of a probable first century performance.[220] In such analyses, the reader will find the scholar observing that "the scene needs to be played so that the audience will feel the connection to other theophanies," a more directive, more fixed interpretation for performance than the fluid nature of performance (which is identified by BPC scholars) would suggest. An Embodied Performance Analysis is more likely to describe the possibilities—if this scene is played in this way, the audience will feel a particular connection, or playing the scene another way, the performer-interpreter notices a different connection to highlight for the audience.[221] In other words, while many Biblical Performance scholars read the text as a script with definite performative intentions embedded in and between the written lines, EPA first lifts the words off the page and into muscle and breath and emotion, allowing that process of embodiment to point to the possibilities for performance and meaning in *this* time and *this* place. The possibilities will be determined by what is embedded in the text from its origins; they will also be determined by the myriad ways in which the composition has been received in different times and places. Further, the possibilities will be determined, as will the choice for the performance moment, by this audience, this performer-interpreter, their contexts, and their relationship with each other and the composition.

Where Boomershine identifies themes within the story and then searches for stories in personal or communal memory that might resonate with those themes,[222] by beginning with the embodiment of the composition my method invites personal and communal stories to arise in response intuitively and instinctively, and perhaps from beyond a thematic connection to an emotional connection. In an Embodied Performance approach, the performer-interpreter will observe the connections that instinctively arise, and critically reflect on those connections for their usefulness and

---

220. Swanson, "'This Is My...'"

221. Noted, but not always fully realized in application, by Ward and Trobisch. "Developing a variety of possible interpretations is a crucial step of scholarly discourse; the performance of texts before an audience helps to achieve this goal": Swanson, "'This is My...,'" 194, 96.

222. Boomershine, *Messiah of Peace*, 153.

appropriateness in influencing the meaning discerned in the composition through performance.[223]

Biblical Performance Criticism is an historical endeavor, and this is not what I expected to find. Whether through the performance mode of thought employed by Giles and Doan, or Rhoads' interpretation for performance as historical re-enactment, scholars employing performance with biblical texts seek to understand the ancient performance events to which the writings point, and thus to understand the biblical writings and the people and situations for which they were composed.

In the field of biblical scholarship, where rational, objective, "criticism"[224] has dominated for a long time, BPC offers a recovery of the embodied, voiced, communal origins of these compositions. BPC is, however, employed in terms of historical, or literary, method; it still presents itself as "criticism." It has not fully embraced the embodiment that is its defining feature, as a tool for interpretation itself. Performance has not been utilized to its full potential, when it has only been employed to test or communicate interpretations arrived at by traditional (albeit adapted) methods. Performance is a lens through which scholars view the biblical compositions *at their origins*.

But what if performers-as-scholars took performance further, in our interpretive encounters with the Bible? What if we listened to the insights of a body, performing; the emotions, inhabiting; the audience, experiencing, these compositions?

Perry begins to do so, in his "performance" stage of analysis. Rhoads acknowledges the question, and points to the potential of performance *as* interpretation. Boomershine presents a commentary with the composition performed, and Perry links to recordings of his performances. Hearon and Mathews both acknowledge the performative re-enactment of these works in communities of faith, making meaning anew on each unique occasion. Students are deepening their engagement and understanding by performing the biblical compositions themselves. Cousins presents an integrated discussion that explicitly draws on insights from the performance events, as well as the reflections of both performer and audience. Interpreter-performers are beginning to pay attention not only to the clues in the texts, but to the responses of their bodies, emotions, and audiences.

Now is the time, it seems to me, for a methodology that supports the work of these interpreter-performers and performer-interpreters. Embodied

---

223. Again, this is similar to the intentionally self-reflective stage of the theatrical interpretation process described by Levy, *Bible as Theatre*, ix.

224. See Levy, *Bible as Theatre*, 9.

Performance Analysis may be the next necessary step in the development of Biblical Performance Criticism, building on the work of scholars and storytellers who have established the inherent performance nature of biblical compositions.

BIBLICAL PERFORMANCE CRITICISM: CONCLUSIONS

The story of Biblical Performance Criticism shows us a field of study applying performance in the interpretation of biblical compositions. It is a field featuring various trends in methodology and application, and two main streams. The dominant stream within NT scholarship is the storyteller's BPC, which emerged from the work of Rhoads and others in Narrative Criticism, and employs narrative methodology and tools along with those of Historical Criticism. The central focus of BPC to reconstruct the performed history of biblical compositions is the second key feature of this dominant stream. It is a focus shared by a second stream in BPC, which I have named the critic's BPC, as employed by Giles and Doan, and others. Biblical Performance scholars either, as Giles and Doan, do not employ contemporary performance in their performance criticism, or, as Rhoads and Boomershine, for example, employ a narrative (or historical) exegesis as preparation for a contemporary performance. Among this latter school, some, such as Ruge-Jones, Swanson, Perry, and Cousins, are beginning to articulate the performance choices they (or their students or actors) make, and how those choices influence the meaning these scholars discern in the text.

Three features of BPC have emerged, in particular for the storyteller's stream in which my work is situated: an emphasis on narrative or story; a focus on reconstructing performed history; contemporary performance as either absent, or the outcome of interpretation (i.e. not *as* interpretation). A further feature of BPC is its inherent mutuality; methods from within biblical scholarship and from other fields of scholarship are incorporated in the analysis of biblical compositions through a performance lens. The method that emerges from my performance practice, Embodied Performance Analysis, is likewise inherently mutual. This approach, however, *begins* with embodiment and performance; focuses on reception of the Bible through performance *today*; and employs narrative techniques only for narrative compositions. So let me now introduce the Embodied Performance methodology, and test case Embodied Performance Analysis of Romans.

4

A New Beginning

Developing an Embodied Performance Method

As Biblical Performance Criticism is an inherently mutual discipline, integrating various approaches from within and beyond biblical scholarship in various ways, so is Embodied Performance Analysis. This new method further utilizes the mutuality inherent to a human being who brings more than cognitive process to interpretation—or whose cognition, as will be demonstrated in this chapter, is not detached from, but indwelling with physical, emotional, and relational meaning-making processes. As I have mentioned, Embodied Performance Analysis *begins* with embodiment; focuses on reception of the Bible through performance today; and employs narrative analysis only for narrative compositions. In short, EPA is "an attempt to articulate meaning in [biblical compositions] in more dynamic and relational terms than those of a disembodied surveillance by a separated *cogito*."[1]

In this chapter I will build a theoretical foundation for an Embodied Performance approach by introducing its tools of body, emotion and audience. To that end, I will engage with such diverse fields as psychology, cognitive science, linguistics, audience studies, and theater studies (for the latter, particular conversation partners will be contemporary performers of the work of Shakespeare). The process of EPA is one of preparation, performance, and critical reflection. The outcome—what might be called a

---

1. To appropriate Welton's aims for his work articulating meaning in theater by paying attention to feeling (*Feeling Theatre*, 11).

commentary—will be an analysis comprised of two elements, Performed Interpretation (presented in Chapter 5) and Critical Reflection (Chapter 6).

In order to understand how body, emotion, and audience might function as interpretive tools, I will examine the way the body "knows" by exploring embodied cognition, observe how emotions communicate meaning to and through a performer, and learn from theater scholarship about the role of the audience. I begin with the body: the physical, sensory organism.

BODY

> [. . .] I held
> My friend's daughter, her blonde hair
> Pressed to my chest, my hand on her sweet
> Head, her eyes huge and lovely as pansies
> After rain, and I remember holding
> My daughter at three in the same way,
> This sweetness that rose off her,
> And I think how my body keeps inside
> Itself the sensory memory of holding a child.[2]

The Body Knows

Scholars across many fields are broadening their perspective on how humans make meaning in and of the world.[3] In contrast to the view of cognition as the brain-based mind receiving and interpreting signs and symbols from the body, many now view the body as a situated organism whose sensorimotor functions not only receive *but also* process information.[4] For example, a person's eyes moving on hearing a sentence that describes movement, such as "the road goes through the desert," suggests that the body must move somehow in order to make meaning. For the body is understood to *know* as an integrated organism: "my body is the fabric into which all objects are woven, and it is, at least in relation to the perceived world, the general instrument of my 'comprehension.'"[5]

---

2. Gillan, "What the Body Knows," 112.

3. Adams, "Embodied Cognition," 619. Adams, however, is not convinced by the connections these scholars make between their data and claims for embodied cognition.

4. Falck and Gibbs, "Embodied Motivations," 253.

5. Merleau-Ponty, *Phenomenology of Perception*, 1962, 235; cited in Gibbs, *Embodiment and Cognitive Science*, 17.

In the past, scholars objectified the body, making the human person out to be an ethereal soul or mind, in some way temporarily inhabiting the material object body.[6] Today, scientists affirm that "what are often thought of as abstract meanings and inferential patterns [in 'higher order' cognition] actually do depend on schema derived from our *bodily* experience of problem solving."[7]

Further, there is wide-spread scientific acknowledgment that old dualisms of body/mind, or matter/soul, do not adequately describe the ways humans interpret their experience, or understand their selves and the world. "Many philosophers and cognitive scientists now reject person-world dualism and advocate that persons be understood, and scientifically studied, in terms of organism-environment mutuality and reciprocity."[8]

How the Body Knows

The study of how the body "knows" (or interprets the world) is being named "embodied cognition." In general, cognitive science sees the mind as somewhat separate from the body, receiving input from the body's senses and movements: the *mind* processes, interprets, knows. But scholarship features varied approaches within diverse disciplines, and, often, interdisciplinary studies, for more integrated and nuanced understanding. Lawrence Shapiro outlines three main trends in embodied cognition—Conceptualization, Replacement, and Constitution. A brief overview of his discussion will serve well as an introduction to the field.

A "Conceptualization" approach will understand that the organism itself makes meaning of, and thus creates its world. There is no independent reality, only what is created by any given organism.[9] Furthermore, a body is constrained in its capacity to know by what kind of body it is.[10] The premise

---

6. Gibbs, *Embodiment and Cognitive Science*, 14. This shift in understanding is ongoing, for humans still "apply our best knowledge and our religious truth" *to* our bodies, rather than listening to the ways our bodies, as subjects, "are seeking knowledge and truth" as bodies: Hefner, *Our Bodies Are Selves*, 9.

7. Johnson, *Body in the Mind*, xx.

8. Gibbs, *Embodiment and Cognitive Science*, 16. Also, Hefner, *Our Bodies Are Selves*, 2. As we have in preaching studies (Lee, *Preaching*), we might observe a similar movement away from dualism in biblical studies with the emergence of ecological readings (see, for instance, the Earth Bible Project, e.g. Habel, ed., *Readings from the Perspective of Earth*).

9. Shapiro, *Embodied Cognition*, 202.

10. Shapiro, *Embodied Cognition*, 112.

of no independent reality is difficult to sustain, and this approach is significantly limited as a result.

The embodiment and situatedness of the person are the core processes in understanding, according to the "Replacement" approach.[11] The concept of "embodiment" thus brings focus to the way a body performs "actions that influence how the brain responds to the world while at the same time influencing how the world presents itself to the brain."[12] The brain or mind is thus equal partner *with the body* in knowing.

In the "Constitution" approach, the body *is part of* the mind. The "constituents of cognitive processes extend beyond the brain" to the *body as a whole*.[13] My work proceeds on this understanding.

As scholarship affirms, humans do not know or understand the self or the world in or with the mind alone. Instead, it seems clear that humans actually understand through complex interrelationships of sensorimotor experience and simulation, imagination and mental processes. An example of research from psycholinguistics examines how a body knows language.[14] In an observation of people who walked slower after a task of reading and unscrambling words like "old," "wrinkled," and "tired,"[15] "people's understanding of metaphorical language" was shown to "recruit embodied meanings that can be tied to specific body actions."[16]

Spiritual knowing has also been observed as an intuitive, embodied phenomenon: humans know God with their whole body. The body "remains the source of many of our deepest joys and delights, and of much of our most cherished knowledge. It is also, we sense, one of the places Spirit manifests itself most deeply and powerfully. And so we continue to listen and attend as well as we can to what the body knows."[17]

---

11. Shapiro, *Embodied Cognition*, 156. Observing the fifteenth century attire of the characters in Funhof's painting of the beheading of John the Baptist, Joynes "reminds us that we are not impartial observers operating in an a-historic space but need to recognize our own situatedness in a particular time and place when we interpret a biblical text": Joynes, "Visualizing Salome's Dance," 159. Further, this is a "positive celebration of our own human identity, our human finitude, as the arena in which we see (and potentially find) understanding": Nicholls, "Is Wirkungsgeschichte."

12. Shapiro, *Embodied Cognition*, 156.

13. Shapiro, *Embodied Cognition*, 158–59. Some go so far as to "claim that the mind extends beyond the body, into the world," in what is named *extended cognition*.

14. Cited in Gibbs, "Walking the Walk," 364. See also Hefner, *Our Bodies Are Selves*, 85.

15. Gibbs, "Walking the Walk," 364.

16. Gibbs, "Walking the Walk," 377.

17. Christie, "What the Body Knows," xi. Donnalee Dox also notes the integrated human understanding: "the experiential synthesis of mind, body, and spirit in vernacular practice has produced a form of knowledge, articulated in language and framed

Further, the language of the body, which is well known as a communicator beyond words, can also communicate to the self a posture, or attitude, that changes a person's own mind, cognitively and physiologically. Amy Cuddy has, with her colleagues, observed the way adopting a posture of "power" can imbue a person with the confidence to perform at the best of their abilities in such heightened social situations as job interviews.[18]

The sciences are demonstrating that the body's very physiology not only experiences the world through sense and movement, but interprets, responds, understands in ways our conscious minds have not the capacity for comprehending. It would seem that scholars are growing in the capacity to observe, acknowledge, and listen to the myriad ways human bodies know. Inspired and informed by this field of embodied cognition, EPA will do just that in encounters with biblical compositions.

How the Body Will Be Employed as an Interpretive Tool

As I discuss the body as a tool for interpretation, we may recall my introduction in Chapter 1 of embodiment and performance as personal and particular, immersive and intuitive. The body is utilized as a tool through the physical immersion in the composition by internalization, rehearsing the composition for performance by heart. Intuition thus helps the performer to know and understand the movement and flow of the rhetoric, when on the page, Paul's arguments may feel disjointed and confusing.[19] The personal and particular embodiment by me—white, educated, ordained, progressive, Australian, female—will explicitly and implicitly shape the meaning I discern as I embody, as I immerse myself in, this letter to mediate it for reception by an audience in Adelaide today.[20]

We will see in the test case: Embodied Performance Analysis listens to the body as the performer—as I—physically inhabit Romans for performance. Storytellers describe the process of learning a biblical text for

---

performances": *Reckoning with Spirit*, 206.

18. Cuddy, Wilmuth, and Carney, "Benefit of Power Posing"; Cuddy, "Your Body Language."

19. For example, Bassler wonders if "the lack of clarity and tortuous logic" in such passages as 1 Cor 11:2–16 "may signal that Paul himself is not exactly sure what is going on": "1 Corinthians," 416.

20. As Lee notes, "we are not neutral" (*Preaching*, 157), so our practice of interpreting and proclaiming scripture must include attending to our own responses (156). Unfortunately, "the homiletical literature of our time shows a diminished interest in introspection as an integral task in preaching" (158).

performance as "inhabiting" or "internalizing" the composition.[21] When I perform, I do not "remember" the words, rather I *know* the letter, in the way one knows one's own story and can tell it without appearing to think about it. I know the letter, because I am immersed in the letter. I will describe in the Critical Reflection a distinct feeling of inhabiting and moving about within the letter as one would inhabit a house, and of the letter simultaneously dwelling within me—the "mutual indwelling" I have mentioned on several occasions already. The process of learning the text is for me profoundly physical, as I feel the text begin to move from my head and a "cognitive" knowing, to my heart, bones, breath, gut, in a fully embodied knowing as if I am experiencing the text acting upon me. For, as storyteller Megan McKenna observes, "Practice makes for knowledge, ease and grace. With time and diligence, the story comes true in you first, inviting all who listen to come true too."[22] Similarly for Brown, the actor of a Shakespeare play will more fully discover the meaning in the words, and in the spaces between them, in the embodied acts of speaking the dialogue and enacting the play onstage.[23] Or consider Buckley's encouragement to storytellers to "absorb" the story: "immerse yourself in the story . . . Sit back and read the story, concentrating on nothing but the feel and sound of the story. Let the characters and words become familiar to you . . . Read the story as often as you are able . . . Read the story out loud, feeling the words coming off your tongue. As you read it . . . listen to yourself read it, you will find that you subconsciously feel the story."[24]

"Subconsciously feel the story"—Buckley effectively describes the learning process as I experience it, and provides helpful preparation for what to expect from the discussion in the Critical Reflection.

I will observe, then, in the test case, my posture, where I stand and at what points I want to move, which will show me something about what the text might mean in my estimation, intuitively and physically. I will observe how my body moves in response to this growing familiarity and mutual indwelling; what gestures I use as I speak the text aloud—gestures that indicate meaning. Ancient orators observe the way that gesture is an intuitive

---

21. Rhoads, for example, describes the process of entering the story of the Gospel of Mark as actually entering the kingdom of God, as walking in Jesus' footsteps: "The New Testament as Oral Performance." See also the website of the Network of Biblical Storytellers, http://www.nbsint.org/aboutus.

22. McKenna, *Keepers of the Story*, 187.

23. Brown, "Learning Shakespeare's Secret Language," 217.

24. Buckley, *Dancing with Words*, 58–59. Swanson has observed his actors and the way the "words change their bodies" (*Provoking the Gospel of Matthew*, 7). For McKenna, the "story becomes incarnated in the heart of the teller": *Keepers of the Story*, 202.

element of spoken communication. Plato notes, for example, that movement can either support or contradict our meaning: "in general, when a man [sic] uses his voice to talk or sing, he finds it very difficult to keep his body still. This is the origin of the whole art of dancing: the gestures that express what one is saying. Some of us make gestures that are invariably in harmony with our words, but some of us fail."[25]

As I observe my body's movements during the learning and rehearsal phase, the body will at times support meaning and show me the way in which I intuitively understand the text. At other times, my intuitive understanding will be at odds with my conscious understanding, posing questions for further investigation. At this point, I will employ other interpretive methods as appropriate—Historical, Rhetorical, Socio-cultural Criticism, for example.

I will also observe the voice, which is embodied beyond merely the larynx and mouth to the intricacies of tongue, teeth, lips, nose, and the very breath that takes the words into the depth of the body to connect with emotion.[26] This "connection between breath and emotion is not to be underestimated. Regardless of whether we are talking about psychic trauma or the lightest of human emotions, the voice is one of the preacher's [performer's] most sensitive instruments—not only for expressing but for knowing."[27] Breath has been employed as a basis for sound mapping and recreating ancient performances, as discussed in Chapter 3, but this is not my method here. I am more interested in the natural and rehearsed intonation and expression of the contemporary performer-as-interpreter, the emphasis and speed of *my* speech in particular as it raises questions and indicates meaning in this composition as I embody and perform it.

The discussion of voice—of pace, emphasis, tone—will be dispersed throughout the discussion of the three interpretive tools in the Critical Reflection, rather than bound exclusively within "body" though I have introduced it here. In particular, as noted, the voice, and the breath on which it is carried, demonstrate the connection of the body with the emotions; the integration of the physical and affective ways in which a human makes meaning.

---

25. Plato, *Leges* 816a. Cited in Shiner, *Proclaiming the Gospel*, 127.

26. For the intricacies of voice mechanics in performance, see Childers, *Performing the Word*, 57–98.

27. Childers, *Performing the Word*, 59.

EMOTION

"Emotion" in Scholarship

Emotion has enjoyed a more respectable position as a field of study in only relatively recent times.[28] "Emotions have been perceived as a subversive force in Western traditions of thought because they are posited in a binary relationship with rationality which corresponds to culture and universality ... This perception made scholarly research on emotions undervalued till recently."[29]

When the term "emotion" was first used in English to refer to the internal "movement" a person experiences, it had been borrowed from the French *émotion*, which referred to any kind of movement, or "motion."[30] Before using "emotion," these internal "motions" had been referred to as "passions"[31] or "humors," and had been understood in many different ways. Based on ideas of how the blood moved through the body, four "humors"—blood, yellow bile, black bile, and phlegm—"were thought to shape personality and mood."[32] Passions were universally recognizable,[33] were external to the person, and could affect trees as much as humans.[34] Although in recent years it seems scholars in the area of emotion studies are reaching greater consensus on key elements of emotion,[35] it has been, and remains, a subject evoking diverse approaches and findings across a wide range of fields,[36] from psychology and sociology, neuro- and biological science, to philosophy; and also *within* each field itself.[37]

28. Cook, "Staging Nothing," 94; Tait, *Performing Emotions*, 4. Tait also refers to Merleau-Ponty's claim that gesture *is* emotion (94)—see Merleau-Ponty, *Phenomology of Perception*, 184.

29. Tait, *Performing Emotions*, 4. Following Jaggar, "Love and Knowledge."

30. Smith, *The Book of Human Emotions*, 15. This marked a shift in interest in emotions to the study of "observable phenomena: clenched teeth, rolling tears; shudders; wide eyes ... understanding how the body's smiles and frowns expressed—and even stimulated—internal emotions."

31. As in Descartes, who talked about passions of the soul; in Gruber, "Human Emotion 1.2."

32. Smith, *Book of Human Emotions*, 14.

33. Cassidy and Cassidy, "Playing Is a Science," 21.

34. Smith, *Book of Human Emotions*, 14.

35. Ekman, "What Scientists Who Study Emotion."

36. Dixon, *From Passions to Emotions*: "the over-inclusivity of 'emotion' has made it impossible for there to be any consensus about what an emotion is" (246).

37. Overviews of the diversity in the field of emotion study are found in, for example, Tait, *Performing Emotions*, 4–5; Feldman Barrett, "Constructing Emotion,"

Early psychological approaches—for example that of William James at the close of the nineteenth century—claimed that emotions were purely physical or physiological responses to environment.[38] Scientists from Charles Darwin[39] to Paul Ekman[40] have claimed varying degrees of innate base emotions as common to all humans. Ekman is a key proponent of the theory of universal human emotions—that all humans experience emotion in the same way.[41] Such theories often propose a core of six or more "basic" emotions that all humans experience—anger, disgust, fear, happiness, sadness, surprise[42]—and, according to Ekman, that all humans express with the same facial and bodily behaviors.[43]

Although a binary opposition between emotion and cognition has long prevailed, many theories today view cognition as a key element of emotion; and challenges to the idea of emotion as purely physical or physiological are many and varied. Cognitive scientists claim there is no emotion without cognitive awareness of it (the Schacter-Singer approach),[44] and cognitive linguistic approaches examine ways in which language functions to complete, define, or describe emotion.[45]

360–61; and more comprehensively, in Smith, *Book of Human Emotions*, and Solomon, *What Is an Emotion?*

38. In his essay, "What is an Emotion" from 1884: see *What Is an Emotion?*, 1, 65–66. Also Feldman Barrett, "Constructing Emotion," 362.

39. Cassidy, "'Playing Is a Science,'" 21; Sweet, "Luxury of Tears"; Solomon, *What Is an Emotion?*, 57–58: Darwin saw emotion in humans as similar to that in animals, having survival value, and as a physiological phenomenon. Much has been discredited of Darwin's conclusions, which have none-the-less laid a foundation for questions and ideas still pursued by scholars today.

40. Gruber, "Human Emotion 1.2"; Solomon, *What Is an Emotion?*, 119.

41. Ekman, "What Scientists Who Study Emotion," 32.

42. Gruber, "Human Emotion 1.3." More complex emotions "arise from a combination of basic emotions or are culturally influenced and constructed." In his study of agreement among established emotion scholars, Ekman notes that five core, or basic, emotions are acknowledged across a broad spectrum of the field—anger, fear, disgust, sadness, and happiness: Ekman, "What Scientists Who Study Emotion," 32. With the Dalai Lama, Ekman has developed an online "Atlas of Emotions" based on this survey: Ekman, Ekman, and The Dalai Lama, "Atlas of Emotion."

43. Solomon, *What Is an Emotion?*, 119.

44. Gruber, "Human Emotion 1.3." Also Solomon, *What Is an Emotion?*, 110. Solomon himself takes a cognitive approach to emotion (*What Is an Emotion?* 224). Ohira cites Spinoza in support of this view: Ohira, "Beneficial Roles of Emotion in Decision Making," 382.

45. Cook, "Interplay," 584, 91; Feldman Barrett, "Constructing Emotion," 370; Welton, *Feeling Theatre*, 23. Smith observes that language and emotion stimulate the brain simultaneously; she also suggests that language dismantles the idea of universal emotions, as different words are found in different languages for the same emotion:

But while some claim that emotion is not "emotion" without conscious awareness, others argue that we feel emotions *un*consciously all the time. As early as James's work we can see the idea of an overall "flow"—or "feeling tone"—of emotion.[46] More recently, Lisa Feldman-Barrett has observed that emotion is both the subconscious continual "flow" of response to experience, *and* discrete, named and cognitively bounded "emotions" that are experiences in themselves—anger, or fear, for example.[47] Her "Conceptual Act Model" is an integrated view of emotion as both natural to humans and shaped by cultural context; as context-specific rather than universal; and as fluid and variable across time, person and situation, rather than predetermined innate response. It also allows for "affect" to be involved in the breadth of human cognition (or meaning-making), not only emotion. Seeing emotion and also concepts themselves as embodied, thus "blurring the boundary between conception and perception,"[48] Feldman-Barrett presents a view of human knowing and meaning-making that is embodied, holistic, and integrated.[49] I find this approach to articulate my intuition based on the experience of making meaning by embodying biblical texts using sensory-motor, emotional, intuitive, and relational modes of interpretation. Artists, immersed in our process, understand the way we make meaning, but cannot (as with the chess player or soldier mentioned in Chapter 1) easily articulate that understanding.

This is, and has been, true across much of human history, although often, and notably in such eras as the Enlightenment, "rational" meaning-making has been significantly favored.[50] As Gisela Kreglinger observes, George MacDonald was a nineteenth-century writer of parabolic fiction heavily infused with Christian spirituality. She describes MacDonald as an artist who could articulate something of his intuitive and imaginative meaning-making process, with resistance to the Enlightenment view of

---

"Buzz Words," 39–40.

46. Henricks, *Selves, Societies and Emotions*, 102; Feldman Barrett, "Constructing Emotion," 362. Cook has observed in Damasio's approach the idea of a "body loop," a system of circulating information within the person to evoke behavior or response: Cook, "Staging Nothing," 95.

47. Feldman Barrett, "Constructing Emotion," 367.

48. Feldman Barrett, "Constructing Emotion," 366. Further support comes from such studies as Ohira's examination of emotion in the process of decision making: "Beneficial Roles of Emotion."

49. In the area of faith or religious experience, Dox describes such holistic ways in which humans know the Spirit: *Reckoning with Spirit*, 206.

50. With this privileging comes "universal claims about the nature of reality and the human condition, and claims regarding certainty and objectivity in respect to knowledge": Cooey, *Religious Imagination and the Body*, 5.

his time, which was inclined to dismiss the emotions and imagination as "irrational."[51] Kreglinger observes in MacDonald's work, and also that of his contemporary Samuel Taylor Coleridge, a celebration of the imagination, bringing the intellect into conversation with feelings.[52] For artistic, creative thinkers, intuition, imagination, and feeling are fundamental to interpreting and making meaning of the world.[53] In the integration of the arts and the sciences deeper insights may emerge into what artists intuitively know from experience.

Theater scholars draw on psychology as well as the experience of actors to make conclusions about emotion.[54] Stanislavski's approach to emotion and acting is the most prevalent subject for discussion, and a dominant method in acting across the world.[55] In short (and discussed further below), Stanislavski advocated for actors to feel emotion in order to communicate it, and in particular to draw on their own emotional memories.[56]

In scholarship, then, emotion is a somewhat elusive concept. It is understood as both innate to human being and learned; involving body and mind and affect, conscious and sub-conscious; useful for interpreting and communicating meaning. How, then, is "emotion" understood as a concept in this project, to be employed as a tool in Embodied Performance Analysis?

"Emotion" in the Current Project

I use the term "emotion" to refer to the *subjective feeling* humans experience in response to the world.[57] As mentioned, I am convinced by arguments for an unconscious flow of subjective response for a human, active all the time.[58] However, the emotion tool in EPA will employ those bounded

---

51. Kreglinger, *Storied Revelations*.

52. Kreglinger, *Storied Revelations*, 99.

53. "Imagining and understanding are the same thing": Cook, "Interplay," 589.

54. For example, Tait, *Performing Emotions*; Cook, "Staging Nothing"; Cook, "Interplay"; Wilson, *Psychology for Performing Artists*; Welton, *Feeling Theatre*; Cassidy, "'Playing Is a Science.'"

55. In particular, Stanislavski, *An Actor Prepares*. See Peta Tait, "Bodies Perform Inner Emotions," for a study of emotion in theater following Stanislavski.

56. See, for example, Wilson, *Psychology for Performing Artists*, 59. This is also held by homileticians to be important for preachers, not only to feel the emotions, but believe what they are speaking: Rottman, "Performative Language," 72.

57. For more on "feeling," see Welton, *Feeling Theatre*, 8. That emotion is a *response* is actually one of the few consistent features in definitions of emotion: Tait, *Performing Emotions*, 15; also, on Damasio's approach, Cook, "Staging Nothing," 95.

58. Feldman Barrett, "Constructing Emotion."

emotion experiences that dynamically engage cognition, sensory-motor, neurological, and "soulful" responses in the naming of the experience as an *emotion*.[59] It is in the naming of the subjective, felt experience that meaning is made clear to our conscious selves,[60] and this is most helpful for the method. And while Perry and Cousins both suggest that the "merely" emotional impact of a composition in performance is not theological interpretation,[61] I wish to affirm the understanding, difficult to articulate as it may be, that is gained through emotional connection, impact, and response in the performance event.[62]

While we experience affective responses constantly, a bounded "emotion" may be understood as *an* experience: "something within your body has been stirred; you are not quite the same as you were in the moments before this encounter."[63] Further, bounded emotion helps us to understand the context to which we are responding, and as such, "emotions are constructions of subjective *meaning*."[64] In naming an emotion, and clarifying meaning, the human person may make connections to other experiences of similar emotion, for further interpretation of the present—as well as past—experience.[65] It may be this that Stanislavski's teaching relies upon: connecting the felt experience of the character with the actor's own experience invites further immersion in the character's "skin," and thereby deeper

---

59. Henricks, *Selves, Societies and Emotions*, 100.

60. Feelings "are linguistically structured interpretations" of experience: Cooey, *Religious Imagination*, 47.

61. Perry, *Insights*, 136; Cousins, "Pilgrim Theology," 214. However, emotion may *be* interpretation or understanding. Later I discuss a contemporary production of *King Lear*, which retained confronting language (for its younger school-age audience) of "bastard," because through the emotional impact of that language, the audience would understand Edmund's position in (or on the edge of) his family: Crouch, "Making Lear Accessible to Children."

62. This may be the knowledge and assumption of composers of biblical compositions. By greater understanding of the oral and performative origins of biblical compositions gained through BPC, we can appreciate the value of embodied performance interpretation of these works, which attends to emotional impact as an expected element of reception and interpretation of the letters, poems, and stories of the Bible. See, for example, Shiner, *Proclaiming the Gospel*, 57–84; Shiell, *Reading Acts*, 34–101; and Oestreich, *Performance Criticism of the Pauline Letters*, 181.

63. Henricks, *Selves, Societies and Emotions*, 98.

64. Henricks, *Selves, Societies and Emotions*, 100.

65. Feldman Barrett, "Constructing Emotion," 372, describes her approach to the role of cognition in emotion as bounding from the constant affective or psychological responses discrete particular combinations as "emotions." She contrasts this with appraisal models that also incorporate cognition into the study of emotion, in which cognition functions to appraise the felt emotion for meaning, but is not required for an emotion to *be* an "emotion."

knowing. The better an actor knows the character, the more effectively he will communicate who that character is to an audience, inviting their connection and meaning-making in the performance event. Acclaimed actor, Simon Callow, describes inhabiting the text, and thereby understanding and embodying the character's movements and emotions.[66] Something similar is true for the storyteller.[67] However, rather than thoughts leading to understanding the emotion, as for Callow, in my process, *emotion* instigates thinking as a way of making meaning.[68]

My experience of embodying texts for performance is that I *feel*, subjectively, internally; I am *moved* in response to the text I inhabit and which inhabits me. This may be similar to the experience of preachers that Childers describes: "for those who hold an incarnational view of preaching, preachers are actors whose own bodies and experience, speech and action participate in the gospel process, i.e., the process by which the Word of God moves forward across the face of the earth from age to age."[69]

It is through my felt responses, then, observed and analyzed, that I understand the text's importance, impact, and message for my audience and me. In this way, I am intentionally and explicitly engaging in a close—and faith-inspired[70]—interpretation of the composition, again the way Childers describes a preacher inviting the composition to get "beneath his or her own skin."[71] For, as Lee observes, we the preacher or performer are also audience to a proclamation of a story "that seeks to form Christian performers who can faithfully and creatively enact their roles as ones in Christ in changing contexts."[72] The confessional nature of EPA will become increasingly apparent as we progress.

---

66. Muir, "Shakespearean Actor on Acting."

67. For Buckley, the storyteller becomes the story: *Dancing with Words*, 84.

68. On emotion as a way of making meaning, see, for example: Hristic, "On the Interpretation of Drama," 350, 52; Brown, "Learning Shakespeare's Secret Language," 219, 20; Wilson, *Psychology for Performing Artists*, 64; Welton, *Feeling Theatre*, 25.

69. Childers, "Preacher's Creative Process," 155.

70. For "Karl Rahner, among others, has observed that the Holy Spirit seems to favor the realm of the human unconscious": Childers, "Preacher's Creative Process," 166.

71. Childers, "Preacher's Creative Process," 155.

72. Lee, *Preaching*, 136, 158.

The felt emotion to which I refer and which I employ may then encompass something of the intuitive,[73] imaginative,[74] and spiritual[75] in this subjective engagement with the composition. Such subjective engagement is the embodied immersion discussed in Chapter 1, which leads to knowing, and successful interpretation of, one's surrounds: in my case here, the letter I inhabited for performance.[76] Naming this second tool in the method "emotion" may not adequately encompass all these elements of human interiority, but to the extent that once made conscious of a subjective response and naming it, a person is making meaning, "emotion" seems the most appropriate term to employ.

How Emotion Will Be Employed as an Interpretive Tool

Emotion I feel in rehearsal is my true, raw emotion.[77] In performance, I moderate the emotion I feel for the performance moment, so that my performance invites the audience to feel for themselves in response to the performance, the message being conveyed.[78] In rehearsal, my emotional responses will connect with my own lived experience,[79] and will raise questions for further investigation through continuing Embodied Performance

---

73. Perhaps in the way that scholars have observed emotion influencing decision making: Ohira, "Beneficial Roles of Emotion," 382.

74. Tait, *Performing Emotions*, 94; Cook, "Interplay," 589. Empathy might be understood as imagining the emotions of another, and is descried as an important element of acting by such actors as Simon Callow in Muir, "Shakespearean Actor on Acting"; or Judi Dench, cited in Wilson, *Psychology for Performing Artists*, 66.

75. For Russians—the context in which Stanislavski worked and developed his method of emotional memory for actors—a lack of emotion is a deadening of one's heart or soul: Wierzbicka, *Emotions across Languages and Cultures*, 18.

76. "The text creates a world for audiences to enter through the performance, a world that includes actors [characters], time, space, point of view, and standards of judgment": Perry, *Insights*, 78–79.

77. Wilson discusses the tension among actors with regard to differing methods, focusing on acting technique or emotion: *Psychology for Performing Artists*, 64–5. From my experience, and this seems also to be Wilson's conclusion, both technique and emotion are at play. For me, in this method, it appears to be that raw emotion felt in response to the text as I embody it dominates rehearsal, as I discover meaning in the text, before technique and prepared emotion are employed in order to communicate meaning in performance.

78. For "the speaker assumes the position of a listener who speaks to facilitate other people's listening": Bartow, "Performance Study," 221.

79. Previous experience and the emotions felt in response primes a person for a new experience, and shapes, unconsciously, the responses of future similar experiences: Feldman Barrett, "Constructing Emotion," 369.

Analysis as well as employing more "traditional" approaches to biblical interpretation.

I noted when discussing the body as tool that particularity can enable not generalization, but points of connection to the particular experiences and memories of the listeners, which becomes a path to understanding. The tension here will be shown, I hope, to be a strength of the method more than a limitation. It offers a challenge to an objective, rational approach to interpretation, but I trust that I have demonstrated the wide affirmation from scholarship for the way in which humans do indeed make meaning by more nuanced, dynamic, and subjective means, including emotion. I need to pay attention to the emotions as they arise in preparation, to discern how I am bringing myself to the composition, and how to make use of my experience, or lay it aside so that it does not inhibit the audience's reception of the composition. Again, this is not necessarily new, but akin to the intentional self-reflection of Levy's theatrical interpretive process, as noted.[80] The audience tool provides an internal balance to this potential limitation in the method, because while my particular emotional responses will be allowed to speak, I will also keep the audience firmly in view throughout preparation for performance, and pose questions regarding meaning from their perspective. The relationality of the human therefore balances individuality, so that meaning is discerned by the one for, and with, the community.[81] Such a process has been observed in the practice of letter-bearers delivering (orally) Paul's letters.[82]

The emotion tool interacts further with the "audience" tool, because through emotion the performer communicates with her audience.[83] It is through emotion that the audience is enabled to identify with the characters in the story:[84] "The emotional goal of theatre . . . is the ability of an audience member to have the same feelings as the character, midwifed through the

---

80. Levy, *Bible as Theatre*.

81. Bartow, "Performance Study," 221. This role as facilitator of others' listening, when taken seriously, moves the performer-interpreter from her initial, personal, response to the composition, to appropriate felt emotions that will evoke meaning-making possibilities for her listeners.

82. Johnson, "Paul's Letters Reheard," 69; White, "Visualising Paul's Address," 5.

83. This is an essential feature of oral communication noted by orators from ancient times: Shiner, *Proclaiming the Gospel*, 57–76. But it is not only in performance. Emotions are integral to human communication, helping to negotiate relationships successfully and to survive: Henricks, *Selves, Societies and Emotions*, 7, 106. Also Clark and Brisette, "Relationship Beliefs and Emotion," 235.

84. Wilson, *Psychology for Performing Artists*, 43. Just as identification is necessary to theater, it is necessary to social living, in the shape of empathy.

performance of an actor."[85] Through such identification, or participation,[86] an audience member can rehearse in the story possible scenarios and their potential responses for lived embodiment in future.[87] An audience member can connect, by feeling the emotions of the story, with moments in their own lived experience of similar emotion, and resolve conflict, discover meaning, grow in understanding.[88] In the case of Paul's letters, Johnson encourages us to consider the performance intent in the written composition: the letter writer expects that the felt emotion will be persuasive for an audience receiving this letter through the embodied performer.[89] Through emotion the audience makes meaning of the story, interpreting the story in light of their own experience.

However, although studies have shown that emotion (as with intuition) has the potential to guide successful decision-making, it is, as with any human process, fallible. For example, the individual's bodily state (such as fatigue) may inhibit successful guiding of decisions by emotion.[90] The integration of a range of interpretive methods through which to explore the insights and questions raised through embodiment in preparation is an important further safeguard built into the EPA method. The third stage of the Embodied Performance process will also be important, for in reflection, with some distance, the performer-interpreter will observe the potential biases and influences affecting both preparation and performance.

Imagination and Emotion: The Performer's Interior World

In the theater, the spaces in the script (a play script is essentially dialogue with a varying level of stage direction) demand that the actor bring themselves to the character and the story, drawing on their own experience in order to enliven their imaginations and bring the character to life on stage.

---

85. Cook, "Staging Nothing," 94. Also, Tait, *Performing Emotions*, 94.

86. A "process of unself-conscious participation and exchange" such as between the performer and the composition: Bozarth, *The Word's Body*, 114.

87. Wilson, *Psychology for Performing Artists*, 2. With particular importance in the context of a faith community, "performance ... mirrors [a] process of 'embodied action', or our ability to *re-present* what we perceive through some kind of embodied enactment," and a way of thinking through performance is found "just beneath the surface of much of the Hebrew Bible text," for example. Giles, *Twice Used Songs*, 14, 15.

88. What Wilson describes as "emotional catharsis": Wilson, *Psychology for Performing Artists*, 7.

89. Johnson, "Paul's Letters Reheard," 69. Paul's letters contain a level of passion that requires a performance, not even simply a recitation.

90. Ohira, "Beneficial Roles of Emotion in Decision Making," 386.

The apparently infinite variety of versions of Shakespeare's plays, for example, may in part be enabled by the space he left for the imaginations of the actors: "Shakespeare identified imagination as the agent whereby a text comes alive in the actor's performances and in the minds of an audience."[91] Stanislavski strongly affirmed this bringing of the individual actor to the theater, advocating "an investigation of the performer's emotional reactions during rehearsal . . . to create a believable style of acting that gave an appearance of social behavior and its emotions."[92] And where an actor's own experience yields no emotional material for connection, experienced actors know they also need to be skilled observers.[93]

Storytelling is likewise highly fluid, with its practitioners recognizing that any story will seem different with each different performer—and even each different performance by the same performer.[94] Intrinsic to the EPA presented here is the fact that I, Sarah, am the one embodying the text, bringing *my* physicality, and *my* interiority to the texts, and the circumstances of the particular audience to whom I perform the letter to the Romans.[95] With the preference for objective and rational approaches to interpretation has come the dismissal of emotion as irrational; but dismissing emotions leaves humans ignorant of their effect and vulnerable to unexpected consequences.[96] Emotions, if observed and acknowledged, can be understood and utilized appropriately as tools for making meaning of experience.

Decisions for the Performance Interpretation will be guided by understanding gained through attending to the raw emotional responses of my rehearsal. In the Critical Reflection, I will attend to my emotions in performance and rehearsal, those of the audience, and any changes in emotional response to the composition in the reflective stage itself.

Of particular interest in the discussion of Romans will be emotions of joy, love, compassion, and disappointment, but above all, love. Love is Paul's message, because it is Jesus' message, because that is the message of Holy One. A storyteller will love the story and their audience, and also be seen to love God, if the story is to be faithfully told and received.[97]

---

91. Brown, "Learning Shakespeare's Secret Language," 217.
92. Tait, *Performing Emotions*, 91.
93. Dench, "Reflecting Nature."
94. Buckley, *Dancing with Words*, 41.
95. "The personality of the storyteller is an integral part of the storytelling": Buckley, *Dancing with Words*, 41. Emotions are also context sensitive: Feldman Barrett, "Constructing Emotion," 374.
96. Schwartz, Melters, and Ritov, "Emotion-Based Choice," 343.
97. Buckley, *Dancing with Words*, 85.

AUDIENCE

Humans are always audience, if performance is doing and being and communicating and acting upon each other.[98] In all these social interactions, the human person watches, receives and interprets in order to respond as they become performer in turn for another's audience. As in our everyday storytelling activity, so in our designated performance events, "storytelling is a relationship between the speaker and the listener . . . No matter the size of the audience, each person experiences the story in a personal way. Sharing story is human-to-human contact."[99]

Scholarship on Audiences

An audience is the group of spectators for a performance. The audience initiates performance,[100] and without them performance does not exist: "a theatre performance that does not take place before an audience is not a theatre performance." Audience is then a "constitutive part of theatre."[101]

Audience studies are primarily conducted within the field of theater theory and practice, for the audience is the theater's very reason for being.[102] Such research primarily focuses on the demographics of audiences: who is attending, where and what and when.[103] Relatively few studies explore why audiences attend the theater, or what happens when they experience a performance.[104]

However, in scholarship that does attend to audience experience, a change has occurred in perspective. For a time seen as passive recipients of what the performers do on stage, audiences are again acknowledged as mutual partners in the performance moment.[105] From the energy the audience feed back to the performer/s,[106] thereby influencing the performance

---

98. See, for example, Freshwater, *Theatre and Audience*, 7.
99. Buckley, *Dancing with Words*, 69.
100. Novak, "Performing the Poet," 373.
101. Beckwith, *Signifying God*, 88.
102. Freshwater, *Theatre and Audience*, 2.
103. Bryan, "Listening to the Audience," 13.
104. Bryan, "Listening to the Audience," 16.
105. Radbourne, Johanson, Glow, and White, " Audience Experience," 16; Saunders, "Revelation and Resistance," 124. Further: "A live poetry audience can be understood as 'participants' in, rather than mere 'recipients' of, a performance": Novak, "Performing the Poet," 372. See also discussion of mutual indwelling of audience and performer in Chapter 1.
106. Freshwater, *Theatre and Audience*, 10–11, 18–19.

in terms of energy, commitment and a shaping of expression and meaning in ways that connect with this audience, to shaping the experience[107] and discovering or making meaning for themselves,[108] the audience creates the performance moment as much as the actors, directors, and theater creative and technical teams.

Interestingly, audiences have been understood at times as a single entity,[109] with significant effect in the sixteenth and seventeenth centuries.[110] In London at that time, audiences were blamed for riotous crowd behavior that caused damage to person and property, and regularly disrupted life throughout the city.[111] Theaters were therefore strictly regulated and under constant threat of closure, and writers could be fined for transgressing these regulations.[112] Many writers were apparently uneasy with such a pragmatic understanding of the theater's relationship with its audience as a single entity to which a performance is "done," and for which a performance ought to be "good" because it will instruct, entertain or transform.[113] They were certainly unhappy with the consequent repercussions for the theater and its practitioners.[114] Eric Dunnum identifies in *The Roman Actor* a timely rebuttal to this view of theater's ability to affect behavior, presenting an alternative picture of theater's potential to change the individual, within. Through theater, so the play seems to say, an individual may come to understand themselves more, know why they do what they do, but, it is careful to demonstrate, not be so moved as to change those actions.[115]

For the performer of biblical compositions, on the other hand, the impact of the performance, the composition, on the audience and on herself is immediate and palpable, with the intention to so move as to change a person's actions. Immersed in the world of the story (or letter or psalm), audience and performer come to know it, its characters, rhetoric, imagery, and meaning, in ways that transform both the individual and the community.[116]

107. Radbourne, "The Audience Experience," 17.
108. Bryan, "Listening to the Audience," 16 (following Barthes).
109. Freshwater, *Theatre and Audience*, 5 (made possible when the audience is understood to be passive, pp. 55–56).
110. Dunnum, "Not to Be Altered," 520.
111. Dunnum, "Not to Be Altered," 520.
112. Dunnum, "Not to Be Altered," 520.
113. Freshwater, *Theatre and Audience*, 55–56; Dunnum, "Not to Be Altered," 518.
114. Dunnum, "Not to Be Altered," 538. Dunnum cites such writers as Thomas Nashe, Christopher Marlowe, Thomas Heywood and Philip Sydney (518).
115. Dunnum, "Not to Be Altered," 535–37.
116. See, for example, McKenna's discussion of the continuing incarnation of Jesus the Christ through the telling of his story for the purpose of inspiring hope, instilling

The intent of these compositions in origin and in reception in faith communities today is to transform.[117] This confessional nature of performance will be intrinsically present in Performance Interpretation and Critical Reflection components of an Embodied Performance Analysis.

Defining "Audience" for This Project

For social scientists, humans are seen to be always performer, and always audience.[118] But here I limit the bounds of an audience to the performance moment, designated and set apart from everyday life. In many instances of my "performance" of biblical portions my "audience" is a worshipping Christian community, and the "performance" is either the Bible reading or the sermon for the day. A congregation is not usually named an "audience," for their purpose is not to receive a theatrical work as such, but to participate in corporate worship. For me, storytelling in these contexts shares the covenantal nature of preaching's covenant between God, preacher, and congregation.[119] Such a covenant establishes kinship, drawing us all into God's Drama, or Story, as its participants. The historic Corpus Christi plays, through "the actor-audience relation, the constitution of community through the obstacles and occlusions of charity as a Eucharistic body,"[120] demonstrate a blurring of boundaries between audience and congregation in the telling of the sacred stories of a community of faith. In these mutually embodied encounters with the story, they become, even more than the involved audience for a theater event, a "community of participation."[121]

Søren Kierkegaard's revisioning of the congregation as the actors, the presider as the prompter in the wings, and God as audience[122] demonstrates the difference between what appear on the surface to be very similar events in theater and corporate worship. With a stage, an individual or small group of people presenting to a larger group of people, and the interpretation of texts,

---

courage, transforming the world, the story "coming true" in each of its tellers: *Keepers of the Story*, 86–108. On which point, we may recall from Chapter 1 the experience of students inhabiting the story of Jesus and understanding with new depth his humanity: Ruge-Jones, "The Word Heard," 106–7.

117. Cousins, "Pilgrim Theology," 69; Mathews, *Performing Habakkuk*, 200.
118. Freshwater, *Theatre and Audience*, 70.
119. Lee, *Preaching*, 138–140.
120. Beckwith, *Signifying God*, 148.
121. Beckwith, *Signifying God*, 148. As Bartow observes, "in speaking texts . . . the speaker assumes the position of a listener who speaks to facilitate other people's listening": "Performance Study," 221.
122. Kierkegaard, *Purity of Heart*, 179–82.

corporate worship does look very much like theater.[123] For Kierkegaard, however, corporate worship is about the performance of the people together;[124] it goes beyond communication to *communion*.[125] I have argued elsewhere for the audience to be seen as participants in the performance event in the theater,[126] participants in a distinctly different role to that of the performer-interpreter. I also draw, there and in this project, on the parallels between presider (in my case, storyteller or performer-interpreter) and actor for examination of the process of performance as interpretation. The difference between worship and theater, between congregation and audience, as I see it, is that in worship the performance of those "on stage" facilitates the congregation in performing the "work" themselves (as in Kierkegaard);[127] in theater, the audience, with its embodied responses, facilitates those on stage to perform the "work."[128]

The audiences for my performances of Romans through preparation and at the Performance Interpretation, for the most part, were audiences much more like a theater audience than a congregation gathered for worship. It is worth noting the difference here, both because the broader context of my work as a storyteller / performer is corporate worship, and because the Critical Reflection is also informed by encounters with Romans in worshipping congregations in the lead-up to the main performances. Throughout these discussions, any group with which I presented the letter to the Romans will be referred to as an audience.

As observed above, theater audiences are now recognized as active participants in the performance and in the making meaning of and through the performance; so too are congregations (noting the stipulated differences) as their sacred works are embodied and given voice in their midst.[129] As I will demonstrate in the test case, it will be important for the Embodied Performance method to include a clear description of the audience for a

123. Childers, *Performing the Word*, 123. In ancient times, synagogue and theater were much more similar in terms of crowd participation, and the practice of Jewish tellings of the story of Esther at Purim continues to include booing and hissing from the congregation to drown out the name of Haman: Shiner, *Proclaiming the Gospel*, 147.

124. Kierkegaard, *Purity of Heart*, 180.

125. Childers, *Performing the Word*, 125.

126. Agnew, "Choice: Stories."

127. In the manner of a "prompter": Kierkegaard, *Purity of Heart*, 180. Lee imagines the congregation as a "company of actors who share the work of interpreting and performing the theodrama": *Preaching*, 119.

128. On the different contributions of performer and audience, see Novak, "Performing the Poet," 363.

129. Lee, *Preaching*, 119; Agnew, "Choice: Stories."

particular performance. In their particularities, both collectively and as individuals, each audience will shape the interpretation of the composition for performance.[130]

How "Audience" Will Be Employed as an Interpretive Tool

The performer mediates the composition for the community, and they encounter the composition together. Before that—long before that—she prepares the presentation for the community, listening with their ears, aware of their stories, context, challenges and joys, and considers how this composition will make meaning of those situations, and how the audience will make meaning of the biblical composition in light of those situations. In this way, the biblical performances in my practice "can easily accommodate many presentations and variations, [so that] no text can be declared to be firmly closed."[131] Attending to the way in which the audience influences these varied presentations is imperative for the Christian church; for each time the Bible is read aloud, this *is* what is happening. Understanding this process will enrich understanding between performers and audiences, and also understanding of the biblical compositions themselves.

The discussion so far has established that audience members bring something to any performance moment. In EPA, the performer's interpretive process uses the audience as a tool in several ways. The performer-interpreter anticipates the cultural capital, the issues and experiences of the audience, and places herself as a receiver in their place. This is akin to the process of reader-response analysis, but with the interpreter imaginatively taking the place of the audience for whom she prepares the performance. In the performance moment itself, audience responses will suggest to the performer the ways in which her anticipation was helpful, or missed the mark, and this may change the interpretation she discusses in the auto-ethnographic style Critical Reflection.

Novak observes that "audience members may be provoked to smile, sigh, or clap enthusiastically by the poet as well as by each other."[132] The physical response of the audience may also come in the "shudder of recognition" that is "a sounding within them by which they are tuned to the experience

---

130. Saunders, "Revelation and Resistance," 124; Freshwater, *Theatre and Audience*, 6–7.

131. As with the text-oriented performances of ancient Jewish letters in Miller, *Performances of Ancient Jewish Letters*, 64.

132. Novak, "Performing the Poet," 361.

of the actor."[133] This may change the performer's pace, tone, volume, or even content; with positive feedback from the audience, a poet will lift her performance for the next poem.[134] Further, "a different audience means a different performance."[135] On one particular occasion, I made a change to a story in performance, which in composition contains lines that depict the rough treatment and deaths of slaves on ships; for an audience that included children, I decided in the performance moment to omit those lines.[136] I felt that to speak those words would not build the relationship I was seeking with an audience with whom I was facilitating several events in the days to follow.

So we establish the audience as a mutual partner with the performer in the performance event. We have seen that audience members bring their embodied selves to the performance, and undergo a transformation in feeling, a metamorphosis in understanding as a result of the encounter.[137] But what does this mean for the performer's interpretation of the text? Acknowledging the role of the audience in the performance moment, the performer will consider her audience at all stages of preparing, delivering, and reflecting upon the performance; this consideration of the audience will influence the meaning discerned in the composition. It is this influence that the Embodied Performance method seeks to foreground, with the audience tool, as the text that is begun on the page is completed in the mutual embodiment of the performer with the audience, in the space that is created between them.[138] Through the body and emotion tools of this method, the performer is like the reader in a reader-response analysis, finding the meaning in and through her own responses to the composition. With the audience tool, the performer understands the way in which audiences respond to live performance—as discussed above—and during preparation imaginatively situates herself in the place of her anticipated audience in order to hear the composition from their perspective. In the live performance, as noted, she will judge from the actual responses how that interpretation has been effective, or differed in performance from rehearsal, in actuality from anticipation, as the audience receives the composition-in-performance. These observations

133. Welton, *Feeling Theatre*, 47.

134. Novak, "Performing the Poet," 373. Indeed, a performer may be considered "impotent unless he or she receives in turn a charge from the audience": Freshwater, *Theatre and Audience*, 10. See also, Ruge-Jones, "Omnipresent, Not Omniscient," 34, as noted in Chapter 2.

135. Novak, "Performing the Poet," 361.

136. Agnew, "Choice: Stories," 129.

137. Bozarth, *The Word's Body*, 116.

138. See discussion of Reader-Response approaches to biblical interpretation in: McKnight, "Reader-Response Criticism," 231.

will shape the discussion of the composition as interpreted in performance in the Critical Reflection, part two of the Embodied Performance Analysis.

The process by which the audience influences the interpretation of a composition is three-fold, and integrates with the performer's own bodily and emotional interpretation of the text. A performer knows her audience, visualizes her audience, and experiences her audience.

The Performer Knows Her Audience

The performer's knowledge of the audience will provoke questions of the text in light of their circumstances and context. Bordieu highlights the question of cultural capital in his discussion of distinctions between population groups; audiences who have attained higher education levels will bring more cultural capital with them, or at least a different content of that cultural capital, than those who have not continued as far with formal education, for example.[139] The consequence is that different audiences will have differing capacities to decipher the social codes embedded in a performance, or work of art, and performers will need to take account of these differences when discerning what a work means for each new audience. We may also recall the concerns of Richard Swanson, noted in Chapter 3, that the communal memory assumed in the composition of the Gospel of Mark is not available to a contemporary audience.[140]

An understanding of the ways in which the performance will likely evoke memories, emotions from current situations, resistance because of present or past conflict for this specific audience will help a performer to shape and adapt both *what* words to use, and the *way in which* to speak them.[141] For Tim Crouch and the "First Encounters with Shakespeare" production of *King Lear*, understanding children and the culture in which they live became a lens for a nuanced interpretation of the play.[142] This production interpreted the play as a story of fathers and children, of family. These themes became pronounced in the abridgement of the play, the abridgements being determined by what meaning this story might hold for its younger audience. Family, in all its variety and complexity, was deemed an experience with

139. Bordieu, *Distinction*, 18–25.

140. Swanson, "This Is My...," 208; also Ruge-Jones, "Those Sitting around Jesus," 51.

141. Buckley, *Dancing with Words*, 79. Further, Jonathan Pryce discusses the importance of such awareness for preparing to perform Shylock in *The Merchant of Venice*; for the long history of persecution of Jews in many times and places problematizes an audience's relationship with Shylock and his foes before the play has even begun: Pryce, "Shylock Played by Jonathan Pryce."

142. Crouch, "Making Lear Accessible to Children."

which their younger audience may connect more readily than with an old man descending into madness.[143] Considering language, the harshness of the term "bastard" applied to Edmund was retained, although it may have been deemed inappropriate for the audience. Crouch describes the importance of the impact of this language on the audience, so as to understand who Edmund is in this family, and why he behaves as he does.

In order to help her audience hear and understand what she is saying, a performer must know the capacity of the audience *to* understand.[144] For the composer of a play script, also, as Raffel observes of William Shakespeare: would he have achieved such enduring success if he had not so effectively connected with his audience?[145] In order to so connect, so evoke responses of appreciation and inspire such insightful meaning-making that his audiences valued his productions, Shakespeare had to have known the capacity of his audience. The structure of his plays demonstrates both guidance for his audience in preparation for a word play or plot-twist, *and* trust in the audience to follow and understand when they get there.[146] For example, in *The Comedy of Errors*, Shakespeare employs an intense phrase of alliterative verse, "four primary alliterating consonants, and two more secondarily alliterating ones, for a total of six alliterating consonants in a line and a half,"[147] to prepare the audience for the twist to come. Shakespeare knew that they would intuitively respond with "a burst of mental speed" at the right time, so as to wrap their minds around the couplet: "Who every *w*ord by all my *w*it being scan'd, / *w*ants *w*it in all, one *w*ord to understand."[148] It is Raffel's contention that Shakespeare employs such word play precisely because he knows the audience will appreciate it, respond, and understand the meaning he wishes to convey, that this husband is not the husband she thinks he is, but a long lost identical twin.[149]

---

143. Crouch, "Making Lear Accessible to Children." Setting the play at Christmas, and over a shorter time frame, supported this interpretation of the play as an exploration of family relationships.

144. Raffel, "Who Heard the Rhymes," 213.

145. Raffel, "Who Heard the Rhymes," 213. While much biblical scholarship is concerned with the words the composers choose in crafting an enduring "script" for performance—see discussion of Rhoads and Philemon in Chapter 3—my practice is to construct the script for my "original" iteration of the composition-in-performance. This insight into the writer's process is instructive background for the discussion of language and abridgements in Chapter 6.

146. Raffel, "Who Heard the Rhymes," 201, 05.

147. Raffel, "Who Heard the Rhymes," 201.

148. Raffel, "Who Heard the Rhymes," 201.

149. Raffel, "Who Heard the Rhymes," 201, 13.

When it comes to the performance moment, a performer's knowledge of the audience is vital for both interpretation and communication. Mariah Gale observed the different ways in which Isabella had been played for audiences over time, as she prepared to take on the role in 2015. She was particularly aware of the different place of nuns in her own time as compared with earlier eras, who are in her estimation more removed and less well understood today. This knowledge of her audience inspired her to visit a convent and seek conversation with practicing nuns to understand the religious life. Gale found that she was then better able to understand her character's choice and commitment to being a nun, and convey her choice and motivations effectively through her performance.[150]

In the test case, knowledge of my audiences led to the omission of the marriage analogy from Rom 7.[151] As Crouch explained the choice to abridge *King Lear* in favor of the family theme rather than that of old age for a younger audience, so I considered my twenty-first-century audience and their ability to connect effectively with an analogy more pertinent for Paul's original recipients.[152] The usefulness of marriage as an analogy is in doubt when marriage is a contested notion, diversely practiced and undergoing radical redefinition at the present time.[153]

The Performer Envisages Her Audience

It is not enough to simply know the audience; a performer must then carry that knowledge into rehearsal, allowing the audience to balance the performer's own intuitive, physical, and emotional responses with a collective reception of the text. By using her imagination, the performer envisages the audience before her during rehearsals, and guided by her knowledge of this audience will listen from their perspective for the humor, the disruptions to the ear, for example. Paapa Essiedou was interviewed about his role as Hamlet:

> you have to get the timing right in the soliloquies, he says. As you share your thought process with the audience, you have to

---

150. Gale, "Isabella. Early Rehearsal Part 1."

151. See Appendix B, Preparation and Rehearsal Notes, for further discussion. I discuss the influence of the audience on choices of abridgements for the script in the Critical Reflection.

152. Crouch, "Making Lear Accessible to Children." Also, Cousins describes the influence of her Australian audience on translation choices when performing the Psalms of Ascent: "Pilgrim Theology," 186, 87.

153. Observable in conversations in various media today, for example: Gross, "Price of Being Single," and the research and writing of Bella dePaulo, http://belladepaulo.com/singles-research-and-writing/.

> take your time to give it truth but if you ponder too long you risk boring them. . . . Every performance is different because the audience is different and each audience deserves as much as the next one. You go in with nothing, no expectations, you go to tell a story and the performance unfolds with the audience.[154]

Cousins describes her experience of internalizing the Psalms for performance as distinct and different from the initial phase of learning the Psalms:

> I could feel the emotions of the text and used gestures naturally to convey them, but I found I had to slow down and "watch" myself to discern how an audience would see or hear what I was expressing. Movement and gestures needed to be developed from my natural body language and expressions into deliberate performance choices. Emotions that I was feeling needed to be conveyed in both my voice and face.[155]

We may recall here the earlier discussion of the body as interpretive tool, the performer observing the instinctive expressions and emphases her voice gives to the words. The performer listens to these instinctive soundings for the meaning, the impact, of this composition for herself, and for *this* audience,[156] and the performer honors her audience by thus allowing the text to speak directly to them.[157] As stated, it is a work of imagination, holding the audience before you in your mind's eye, looking at them through the text and anticipating response and reception, understanding the potential impact of the words I am embodying to bring alive in their midst.[158]

I will discuss in the Critical Reflection the challenges I faced as I rehearsed Rom 1, listening with my audiences' ears; I could not hear Paul's words about unhealthy sexual passion without hearing the voices of those whom I have heard speak those words in judgmental condemnation. My audience's context, our shared commitment to the dignity of humans of any sexual orientation, challenged Paul's words, and history's interpretation of

---

154. Graver, Pathways to Shakespeare, Papa Essidou.

155. Cousins, "Pilgrim Theology," 183. Peter Perry imagines particular people he knows, and anticipates their responses as a way of determining how he will communicate with his body for that audience: *Insights*, 87.

156. As discussed earlier, each audience is particular, distinct, and in their difference, and the differences in situation for the performer on each new occasion, each performance is unique, the same story and also not the same as it was when told before. See also, Childers, "Preacher's Creative Process," 165.

157. McKnight, "Reader-Response Criticism," 240. See also Childers, *Performing the Word*, 117 ff.

158. Because words act in performance: Miller, *Performances of Ancient Jewish Letters*, 33. Also, as above, Perry, *Insights*, 87.

them. This will become an example of the way in which performance alone is not always the appropriate approach for receiving biblical texts today; but the components of the Embodied Performance Analysis together may even so offer a rigorous, if uncomfortable, method of interpreting those compositions, and may do so by incorporating different forms of performance for the Analysis.

The performer has to imagine herself also, in the anticipated performance moment, in which she will be mediator of the text. Speaking these words *to* these particular people demands that a performer understand what she is saying to them. Jonathan Pryce and his company, imagining the audience's interpretation of Shylock and responding to the character themselves, in their cultural context of anti-Semitic history, adapted the play to show more of Shylock and Jessica at home, to highlight their context within a minority group in the story. Adding a scene between father and daughter, their production offered "a glimpse of the home life of Shylock where Jessica and Shylock converse in Yiddish. And that I think is quite telling about their family situation and emphasizes to an audience that these are truly outsiders, locked away in a ghetto."[159]

As I describe the Embodied Performance process, it will become apparent that in my practice I attend to intuition as I speak and listen to the words, in order to identify language and ideas that confuse, or that do not effectively convey meaning. During preparation of Romans I found myself stopping and asking myself, what am I saying? What does that *mean*? The Critical Reflection will describe ways in which such questions provoked experimentation with different techniques by which to voice the text, and sent me back to the scholars and to the original language, searching for meaning in what others have said and for more helpful ways to render the Greek into the English that is spoken by my audience. This may result in changes in language or delivery that I incorporate into this generation of the composition.[160] I then rehearse this interpretation I have discerned, imagining my audience, in a process such Cousins' "hermeneutical circle," in which translation is performed, then revised following the experience of the performance, to then be performed again.[161]

---

159. Pryce, "Shylock. Pre and Early Rehearsal."

160. Wire, *Holy Lives*, 8: describing each performance as a creative moment that regenerates a tradition.

161. Cousins, "Pilgrim Theology," 185.

The Performer Experiences Her Audience

That brings us to the third way in which the audience influences the interpretation of a story: as the performer experiences them and experiences the composition live and embodied *with* her audience. On this point, the experience of accomplished performers of Shakespeare's plays again illustrates the way that the audience shows a performer something new in the play, each time it is performed. The audience's responses, or the context of the moment, will enhance meaning. For example, the actual "trick" of a helicopter in the sky that augmented the impact of a moment in an open-air performance of *Measure for Measure*. Recall from Chapter 1 the actor describing the moment when the character said "Play such fantastic tricks before high heaven, as makes the angels weep," and she indicated above her as if to say, such fantastic tricks as this helicopter.[162]

The live audience may change the mood of the performance, especially if they know the story already. This was the case in a performance of *The Taming of the Shrew*, in which people anticipated before they had seen this actor's interpretation of her character, and shouted as Petruchio demands she kiss him in the street, "Don't do it, Kate!"[163]

For some actors, the audience completes the character, by providing the missing ingredient with their energy and responsiveness. This helped Lucy Ellinson make the character of Puck finally "soar": by which perhaps she means that Puck needed an audience to play to, in order to come fully to life on stage.[164]

It is for this reason that I have included a test case Embodied Performance Analysis, and engaged with several audiences in the preparation stage: for I did not know what Romans would mean, embodied for audiences today, until I embodied it *with* audiences today.[165] So, as I have noted earlier, the audience is participant in the performance, receiving what the performer has to offer to them, and giving back with their presence and embodied responses. The performer feels her emotional response through her rehearsal

---

162. Gale, "Isabella: Performance 1."

163. Duffin, "Katherine: Interview with Rona Kelly."

164. Graver, "Lucy Ellinson."

165. Perry observes that multiple performances may also be helpful for particular audiences, giving them time to become familiar with, and more fully immersed in, a composition: *Insights*, 99. Cousins, too, noted that audiences did not experience the composition with the same depth as the performer, and suggests that group performances will provide something of this experience for more people in communities of faith: "Pilgrim Theology," 226.

and preparation phase; in the performance moment, she will feel a range of her own emotions, and also the emotional response of the audience.[166]

In order to gain some insight into what I perceived from the audiences in our encounters, I invited audience members to record their responses on pieces of card during the performance.[167] I do not present these responses in the discussion, as this is not a study of the audience *per se*. The audience as interpretive tool in this method utilizes the influence of the audience *on the performer,* as my knowledge, imagination, and experience of live, embodied people shaped the meaning I found in the composition I had embodied to speak in their midst. Thus, audience feedback informs and enriches my reflection upon what I thought I was receiving from the audiences at the time, by hearing their experiences in their own words. One example I will discuss in the Critical Reflection will be of the first audience in the performance schedule, whose response helped to shape a revised translation of ἀσπάσασθε in Rom 16.

Although for some of the "preview" performances I engaged in conversation with the audience, my inquiry and approach for the test case proper differ from those of Perry and Cousins, discussed in Chapter 3, both of which included discussion in the performance events, and written feedback from the audiences. As we will see, the more complex mechanisms utilized and suggested by these scholars for gathering responses will be required if the depth of meaning-making for audience members themselves to a performance of biblical storytelling is to be understood. Possible ways forward in gleaning the insights of audiences include more scholars writing, as Hearon does, from the perspective of the audience for performances of biblical compositions; development of the audience feedback described in Perry's method; or analysis of audience feedback as for Cousins.[168] To reiterate: the purpose of audience as a tool in the EPA is to articulate the way the particular audience shapes the performer-interpreter's decisions, not to articulate the experience of the audience.

---

166. Again, this is what Niamh Cusack describes: not knowing, really, how to play the character until she has experienced the audience: "Paulina. Performances."

167. These were blank cards, and I invited people to record images or words, in the flow of the performance, or on reflection immediately afterwards.

168. Hearon, "Characters in Text and Performance"; "From Narrative to Performance"; Perry, *Insights*, 88–92; Cousins, "Pilgrim Theology."

SUMMARY: EMBODIED PERFORMANCE METHOD

The Embodied Performance methodology takes the following form:

> *Through preparation, performance, and reflection, the performer-interpreter employs tools of the body, emotion, and audience, integrated with a range of pertinent exegetical approaches, to discern meaning in a biblical composition, presented in an Analysis comprised of Performance Interpretation and Critical Reflection.*

Embodied Performance Analysis emerges from the storyteller or insider approach to Biblical Performance Criticism. It develops the BPC field further by offering a method that *begins* with the embodiment of the composition for performance, which is normally the end result of a "storyteller's" BPC analysis.

I described this embodied and performed approach to interpretation in Chapter 1 as one that embraces the personal and particular nature of any interpretive engagement with the Bible. It does so in order to appreciate what the composition means in its particular reception context, through the personal relationship of the performer with the composition and the audience. This approach is also immersive and intuitive, for as physical, emotional, and relational beings, humans develop deep knowledge through immersion in our environment, which shapes our intuitive responses to the world we inhabit.

Body, emotion, and audience will be employed as tools for interpretation in a process that begins with preparation, proceeds to performance, and culminates in reflection. As we consider my choice of Romans with which to test the application of EPA, I will outline what to expect from the method in practice.

THE TEST CASE: ROMANS

To explore the potential strengths and limitations of this Embodied Performance methodology, I performed the letter to the Romans. The performance was to last one hour, which required some abridgement of the letter, and the Performance Interpretation was to be presented to an audience in Adelaide, Australia.

Why Romans?

We have seen from the story that storytellers' BPC is predominantly employed with Gospels, and we saw that performance as a lens for interpretation has been established as a worthwhile approach to these narrative texts. The first factor in choosing Romans as test case, then, was to further explore the potential of performance as an interpretive approach for non-narrative texts.[169] It will be useful in future to take this Embodied Performance approach and apply it to Gospel compositions, as an approach more focused on reception today, alongside the predominantly historical focus of BPC discussed in Chapter 3; and as an approach foregrounding the insights gained through embodiment, alongside approaches for which performance is a tool for communication, as discussed in both Chapters 2 and 3.

As I introduced myself as the protagonist in this story, I described a key feature of my storytelling practice to be a strong focus on themes of human wellbeing as found through mutuality. The theme of mutuality has been observed in Romans,[170] and it seemed an interesting theme to explore through a method that is itself intrinsically mutual, within and between human beings, and between interpreter and composition.

Finally, Romans is a book I know I have resisted because of its interpretation and application in past (and present) experiences, to judgmental, anti-Jewish and anti-LGBTQI ends. I wanted to seriously engage with this letter as a part of the sacred inheritance of the Christian tradition, to discover anew what meaning it might offer for the communities in which I live today. Could a different, more holistic approach to interpretation overcome some of the potential for harm that has been demonstrated from this letter?

Audiences

The letter was performed in two countries. Performances during the rehearsal stage were predominantly held in Scotland, with the full performance presented for the first time at the Scottish Storytelling Centre in Edinburgh. This city, this country, I had chosen for the established practice, the art and craft of oral storytelling, in great part encouraged through the Scottish Storytelling Centre. This is a more established culture than in Australia, where songwriters will call themselves storytellers, but where those practicing the art form of oral storytelling are rare; those doing it

---

169. Of course, as we saw in Chapter 3, Biblical Performance scholars have not entirely neglected the Epistles.

170. For example, Ehrensperger, *That We May Be Mutually Encouraged*.

for a living even rarer. The performance in Edinburgh would thus enable me to learn from an audience not only in the performance moment itself, but also in rehearsal and previews; and learn not only about Romans and performance interpretation, but also more about the craft of storytelling/performance generally, and myself as a storyteller.

After one more preparation performance, which also experimented with a different format,[171] the second full performance, the Performance Interpretation for the Analysis, was held at Blackwood Uniting Church in Adelaide, Australia. This church is my home church in Australia while I do not serve elsewhere as a minister in placement. I was a member of this congregation for more than ten years, and they supported my candidacy for ordained ministry. The relationship had continued with their support for my PhD through financial donations from individuals in the congregation, and the prayerful support of the community as a whole.

The shorter performances presented in the preparation and reflection stages of the process yielded further opportunities for observation and interrogation of my practice as a performer-interpreter. Contexts for these performances have included Divinity colleges, sermons in congregations, presentations at conferences, and a digital performance of Rom 1:20–32.[172]

As noted, the Performance Interpretation component of the Analysis, presented in Chapter 5, is that offered in Adelaide. Although this Performance Interpretation forms the basis for the Critical Reflection in Chapter 6, the full range of performances directly and indirectly influence that discussion.

Audiences at both full performances, and at the performances in the schools of Divinity, were invited to respond to the performance with comments, questions, or observations, on small cards during the performance, to be placed in a box as they departed. As noted, these responses were not collected as data for discussion in the Critical Reflection, but as a way of providing insight into the experience of the audience to inform my own reflections on my experience of the performance moment.

---

171. See tack 24 in video files at https://sarahagnew.com.au/embodied-performance/: the imagined story of Phoebe as letter bearer to Rome, then picking up her performance at Romans 12.

172. Digital performance: track 3 of video files at https://sarahagnew.com.au/embodied-performance/. My article "Romans 16: a call to embrace one another in love" is based on the presentation of the same name to the *British New Testament Conference* (Chester, England, 2016).

EMBODIED PERFORMANCE ANALYSIS: PROCESS

Preparation

The first step was to develop the "script" for the performance. In consultation with my supervisor, it was decided that a performance of one hour would be most appropriate for audiences, for the original PhD thesis, and for me as performer. The letter would therefore need to be abridged, as it would take closer to 90 minutes or two hours to perform the whole letter.

Interpreter-performers such as Cousins, Perry, Rhoads, and Boomershine, as we have seen, translate their chosen composition for performance. However, as this project is an examination of my usual practice as a storyteller, and in general for performances in Christian worship gatherings I use the commonly accepted translation of the NRSV, I used the NRSV as the basis for my performance of Romans. As I will describe, I abridged the letter, and made some adaptations to the translation for this performance series.

I typeset the full letter into the format I employ for learning biblical stories for performance and began to read through the letter aloud, as a whole.[173] I began noting language difficulties, and making choices about material to cut. I edited, re-read, and revised this script over the course of several months. I discuss my decisions concerning abridgements in the Critical Reflection.

The next step was to rehearse. Rehearsing began with "chunking" the text—taking smaller chunks of text, I read the section aloud over and over, until I could begin to speak it from memory without looking at the words on the page.[174] As I did so, I became immersed in the letter, and grew to know it better. As I grew to know it, I grew in my understanding of its meaning for this performance context.

I continued to rehearse from memory, daily, over several months. During this process, the text moved from merely "memorized" to embodied, as the words and their meaning became known, and came to inhabit my mind, my body, my emotions. Cousins articulates a sense of "owning" the psalms as she "engaged with them with my emotions and imagination as well as my understanding and the words became my own."[175]

---

173. The performance script is found in Appendix A, in the format used for rehearsal.

174. Boomershine, "Teaching Mark as Performance Literature," 82: chunking is a "basic technique of memory processing . . . in which several items are linked together and are thought of as one item." See also Perry, *Insights*, 86.

175. Cousins, "Pilgrim Theology," 183.

During this phase, questions arose. Questions of language in the NRSV translation arose when a word seemed unclear in its meaning, perhaps having changed in its usage in the English of my audience.[176] When I found the NRSV language inadequate for conveying meaning, I returned to the Greek and explored the range of meanings for re-translation informed by my understanding of the letter and audience. Again, I discuss this process in relation to specific passages in the Critical Reflection.

Questions of meaning also arose as I observed the movements of my body, or the emotions I felt. Many times, these questions were instigated by what poets call the "aha" moment, when a poem twists and meaning becomes apparent. Such moments of clarity cannot be easily expressed in words, and this tension is a feature of EPA to embrace rather than resist. As the performer-interpreter immerses herself in the composition, the words are allowed to impact her as receiver—emotionally, subjectively, intuitively. A key aim of this project is to discover whether such understanding can be articulated beyond the performance moment, in discussions that contribute to the broader conversations about the biblical compositions.

From chunks, I built to chapters, and as I moved from one chapter to the next, I included the final line of the previous chapter in the first chunk of the next, to aid with the flow of the argument in learning and interpretation. In the Critical Reflection I will note several specific points in the letter at which this provided particular insight.

Throughout the entire rehearsal stage, the audience was forefront in my mind. As described above, I paid attention to the contexts in which my audiences are living in both Scotland and Australia, and the stories affecting these communities; I imagined my audiences before me, and knowing the spaces in which I would be performing, I placed myself and my audiences there in my imagination as I rehearsed. The smaller performances along the way helped to test my interpretations, as I will discuss with relation to Rom 1:26–27.

Performance

From rehearsal, I moved to performance. The four main performances were:

- 18 February 2016: preview, Rom 1–7, New College staff and students (n=30); in a lecture room at the college, with conversation to follow.

- 9 March 2016: full performance, Rom 1–16, Scottish Storytelling Centre, Edinburgh, mixed, general audience (n=65); in a theater, with dimmed lighting, a stage with black backdrop, the center's "storytelling" chair

---

176. See Cousins, "Pilgrim Theology," 187.

with a Bible on one arm on stage, no discussion afterwards, but some greeting conversations beforehand.

6 April 2016: Phoebe's story and Rom 12–16, Flinders University / Uniting College staff and students (n=25), Adelaide; in a lecture room, people at desks, conversation to follow, and a further session on Biblical Performance Criticism.

17 April 2016: full performance, Rom 1–16, Blackwood Uniting Church, Adelaide, predominantly Uniting Church members with a large contingent from the Blackwood congregation itself (n=85); in a church, chairs in a semi-circle, performance lighting, two videographers, no formal discussion but informal conversations after, greeting beforehand, and a workshop was held in the afternoon at the church prior to the performance.

After each performance, I reflected in my journal on what I had experienced in the performance moment.

Reflection

These reflections evolved into the final stage of reflection, during which I watched the recordings, reviewed notes from rehearsal and performance stages, and drew together insights from the integration of embodiment and performance with textual, literary, rhetorical, socio-critical, and historical analysis. In this focused stage of reflection, I clarified the major themes and key insights that had emerged in the Performance Interpretation.

Outcome: The Analysis

The Embodied Performance Analysis of Romans consists of two elements: Performance Interpretation (Chapter 5) and Critical Reflection (Chapter 6).

Chapter 6's discussion presents reflection not only on the meaning discerned through embodied performance of the letter to the Romans, but also *how* that meaning was discerned through the tools of the body, emotion, and audience.

Part 2 consists of the Analysis and a critique of the method. In Chapter 7 I will summarize the strengths and limitations of this Embodied Performance approach, place it within the context of the field of BPC and identify the questions still to explore, and suggest ways in which EPA may be applied in full or in part.

PART 2.
IN PRACTICE:

Embodied Performance Analysis of Romans

5

Performance Interpretation of Romans

"WELCOME ONE ANOTHER IN LOVE"

Blackwood Uniting Church, Adelaide
17 April 2016

Please watch track 00, found at sarahagnew.com.au/embodied-performance/, for the Performance Interpretation.

Please note that the most complete experience of an embodied interpretation is to watch the performance without referring to script or Bible, in the first instance.

As Perry notes, however, multiple viewings will no doubt familiarize audiences with both the mode of delivery and the content of the letter in performance.[1]

---

1. Perry, *Insights*, 99.

6

Critical Reflection

ROMANS: A CALL TO MUTUAL EMBRACE

We come to the Critical Reflection having experienced the Performance Interpretation of Romans. We have observed Rom 16 in this reception as the climax, claiming the letter as a call to mutual embrace within the community of Jesus' followers, inspired by the embrace of all through Jesus Wisdom.

A Performance Interpretation aims to stand in its own right. All who experience the composition in performance receive that interpretation of the composition by the performer-interpreter in that moment. Embodied Performance Analysis seeks to bring the insights of that moment, and of the performer's decision-making through preparation, into the scholarly forum. By so doing, EPA invites the physical, emotional, and relational aspects of human meaning-making to contribute to conversations generally dominated by rational objectivity.

In order to allow the insights of the Performance Interpretation to contribute to scholarly discussion, the Embodied Performance Analysis includes a second component. The Critical Reflection presents a discussion of the preparation and performance of the composition, and describes the way in which broader scholarship and other methods have been integrated into that process. In this chapter, then, is the Critical Reflection of Romans in performance.

Introducing the Critical Reflection

As anticipated in Chapter 1, the tone of the Critical Reflection is more akin to auto-ethnographic reflective writing than the established tone of a biblical commentary. This is necessary and appropriate for a discussion that reflects on my experience of mediating the composition for an audience, describing the physical and emotional impact I felt as I inhabited the letter and it simultaneously inhabited me. Particular insights may resemble interpretations arrived at through "conventional" exegetical methods: the innovation in the Embodied Performance method is in the *experience and* discussion of a composition, so that the whole human person is allowed to participate in that discussion.

The particular insights of audience, body, and emotion structure the discussion of Rom 1–15. I begin with broad influences of the audience on language, translation, and omitted passages, which will demonstrate the influential consideration given to the audience in EPA, which seeks to enable reception of the composition with particular meaning for a particular community of faith. My challenge was to enable the letter in performance to be received without comment or clarification, with nothing but the performer to bring it to life in a meaningful way, to allow the composition in performance to be an interpretation that stands alone in that reception context. Knowing there would be no discussion or comment in the performance event, I found analogies and questions pertinent for a first century audience wrestling with Holy One's welcome of all to be ineffective in communicating meaning in this specific reception of the composition today. In particular, the question pertaining to the place of Israel (in Rom 9–11) has been problematized for audiences today by a long history of anti-Semitic application of Paul's question, and developments in understanding and expression of human sexuality have created divisions within the church as Paul's words on this issue (Rom 1:26–27) have been invoked in unhelpful ways.

As my body moved, taking steps, turning, and making gestures, I saw and felt meaning in the letter. Different voices became apparent, creating texture in the performance, and arguments in a complex composition on the page resounded with new and renewed meaning on my voice. Notably, a repeated gesture accompanying certain words and phrases visually highlighted the theme of mutuality.

Emotionally, I participated in Paul's argument, in his love for Holy One and the people of Holy One. Although it is the most challenging of the tools to articulate in the Critical Reflection, emotion remains, as anticipated in Chapter 4, a most profound tool in the Performance Interpretation for its impact on audience and performer, as we make meaning through an intuitive apprehension of Paul's emotion.

When I discuss Rom 16 I do so integrating the tools in a more systematic section-by-section discussion of this part of the letter. This chapter had a significant impact in performance, and on the meaning of the letter in performance as a whole. From the presentation of Phoebe as exemplar member of the Christian community and participant in mutual relationships, to the translation of ἀσπάσασθε (*aspasasthe*) in light of performance experiences, Performance Interpretation found Rom 16 to be the climax of a letter calling its recipients to enact mutual embrace in community.

INTERPRETING ROMANS THROUGH THE AUDIENCE

If the audience does not trust the speaker, they will not receive what she says.[1] The opening of the performance event is important for establishing the relationship of performer and audience. As in my practice (as possible) when presiding in a worship gathering, facilitating a workshop, or speaking at another event, I walked around the church spaces greeting friends and strangers. In this way, I saw participants up close, and let them see me: I invited them to connect with, and to trust, me, before I spoke the letter in their midst.[2]

A relationship of trust existed already with many in the audience, as we have participated in communities of faith together for a number of years. I had been away for some time, so this welcome was an opportunity to re-establish our connection and trust.[3] In particular, many there had experienced my previous performances, my writing, or online presence, and come to know my commitment to the dignity and mutuality of humans together. This relationship with my audience forms the basis of their trust in me, and therefore decisions I made about how to perform the letter to balance its integrity and my own. As mutual welcome, listening, and trust are also features of the Christian community encouraged in the letter, maintaining my integrity is intertwined with maintaining the integrity of the composition.[4]

1. See, for example, Freshwater, *Theatre and Audience*, 73; Pasquarello, "Narrative Reading, Narrative Preaching," 177; Kemp, *Embodied Acting*, 34; Buckley, *Dancing with Words*, 84–87; and discussion in Chapter 4.

2. As noted in Chapter 3, the introduction with the audience is considered vital for Perry in his Performance Criticism practice: *Insights*, cf. 88.

3. I have left in the recording the opening remarks and explanations before beginning the letter, to show you the relationship between my audience and me.

4. Ehrensperger, *That We May Be Mutually Encouraged*, 118. On the integrity of the

The context of my audience as a faith community offering radical welcome to those in the LGBTIQ community and building inter-cultural and inter-faith relationships was congruent with my own commitments. This became particularly important when interpreting passages with problematic history of reception, such as condemnations of homosexuality based on 1:26–27,[5] applications of the dualistic pitting of flesh against spirit in Rom 7 in a diminishment of the human body,[6] and the perceived anti-Semitism of 9–11.[7]

Furthermore, the project itself had been introduced to my audience as one that values the whole, human person in the task of interpreting biblical compositions. This meant that maintaining my own integrity and that of the composition in performance would also preserve the integrity of the method.[8] Already we can see how the inherent mutuality of the method is evident in practice.

Speaking Language We Can Understand

Many of the scholars discussed in Chapters 2 and 3 translate their chosen composition for performance themselves.[9] As the current project is an examination of my practice as a biblical storyteller, I have approached the test case as I would approach any performance of a biblical composition. My practice is to use the translation most familiar to, or accepted by, the community: in this case, the NRSV. As I learn a composition in this translation, I inevitably find words in the English that have changed or nuanced meaning, broadly, or for a specific cultural context. For "words are never imprisoned in the expressions of a single author or a single age—they break out with explosive force—they reveal possibilities of meaning that cannot be

---

performer, see also Shiner, *Proclaiming the Gospel*, 25; and Cousins, "Pilgrim Theology," 74, 78, 82. Lee stresses the importance of maintaining integrity of audience and Scripture for a preacher (*Preaching*, 146), which is no less important for a storytelling performer-interpreter.

5. Martin, *Sex and the Single Savior*, 67.

6. Even when noting Paul's affirmation of human as both body and spirit, scholars such as Luther and Calvin still diminished the "flesh," describing it as like a wound (Luther) or as the inferior element (Calvin): Elliott, "Romans 7 in the Reformation Century," 172–73, 83–84.

7. Gaventa, *Our Mother Saint Paul*, 126.

8. Lee notes the explicit and implicit proclamations received from any presentation of the Word, to which a performer must pay attention: *Preaching*, 84.

9. For example, Perry, *Insights*; Swanson, "'This Is My . . .'"; Cousins, "Pilgrim Theology."

suppressed or be straight-jacketed by any single interpretation."[10] Because my audience and our culture have not "straightjacketed" our English language to any one meaning, I found certain words or phrases inadequate or inappropriate for this reception. For example, some language might carry the memory of an interpretation that will inhibit my audience's ability to "hear" those words in this performance.[11] In such instances, I return to the original language to revisit the semantic range, and translate anew to more effectively communicate the intent of the original language in contemporary English.

My first rendering of Romans into the script format gave me the opportunity to read the letter several times through in the NRSV translation as I typeset it for rehearsal. I do generally read biblical compositions aloud from the start of the process, seeking to vocalize the composition and hear it, and as I spoke Romans aloud in these early readings, I identified difficulties with the language. I made some translation choices at this very early stage, to be revised during rehearsal when I could feel the new language in my body and on my voice, with my particular audiences in mind.

The table below presents selected translation choices, and further discussion follows. The full script is presented in Appendix A, and Appendix B presents notes from preparation and rehearsal, in which further translations are discussed. It is important to remember that translation choices were made for a particular performance, on a particular occasion, for a particular audience. They were also made in the context of testing a new method, and are therefore intentionally experimental, often with an expectation of "failure," in order to identify the structural limits for practitioners of this method in future.

---

10. Hefner, *Our Bodies Are Selves*, 149. Following Ricoeur, *The Rule of Metaphor*.

11. "The story one hears in the present performance echoes against all earlier performances": Foley, "Man, Muse, and Story," 95. Of course, I cannot anticipate every association that individual audience members may make, but it is vital to attend to the collective memory and shared history of composition and language, to remove what inhibitors I can.

Greek[12]	NRSV translation	SA transposition	Notes
Θεός	God	Holy One	
πατερά	Father	Creator	
	He	They	In relation to Holy One / God
	His / God's Son	Their Son	
Χριστὸς	Christ	Wisdom	
κυρίος	(the) Lord	(the) Liberator	
δικαιοσύνη	Righteousness	Holiness	
δικαιόω	Justify / justified	(to) welcome into holiness/ Welcomed into holiness	
ἅγιος	Saints	The devoted / devotees	
μετάνοια	Repentance	Turn towards holiness	
ἁμαρτία	Sin	Tyrant	When sin is the noun
ἁμαρτία	Sin	Participating in tyranny	When sin is the verb
ἁμαρτωλὸς	Sinner	Participant in tyranny	
ἁγιασμός	Sanctification	Liberation from tyranny	To be sanctified is to be made pure / free from sin
λογίζομαι	Reckoned	Credited	Colloquial use of language with an accounting sense
ἀσπάζομαι	Greet	Embrace	

Holy One: Creator, Wisdom, Spirit

My translations of the Divine names are among the most contestable in the script. If I had been "acting" as Paul dictating the letter to Tertius, or Phoebe delivering it in Rome, I would have left the Divine names in their more conventional translations. As mediator of the composition in the context of my broader faith community, I needed to convey my commitment to

---

12. Greek transliterations: *Theos; patera; Christos; kurios; dikaiosune; dikaioo; hagios; metanoia; hamartia; hamartolos; hagiasmos; logizomai; aspazomai.*

the faith that this letter seeks to encourage.[13] A lack of confidence would show in my voice, and may have caused audiences to mistrust my commitment, and thereby mistrust the message.[14] I allowed my personal theological convictions to explicitly shape the choices for the Divine names, because I could then speak them with confidence and integrity; this would allow my commitment to faith in Holy One to resonate throughout the whole letter in performance. "Before I can believe any idea, it has to authenticate itself to me personally; and before you can be expected to believe it, it must become self-authenticated to you."[15]

A further consideration was the aim of enabling meaningful reception of the letter by *this* audience. As I was seeking to enable a 21st-century audience to hear an ancient letter with a long, and provocative, history of interpretation, I chose to be provocative with some of my translations. I sought to jolt my listeners into a state of novelty in their hearing of the letter, in order to discover anew meaning for themselves in their context.

Rendering "God" as "Holy One" was a decision influenced by liturgist Stephen Burns, who I heard use the phrase "Holy One, Holy Three," where more traditional liturgy would use "Father, Son, and Holy Spirit." This has been a helpful picture of the Trinity for me, with "Holy One" representing the three "persons" together, and Creator, Wisdom, Spirit, naming my experience and understanding of the three distinct "persons."[16] As "Holy One" is in my mind the three persons of the Trinity in their wholeness, it therefore made sense to use plural pronouns. This provided a way of avoiding either gendered language or the overly repetitive use of "Holy One" in the place of a pronoun.

It is also important for the language to be appropriate for the listeners, if they are to be effectively drawn into the impact, meaning, and transformative purpose of the letter. As Cousins notes, "translation for performance must carefully understand *how* the text in its original language seeks to inform and influence and then find corresponding ways of achieving the same effects

---

13. Jeff Lawrence encourages the spirituality of biblical storytellers as sacred tellers of God's story, rather than tellers of a sacred story: "The Spiritual Pilgrimage of a Biblical Storyteller." And Buckley notes that storytellers in faith communities "are sharing the stories, and creating stories, that contain the essence of what we believe. Our primary purpose is to share and continue our faith . . . We must be credible in our personal faith," *Dancing with Words*, 55.

14. As with preachers, whose lack of investment in what they are saying is evident in their voice, posture, expression: McKenzie, "Intersection of *Actio Divina* and *Homo Performans*," 58. Also see further discussion of the voice below.

15. Stott, *Between Two Worlds*, 55–56; cited in Lee, *Preaching*, 65.

16. See Agnew, "Every Mistake We Make."

in the language of the audience."[17] I anticipated mixed responses whatever names I chose for God: this is something quite personal for people of faith.[18] One of the potential pitfalls of the Embodied Performance method, however, is the inappropriate injection of the performer's self and own theology in such a manner as to obstruct the theology of the composition and its author. For, as in the preaching event, the performance event is an occasion for "divine self-disclosure,"[19] and the performer, as the preacher also, who remembers this purpose will be more likely to act with faithfulness not only to the text, but to the role of the speaker, their listeners, and the occasion.[20]

I decided that in this experiment with a new interpretive method it would be helpful to explore the effect of such a transgression *by committing it*, and chose to do so with the Divine names, as they recur throughout the whole letter, in different contexts and combinations. In particular, the choice to use "Wisdom" where the Greek and NRSV use "Christ" was a strikingly obvious overlay of my personal theology; such a choice foregrounds myself in a role that requires I foreground the community and the Divine. Further, "Wisdom" is not consistent with Paul's use of language, or his Christology:[21] it therefore presents an obvious insertion of the performer's self for an examination of the effect.

In the event, I found "Wisdom" personally helpful; "Wisdom" also resonated well with some listeners. However, on the one occasion when I used "Christ" rather than "Wisdom" I felt more confident in my connection and communication with the audience more broadly, perhaps because I had more appropriately foregrounded the community and the integrity of the letter.[22] For this reason, in future performances of Paul's letters I would most likely use "Christ."[23]

Transposing "Creator" for "Father" helps move away from patriarchal language. This is also not an entirely accurate representation of Paul or his

17. Cousins, "Pilgrim Theology," 84.

18. Any name we use for God is inadequate. Early fathers Aquinas, Anselm, and Augustine are for Hefner et al. "reminders that our talk about God is not straightforward and direct . . . when we do speak about God it is against a background of unspeakableness": *Our Bodies Are Selves*, 127.

19. McKenzie, "Intersection of *Actio Divina* and *Homo Performans*," 60.

20. McKenzie, "Intersection of *Actio Divina* and *Homo Performans*," 64–65.

21. Although it might be reasonable to say that Paul's language use in some letters resembles the Wisdom tradition of the Hebrew Scriptures: Hill, *Paul and the Trinity*, 8–9. See also Dunn, *Christology in the Making*.

22. Uniting College / Flinders University, 6 April 2016.

23. Note that I use "Wisdom" throughout the Critical Reflection, however, for that is the term used in the Performance Interpretation.

context, but is appropriate for twenty-first-century audiences. "Father" appears only four times in Romans (1:7; 6:4; 8:15; 15:6),[24] making this a less prominent change. Twice I used "Creator" where the NRSV uses "he" (both in 1:20), when Paul is speaking of Holy One as Creator of the world.[25]

Through my relationships with the many questioning, liberal to progressive people within my Adelaide audience, I was aware of their discomfort with "Lord." It carries connotations for them of hierarchy and patriarchy that would create a barrier to their finding meaning in the letter.[26] Using lexica for the Greek κύριος (*kurios*), and a thesaurus and dictionary for the English "Lord," I settled on "Liberator" as representative of the kind of "lord" (leader, ruler, king) I understand Jesus to be in the gospel according to Paul.[27] As some of my other translation choices are influenced by Gaventa's apocalyptic interpretation,[28] understanding Jesus to be the liberator of all from the power of Tyrant (Sin) also factored in this translation choice.

Of Sin and Sinners

I got stuck whenever I tried to speak the language of "sin." I was preparing for an audience who have experienced overly judgmental uses of "sin" and "sinners," and the subsequent view of a "fallen" humanity that is neither redeemable nor good. I looked for what others might have done with this language, to see if an alternative was possible.

Beverly Roberts Gaventa, understanding the cosmic battle between Holy One and the forces of evil to be the background for Paul's letter to the Romans, renders Sin as a proper noun, one of the powers in conflict with Holy One.[29] Gaventa notes that "sin is Sin—not a lowercase transgression, not even a human disposition or flaw in human nature, but an uppercase Power that enslaves humankind and whose final defeat the resurrection of

---

24. At 8:15, my "Creator! Maker!" replaces the NRSV's "Abba! Father!"

25. Further, my "Creator" at 1:25 appears as "the Creator" in the NRSV.

26. Again, community context came into conversation with the letter and moderated my own responses. Childers notes the importance for a preacher to know the audience, in order to discern what and how they may hear; this attention allows mediation of the composition to be helpful and effective for reception by the audience. Childers, "Preacher's Creative Process," 165.

27. Lampe, ed. *Patristic Greek Lexicon*, 787; *A Greek-English Lexicon*, 577–78; "Oxford Dictionaries," "lord."

28. Gaventa, "Cosmic Power of Sin"; Gaventa, *Our Mother Saint Paul*.

29. Gaventa, *Our Mother Saint Paul*; Gaventa, "The Shape of the 'I.'"

Jesus Christ inaugurates and guarantees. That larger picture of the cosmic battle is necessary to understand Paul's language in Romans."[30]

However, while the capitalization of "Sin" is helpful for a reader in denoting something different in an author's interpretation, it is less clear for a listener. Having chosen to follow Gaventa and personify "Sin" as a way of evoking some new and nuanced meaning from the letter,[31] I not only capitalized the noun, but also changed it to "Tyrant."[32] I felt this would make it clearer for a listening audience that I was interpreting "sin" as a personified opponent against Holy One, whether or not they were consciously aware of the cosmic battle at play. Using "Tyrant" as the proper noun also enabled me to use the common noun "tyranny" for language describing human "sin." I therefore changed the NRSV from "sin" to "Tyrant"; "sinner" to "participant in tyranny"; and "sinning" to "participating in tyranny." "Sanctification" is also brought into the word group of "Tyrant," rendered "liberation from tyranny," for I understood the process of being made holy (see below) as extrication, by the Liberator, from the grip of Tyrant. This also resonates with the sense of salvation as something that has been accomplished through Jesus Wisdom, but is a process not yet complete, as intimated in the "I" discourse of Rom 7.

The Holy Action of Holy One

The language for Holy One's action in this cosmic battle, for the changed status of humans being liberated from Tyrant, has been in the NRSV and other translations "justification" and "righteousness." Speaking it aloud, I felt the weight of the significant baggage that accompanies this language. This baggage is expressed as a "legalism" that Langton notes is divided when observed in certain attitudes to Torah[33] and may also feature in the Christian applications of theologies even of justification by faith or grace. Listeners today hear much when the words "justification" and "righteousness" are

---

30. Gaventa, *Our Mother Saint Paul*, 127.

31. In Chapter 2, I noted Hearon's observation of the nuanced meaning that differs in each performance of a composition, although the structure remains the same: Hearon, "From Narrative to Performance," 129.

32. "Tyranny" is cruel and oppressive rule. While synonyms for sin include evil, wickedness, and transgression, the dictionary definition focuses on the *act* of sinning. "Tyranny" carries the sense of oppressive power that can, as Tyrant, become a proper noun functioning in the way that Gaventa's capitalized "Sin" functions, and the word group of participants / participating in tyranny further expresses this understanding of the human captured and under the power of Tyrant. Definitions: "Oxford Dictionaries."

33. Langton, *Apostle Paul*, 18.

spoken, and not all that is heard will be consistent with the meaning Paul may have sought to convey. Considering my audience, and seriously seeking to help them receive meaning in this letter, I rediscovered the life-giving potential of Paul's theology by using different language in translation.

I chose to include these terms in the "holiness" word group. Holiness was explicitly stated or implied in the dictionary, thesaurus, and lexicon entries I consulted for these terms. I found "justification" to be "the action of declaring or making righteous,"[34] and "righteous" to be faultless, saintly, sinless.[35] That I had chosen Holy One as the Divine name led me to explore the synonyms of "holy," and found one of its major synonyms to be "righteous."[36] BDAG, for δικαιοσύνη (*dikaiosune*), gave the meaning as fulfilling divine expectation[37] or meeting God's standard.[38] If Gorman is right in observing that "a central theme of Romans is *theosis*, becoming like God by participating in the life of God,"[39] and I was naming "God" as "Holy One," then to become like God or to meet God's standard could be understood as "becoming holy."

Others have noted the significance of holiness language in Paul's writing. Although they make different observations and draw different conclusions, some overlap is discernible with what I was feeling and seeking to convey in my translations. My decisions may therefore be considered appropriate in light of broader understandings of Paul's theology. For example, Sarah Whittle notes Paul's use of ἅγιος (*hagios*) language throughout Romans, in particular linking 1:7 and 1:4 with 15:15–16.[40] She notes that the Spirit makes holy in 15:15, 16, and 19, and "this completes and explains, or summarizes, that which was introduced by Paul in 1:7: the Romans are called as holy, or called to be holy."[41] Noting, with Oakes, that Christians are described as holy "no fewer than eight times in Romans," and that bodies are also holy (12:1) and Gentiles are holy (15:16), Whittle states that "Paul is evidently concerned with the holiness of people."[42]

---

34. "Oxford Dictionaries," "justification."
35. "Oxford Dictionaries," "righteous," "righteousness."
36. "Oxford Dictionaries," "holy."
37. BDAG, 248.
38. BDAG, 249.
39. Gorman, *Becoming the Gospel*, 261.
40. Whittle, *Covenant Renewal*, 177.
41. Whittle, *Covenant Renewal*, 178.
42. Whittle, *Covenant Renewal*, 177.

Not only does the Spirit, Holy One, "make one holy," but this is "God's gift and nobody can earn it."[43] Further, "in contrast to the individualistic tradition of interpreting [15:15–16], it is the presence of the Holy Spirit *within Christian communities* that makes them holy."[44] For Paul, as we have and will continue to see, the mutuality of humans is indeed a key feature of the transformative work of Holy One in Jesus Wisdom. Whittle notes, further, that this work of Holy One, for Paul, is a broadening of Holy One's welcome into holiness to Gentiles, a welcome already extended and enjoyed by Jews for many generations.[45]

Arguably, Paul distinguishes "holiness" from "righteousness" in his use of consistent, specifically different language. For Oakes, the perfect participle ἡγιασμένη (*hegiasmene*) connotes "a change in status that comes about at conversion: the move from the ordinary to the holy."[46] This understanding of the work of Holy One in people resonates with my word choices, even if I have lost some of Paul's distinction in terminology. Perhaps on another occasion I might choose the "justice" word group. Alternatively, I have in the past substituted "right relationship" for "righteousness," but on this occasion, that felt a cumbersome option.

Along with theological considerations, the influence of my practice as a poet is particularly evident in my translation choices here, as I paid particular attention to the sound of the repeated language of "holiness." Cousins also altered her "translation after hearing and performing the text out loud to provide the audience with some sense of the aural poetic or alliterative effect of the text."[47] Some in my audience found the repetition of "holiness" overwhelming or distracting; many expressed appreciation for it. On reflection I noticed a cumulative effect in this repeated language, a subtle suggestion, perhaps, of the silencing of Tyrant by Holy One or holiness.

The Process

Envisaging the Adelaide audience, with whom I have a long relationship and therefore who I know well, influenced the language choices I made. We have noted that the process began with speaking the text aloud, listening to and feeling the sound and impact of the words.[48] As the words provoked

---

43. Ehrensperger, *That We May Be Mutually Encouraged*, 170.
44. Jewett, *Romans*, 908 (my emphasis).
45. Whittle, *Covenant Renewal*, 180.
46. Oakes, "Made Holy by the Holy Spirit," 171.
47. Cousins, "Pilgrim Theology," 185.
48. Childers, *Performing the Word*, 59.

reactions against an unhelpful reception history, I sought alternative translations, consulting lexica, dictionaries, and scholarship, for clues to the semantic range. I drew on my practices as performance artist, poet, storyteller, and scholar, to discern, test, revise, and settle on the words I would use for this performance interpretation.

Further comments on translation choices can be found in the Preparation and Rehearsal Notes, as mentioned, in Appendix B. Translations of 1:26–27, and ἀσπάσασθε (*aspasasthe*) (Rom 16) are included in discussions below.

Abridgements

The script for the Performance Interpretation is an abridged version of the letter to the Romans. This was necessary to fit the performance into the chosen time of one hour. As with translation choices, specific omissions and adaptations were in large part determined by the audience and my task of enabling them to receive this text with meaning for today. To summarize, Rom 1–2 and 12–16 were presented in full; 3–8 were abridged; 9–10 were not presented at all; and Rom 11 was omitted except for verses 1–2 and 33–36. Rather than discuss each one, I will focus on the major abridgement of 9–11. I will then discuss the decision to leave one of the most problematic passages (1:26–27) in the script. For discussion of other omissions, please refer, again, to the Preparation and Rehearsal Notes.

Staying Silent on the "Israel Question"

Watching the Performance Interpretation and the repeated steps I take to the position of the Jewish community (the audience's right), it is visibly evident that the issues of Jews and Gentiles being together the church in Rome are a central concern in this letter.[49] How are the Jews to relate to Holy One if the realm of Holy One is now open to all the nations (Rom 9–11)? What is their relationship to Torah, their ancestors and traditions (Rom 3–4)? How do followers of Jesus of Jewish and Gentile identity function as one community with all that differentiates them from one another (Rom 12–16)? For this performance, I chose to give voice to select questions. On the issues of circumcision (2:25–29), and food and Sabbath (14:1–23), I spoke Paul's wrestling and encouragement. As for the place of Jews within

---

49. As noted by, for example, Stendahl, *Paul among Jews and Gentiles*, 3: "Paul was chiefly concerned about the relation between Jews and Gentiles."

the salvation of Holy One, however (9–11), I left Paul's responses almost entirely in silence. Language of circumcision, and the questions of food and Sabbath are removed enough from my audiences' experience of church today that I could confidently trust them to make alternative meaning by replacing first century issues with those of their twenty-first-century contexts—again, recalling my earlier discussion of the particular and the personal. Issues of food still challenge churches today, for example, and although the questions differ, the issue of hospitality for the other is as pertinent for vegetarians and those with various allergies and intolerances as for "those who abstained" in the Roman churches (14:6, discussed below).

Concerning the place of Jews in the redeeming work of the Divine, however, I was aware that scholars in the past have "all too readily interpreted Paul's letter as a reasonable and reliable indictment of Jews and Judaism."[50] The anti-Semitic application of these words must be acknowledged if the words are to be spoken in community: one must identify the "elephant in the room," or it will block the view.[51] Here I may have identified a limitation to the Embodied Performance approach. It seems there may be some passages in biblical compositions not suitable for Performance Interpretation, or perhaps not suitable in certain contexts. A problematic discourse such as Paul's extended pondering of the place of Israel in Holy One's redeeming action in Rom 9–11 seems more suitable for reception and interpretation in written commentary, or if in an oral context, in sermon or Bible study, or the theology classroom, where the issue can be more fully discussed. I found that any expression I gave to these words seemed to interpret Paul's questions as a denigration of Israel or the Jews. My instinctive desire was to stop and explain, but that was not the mode of reception I had chosen for the letter on this occasion. As there would also be no discussion following the Performance Interpretation, I felt it was most appropriate to leave these provocative chapters unspoken. Having read the experiences of other performers who do invite audience conversation and reflection as part of the performance event,[52] and experiencing this myself in earlier performances

50. Gaventa, *Our Mother Saint Paul*, 126. See also Ehrensperger, *Mutually Encouraged*, 168; Heschel, *The Aryan Jesus*, 109, 63; and Eisenbaum, "Is Paul the Father of Mysogyny and Antisemitism?," 506.

51. "Those experiencing a performance of a text not only participate in its enactment together but can recognize their connection to a history of performances that come before and after": Cousins, "Pilgrim Theology," 86. That history may be helpful or harmful, for "the story one hears in the present performance echoes against all earlier performances and the Gestalt that is the experience they provide": Foley, "Man, Muse, and Story," 95. The use of Paul's arguments in harmful rhetoric is one of the collective "performances" of Romans inextricably woven into the letter in every reception since.

52. For example, Perry, *Insights*; Cousins, "Pilgrim Theology."

in the project,⁵³ I have since determined that such discussion is important to include in a Performance Interpretation event, to better enable the audience's reception and understanding of the composition-in-performance.

In this Performance Interpretation, although I did make some alternative choices regarding translation of key terms and the Divine names in order to provoke a hearing of the letter anew, these changes generally sought to render Paul's meaning into contemporary use of the English language. However, I could not alter the language of Paul's discussion in 9–11 without changing Paul's meaning. This is the limit of faithful interpretation I deliberately transgressed with the transposition of "Wisdom" for "Christ," so as to identify it. Here, I wished to remain with the bounds of a faithful and appropriate interpretation, the more usual goal of any exegetical work.

I left six verses of Rom 11 in the Performance Interpretation as a way of respecting Paul's question as appropriate and necessary for his context. I was not aware until I rehearsed and performed the letter of the way in which the silence itself would also speak, not only Paul's question, but also an acknowledgment of the distance my audience and I have travelled from the context of Paul's original recipients. I discuss silence below, and there return to this discovery.

Giving Voice to the Difficult Passages

> Many readers have taken Paul's comments in Romans 1 to refer only to homosexual desire . . . this is a tendentious reading prompted by a modern urge to condemn homosexual desire while sparing heterosexual desire. Paul's argument actually does not differentiate between the two kinds of desire, which is understandable when we recognize that desire itself is the problem for Paul, not just what moderns call "homosexual" desire.⁵⁴

One of the most problematic portions of the letter in performance was 1:26–27:

> 26. For this reason God gave them up to degrading passions. Their women exchanged natural intercourse for unnatural, 27. and in the same way also, the men, giving up natural intercourse with women, were consumed with passion for one another. Men

---

53. See Appendix D.
54. Martin, *Sex and the Single Savior*, 67. See also Parker, "The Teratogenic Grid," 47, 60.

committed shameless acts with men and received in their own persons the due penalty for their error. (NRSV)

Speaking these words aloud, my voice, my body, my whole being, wanted to stop, every time. I discussed in Chapter 4 the way that a person, immersed in experiences, develops a deep knowledge that informs instinct and intuition. Immersed in the community of Blackwood Uniting Church for many years, I know deeply the commitment of that community to embrace LGBTIQ folk. Further, I had been on a committee more than ten years earlier that issued a call to a new minister for this congregation, a minister in a same-gender relationship. I know this congregation's story from inside, from my experience with them of radical mutual embrace, encouragement, and care across difference. This embodied knowledge leads to an instinct of resistance with and on behalf of my audience to these words and the history of consequences they carry with them.[55] I asked myself, "How can I speak these words in my community, when we do not condemn the kind of 'intercourse' Paul appears to name as contrary to nature?" When face-to-face with people bearing the consequences of the history of interpretation of these verses, one understands that "topics like same-sex marriage are not just issues, but are about real people who matter."[56]

Early audiences shaped my Performance Interpretation of this passage, in a process Cousins names as a "hermeneutical circle."[57] The audience at the preview performance at New College observed the way I stumbled over these verses, uncertain of my interpretation. They told me to "Push into the discomfort; see what you find there; do not back away from this challenge." With their encouragement, I continued to engage with these verses, rather than omit them. Within my active resistance I found the possibility of a more nuanced meaning in the Greek, and chose to give voice and body to that interpretation.

Leaving a silence would have been (as with Rom 9–11) comment itself on the distance travelled in human understanding of relationships from Paul's context to our own. However, the challenge to find a way of giving voice to these words, to find in Paul something more than a demonization of homosexuality, as such passages have come to be interpreted and applied,

55. Professor C. L. Seow claims the distinction between interpretation and reception is false and elitist, for "it is not true that artists only receive." Further, there is no original text, for all texts are themselves interpretive, and understanding is always historically affected. Seow suggests an approach to studying the history of biblical texts that examines the consequences of these historically affected interpretations, receptions, and applications of the Bible. Seow, "Consequences of Scripture."

56. Hefner, *Our Bodies Are Selves*, 67.

57. Cousins, "Pilgrim Theology," 185.

was enticing; for, surely, "to use this passage to justify the exclusion of persons who are homosexual would be the grossest distortion of Romans and its claims about God's radical and universal grace."[58]

My translation pushes the limits of meaning in the Greek, perhaps further than is supportable; but again, this translation was for a particular audience in a particular moment. I do not claim that this is the best, or an enduring, translation.

> 26. And so they were given up to endured dishonor. Their women exchanged natural relations for unnatural; 27. Men with women, exchanged natural relations for unnatural. They became consumed with passion. Men conquered men, shamelessly; they suffered in their own person the penalty of their actions. (Track 1)[59]

While we examine the translation choices, we must also recall the interpretation-in-performance: how I gave voice to these words is part of the translation, expression inherent in the meaning I discerned and sought to convey.

I translate εἰς πάθη ἀτιμίας (*eis pathe hatimias*; v. 26) as "endured dishonor." πάθος (*pathos*) can be understood as suffering, or "that which is endured."[60] In Ancient Rome, to describe a man being penetrated sexually literally meant "to have a woman's experience" (further, for a woman to be penetrated anally, she was linguistically situated as a boy—something other, and less, than she was).[61] Walters argues that the Greco-Roman idea of sex was something one person did to another, and the only appropriately active partner in sexual intercourse was a *vir*.[62] *Vir* "refers specifically to those adult males who are freeborn Roman citizens in good standing, those at the

---

58. Gaventa, "Romans," 407.

59. Track numbers for videos found at https://sarahagnew.com.au/embodied-performance. See Appendix C for a full list of tracks for Chapter 6.

60. BDAG, 748. Reading Lampe (*Patristic Greek Lexicon*, 992–98), I was struck by the diversity in meaning for πάθος, from suffering, in particular of Christ and the martyrs and spiritual nature of that suffering, to the kind of "passion" that is particularly sexual, and negatively so, as found in the entry in BDAG (478), which, noting a connotation to πάθος of strong sexual desire or passion, translates Rom 1:26 as "disgraceful passions." πάθος does have a passive sense about its range of meanings, although that passivity need not be negative. The range of meaning includes "what one has experienced," "emotion," "a state or condition," and the rhetorical "emotional style or treatment": Liddell, Scott, Jones, and McKenzie, *Greek-English Lexicon*, 1285.

61. Walters, "Invading the Roman Body," 30.

62. Walters, "Invading the Roman Body," 31.

top of the Roman social hierarchy."⁶³ To be penetrated was to suffer shame, and thus to move lower in the social hierarchy. I found this to support my translation of ἀτιμιας (*atimias*) as "dishonor."⁶⁴ Further, rendering the Greek as "dishonor" provides an aural contrast with "honor," a key feature of the relationships of mutual embrace that Paul encourages (e.g., 12:10; 13:7; also 15:6, "love and honor Holy One").⁶⁵

ὀρέξις (*orexis*, v. 27) has "a connotation of strong desire," and is only used in an unfavorable sense.⁶⁶ Paul's views on "passion" in the context of sexual activity are generally negative. In 1 Cor 7, for example, Paul encourages marriage as the preferable and necessary location for sexual activity, but not to *express* passion or desire, rather to *contain* it as the duty of care from one spouse to another.⁶⁷ Paul sees marriage as a safe space in which to dispel sexual passion (in the form of passionless sex) in order to keep the passion from becoming an idolatrous distraction from the worship of God. Further, if the sexual activity of Ancient Roman culture was not an expression of mutual love, not a sharing in mutual pleasure,⁶⁸ Paul's preference for celibacy may be located within his broader understanding of the counter-cultural mutuality of Christ-inspired relationships.⁶⁹ Celibacy or marriage would transform unhealthy relationships based on the power structures of Greco–Roman society to counter-cultural mutual care and respect.⁷⁰

The NRSV's translation of ἐξεκαύθησαν (*exekauthesan*) as "consumed" felt right,⁷¹ and my aim in performance was to highlight the "being consumed with" rather than the "passion" itself, placing emphasis on "consumed," and employing a gesture closing in on myself. For Paul, "the passion of sexual desire is part of the polluting complex of the cosmos that threatens

63. Walters, "Invading the Roman Body," 32.

64. Within the range of meanings in BDAG, 149; see also Friberg, Friberg, and Miller, *Analytical Lexicon*, 80.

65. As noted already, Cousins also considered aural effect in her translation of Psalms for performance: "Pilgrim Theology," 185.

66. BDAG, 721–22.

67. Martin, *Sex and the Single Savior*, 66.

68. Parker, "Teratogenic Grid," 57.

69. Paul's approach to the problem of sexual desire, which was viewed by medical and Stoic writers of the time as a disease, was unique, as was his rejection of the idea of the self-sufficiency of a human being, the goal for a Stoic. Martin sees in Paul's writing (2 Cor 3:5–6; 2 Cor 5:15) an affirmation of "thick interconnections of being"; because Christ died and lived for others, the others do not live *for* themselves: Martin, *Sex and the Single Savior*, 71–74.

70. Martin, *Sex and the Single Savior*, 71–74.

71. Longenecker translates as "inflamed with lust": Longenecker, *Epistle to the Romans*, 189.

the church."[72] As noted, Martin sees a particular connection between desire and idolatry as sources of sin (or participation in tyranny); this sense of idolatrous relationships that put desire, pleasure, or power (if Walters' argument is correct) above God and respect for others, was what I felt, internalizing Paul's rhetoric.

χρῆσις (*chresis*) can connote relations that are usually intended as sexual.[73] The translation in NRSV as "intercourse" does clarify this for an English-speaking audience. The more suggestive "relations"[74] is often used in contemporary English as a circumlocution for talking about sex, but is not limited to sexual relations. In light of the broader theme of mutual relationships, this broadens the meaning to include relation(ship)s of a non-sexual nature,[75] for unhealthy sexual activity seemed in the Performance Interpretation to be one example within a breadth of harmful exchanges evident in the behavior of "*all* who by their un-godliness and wickedness suppress the truth" (v. 18).

Reflecting on the Performance Interpretation, I noticed again the build-up of three "exchanges" that Paul lists (1:20–27, track 2): glory for idolatry (v. 23), truth for a lie (v. 25), and natural relations for unnatural (vv. 26–7). Paul seems to say "exchange your God for an idol, and you will exchange your genuine humanness for a distorted version, which will do you no good."[76] The implicit exchange at the close of Rom 1 is the way of Holy One (or the law / love) for the way of every kind of wickedness; and

> the punishment not only fits the crime, but directly results from it as well: Those who worship images of their fellow creatures must not be surprised if their own bodies are dishonored as a result of the lusts . . . of their hearts.[77]

When I discuss emotion below, I include Paul's disappointment. I want to note that I felt Paul's dismay here at the turning away from Holy One's way

---

72. Martin, *Sex and the Single Savior*, 67.

73. Although its general meaning has to do with use or usefulness: BDAG, 1089; Liddell, *Greek-English Lexicon*, 2006.

74. BDAG, 1089.

75. Walters observes the framing of sexual activity in the ancient world by the broader relationships and social hierarchy: Walters, "Invading the Roman Body," 30. For Gaventa, "Cosmic Power of Sin," 233, the debate on homosexuality has confined this passage to "questions of sexuality. That debate thereby obscures Paul's powerful depiction of humankind that refuses to acknowledge God or its own status as creature." Ehrensperger notes that "sin has to do with the unrelatedness of individuals as well as systems of oppression": Ehrensperger, *Mutually Encouraged*, 120.

76. Wright, "Romans," 434; Martin, *Sex and the Single Savior*, 67.

77. Wright, "Romans," 433.

by "those who suppress the truth" become pointed disappointment in Rom 2, when "you" are named as not so innocent yourselves.[78] I felt what others have observed: this "passage turns out to be one long, clever set up to rebuke religious people for feeling superior to others."[79]

An Alternative Performance Interpretation?

I was still unconvinced by my interpretation, however, and wondered if biblical storytelling might yet present this portion in a way that enables meaningful reception today. In the multi-media context of the twenty-first century, another option for reception of biblical compositions is through recorded performance. In track 3 I present a digital storytelling of Rom 1:20–32.[80] This format offers the option to overlay text, intersperse the telling with scenes from other stories, or to use music. I found these means helpful ways to offer comment without presenting a written commentary.[81] The format of Performance Interpretation may therefore vary in an Embodied Performance Analysis, and this will be a fruitful area for further exploration, utilizing the breadth of communication media of our time.

To Whom Paul Wrote

My Audience: Paul's Addressees

These choices about omissions and translations were all made in the interest of interpreting the letter *as received by twenty-first-century audiences*. However, as the letter is unavoidably addressed to a specific group of people, all those beloved of Holy One in (first century) Rome (1:7) were also experienced as somehow present in the performance moment.

---

78. The rebuke of those judging others sees their actions as another "form of the denial of God," and could be an anticipation of Rom 14. I was disappointed to discover after the event Richard Longenecker's comment on the vocative ὁ ἄνθρωπε (*ho anthroupe*) at 2:1, 3 (*Epistle to the Romans*, 235–38.). I felt I had missed an opportunity for the performance, as his "You, therefore, O man or woman, whoever you are" (232) would have great rhetorical impact in oral performance. This offers further encouragement for performer-interpreters to translate a composition for themselves.

79. Otto, *Oriented to Faith*, 81; also, Gaventa, "Cosmic Power of Sin," 233.

80. Decisions made for the editing of the film find support in the observations made by Walters, "Invading the Roman Body," 30; also, Gaventa, "Cosmic Power of Sin."

81. For further examples, see the #BibleUnplugged series from The Slate Project Baltimore.

Observing my gesture at 1:7 (track 4), with arms open wide for "all," I seemed to encompass *that* audience in Adelaide, and my audience thus became situated as both their twenty-first-century selves receiving this ancient letter, *and* also the first century Jesus-followers Paul addresses in Rome. This appears to have given individuals the impression of becoming, or at least sitting alongside, the first century addressees of the letter for that one moment or for the whole performance,[82] and may resemble Boomershine's "rhetoric of implication"[83] discussed in Chapter 4. As the performer, not only did I see before me my audience, for whom I was concerned to discern meaning in, and through this ancient letter, I also instinctively visualized Paul's addressees, Phoebe's audiences.

To Jew and Gentile

Commentators might focus on the question of whether and to what extent the audience of Romans was Jewish or Gentile.[84] To whom does Paul speak in any given portion of the discourse is also a question raised.[85] Further, the names in 16:1–16 have been analyzed for potential clues to Jewish or Greco-Roman ethnicity.[86] Such scholarship illuminated possibilities for the letter that did assist my embodiment of it for performance.

That the Roman churches may have been struggling with the consequences of a mass deportation of Jews and their subsequent return to Rome[87] helped me to imagine heightened tension when Jews returned to find the Jesus-community departing from their preferred Torah-shaped practices. That the Jew/Gentile divide might be more complicated than often assumed[88] resonated with my sense of the ethnic divisions of Jew

---

82. See discussion below of 16:16 as a bookend to 1:7.

83. Boomershine, *Messiah of Peace*, 394–5.

84. For Wright, there are two situational emphases that address "Gentile Christians faced with non-Christian Jews," and an "uneasy coexistence" between Jewish and Gentile Christians: "Romans," 406. See also, Park, *Either Jew or Gentile*; Gamble, *Textual History*.

85. Wright, "Romans," 406. Also, Donfried, "A Short Note on Romans 16," 49; Lampe, "Roman Christians," 219; Oestreich, *Performance Criticism of the Pauline Letters*, 152–90.

86. As mentioned by Witherington, *Paul's Letter to the Romans*, 382.

87. Witherington, *Paul's Letter to the Romans*, 8, 376; Wright, "Romans," 406.

88. Park, *Either Jew or Gentile*, 2. The "Torah-free" gospel was not necessarily non-Jewish, nor was it anti-Jewish. Indeed, "Paul was not a champion of 'Christianity against Judaism.' The dichotomy between Judaism and Christianity should not be anachronistically imposed on this distinction between the two gospels [Torah-free and Torah-bound] of early Christianity."

and Gentile when Jewish followers of Jesus are tempted to feel superior to Gentiles, having been the chosen holy people of Holy One for countless generations, and the distinct issue of religious differences apart from ethnicity, particularly with Gentile proselytes.[89] Perhaps Paul proclaims such mystery concerning Israel's future (Rom 9–11) in hopes of guarding against feelings of superiority from the Jesus-followers.[90]

Ultimately, I understood Romans to have been sent to *all* the church in Rome—Jew, Gentile, Torah-observers and not.[91] I spoke the letter to "all" (discussed below) as I spoke it for an audience likely to experience different types of divisions today (inevitably, as in 16:17–20).

INTERPRETING ROMANS THROUGH THE BODY

Although even the "full" performance for the test case was abridged, performing a composition as a "whole" is a major feature of the Embodied Performance Analysis, as for BPC. Embodying the letter from start to finish, I experienced the development of the discussion and appreciated how the various elements of the letter spoke to one another. Audience members also expressed appreciation for hearing the breadth of the letter as having enriched their understanding of it in some way. Further, the physical act of speaking the letter aloud in itself enables a different encounter with the discussion, because the ear hears differently to the reading of the eye, and the body communicates differently to writing on a page.[92] I gained an experience of the major themes of the letter by hearing and feeling the repetitions and returns to various ideas with repeated gesture, and envisaging the audience in order to consider what, and how, they might hear.

---

89. Lampe, "Roman Christians," 225.

90. Stendahl, *Paul among Jews and Gentiles*, 4; Nanos, "Romans," 261.

91. Although some scholars even doubt that the church in Rome was the intended audience at all. Putting the argument for Jerusalem as addressee of the letter is Jervell, "Letter to Jerusalem." Examples of those arguing for the Ephesus church as the intended addressee include Goodspeed, "Phoebe's Letter of Introduction"; and Whelan, "Amica Pauli." My embodied performance interpretation, particularly at Rom 16, challenges both these assertions.

92. Maxwell, "From Performance to Text to Performance," 166–67. Not to mention the different assumptions made of a written text and its fixed permanence (162–63).

Gesture: That We May Be Mutually Encouraged

At 1:12 (track 5)—"that we may be mutually encouraged by each other's faith, yours and mine"—my body naturally gestured by moving my hands alternately towards the audience and towards me, one each way simultaneously, back and forth. Slowly, and with palms turned upwards and hands open, I detected in this motion an intuitive understanding of mutuality as a simultaneous giving of oneself and receiving from another. I employed this gesture at various moments throughout, and not only with the "mutuality" word group (e.g., 1:12, 14:19). In phrases such as "members of one another" (12:5), "welcome one another" (15:7), "love one another" (12:10; 13:8), "love your neighbor as yourself" (13:9) "live in harmony with one another" (12:16; 15:5), "not pass judgment on one another" (14:13), "accommodate one another" (15:2), and "instruct one another" (15:14), this theme of mutuality was supported and enhanced through my body's movements (track 6).

This gesture conveyed the act of giving, accommodating, loving, or upholding one another, as my body demonstrated the physical reality of mutual relationship. My expression and emotion, evident in the slowing down, the attending to the movement of my hands, the smile at this enactment of mutuality, evoked the compassion and love intrinsic to relationships of mutual care. In our own giving and receiving in the performance moment, implicitly referenced in the gesture from me to the audience and back—my giving in performance and their receiving, and their giving attention and energy and my receiving—audience and performer were ourselves drawn into the enactment of mutual embrace that Paul encourages for communities of Jesus-followers. The impact this has on both performer and audience, moved, inspired, challenged by the call to enact mutual care for one another *is* the meaning received in performance. As one audience member stated, "I felt the love; I felt welcomed."

I discuss below the way in which adaptation of the gesture of mutuality became the gesture of embrace in Rom 16, drawing the theme of mutuality into this climactic call to *embody* mutual embrace in the church of Jesus.

Movement: The Interlocutor and the "I"

As I spoke the questions and responses of Rom 3–4, standing, in rehearsal, I intuitively stepped to the left and slightly forward, as if taking the place of the questioner, and back to "center" to reply. Although not always obvious in the video editing, similar movements can be observed at 7:15–25 and 16:22, and to both of these occurrences I will return. For each of these movements, I stepped in a different direction (always the same pattern each performance), so as to differentiate between each persona. This helps me to know in whose "voice" I am speaking, and the audience to recognize shifts in persona and thus in rhetoric and discourse.[93] The step to my left / audience right for Rom 3–4 was a movement in the direction to which my gestures for Israel and the Jews had indicated in Rom 1–2.[94]

The Interlocutor: Romans 3–4

Even if it is Paul himself posing rhetorical questions,[95] my stepping from side to side represents the interrogative rhetoric here (track 7). It seemed to me in rehearsal and performance that Paul brought into the discourse a representative Jewish believer, or perhaps collectively, "the Jesus-following Jews." In my experience of the letter, the author-voice utilizes the voice of an interlocutor in order to attend to the questions of the Jewish followers of Jesus.[96] This may be an application of an intra-Jewish argumentative approach typical in Hellenistic Jewish texts.[97] As I heard the questions and Paul's responses

---

93. Ruge-Jones observes use of gesture or movement to indicate a transition from narrator to character voice: "Those Sitting around Jesus," 41.

94. A gesture with my left hand, but much closer to "center," will later be described as indicating the Jesus-followers who followed the Torah, whether Jew or Gentile in their ethnicity, still on the left to indicate the association of Torah with Israel. I made such movements in rehearsal intuitively, visually reinforcing for myself the connections I was making between sections of the letter; I then communicated this meaning I had physically identified with the audience in performance through those same gestures and movements.

95. Wright seems to understand that Paul is posing the questions himself: "Romans," 454. Longenecker (R), although more in favor of Paul himself naming possible objections to his reasoning, acknowledges the possibility of an interlocutor persona in an adaptation of the Greek Diatribe form: *Epistle to the Romans*, 333–34.

96. "Paul employs the rhetorical technique of diatribe here and throughout Romans. Like character portrayals in a drama, diatribe, which is speech-in-character, creates attitudes to which the audience is expected to relate, whether positively or negatively. . . . Thus, Paul may be asking the questions, or putting them in the mouth of the interlocutor . . . The original letter was probably delivered by a letter carrier (Phoebe; cf. 16.1) in a way that included acting out the parts": Nanos, "Romans," 257. However, Nanos does not see the interlocutor here as a Jew, because of the use of the third person plural pronoun in 3:2 (259).

97. Fredriksen, "Jewish Romans, Christian Romans," 24–25. Fredriksen describes the antagonism of later Christian rhetoric "*contra Iudaeos*." In my embodiment of the letter, I do not experience Paul's use of interlocution as antagonistic towards the Jews, in the kind of anti-Jewish rhetoric of the late first century and afterwards, inspired by Greco-Roman adversarial conventions, and perhaps even a misappropriation of Paul's discussion here.

on my voice, I heard Paul wanting to acknowledge very real concerns; concerns about the Jewish believers which were held by both the Jewish and non-Jewish followers of Jesus—what does the life, death and resurrection of Jesus *mean* for us? What does the covenant mean in light of the gospel of Jesus? Who are we, now, if we are not the set apart people of Holy One, made holy because Holy One is holy?[98] Like a minister of a congregation, or in this case perhaps a visiting preacher in someone else's pastoral context, when that congregation is facing change or conflict, I felt Paul seeking to comfort, reassure, and gently but firmly guide the people to the best of his ability as one called by Holy One for just that purpose (Rom 1:1; 15:16).

The "I" of Romans 7

In this Performance Interpretation of Romans, the "I" discourse follows directly from 6:23, beginning at 7:15.[99] I inserted "Even so" as a link, for what follows becomes in this iteration a "but" to the affirmation of Rom 6.

My step forward (track 8) was an instinctive move as I learnt the words and connected the blocks of Rom 6 and 7 together. I described earlier the process of rehearsal as "memorizing" words in small chunks, connecting the chunks together, and then, as I become confident that I know the words, rehearsing over and over to allow the words and meaning to become internalized in a mutual indwelling of letter within me and me within the world of the letter. This incarnation of the word is a "process of unself-conscious participation and exchange"[100] between composition and performer, resulting in an existential knowledge that "is based on an encounter in which a new meaning is created and recognized."[101]

Instinctively this felt like a discrete, new, voice. As I consulted scholars for the ways in which others have understood Paul's rhetoric here, I was surprised at the ways in which some commentators want to dissect this passage. The "I" may be Paul, Adam, or an "every-person." If the "I" is Paul speaking for himself, scholars wonder if he is speaking of his experience as a Jew, before God calls him as an apostle of Christ,[102] or after, expressing the

---

98. For Nanos, Paul affirms that neither Jewish nor Gentile follower of Jesus is superior or inferior to the other: the point is that *both* are now "equal recipients of God's benefaction in Christ" (Nanos, "Romans," 261).

99. Comments on the omission of 7:1–6 can be found in Appendix B. Comment on omitting 7:7–14 is found below.

100. Bozarth, *The Word's Body*, 114.

101. Tillich, *Courage to Be*, 124.

102. Stendahl, *Paul among Jews and Gentiles*, 7. As an aside, I quite like this idea of Paul being "called" into a new relationship with God, rather than "converted" out of

ongoing struggle between the path he wants to walk, and a path in another direction. Perhaps due to my abridgements, the connection to Adam (and Eve) escaped me entirely, as did any associated reference or insinuation of Eve's trespass as sexual.[103] It may be that sexual desire receives a significant amount of attention in this or other letters, but my experience of Romans suggested that there is greater interest in this letter in the extended invitation into holiness beyond Israel alone to all the nations, and in the mutual embrace of humans for one another in response to Holy One's embrace.

Gundry sees the αὐτὸς ἐγώ (*autos ego*) of 7:25 as "emphatic self-reference" on the part of Paul.[104] As the NRSV does not reflect this emphasis found in the Greek, I did not encounter it in preparation. Although Gundry notes the theatrical impact of this emphatic "I myself," "combined with the pathos of the preceding oratory" in v. 24, he seems distracted by the implied autobiographical reference.[105]

In my Performance Interpretation, the biography of Paul was not as important as the rhetorical impact itself, which I felt, as Gaventa also observes, catches the audience up in the "I" in a mutual expression of the anguish of the human situation with Tyrant (or Sin) grasping for power.[106] When I inhabited the letter and spoke the words aloud amongst a community of faith, the "I" was an "every-person" caught up in the cosmic battle of good and evil; we participated in the letter and the anguish it expressed, together, and together with Paul and his addressees. This participation itself was the meaning of this passage.

Sin: Spirit vs. Body

The dualism pitting spirit against flesh in Rom 7:7–14 felt unhelpful and even harmful,[107] preparing for reception by an audience in a culture so dominated by unrealistic images of "beauty."[108] Not only that, but the very methodology I propose through this test case is an *embodied* performance hermeneutic, placing a high value on the body and its ability to discern

Judaism and into Christianity; such language better recognizes the continuity of faith for Jesus followers in the first century, out of the tradition of Israel and Judaism.

103. Discussed, for example, by Gundry, "Moral Frustration of Paul."
104. "Moral Frustration of Paul," 229.
105. "Moral Frustration of Paul," 229.
106. Gaventa, "Shape of the '"I,"' 80. Also, Longenecker (R) sees in 7:24 a "universal cry of despair": *Epistle to the Romans*, 667.
107. Ehrensperger, *Mutually Encouraged*, 165–6; citing Castelli, "Romans."
108. Hefner, *Our Bodies Are Selves*, 70.

meaning in biblical texts. Here, I was aware of what Lee refers to as implicit proclamations in the embodied performance of the Bible.[109] Thus, although retaining the section 7:15–25, I removed verse 18, as I found I could not stand before an audience today and speak the words "For I know that nothing good dwells within me, that is, in my flesh" with any intonation that illuminated meaning with integrity for my audience.[110]

The very first thing Holy One says of humans in the Jewish and Christian sacred texts is that humans are blessed (Gen 1:28). Further, "because God became incarnate in Christ and Christ in us, we can experience the joy and pleasure of our bodyselves, gifts from our Creator God."[111] In a commentary or sermon, one could "flesh out," as it were, Paul's discussion of the struggle between good and evil in less figurative language, but even then the argument still relies on a negative view of humans in a rhetorical emphasis on the gift of Holy One and holiness.

I spoke the words "I do delight in the law of Holy One in my inmost self, but I see in my body another law at war with the law of my mind," although here, too, is a tendency towards dualism. And while I did speak verses 22 and 23 (track 9), I omitted "that dwells in my members" after "making me captive to the law of Tyrant," so as to present the conflict between good and evil without demonizing the body as inherently associated with sin.[112]

Further, speaking the words "Who will rescue me from this body of death?," I was careful to place the emphasis on "death," not "body," in an attempt to link back to Tyrant's body (6:6), the follower of Jesus being "crucified with him [Jesus] so that the body of Tyrant might be destroyed." In this emphasis on "death" rather than "body" we can see the way that expression and the voice carry meaning in a performed interpretation.[113]

---

109. Lee, *Preaching*, 84.

110. Boyarin notes the dualism in Paul's writing, and his privileging of spirit over matter (*A Radical Jew*, 7). In an acting performance as Paul or Phoebe, these words would be more clearly be spoken in a first century "voice." As I am mediator of the letter, however, my voice is heard as well as that of Paul; and as I am inviting my audience to receive this letter as holding meaning for them today, what they hear must be considered. The body–spirit hierarchy is something to discuss as a feature of Pauline theology and rhetoric; it is not appropriately received in a performance without discussion.

111. Hefner, *Our Bodies Are Selves*, 161. The process of becoming to which Holy One calls us is evident in the understanding of Iranaeus and Athanasius, whose ideas "later developed into the Orthodox notion of *theosis*" (161), which I discussed in relation to my translations using the "holiness" word group (cf. Gorman, *Becoming the Gospel*, 261ff).

112. I likewise omitted 13:14, for its exhortation to "make no provision for the flesh."

113. Track 10 of the videos online, https://sarahagnew.com.au/embodied-performance/. Further discussion of this decision is included in Appendix B.

Such omissions of language as I have discussed, language that has been used to construct boundaries between "body" and "soul,"[114] represents a challenge to this unhelpful dualism, in an interpretation designed to assist in the letter's reception today. My hope is that the methodology itself is a reimagining of body and spirit as not in dichotomy, but as integrated and mutually interrelated.

INTERPRETING ROMANS THROUGH EMOTION

The Voice Says More Than Words

When I spoke Rom 1:26–27 at the preview performance at New College, I faltered, not forgetting the words, but somehow in the moment unable to actually articulate them. That Performance Interpretation I thus presented was unambiguous: in my faltering I said, "I do not agree with these words and I do not know how to speak them in your midst." This is not what I had intended to say. I thought I had determined a clear interpretation of the words as non-anti-homosexual. But the voice, the most personal tool, will "reveal more about us than any other single aspect of our communication style. Why? Because our words are made of breath. There is nothing more intimately ours—more interior to us—than our voices."[115]

I did not yet know what meaning could be found in these words for an audience today, to speak them aloud and invite them to stand without comment, and my voice told me (and my audience) so. I have described my continued embodiment and reflection on these verses above; I have also discussed the insights gained from expression and emphasis, the different intonations of the voice. I have not located the voice specifically within any one tool, because through the voice we can see the interrelation of the three tools of Embodied Performance Analysis, especially this intimate connection between body and emotion through the breath and voice.

Participating in the Rhythm of Paul's Words

Although there were times when I found Paul's words to be inappropriate for reception through performance, when I put Paul's words onto my voice, I did identify with his perspective, and participate in his communication efforts. Childers observes the way in which "disciplined, sensitive reading

---

114. Christie, "What the Body Knows," x.
115. Childers, *Performing the Word*, 58.

of a text . . . may reveal something of the writer's heart and mind."[116] Such disciplined reading, for Bozarth, demands a generous "at-onement . . . between poem, performer, and audience."[117] As the performer experiences the "text's rhythms, word colors, and 'mouth feel', and through the kinesthetic experience of linking the reader's breath and the writer's phrase, a process of identification" occurs.[118] Aligning your voice with that of the writer through immersion in the composition illuminates otherwise inaccessible aspects of meaning. It was through this embodied, intuitive, participation in the rhetoric and emotion of Paul's letter that I understood Rom 13 to offer an example of the way that good might overcome evil (12:21).

As I spoke "Let every person be subject to the governing authorities" (13:1), I placed the emphasis on "be." As I developed the performance, scaffolding Rom 13 onto Rom 12, I became aware of the progression from one argument to the next (track 11). "Overcome evil by good" led into "let every person be subject to governing authorities," which seemed to align the authorities with the evil to be overcome. Romans 13 then became an example of overcoming evil with good: do not buy into the evil ways of the rulers, their greed and power, but rather, do good, take care of your soul by living according to the rule of love and honor—and thus "heap burning coals on their heads" (12:20).[119]

Through the mutual inhabitation of letter and performer, I understood it intuitively, and it flowed with revelatory intonation. In this process *how* I embody one section is influenced by, and flows from, the embodying of the previous section. The rhetoric flows, the argument builds, scaffolding pieces to make sense of each other as they build in my knowledge, and it is as though I am an architect decoding a building. Kelly Wilson observes that a reader may see the whole script, sections nested within one another, yet in a theater, the audience experience the building, the growing of the composition into a whole.[120] As a performer-interpreter, I move from seeing the whole, to deconstructing the nests into parts, then building it again in

---

116. Childers, *Performing the Word*, 59.

117. Bozarth, *The Word's Body*, 114. Bozarth uses "poem" as I use "composition."

118. Childers, *Performing the Word*, 59. Although "identification" might not quite express this process, if, as Bozarth observes, the integrity of both poem and performer are preserved even as the two combine to create something new and distinct out of their mutual inhabitation: Bozarth, *The Word's Body*, 38. Bozarth prefers the term "participation" (35). Gorman, too, in his discussion of Romans through the lens of mission, sees *theosis* as a central theme; *theosis* as more than identifying with Christ / God, but "becoming like God by *participating* in the life of God" (my emphasis): Gorman, *Becoming the Gospel*, 261.

119. See also Esler, "Social Identity, the Virtues, and the Good Life," 60.

120. Wilson, "Performance Critical Analysis," 161.

my body, in the embodied space between my audience and me. I see from within how it works, and from there can invite others inside, show them how and what I see, using the mutual embodied moment and imagination to bring the letter to life in our midst.

Silence Also Speaks

Communication and meaning also happen in the silences, and in the performer-interpreter's use of pause. After Rom 8:39 and the doxological "nothing can separate us from the love of Holy One in Wisdom Jesus our Liberator," I paused for several moments before saying, "And yes, I do ask, has Holy One rejected their people, Israel?" (track 12).

Paul has just made his joyful declaration regarding the love and grace of Holy One through Jesus. In this performance of the letter, Paul's three-chapter wrestle with the question of the place of Israel in relation to that grace was articulated in six verses and a poignant pause.

The pause did at least two things.

First, it acknowledged the missing material of Rom 9–11 by creating a space where it might have been.

Second, which has to do with what I, the performer, *did* with the pause, it conveyed the conflict within Paul that he himself conveys through Rom 9–11. As discussed, I had omitted these chapters because I felt their anti-Semitic history of consequences could not be adequately addressed, nor could the doubts of the audience be articulated, in any expression of those words alone.

But in that pause and the framing of the silence in place of Rom 9–11, as I reached a hand towards the side on which the Jews / Israel had been represented so far in the performance (the audience's right), I did give voice to Paul's question, and honored it. The silence acknowledged the history of reception, rather than removing that history altogether from this reception of the letter. I reached a hand, and I turned my gaze, as if Paul was looking at Israel, and I looked with love, concern, and some anguish; actually, in the moment I felt as one on the verge of tears. I represented Paul looking at Israel and then his audience, not knowing the answer to his question, but acknowledging that he *had* asked the question. Proceeding from there to the doxology, the only answer given in this interpretation is awe at the mystery of Holy One's generous embrace of all.[121]

---

121. This embrace of all is, as we have seen, a key concern of Paul's letter to the Romans.

Not only did my silence "give voice" to Paul's anguish, but it also acknowledged the traumatic consequences of interpretations of these chapters through history. My voice expressed Paul's complex emotions, his love, his compassion, for Israel; and it expressed my own love and respect for our Jewish brothers and sisters today. Inhabiting the letter, I participated in Paul's love; interpreting the letter through emotion, through that love, I understood Paul's purpose in writing to Rome.[122]

Disappointment and Compassion: When Embrace Is not Offered

Embodied performance is the inhabiting of a composition that is held by my community and by me to be sacred, to have held meaning for generations before us. When I bring these words to life in the midst of community, I do so expecting to encounter the Sacred, and invite my audiences to encounter the Sacred in that moment.[123]

So when Paul is disappointed with the people's turning away from the Way of Holy One ("why do you pass judgment on your brother or sister," 14:10; "we must accommodate our neighbor, not ourselves," 15:1–2), and I spoke those words amidst my fellow people of Christian spirituality, I felt his disappointment as my own. I understood that we, too, have experienced the captivity that is the grip of Tyrant (5:12; 6:6; 7:23), evil lying close at hand (7:23), pulling us from the good for which we yearn (7:19). We, too, have judged our neighbors (14:3–4, 10), put stumbling blocks in their way (14:13, 21), and not made space for them to flourish (12:3–18; 13:8; 14:19).

In the discussion of weak and strong through Rom 14–15, those who abstain and those who eat anything, I particularly felt this disappointment; even more, I felt compassion. As I spoke, I brought my hands closer together, while still representing the two broad groups of these divisions on either side of me as I had in earlier discourses.[124] On audience right, I associated "those who abstain" with Jews / the circumcised / Torah observers, and on audience left, "those who eat anything" with Gentiles / the uncircumcised

---

122. As Boomershine notes concerning the embodiment of characters in performance, so I discovered, that inhabiting his words, I could not hold Paul at a distance for objective critique. See Chapter 2, and Boomershine, "Audience Address," 119.

123. Scripture may be understood as the self-performance of Holy One; the proclamation of preacher or performer-interpreter "an extension of the Word that continues to speak and perform in our world" (Lee, *Preaching*, 36).

124. At 3:29, for example (track 14) as I spoke, "are they [Holy One] not the Holy One of Gentiles also? Yes! of Gentiles also," I moved my hands together from left side and right, raised just below shoulder height, bringing both groups to equal standing in the welcome of Holy One, on which their welcome of each other is founded.

/ non-Torah observers (track 13). I brought them closer together than the earlier gestures, because I could see these groups as being within the one community, rather than the distinctly separate Jews and Gentiles in the more historical story to which the first part of the letter refers. I was aware through this embodiment that those who eat or abstain were not necessarily determined by ethnicity.[125]

Oestreich imagines the original performer of the letter employing gestures in a manner somewhat akin to the gestures I adopted.[126] He notes as a feature of oral performance the parallelism in Rom 14, which he sees as signifying Paul's desire to "treat both sides in the same manner."[127] It is the responsibility of the "strong" to care for the "weak"; it is not Paul's aim, nor is it the task of the community, to denigrate a faithful minority who have doubts about the practices of the majority.[128] This resonates with the compassion I felt.

The disappointment I felt was also shaped by the context of my audience. In the discussion of food practices, I thought of the treatment of vegetarians and vegans; in my experience of church, those who have abstained from meat have both been denigrated by, or themselves been disdainful of, "meat eaters." Although awareness of various food-related health circumstances is growing, along with acceptance and even generous hospitality in many places, I wondered, do *we* define the realm of Holy One on the basis of "food and drink" rather than "joy and peace" (14:17)? I also thought of the judgment from both sides over welcome of those identifying as LGBTIQ today. I participated in Paul's disappointment and compassion, both for those who have been poorly treated through judgment and exclusion, and for those who feel under attack for their traditional or conservative views.

In 14:7-9, where Oestreich sees Paul as now addressing all, leading them from their differences to what they have in common, I saw my audience, and addressed them as one group, rather than identifying discrete sub-groups. The potential lines of difference they would experience in their own communities were not described in the particular words I spoke; but

---

125. Some Gentile believers were following Jewish practice, as boundaries between Jewish and Gentile Christian groups remained fluid for some time: Ehrensperger, *That We May Be Mutually Encouraged*, 182. Also, Park, *Either Jew or Gentile*, 2.

126. Oestreich, *Performance Criticism of the Pauline Letters*, 164. I disagree, however, with his conclusion that this would not have been Phoebe (73).

127. Oestreich, *Performance Criticism of the Pauline Letters*, 164. Further, Paul uses what may appear to be deprecatory terms at a point in the discussion "when he wants to elevate the status of people": Oestreich, *Performance Criticism of the Pauline Letters*, 159.

128. Oestreich, *Performance Criticism of the Pauline Letters*, 159, 60.

through emotional connection, they would make associations with their lived experience (as I had).

This is a helpful contrast of the outsider and insider approaches to performance analysis I discussed in Chapters 2 and 3. Oestreich (in an outsider approach) seeks to construct a probable performance scenario for the first century in Rome; he looks back through time to a context specified in this letter written for those audiences. He imagines that "the presenter would have continually intensified the volume and expression in his voice"; and that, supported by the performer's gestures, the "parallel lines give the words a pulsating rhythm, which alternates between two extremes: life and death."[129] In my Performance Interpretation (an insider approach), I modulated the rhythm, for example speaking slightly faster at 14:8c, and slowing for 8d to underline those words. Oestreich, too, has the performer arrive at an "underlining [of] the concluding words,"[130] but Oestreich and I emphasize different "conclusions." For me the strong point from these verses was less the pulsating extremes of life and death observed by Oestreich, and more that *we are* the Liberator's" (14:8d)—we, all who have chosen to follow Jesus, embraced regardless of ethnicity or religious practice.

Open to Others: Joyful Exhortation to Embrace the Neighbor

In the performance of the doxological moments in the letter (track 15) I instinctively assumed an elevated posture—my back straightened, my head lifted, eyes opened wider, and I often stood on my toes. The expression in my voice was light and bright, and I beamed. I *felt* joy, love, and gratitude. In such emotions it is particularly evident that Performance Interpretation is confessional for the Christian performer-interpreter.[131] The Christian performer-interpreter, like the preacher, performs in order to model the performance to which God, through Scripture, calls God's people.[132] The theological reflection carried out in performance is the enactment of Scripture.

I employed this elevated posture at, for example, 1:7, which I spoke with a benedictory tone, as when I preside as a minister. Romans 6:23 offers a further example of the elevated tone, where Paul describes the effect

---

129. Oestreich, *Performance Criticism of the Pauline Letters*, 174–75.

130. Oestreich, *Performance Criticism of the Pauline Letters*, 175.

131. These compositions are designed for transformation, and perhaps more than any other way of engaging with them, in embodied performance there is no distancing yourself from the impact of the composition.

132. Lee, *Preaching*, 117.

of Jesus' life, death and resurrection as leading to welcome into holiness (justification) and life for all (*life,* spoken with a particular emphasis and elevation). Romans 15:5–6 also evoked the same posture, in a prayerful hope for corporate love and honor (glorification) of Holy One.

Even more, speaking 8:38–9 I was on my toes.[133] With a big smile and open arms, I sought to catch audience members up in the joy of life with Jesus, Wisdom, Holy One. This significant elevation in posture and emotion of joy demonstrates why the pause that follows, discussed above, was so important. Pausing provided the contrast between this joyful affirmation of salvation in Holy One for all, and Paul's doubts and concerns for whether Israel is in fact included. Even more, perhaps, evoking his desire that Israel, his people, will not be excluded from this joy and life with Holy One.

SUMMARY

The Critical Reflection so far has identified discrete ways in which audience, body, and emotion have shaped interpretation of the letter in performance. In particular we have noted the theme of Holy One's welcome for all, Jew and Gentile, from which the Jesus-community is to offer to one another a mutual embrace. Next, the discussion of Rom 16 notes the way in which the final chapter of the letter in performance is a call to *enact* this mutual embrace. This discussion presents an alternative form for the Critical Reflection element of an Embodied Performance Analysis more akin to verse-by-verse commentary.

MUTUAL EMBRACE: CLIMAX, IMPACT, AND MEANING FOR TODAY

The letter in performance opened with Paul's own commitment to a relationship of mutual encouragement with the churches of Rome in 1:12. From there, the letter developed from expounding the implications of Holy One's welcome for all, through "our" welcome of each other in our diversity. It culminated in Rom 16 with profound meaning and impact for audience and performer alike, in the practical, repeated request for actual, enacted embrace.

---

133. Track 12, https://sarahagnew.com.au/embodied-performance/, which also includes the doxology of 11:32–36.

Phoebe: Commended[134]

From the performance at Uniting College, which told Phoebe's story, one audience member saw "Phoebe as an embodiment of Paul's meaning." This is how I had come to understand her, as I inhabited the letter for performance.

Phoebe's introduction, when spoken within the context of the letter as a whole, shows her to be an influential leader in the church in a relationship of mutuality with Paul. Phoebe is Paul's superior, socially, which makes him dependent on her.[135] In turn, Paul entrusts Phoebe to perform "a specific function as a transmitter of a letter, which included the role of transmitter of the message itself."[136] Paul presents Phoebe with commendation—with honor—as if to say, here is one who does embrace others (sister), welcome others (servant), and love others (benefactor) with openness and generosity.[137] In Phoebe we see exemplified Ehrensperger's observation that "in a local ἐκκλησία [ekklesia] or as itinerant συνεργοί [sunergoi]," women were "entrusted with special tasks within the movement"; *were* leaders.[138]

Our Sister Phoebe

Introducing Phoebe as "our sister," ἀδελφὴν ἡμῶν (*adelphen hemon*), Paul affirms her place within the broad Christian community. This is an identity marker, a claiming of Phoebe as a person within this people of Holy One.[139] "The use of the sibling metaphor throughout the letters in addressing the members of the ἐκκλησία [ekklesia] indicates that Paul and the co-senders stressed from the very beginning that they were all bound together in a relationship which is or should be characterized by mutual responsibility and solidarity."[140]

---

134. Tracks 16 and 17.

135. Ehrensperger, *Paul and the Dynamics of Power*, 54. She is "described as a great supporter of Paul" (52).

136. Ehrensperger, *Paul and the Dynamics of Power*, 54. The latter is not a universally accepted position: Oestreich, for example, does not believe Phoebe would have read the letter to the church in Rome: *Performance Criticism of the Pauline Letters*, 73.

137. Robert Jewett also sees Phoebe's introduction as indicative of her high importance, albeit for a different purpose (as patroness of the Spanish mission): Jewett, "Paul, Phoebe, and the Spanish Mission," 148.

138. Ehrensperger, *Paul and the Dynamics of Power*, 55.

139. Ehrensperger, *Paul and the Dynamics of Power*, 60. *ekklesia* = assembly; *sunergoi* = fellow workers.

140. Ehrensperger, *Paul and the Dynamics of Power*, 60.

In the recommendation of a letter bearer, it was "customary, as we can see in the Christian papyri and here, to call the bearer a brother or sister, making clear that the person should be received as a fellow believer."[141] The aims of the transformation in their baptism is to become equal, siblings together.[142] As I discuss below, kinship language will be employed throughout the invitations to embrace. This again established Phoebe in my embodied understanding as the example kinsperson, trusted, generous in support and service, in whatever differences she may have from other kinsfolk.

"Deacon"?

Thurston sees Phoebe as a "pastoral assistant" to Paul,[143] but Collins claims that the broader Hellenistic use and understanding of διάκονον (*diakonon*) as "messenger" provides a better context in which New Testament usage of the word can be understood.[144] Garroway argues for the description of Christ as διάκονον in Rom 15:8 to be as an *agent* (rather than servant) of circumcision, one who offers it to all,[145] a reading that receives support in BDAG.[146] In this way, followers of Christ described as διάκονον may be *agents* of the gospel.[147] Such "agency" may be understood as being carried out through acts of service described by the διάκονον word group, as seen for example in the story of Stephen (Acts 1:1–6).[148] I chose "servant" rather than "messenger" or "agent," as the context of her service alongside being "προστάτις (*prostatis*) to many" suggests that in self-giving to others Phoebe indeed has resources from which to give.[149]

The "other-regard" (or mutuality) central to Paul's letter to Rome is a Christ-inspired way of engaging in relationships, with particular emphasis on support of the vulnerable (as noted in discussion Rom 14). "Self-sacrifice is commendable in situations where human relations are distorted, and . . .

---

141. Witherington, *Paul's Letter to the Romans*, 382.

142. Ehrensperger, *Paul and the Dynamics of Power*, 62.

143. Thurston, *Women in the New Testament*, 54; Collins, "'Envoys' in 2 Cor 11:23," 93.

144. BDAG, 230–31. See also "'Envoys' in 2 Cor," 93, 96.

145. Garroway, "Circumcision of Christ," 304; BDAG, 230. So, too, Osiek: "Diakonos and Prostatis," 364.

146. BDAG, 230.

147. Garroway, "Circumcision of Christ," 303.

148. In the story of Stephen we might also find indications that the role of serving does not refer to material service only, as Stephen clearly has a spiritual serving role as well as "serving tables": Hiebert, "Behind the Word 'Deacon,'" 155.

149. Witherington, *Paul's Letter to the Romans*, 383.

the aim of such action is to restore or create a form of equitable solidarity within which such self-sacrifice will no longer be required."[150]

Further, I chose to say "servant" rather than "deacon" because it is unlikely the latter term was used in an official specified ministry, which might be an association made by my audience, familiar with such a role in their traditions.[151] Note, however, that "the fact that Phoebe is a 'deacon' (not a 'deaconess'. . .) surely means that she serves in some significant leadership role in the congregation at Cenchreae."[152]

Benefactor to Many, Including Me

This designation as προστάτις (*prostatis*) is the most problematic of the descriptors Paul uses for Phoebe. Unique in the New Testament, and comparatively rare beyond it,[153] προστάτις is still much debated.

BDAG suggests for προστάτις and προστάτης (*prostates*) that the gender of the subject actually changes the meaning of the word.[154] προστάτις is specifically translated as "a *woman* in a supportive role, patron, benefactor," while προστάτης is "one who looks out for the interests of others, defender, guardian, benefactor."[155] But Paul models significant affirmation for women in Rom 16; moreover, it is only through the words of Paul, her ministry partner, that we know Phoebe. Indeed, it is this partnership and the community within which their ministry is exercised, to which Phoebe's introduction points. This relationship, as much as Phoebe herself, may be seen as an example of the goal for which Paul argues throughout the letter.[156] For example, in the phrase, "including me," we see from Paul his willingness to be the recipient of the ministry of others, regardless of gender.[157]

Phoebe is the only person he describes as προστάτις;[158] she is the person with whom he trusts the letter and its presentation to the community, and thus to represent him. A significant proportion of the others he names are

---

150. Horrell, *Solidarity and Difference* 245.
151. Reid, *Wisdom's Feast*, 79–80 (although Reid still translates as "deacon").
152. Gaventa, "Romans," 410.
153. Garrison, "Phoebe," 70; Mathew, "Women in the Greetings," 120.
154. MacGillivray notes the shift away from such interpretations: "Romans 16:2," 184.
155. BDAG, 885.
156. For the flow of the argument through to Rom 16, see, for example, Witherington, *Paul's Letter to the Romans*, 376.
157. Ehrensperger, *Paul and the Dynamics of Power*, 54, 55.
158. The word occurs nowhere else in the extant letters, or the wider NT: Mathew, "Women in the Greetings," 120.

women, and he affirms their leadership and service without reservation.¹⁵⁹ The mutuality modelled in his relationship with Phoebe in particular is one that, as in his now famous words from Galatians (3:28), does not see gender as a dividing line for full participation as members of the ecclesial body.¹⁶⁰ The picture of Phoebe thus emerges as one of acknowledged and trusted minister to the community, and to individuals within the community.

But how would I best translate this term? How was I to imagine the woman Paul commends? This would shape my expression, tone, and gestures as I introduced her to my audience.¹⁶¹

A translation as "helper" may give the impression of subservience or lowliness, "mere" assistance to the "real" minister, Paul.¹⁶² However, attempts to recover the autonomy, status, or authority of Phoebe's role may claim *too much*, when scholars argue for a translation of προστάτις as the presider or president of the congregation.¹⁶³ Carolyn Osiek suggests that such liturgical presiding, although not entirely ruled out, is not the most likely meaning.¹⁶⁴ She argues, instead, for Phoebe as patron or benefactor, drawing on extensive evidence for women in patronage roles at the time.¹⁶⁵ It is helpful to remember, however, the distinction between "mutuality" and "reciprocity" described in Chapter 1, and that the relationships encouraged in Paul's letters are counter-cultural in their other-regard.

After considering the options for its meaning, and the socio-cultural context of benefaction and patronage, I have retained the NRSV's "benefactor" as a term that as accurately as possible reflects in contemporary English what I understand her role to have likely been.¹⁶⁶ Filling in the gaps,¹⁶⁷ I imagined Phoebe the προστάτις as one of significant means, who shared

---

159. Ehrensperger, *Paul and the Dynamics of Power*, 55.

160. Loveday Alexander presents evidence from the letters of this ideal in practice; although it did, over time, give way to the practice in broader society of a hierarchy of genders (Alexander, "Women as Leaders").

161. See, further, Mathew, "Women in the Greetings," 121 (also Appendix B).

162. Ng, "Phoebe as Prostatis," 4.

163. Ng, "Phoebe as Prostatis," 4.

164. Osiek, "Diakonis and Prostatis," 364.

165. Osiek, "Diakonis and Prostatis," 365. Also MacGillivray, "Romans 16:2," 199.

166. Translating as benefactor maintains "the correct implications that Phoebe's help, or assistance, was significant, while also avoiding any unhelpful connotations of servitude" (MacGillivray, "Romans 16:2," 199).

167. In prompting an audience to recognize such gaps, in finding them and filling them intuitively with the body and emotions, a performer provides an invaluable input for the interpretive conversation. Following Joynes, "Visualizing Salome's Dance," 162. Also, Gaventa, "Romans." See also "Phoebe's story" in track 24.

alher wealth with others: this may have been through hospitality in her home, advocacy, money, food or other resources, or her time.[168]

In my Performance Interpretation, then, I introduced Phoebe as our sister, servant to the church in Cenchreae, a benefactor to many including Paul himself. I did so employing an elevated posture that holds her before the community as a representative not only of Paul, but also of the kind of Christian Paul has encouraged the first recipients to be, and through this performance reception, encourages these twenty-first-century recipients to be.

Mutual Embrace

ἀσπάζομαι:[169] Gesture, Audience, and Translation

Throughout Rom 16, as Paul exhorts the community repeatedly to ἀσπάσασθε (*aspasasthe*; NRSV, "greet") various members, I employed an abbreviated form of the gesture of mutual love and welcome I had employed throughout the letter in performance (track 18). This gesture both highlighted for me in rehearsal the recurring theme of mutual embrace, and linked the theme visually for the audience in performance. Paul signals from the beginning that this is a direction towards which his argument will move, though for much of the first half it remains implied. It is much more apparent in the later chapters, where we see the gesture and theme of mutuality in 12:5, 10 and 16, with that chapter's strong affirmation of the dignity and value of all within the community. We see it again at 13:8–9, 14:19, and 16:16a.

As noted, beginning with "our sister" Phoebe there is much language of love and kinship throughout Rom 16, and I have mentioned the function of kinship language as an identity marker. My body's movement in response here suggested to me that the welcome and embrace to offer, that will be "fitting for the devoted" (16:1), is the welcome and embrace one offers to family—like a big warm hug, or a gentle but intimate cupping of the face of a beloved sister or brother.

For this "welcome" he encourages throughout the "greetings" of 16:3–16, 21–24, Paul employs the language of ἀσπάζομαι. For Witherington this term "literally means to wrap one's arms around and embrace someone, and when coupled with the command to offer the holy kiss as well (v. 16),

---

168. MacGillivray, "Romans 16:2," 197: observing the link with παραστῆτε (*parastete*), the help Paul requests for Phoebe; see also Alexander, "Women as Leaders," 17.

169. *aspazomai*.

it amounts to a command to treat those named as family, to welcome them into one's own home and circle."[170]

Baptism into the one body and one Spirit is a baptism into family. It is a transformation of relationships from the social stratification of Greco-Roman culture to mutuality and other-regard that sees one's wellbeing as entwined in the wellbeing of another.[171] It is a reaching for, a drawing together—an embrace.

In my earliest performance for the project, of Rom 16,[172] I felt that "greet" in the NRSV was not expressing the meaning I had discerned. Even with (or perhaps by way of) this gesture demonstrating a reaching towards those to be "greeted," I felt the language needed to be more dynamic.[173] As noted, this letter is woven through with the theme of mutuality, and the repeated invitation in Rom 16 felt to me to be a culmination of that message "to welcome one another in love, as Christ has welcomed you" (15:7). This welcome seemed to be concerned with making space for each other's differences, accommodating the neighbor (15:2). So I experimented with possible translations for ἀσπάσασθε, and settled on "embrace."[174] Moreover, it felt like a joyful embrace; a celebration of the various gifts each member brings into a vital, dynamic, and healthy community.

In this way, we can see how embodied interpretation, with body, emotion, and audience, influences translation choices. The process was to observe the intuitive response (here, the word in conjunction with the gesture), note the meaning or question thereby suggested (is this what "I" / Paul means?), return to scholarship (here, engaging in translation work), and consider the whole letter and the theme of mutual embrace. This process led to an "aha" moment: I heard for my audience today Paul encouraging followers of Christ to embrace one another, physically, emotionally, relationally—in other words, as and with one's whole being.

---

170. Witherington, *Paul's Letter to the Romans*, 380.

171. A transformation that sees mutuality even in asymmetrical relationships, or relationships in which power oscillates, so that what power is exercised is so to "render itself obsolete": Ehrensperger, *Paul and the Dynamics of Power*, 61–62.

172. Church Service Society Study Day, Paisley, September 2015.

173. In the *Oxford Dictionary*, "greet" is "To give a polite word of recognition or sign of welcome when meeting (someone)." It is the "polite" element of the contemporary meaning that felt inadequate.

174. BDAG defines ἀσπάζομαι (*aspazomai*) as "to engage in hospitable recognition of another," and offers translations of "greet, welcome": 144. For Lampe, options include the formulaic "welcome readily" or "greet" of letters; "receive with joy" or "embrace" teaching or virtues; and "embrace" or "kiss" in a liturgical setting: *Patristic Greek Lexicon*, 245–46.

"Embrace" is within the range of meanings for the Greek here, although the meaning I found differed from the sense of embracing a teaching or virtue, or the kiss of peace as part of religious liturgy.[175] The more deeply I embodied the letter, the more I understood actual physical embrace of estranged brothers and sisters to be the message to receive from Rom 16, and thus of the whole letter. This may be the most significant new insight to emerge from this Performance Interpretation of Romans.

Joyful Embrace

Feeling and expressing joy at Rom 16 linked the embrace of these members with the joy of Holy One's welcome for all, experienced in the letter's earlier doxological moments of joy and gratitude already discussed. As audiences received it in these performances, Rom 16's repeated invitations to embrace were heard as an invitation to embody Paul's teaching—the Way of Jesus Wisdom—in our living, in our relationships with one another.[176] And it *is* a joyful invitation. I instinctively spoke "Embrace the beloved Epanaetus," or "Embrace Rufus's mother who has been a mother to me also," with a smile that I beamed around to the whole audience. As I embodied the letter to Rome, the "greetings" of Rom 16 became not a formality, but rather a fulfilment of the letter's very call.

Love and joy are among the strongest emotions to stir in an audience, if a *rhetor* wishes to evoke a change in behavior. Rhetoricians dive deep into the emotions of love, hate, grief, joy, anger, pity, "and so create *pathos* in the audience in order for the hearers to embrace the arguments not merely intellectually but affectively as well. When that happened the act of persuasion had achieved its aim of winning over the whole person or group—body and soul."[177]

My audiences did respond to the love and joy in Rom 16, and indeed the whole letter. Many spoke of their envisaging of the people named, or of calling to mind certain people in their own communities. They even stated that they understood the function of Rom 16 and found meaning in it for the first time. My experience of audiences when performing Rom 16, either on its own or as the culmination of the broader letter, was a palpable positive energy, resounding applause, broad smiles, and sighs of appreciation

---

175. Lampe, *Patristic Greek Lexicon*, 246.

176. This is the call Lee hears from theodramatic preaching or proclamation of the Word generally: the Bible is intended for enactment, the people for performance within God's Drama (Lee, *Preaching*, 114, 136).

177. Witherington, *New Testament Rhetoric*, 16.

that made me feel as though we had together been caught up in the embrace of Holy One and each other.

Love Makes Sense

Paul's love is for Holy One and for the people to whom he writes. I found my participation in this love through the internalizing of the letter helpful when I performed 16:17–20 (track 19), verses that have struck many interpreters as an interruption.[178] My Performance Interpretation provides a contrast with such readings, and their reasoning for viewing 16:17–20 as an interpolation. It did not occur to me in voicing these words that those accused in 16:17–20 are the "weak" (or uncertain) of Rom 14; the clarification that they are not is one Keck seems to think is necessary.[179] For me, Paul's call to embrace one another reminds him of those who would, as he says, "cause dissensions and offences" (16:17). In my imagination, he has to express again his concern for these followers of Christ that they would protect themselves and each other[180] from those who would do harm with their selfishness and deceit (16:18). Wright also views this interjection functioning "rhetorically like the sudden reminder that breaks into a family farewell scene," noting further that "it is clearly heartfelt; Paul knows that troublemakers will surface in any church."[181]

In performance I paused after 16:16. As I spoke 16:16—"all the churches of Jesus embrace you"—and my arms swept wide, it felt like an embrace, a holding of one community in the arms of another. Thus "holding" this audience in that embrace, simultaneously holding the Roman church in the embrace of "all the churches," I saw them, and I saw (with my own eyes and the eyes of Paul) the wolves coming for the sheep.[182]

Paul's embrace for the church here forms a parallel with the greeting to all the church in Rome at the opening (1:7), for I observed in this performance similar gestures of arms open wide (track 20). Romans 16 thus offered a closing bookend to Rom 1. A more apt metaphor might be Rom 1 and 16 as two arms holding the letter and holding its recipients in an embrace of mutual welcome. Rhetorically, Rom 16:17–20 may be understood

---

178. For example, Jewett, *Romans*, 986–96.

179. Keck, *Romans*, 377–8.

180. Keck, *Romans*, 376. For he has confidence of their ability *to* instruct one another (15:15).

181. Wright, "Romans," 765.

182. Wright also sees this imagery, and a parallel in Acts 20:29–31: Wright, "Romans," 764.

to function as the *peroratio* (conclusion) of Paul's rhetorical structure within the letter, as he "makes a final appeal to the deeper emotions to make sure the argument persuaded"[183] the churches in Rome of his care for their well-being as communities of Jesus-followers.

Into 16:17 I inserted "do": "My beloved, do keep an eye on . . . ," and internalized the language so that it became fluid. I understood Paul to be saying, "be careful," for he has such a parent-like concern for the churches of Jesus,[184] even the churches of Rome, which he himself did not birth. As Paul wrote, so too I spoke, with love as I looked at these people: my community, my audience, *my* beloved.

Mutuality of Paul with His Co-workers

I paused again after "crush Evil One under your feet," and my use of expression and pause connected 16:20b with 21–23 (tracks 21 and 22). "The grace of our Liberator Jesus Wisdom be with you" felt like a prelude for the messages of embrace from Paul's co-workers, and so, their embraces (though *in absentia*) became an embodiment of the grace of Jesus. As with the earlier imperatives to embrace, my chief emotions were joy and love. I felt as though I was speaking my embrace for my audience, as much as I was expressing the embraces of these people of Holy One from so long ago.

I took a step forward and to my right as I spoke Tertius' message of embrace.[185] The only differentiation I sought to make here was in voice: I spoke with Tertius' voice from a position I had not used for Paul's own or rhetorical voices. I observed audience responses (smiles, nodding heads) that indicated their intuitive understanding that Tertius "spoke" for himself. By giving Tertius a message in his own voice, I felt Paul's embodiment of the mutuality he has encouraged in the letter. This collegiality compliments his desire for mutuality in 1:12; Paul has in this letter asked nothing of the church that he himself did not strive to accomplish.[186] Although Ehrens-

---

183. Witherington, *New Testament Rhetoric*, 16.

184. He has become a father to Onesimus (Phlm 10); he describes the care he and his co-workers have for the Thessalonians as "like a nurse tenderly caring for her own children: (1 Thess 2:7); and in Galatians, he is "in the pain of childbirth" for his "little children" in 4:19. Ehrensperger reminds us that this is not common language for Paul, is often metaphorical, and seems to be used with care in order to maintain the distinction of God as father: Ehrensperger, *Paul and the Dynamics of Power*, 126–28.

185. I made it an angled step, as I did not interpret Tertius as aligned with the Gentile or non-Torah observers who were directly on my right throughout.

186. This resonates with Martin's affirmation of the counter-cultural nature of Paul's mutuality when Stoics, for example, pursued the goal of self-sufficiency: Martin, *Sex*

perger argues for Romans as unique, with no specifically named co-sender as in his other letters,[187] there was still for me a sense of the letter being sent from a collective, especially when "greet" became "embrace."[188] Ehrensperger challenges the portrayal of Paul as "an independent hero," and my embodied understanding affirms her observation "that Paul does not claim to address the recipients [of his letters] as a lonely voice."[189] In Ehrensperger's estimation the letters are part of the ongoing relationships between groups, rather than individuals.[190] Furthermore, Rom 16 contains not only an invitation to the people of the Roman churches to embrace one another as individuals or even as groups, across their differences, it contains a warm embrace of the Roman churches by their kin, the churches in Cenchreae/Corinth. My imagination saw a broader picture of the body of Jesus Wisdom as not only a local church, but as the broader church, each congregation a member of the body, loved and needed for the body's wholeness and health.

Doxology: Genuine Praise

In Rom 16:25–27 I employed again the elevated tone and posture for another doxological moment, the final ascription of glory to Holy One for this letter (track 23). Every time I performed these verses, the words elicited from me genuine praise, and my gaze turned "heavenward." I sensed the audience following that gaze, and, I hoped, entering into that moment of praise themselves. Again we see the confessional nature of a Performed Interpretation; and see it as authentic to the material being received and interpreted, and to the role of the Bible in the receiving and interpreting community.

Implications from Romans 16 for the Whole

I have noted the gestural bookends—or embrace—formed by Rom 16 with Rom 1. This Performance Interpretation treated and presented Rom 16 as integral to the whole, in contrast to text-bound readings that separate it, perhaps even claiming it for an entirely different audience.[191] Embodying

---

and the Single Savior, 71, 74.

187. Ehrensperger, *Paul and the Dynamics of Power*, 35.

188. On observing in the letters the collective thinking of Paul with co-workers, see, for example, Byrskog, "Co-Senders, Co-Authors," 249.

189. Ehrensperger, *Paul and the Dynamics of Power*, 35.

190. Ehrensperger, *Paul and the Dynamics of Power*, 56.

191. Whelan, "Amici Pauli."

the letter, gestures indicated a movement from the exclusiveness to inclusiveness of Holy One's welcome into holiness; audience and addressees were invited into relationships of mutual embrace across difference; love unified Paul's concern and his joy, his warnings and his affirmations. Integrating rhetorical interpretation into this Analysis revealed several affirmations for the integrity of Rom 16 with the whole, from its role in framing the letter with Rom 1, to its function with Rom 12–15 as the particular implications for Rome of the earlier discussion of Holy One's open invitation.[192]

The rhetorical structure of the letter in performance was comprised of two parts, Rom 1–8 (with 11:1–2, 33–36) and 12–16. I understood Paul's concerns in part one to be the unity of the whole church and the transformation of baptized persons. The concern for unity was evident in the language of Jew *and also* Greek (1:16; 2:9, 10; 3:9, 29; 4:24; 9:24), "all" (1:7; 3:9, 30; 4:11; 5:18; 8:14, 28; 10:12; 11:32), "no partiality" (2:11), "no distinction" (3:22; 10:12), "participation through faith" (4:16; 10:4), and the action of Holy One, Spirit, and Wisdom (8:15, 16, 17, 35–39; 11:29, 32). Transformation was a particular theme in Rom 8, but featured throughout part one: Holy One's kindness leads to repentance (2:4); appropriate boasting in Holy One brings about endurance, character, and hope (5:1–5); baptism leads to life (6:4, 8, 11; 7:4); and living according to the Spirit is living fullness of life (8:1–13).

Transformation persists through the particular implications of part two: 12:2 "be transformed"; 13:11 "wake from sleep"; 14:7–8, living and dying with Wisdom; and in 15:3, 5 and 7, with Wisdom as the example for relationships of harmony and welcome. The rhetorical movement of the letter proceeded from the foundational unity of all who believe in Wisdom, and the transformation that comes through baptism into Wisdom, through Rom 15 and the Wisdom-example for relationships of mutual welcome and responsibility, to Rom 16 and the embodiment of that mutual welcome from those with the power or strength in the community, towards the vulnerable minority.

If ἀσπάσασθε (*aspasasthe*) means "hospitable recognition of one another"[193] through "greeting" or "embrace," then mutuality is implied. As such, it embodies the mutuality that is evident in the language of unity and transformed relationships of love for one another. This term, as imperative and as present active, occurs twenty-one times in Rom 16. Presupposing,

---

192. For example, the rhetorical connection between the *exordium* (introduction) of Rom 1:1–15 and the *peroratio* (conclusion) of 15:14—16:23: Wuellner, "Paul's Rhetoric of Argumentation," 136.

193. BDAG, 144.

and presupposed by[194] the Wisdom-examples of Rom 15 (vv. 3, 5 and 7) and Paul's own hopes for mutual care ("I might be refreshed in your company," 15:32), Rom 16 offered to hearers an invitation to embody the mutuality at the letter's core. It thus became the emotive climax of the letter as a whole, Paul going "all out to create a new social situation" within the Christian community.[195]

The rhetorical effect of the so-called "greetings" in Rom 16, which became clear in performance, was to lead the audience to conclude that welcome and gratitude is due to these Christians who are in Rome, Paul (and his emissary Phoebe) are not entirely strangers, and the Roman church is part of a larger entity.[196] For Paul does not simply send his greetings to these people, he asks the recipients of the letter to embrace them, with the repeated use of the second person infinitive ἀσπάσασθε.[197] In this repeated call to embrace each other, Rom 16 in performance built on the theme of mutuality throughout the letter and achieved the climactic function of exhorting the community's holistic embodiment of unity in diversity:[198] you are kin, you are one, as brothers and sisters in Wisdom.[199]

FINDING MEANING ANEW, PERFORMING ROMANS

Embodied Performance of Romans illuminated the nature of Paul's encouragement of relationships of mutual encouragement to be not simply idealistic, but profoundly enacted. In performance, interpreter and audience participated together in this mutuality, giving and receiving with each other in a moment of embodied presence, imagination, and meaning-making. Through the performance, interpreter and audience participated in the emotional ebb and flow of the rhetoric, the emotional tapestry of Paul's commitment to Holy One and the gospel of Jesus, and his commitment to the church of Jesus. In the live embodied encounter with this letter, performer and audience encountered Paul, Phoebe, their friends, and the

---

194. Lampe, "Roman Christians," 217.
195. Witherington, *Paul's Letter to the Romans*, 380.
196. Witherington, *Paul's Letter to the Romans*, 381.
197. Kennedy, *New Testament Interpretation*, 156.
198. Following on from passages such as 12:4–5 and the one body with many members, 12:9–13 and the list of ways in which to build up the community as a whole, echoing Jesus' teaching that love fulfils Torah in Rom 13 (Witherington, *Paul's Letter to the Romans*, 376). Also visible in the language of "Jews *and also* Gentiles" in part one (1:16; 2:9, 10; 3:9, 29; 9:24) and "(loving) *one another*" in part two (12:16; 13:8; 14:5; 15:5, 7, 14; 16:16).
199. Wright, "Romans," 710–11, 24–25.

churches of Rome, as we also encountered each other, as the "other" with whom we experience mutual embrace.

Embodied Performance Analysis is profound in its affirmation of the potential of relational encounter, mutual embodiment and imagination, and emotional, intuitive participation, for making meaning of biblical compositions. It is unapologetically, and necessarily, confessional. Performance Interpretation and Critical Reflection together illuminate mutual embrace as a necessary feature of the churches of Jesus today as it was in the first century. Received in performance Romans made meaning of the lived experience of audiences today, and in light of their experience, Romans in performance also helped an audience today to make meaning of the lived experiences of the original recipients.

Interpreting Romans through the lens of a twenty-first-century Australian audience, predominantly comprised of Uniting Church members of congregations I know well, I discovered new meaning through the language of Holy One and holiness, and Tyrant and participation in tyranny. Participation itself as a feature of EPA helped to highlight the nature of "righteousness" and "justification" as participation in the holiness of Holy One. The audience highlighted the need for new metaphors for church and for our relationship with Holy One; but this may be a task for a different mode of Performance Interpretation. Reimagined scripts and ensemble drama, such as we observed in the approach of Richard Swanson and the Provoking the Gospel project (Chapter 3), or digital storytelling (as in the example in track 3), might be such modes of reception that could fruitfully combine with Embodied Performance Critical Reflection employing body, emotion, and audience as tools for articulating the performed interpretation. Further, the particular mode of Performance Interpretation employed in this test case may yet have the capacity for mediating difficult passages, passages of ancient cultural specificity, or a problematic history of interpretation. The attempt to do this with Rom 1:26–27 was inconclusive in its success in offering a helpful interpretation for an audience today. The use of pause, gesture, and abridgement was more successful in framing a silence that still gave voice to the omitted complex discussion of Israel in Rom 9–11 and its problematic history of interpretation.

Although the EPA focuses on an interpretation for reception by an audience today, my audiences and I did find that the first century recipients of the letter were present in the live performance moment. Through our imagining the church in Rome, I gained insight into the original context of the letter. Complexities of diversity that ran not only along ethnic lines of Jew and Gentile, but also along lines of practice for Jew and Gentile Torah observers, and Jews and Gentiles not practicing Torah observation, became apparent. My contemporary audience helped form an understanding of Holy One's work through Jesus as the liberation of creation from the grip of Tyrant, a process of making holy not only those in Israel, but all who choose to accept the invitation.

Interpreting Romans through the body, that thread of mutuality was held up in my hands in a repeated gesture of giving and receiving between one another. Taking steps within the performance space, I distinguished the voices that spoke along with Paul's, adding texture, representing community, and the mutuality Paul sought to encourage. Body and audience together shaped interpretation of the letter for today, deeming the dualistic body-versus-spirit rhetoric insufficient for the encouragement of human flourishing: a human whose body is acceptable as spiritual worship before Holy One.

Body and emotion combined to interpret through the voice, with faltering and emphasis, and just as much in silence. Interpreting Romans through emotion I found myself participating in the emotions of the letter and its author; seeing my audience through Paul's love, I also came to understand Paul's love for the Roman church. I felt his disappointment at the divisions in the community, and his compassion for the marginalized. Paul's compassion for the vulnerable made further impact on the encouragement of the mutual embrace of all. His joy at the generous embrace of Holy One became my joy, my gratitude, my praise. The Performance Interpretation is shown in this test case to be unavoidably and necessarily confessional, for the integrity of the composition, credibility of the performer-interpreter, and the trust of the audience in the mediator of biblical compositions as their spiritual inheritance.

Embodying the letter to the Romans, with its movement from separated Israel and Gentile nations, to unified Jesus-followers who are *all* the Liberator's *in* their differences, transformed by baptism into kin to embrace joyfully, I understood the *letter's* unity. I was aware of speaking this letter to Christians today, 2000 years on from the emergence of Jesus-following Jews and Gentiles within, on the fringes of, and eventually distinct from, Jews following the way of Moses. That meant I did not articulate Paul's question concerning the redemption of Israel, but instead allowed silence and the praise of Holy mystery to be comment on harmful implications of the question, and the only helpful answer the question really needed in this performance: it is for Holy One to determine.

I did not rewrite the letter for a new day, but did seek to allow this letter, our inheritance, to speak anew in our time, in part through omissions of content and adaptation of language. I provoked the letter and my audience with revised translations, to embrace the newness, the uniqueness of this letter in this particular performed interpretation. On reflection, I have determined that the audience would have been further assisted in their reception of the letter with some discussion following the performance. I may not use the more provocative translations of Wisdom or Tyrant in future; future audiences will determine my choices as this audience shaped this interpretation.

Embodying the letter to the Romans, an inherently mutual approach to interpretation within and between humans, between composition and receivers, between receivers and Holy One, did indeed further illuminate the centrality of mutuality as a concern for Paul in this letter. Also, the letter's affirmation of difference, diversity, wholeness, and the importance of mutual respect and responsibility describes the theological significance of an inherently mutual, embodied approach to interpretation. Welcome each other as Jesus welcomed you, Paul says (15:7): Jesus welcomes as one incarnate, through the mutual indwelling of Holy One with creation.

So it is that communities of faith welcome Holy One through the word incarnate, a mutual indwelling of composition and performer, mutual inhabitation of the performance space and the world of the composition by performer and audience, mutual encounter of Holy One and humans in the live embodied performance event. That event will provide the circumstances for interpretation, for making meaning of the Bible and our own experience. Those insights will enrich the study of biblical compositions with the fullness of human being, which is the purpose of those compositions, and is achieved through the mutual indwelling of an Embodied Performance Analysis.

7

A Story of Mutual Indwelling

THE POTENTIAL OF MUTUALITY

This has been a story of mutual indwelling, and in telling it, I have told of identifying and exploring unrealized potential. The potential I saw in Biblical Performance Criticism was to use performance *to* interpret biblical compositions. Some BPC scholars do acknowledge this potential. Some, in approaches approximating my own, have begun to describe the performance event, the movement of the performer's body, the emotions of performer and audience, and even the influence of particular audiences and their circumstances on the meaning discovered in the composition. I felt, however, that the fullness of human epistemology, the meaning-making processes of a physical, emotional, relational being, were not fully incorporated into a coherent performance interpretation methodology, and from my experience I suspected it could be. Observing my practice, building on the insights of biblical performance scholars, and learning from the breadth of scholarship into human epistemology, I have developed a new method for biblical interpretation that seeks to realize this potential of embodied performance to interpret biblical compositions. It is a method that embraces the fluidity and of-the-moment quality of live performance; it is a method that allows for confessional involvement of the interpreter. Within the method, an inherent mutuality between performer-interpreter and audience/reception community, and the incorporation of multiple methods of analysis, provide accountability for the overt involvement of the performer in the interpretation, and thus the subjectivity of this approach partners with objective reflection to present a rigorous and balanced method for biblical interpretation.

I also sought to more fully realize the potential of Paul's community ethic. Scholars have identified the mutuality of this community ethic, and begun to extricate Paul's letters from generations of interpretations both faithful and harmful. I, and others in my communities of faith in recent decades, have nevertheless still felt considerable resistance to Paul's letters, because of the potential for harm that has been demonstrated in some interpretations. Can we hear this letter without a condemnation of homosexuality? Can we receive this letter without anti-Semitic application of Paul's words? I sought to explore the potential of this letter in a new reception with a live, embodied community. The Embodied Performance Analysis did realize the potential for encouragement of mutuality and a diverse unity within the church, through gesture, movement, emotion, and the relationship between audience and performer. The Embodied Performance Analysis did respond to the history of consequences arising from this letter, and in reception that history was acknowledged, and the words of Paul heard anew.

Unrealized potential for performance interpretation of this letter yet remains, especially regarding the reception of Rom 1:26–27, and I have presented a further experiment in performance reception of this passage with a digital Performance Interpretation. There is also potential to be realized in the role of the audience in embodied performance interpretation, and the further application of Embodied Performance Analysis with the range of genres in the biblical corpus.

EXPLORING THE POTENTIAL OF ROMANS

The Performance Interpretation presented in the Analysis of Romans was given in Adelaide, with a core audience from Blackwood Uniting Church, who were joined by friends and strangers, members of other churches and denominations or none. In the Critical Reflection I noted the influence of this audience's context and story, of welcome for those identifying as LGBTIQ, and a history of interfaith conversations and relationships, on choices to leave silence where Paul's discussion wrestles with the place of Israel in Holy One's redeeming work (9–11), and to re-translate 1:26–27 seeking to liberate the letter from harmful anti-homosexual rhetoric. In this way, EPA overcame the letter's potential for harm, or at least acknowledged it and responded with a new interpretation in reception.

The audience tool interacted with the body and emotion tools in these interpretive decisions, as I noticed my own resistance as a person committed to affirming the dignity of all races, faiths, gender identities, and sexual preference. I have noted that in a performance during the preparation stage, the audience expressed their appreciation for the uncertainty evident in my voice at 1:26–27, seeing it, in this instance, as a measure of integrity. In my hesitation they found permission to question highly contextualized and sometimes inappropriately interpreted portions of the Bible as a faithful process of discerning meaning.

The body's movement, to take steps and allow variation in voice to illuminate the rhetorical effect of Paul's arguments, and gesture to highlight the central theme of mutuality, offered nuanced interpretation of the letter in performance. In the performance moment, the feedback I received from the audience by way of their physical nods of assent and understanding told me that in the steps I took to represent the different voices, my audience moved with me, and appeared to be helped in their understanding of the rhetorical movement of the discussion.

The emotional impact of the letter would appear to be a key element in this measure of success of the Performance Interpretation. It is difficult to describe the emotional atmosphere and energy in a room, but at the close of the Performance Interpretation, I felt a warmth that seemed to communicate appreciation and a feeling among the audience of being "uplifted."[1] My intuition on this point was affirmed by the responses from the audience, which included comments about feeling "loved," "welcomed," and "embraced." There were expressions of gratitude for the language choices, including the more provocative and experimental "Wisdom" and "Tyrant." Even from audience members who preferred more traditional language, I received comments acknowledging the effect I had sought, which was to provoke listeners to hear the letter as if for the first time, so as to discover new meaning in it for their time.

As discussed, interpreters such as Perry and Cousins have also noted the emotional impact of a performed interpretation, and the ways in which the audience for whom the performance is prepared shape the interpretation that is presented.[2] EPA seeks to harness the potential of such community interpretation by observing the interpretive decisions that are made

---

1. Even more so in workshop presentations of Rom 16 for discussion of emotion in storytelling in August 2016.

2. Perry, *Insights*; Cousins, "Pilgrim Theology."

for this particular performance, for this particular audience, and discussing those decisions in the context of the history of reception. A strength of this method is that it attends to a feature of reception that is often overlooked: that is, that every time the composition is received, it is interpreted. By attending to the particular audience, a performer-interpreter learns from the contextual influences on interpretation, and articulates those influences for richer, clearer contribution to the ongoing conversation that happens as the compositions continue to be encountered in various ways and contexts.[3] We noted in Chapter 4's discussion of the various ways humans "know" that particularity invites identification and the discerning of meaning for the receiver's own context.[4]

Love gave deeper meaning to Paul's disappointment, warnings, and compassion. Love invited me as performer and, through my embodiment of love the audience, to participate in the transforming work of love, and of the letter. Such participation and transformation are also at the heart of my translations of Divine names and the language of "righteousness" and "justification" into the word-group of "holiness." Possible meaning and impact of the letter in intent, its movement from division to unity with vital diversity, were thus in synergy with the theology of the letter in this performance.

Embodied Performance Analysis involves the whole person. The Performance Interpretation requires commitment, not only to a performance, and not to a character as in acting, but more—to the claims of the composition as a sacred work of the performer-interpreter's community of faith. EPA is for performer-interpreters who are members of the Christian community, for whom the Bible is the "Sacred Story." Doxological moments, such as those of Rom 8, 11, and 16, evoked exaggerated movement and elevated posture as if my heart was bursting through into the space between us.

I noted actor Aoife Duffin's observation that as a performer one must experience the emotions oneself, "because people check out if they think that you as a performer are not properly doing it."[5] In this, a performance event is similar to a preaching event, and the insights of homileticians proved insightful for articulating the experience and ethos of a performer-interpreter, noting the communication through the body of a preacher the depth (or otherwise) of their investment in the message they proclaim.[6] My

---

3. Seow, "Consequences of Scripture."

4. With scholars such as Bartow, "Performance Study," 221; and Joynes, "Visualizing Salome's Dance," 159. Also in Chapter 1, with such scholars as Wire, *Holy Lives*, 9; and May, "'A Body Knows,'" 347: "To claim my body as knower is to claim epistemological physicality and possibility."

5. Duffin, "Katherine: Interview with Rona Kelly."

6. McKenzie, "Intersection of *Actio Divina* and *Homo Performans*," 58. Storyteller

participation in the confessions of faith in the letter established my integrity and authority for my audience. Without such trust, an audience's reception of the work, and its meaning, may be inhibited.

To safeguard against a manipulative interpretation the Embodied Performance method integrates multiple interpretive approaches and broader scholarship into the preparation and reflection stages. As questions are raised by the inhabitation of and response to the composition, the method requires the performer-interpreter to check those questions and responses through historical, socio-critical, rhetorical and other methods, and in conversation with other scholars. The Embodied Performance approach is intrinsically particular to the performer-interpreter mediating the text.[7] It is also intrinsically mutual, integrating community perspective and scholarly insights into the development, delivery, and discussion of a faithful Performed Interpretation.

Embodied Performance Analysis involves the whole person *and, with,* the community. The community moderates the potential risks of imposing too much of one's self onto the composition, of making choices based on personal preference rather than the meaning of the author and the composition. That the Embodied Performance method involves an audience tool builds into this approach a way to further maintain integrity. The letter to the Romans and its theme of mutuality thus, in turn, helped to demonstrate the potential of performance *as* interpretation through reception in community. The audience require integrity in the performer as a person of faith and commitment in line with the message of the composition; if she cannot speak the words with commitment, she may do better not to speak them at all. Again, in such portions as Rom 9–11 and the articulation of a deliberate leaving of Israel outside the redemption in Christ for now, and its implicit assumption of the salvation through Christ as the only way into the heart of Holy One, I found that I, as mediator of the composition, was at odds with its message. For the smaller portion of 1:26–27, I found a way to, although still somewhat inadequately, express the broader argument of unhealthy priorities, idolizing human self and pleasure rather than worshipping Holy One, with a translation that pushed back against harmful applications of these verses. But for 9–11, I could not find a way to give voice to the argument and also to the questions my community and I might have with that first century pondering of a first century question. Paradoxically, I found on reflection that the silence itself seems to have, after all, allowed me to

---

Ray Buckley also provided insight into the role of a storyteller within a community of faith (*Dancing with Words*, 54–56).

7. The method thus embraces as a strength the reality of experience—that we are not neutral—rather than diminishing the value of introspection (Lee, *Preaching*, 157–58).

name Paul's question and acknowledge the distance and difficult history of consequences from these chapters, in the Performance Interpretation.

The Performance Interpretation of Romans was a presentation of the letter as it appears in the Bible; it was not converted into a conversation or dramatic presentation of the story behind the letter.[8] I did not rewrite the letter into a piece of rhetoric for today, but sought to explore the way the letter itself, as it is found in the Bible as the sacred writings of the Christian community, may be received in performance today.

In order to focus this study's examination on my practice as an interpreter through performance, we did not include conversation with the audience in the main Performance Interpretation event. However, although I did find in the Critical Reflection that silences and retranslations were effective in communicating meaning, I am convinced that conversation in some form does enhance a Performance Interpretation for both audience and performer-interpreter. Such direct engagement with the audience provides further insight and reflection for the performer-interpreter,[9] and, importantly, enables deeper meaning-making for the audience. For, as Cousins observed, audience experience of the composition in performance is less effective in enhancing "theological exegesis," and more in deepening emotional and imaginative engagement with it.[10] And as this study attests, emotion and imagination may themselves be understood as interpretive tools: therefore discussion following performance will help audience members to identify and articulate the understanding they have begun to discover through their embodied experience of the composition mediated through the performer.

Summary: Embodied Performance Analysis of Romans

Through gesture, and in particular a gesture that incorporated performance and audience into Paul's language and encouragement of mutual embrace, this analysis demonstrated the centrality of mutuality as a theme, and a purpose, of the letter to the Romans. The gestures that identified "Jews" and "Gentiles" as separate ethnic groups, became closer distinctions of Torah

---

8. However, in the preparation stage, I did experiment with such imaginative retelling for the Uniting College presentation.

9. Cousins, "Pilgrim Theology," 93. However, for Oestreich, as noted in Chapter 3, the emotional impact of the letter to the Romans in performance is understood to be the first century audience's understanding, interpretation, of their situation in light of the gospel and the scriptures of Israel: Oestreich, *Performance Criticism of the Pauline Letters*, 181.

10. Cousins, "Pilgrim Theology," 214.

and non-Torah observing groups within the one community. Embodiment thus interpreted the movement of the letter from division to a unity incorporating vital difference, in a profound demonstration of observations made from the outside of the letter looking in, by scholars such as Oestreich.[11]

I was surprised by the way that my omission of Rom 9–11 was not only protest at the anti-Semitic application of Paul's contextual question through history. This choice actually worked as interpretation, with the words I did speak from Rom 8 and 11 framing a silence that held emotions of love, confusion, concern, and hope.

With a new translation of Rom 1:26–27, made because I was committed to faithful reception of the letter for an audience today, my audience was invited through me to nuance their reception of the letter. My interpretive work was forced back beyond the history of consequences, to explore the original context, so as to hear these verses again for the first time. Perhaps this passage can only be received with question marks, with uncertainty, with the recognition that it is of its time. Perhaps, as for Rom 9–11, this passage may be most helpfully received in performance with silence. It would be insightful to explore this further in a performance that omits Rom 1:26–27 in order to discover what meaning might be conveyed through such silence.

The impact of Romans in performance also took me by surprise, somewhat, with its climax of mutual embrace. Romans 16 as the crux, the climax of the letter in reception, rather than a separate, form letter of "greeting" and introduction, emerged as a radical new interpretation of the letter through this Embodied Performance Analysis. This climax of "embrace" challenges claims of Paul's purpose in writing to Rome to introduce himself in order to gather financial support: if mutuality is the purpose, his desire in Rom 15 to be encouraged by their fellowship is far more important than their financial support. The mutual "embrace" encouraged in Rom 16 helps to integrate Rom 16 with the whole, as it was received in the live, embodied Performance Interpretation, and as it is received in the biblical canon. Such integrative consequences of performance interpretation mirror the integrative aims of Narrative Criticism of Gospels, which we have understood to be the beginning of the storyteller's BPC. The climax of the letter is the repeated call to "embrace," and if that call is heeded, the letter's potential, when realized, *is* the physical, emotional, relational embrace of members of the body of Christ in their differences, as Christ has welcomed them all.

---

11. Oestreich, *Performance Criticism of the Pauline Letters*, 152–89.

EMBODIED PERFORMANCE ANALYSIS: REALIZING POTENTIAL

Subjectivity and Mutuality as Strengths

Embodied Performance Analysis is inherently subjective. The risks of such subjectivity are balanced by the strengths of the method's inherent mutuality, so that this approach is subjective *and also* objective. As many "objective" approaches ignore the inherent subjectivity of any human interpretive endeavor, this method may offer a more complete approach to biblical interpretation. This approach *is* embodied, and so is cognition, as we observed in Chapter 4, where we also noted that much scholarship appears to ignore this fact and proceed on the false assumption of a disembodied higher cognition that dismisses and diminishes the physical, emotional, and relational interpretive work in which every human being engages. These interpretations are performed in *a* moment, and so are all interpretations *of their* time, rather than *for all* time.[12] Perhaps this is a method that, along with newer approaches to preaching and other developments in associated fields, will facilitate appreciation for our interpretations as tentative, rather than expecting to make pronouncements of meaning that remain true across time.[13]

At the very least, Embodied Performance Analysis may bring some necessary balance to scholarly discussion of the Bible. The Bible's compositions are designed to transform its readers, and this transformation is by nature of the whole person; it is embodied, it is emotional, it is relational. EPA attends to the transformative work of a composition on the performer-interpreter as mediator of the work in performance, and on her audience, and allows those responses to speak the valid meaning highlighted in, of, and through biblical compositions that change with every encounter. In this way, EPA affirms, celebrates, and learns from the fullness of the work of a biblical interpreter, where many other approaches may be limited in their assumed objectivity and disembodied cognition.

The story of this project began with a biblical storyteller noticing that her body, emotions, and audiences were showing her meaning in the compositions she brought to life in performance. The question: could a performer-interpreter articulate the insights thus gleaned in a way that

---

12. Porter observes that "all exegetical approaches and methods are located in relation to other methods and in relation to the times and places in which they have developed" (Porter, *Linguistic Analysis*, 95).

13. Cf. Lee, *Preaching*, 41, where she refers to earlier homiletics scholar, Lucy Atkinson Rose (*Sharing the Word*), among others.

would allow fuller participation of the whole human person in scholarly conversations about the Bible?

I had hoped that Biblical Performance Criticism would help to articulate my experience of interpretation through the mutual indwelling of performance and composition. I discovered that BPC has different aims and purposes to my expectations. But the work of scholars in that emerging field has built a foundation from which the EPA has developed. This foundation begins with story, and story is the foundation of my own process. Storytelling is the art form and the practice that leads me to embodied performance interpretation. Biblical scholars such as Rhoads and Boomershine understood and explored the nature of the Gospels as story, and began to appreciate the origins of those stories in live, embodied performance situations and developed what I have named the storyteller's BPC. Other scholars arrived at similar conclusions about the performed origins of other biblical compositions through the application of a performance critical approach that had been developed in the social sciences, to develop what I named the critic's BPC.

The critic's approach is most prevalent within Old Testament/Hebrew Bible scholarship, and focuses on identifying the evidence in the text for the performed history of that text. We observed the work of Giles and Doan as key exemplars of this stream,[14] and Oestreich was an example of "outsider" BPC scholars working within the NT.[15] The storyteller's approach is most often employed for New Testament, and particularly Gospel, compositions, and evolved out of Narrative Criticism with such works as the foundational *Mark as Story*.[16] That book, and its subsequent volumes, framed the discussion of the narrative origins of BPC, as I identified one of the key features of the approach, which is to begin with an exegesis of the text (or composition, and usually a narrative exegesis), and then to perform the text based on that interpretation. Rhoads and Boomershine may be considered the founders of this stream of BPC;[17] Ruge-Jones and Hearon were among others who provided further examples of this approach, including in the HB/OT Cousins' recent work with the Psalms.[18]

---

14. Giles, "Performance Criticism"; Giles, *Twice Used Songs*; and Giles, *The Naomi Story*.

15. Oestreich, *Performance Criticism of the Pauline Letters*. White ("Visualising Paul's Appeal"), noted in the discussion, may also be considered as conducting performance criticism of Philemon from "outside" the letter.

16. Rhoads, *Mark as Story*.

17. Boomershine, "All Scholarship Is Personal"; Boomershine, "Mark, the Storyteller"; Rhoads, "Narrative Criticism."

18. Ruge-Jones, "Omnipresent, Not Omniscient"; Hearon, "From Narrative to Performance"; Cousins, "Pilgrim Theology."

Historical re-enactment is the goal of most BPC endeavors, whether from a storyteller's or critic's stance. The orality debate has shaped scholars in this endeavor; translation has been influenced,[19] and we noted the sound mapping[20] approach, particularly as employed by Boomershine.[21] Exemplar scholars in this discussion again included Rhoads,[22] Hearon,[23] and Ruge-Jones,[24] along with Shiner[25] and the unique approach of Swanson's Provoking the Gospel project.[26]

As I moved towards the introduction of EPA, I discussed the work of Perry[27] and of Cousins.[28] The methods of both of these scholars share much in common with the method that I employ, with consideration of the way in which particular audiences and contexts shape interpretation, and discussion of the body and emotion, although often from the perspective of *communication* rather than *interpretation*. With Perry's overview of BPC, we have a rare articulation of a methodology from within the storyteller stream. For many scholars in this stream, BPC is viewed as shifting the (narrative and/or historical) interpretive paradigm rather than establishing a new discrete methodology, and this is evident in their practice.[29] Perry's method follows a process of Preparation, which is to say the exegetical work, including a new translation; Internalization, learning the composition by heart and making decisions about how to employ expression, tone, gesture, emotion, and movement so as to communicate effectively; and Performance, including audience participation in discussion at the performance event.[30] By contrast, we have seen in theory and practice that Embodied Performance Analysis begins with internalization, integrating scholarship and other interpretive methods; presents performance in the center of the

---

19. See Maxey, *Translating Scripture for Sound and Performance*.
20. Lee, *Sound Mapping*.
21. Boomershine, *Messiah of Peace*.
22. Rhoads, "Emerging Methodology Part 1"; Rhoads, "Emerging Methodology Part 2."
23. Hearon, "Characters in Text and Performance."
24. Ruge-Jones, "The Word Heard"; Ruge-Jones, "Those Sitting around Jesus."
25. Shiner, *Proclaiming the Gospel*.
26. Swanson, "'This Is My . . .'"
27. Perry, *Insights*.
28. Cousins, "Pilgrim Theology."
29. Led by Rhoads: see, for example, Rhoads and Dewey, "Performance Criticism"; and the method that begins with interpretation to prepare for performance, resulting in a commentary that includes directorial notes for performance, rather than particular insights from a particular performance (e.g., Boomershine, *Messiah of Peace*.)
30. Perry, *Insights*, 39–72.

process; and explicitly concludes with reflection that again integrates scholarship in the exploration of interpretive decisions and the relationship with the audience in performance.

Human Meaning-making Potential

Part of the foundation that BPC scholarship has established for EPA has been the recovery of the inherent performance nature of biblical compositions. To fully realize the potential, the intended reception experience of the compositions of the Bible, the Bible's composers expected performance, proclamation, the embodiment of performer and audience together. Consequently, we *ought* perhaps to expect interpretation to be fluid, of-the-moment, contextually nuanced, and the composition to be new and original with each embodied reception. I suggest that BPC has not fully realized *this* potential in its use of performance as a lens for interpretation, or a test or presentation of interpretation by other (e.g. Narrative) methods. EPA, as applied here in Romans, does. In order to develop the methodology that would make fuller use of the body's physical, emotional, and relational meaning-making processes, and attend to the particular insights of an original composition in performance, I needed to learn more about human epistemology.

I needed to understand more about how humans make meaning as physical beings. I learnt that there is growing acknowledgment of more integrated processes of human knowing and understanding than old dualisms of body/mind or matter/soul. Further, the human person is understood to be integrated not only within themselves as physical, emotional, relational, cognitive, spiritual beings, but as participants in an "organism–environment mutuality and reciprocity."[31] I found the approach of embodied cognition to articulate something of my intuition and experience of knowing through the physical body.

I proposed to employ the physical body as a tool for interpreting biblical compositions by "internalizing" the composition and observing my physical movement in response. As I gestured and took steps intuitively, I reflected on what meaning might be represented in such movement.

I needed to understand how emotions *are* interpretive, determinative, useful. I learnt that "emotion" is a challenging concept to define, and there is little consensus on a definition across the various fields in which emotion is under examination. Further, I learnt that the emotions we feel involve physicality and cognition, and a more elusive "soulfulness" or "affect." I

---

31. Gibbs, *Embodiment and Cognitive Science*, 16.

found that the terminology for describing the internal movement or feeling humans experience is complex and varied. I chose "emotion" as the name for this tool, because although humans continuously and subconsciously respond subjectively to the world, EPA would employ the discrete felt experiences that are recognizable between humans as "emotions." To apply this tool, I observed through internalizing the biblical composition the feelings that arose within me in response to what I was speaking. I questioned the feelings for what they might say about me, as much as for what they illuminated about meaning in the composition.

For audiences, the emotional impact of a Performed Interpretation is the dominant form of meaning-making in the performance encounter.[32] Further study may illuminate the ways in which this emotional impact develops over time into conscious and articulated interpretation. That the emotional interpretation is felt, and to a large extent unable to be further discussed, does not, and should not, designate these experiences as unimportant or without meaning.

I was more focused here on understanding the relationship with my audiences, how they were in various ways shaping the meaning I discerned in a biblical composition. I learnt that humans are audiences all the time, always watching, responding, offering feedback to one another and making meaning from experience. I learnt from actors more about the process of preparing a performance for an audience, and found in their reflections an articulation of my own experience that the performance is incomplete until it is brought before the audience. I also learnt from theater studies the way in which audiences participate with performers in the creation of meaning through energy and physical and emotional feedback.

I defined audiences for this project as bounded gatherings similar to theater audiences, although the context for my biblical storytelling is usually the "congregation." A theater audience facilitates the work of those on stage, while it is the performer who facilitates the work of the gathered people together in the context of a congregation. Perhaps the phenomenon of interpretation by performance includes aspects of both these relationships. In practice, the audience shapes interpretation in three ways: through the performer-interpreter's knowledge of the audience; her visualization of the audience in preparation; and the mutually embodied experience with the audience in performance.

This learning established a foundation for using body, emotion, and audience as tools in an interpretive methodology of preparation, performance, and reflection. The outcome, as we have seen in this thesis and its

---

32. Perry, *Insights*, 136.

test case, is an Embodied Performance Analysis composed of a Performance Interpretation and Critical Reflection.

APPLYING THE ELEMENTS

The learning from this study in human epistemology and biblical scholarship may transform scholarship even without the need for scholars to become performer-interpreters. I will now consider ways in which scholars, and also readers and preachers in gathered worship, may apply elements of EPA to enrich their encounters with and understanding of biblical compositions.

Embodied Scholars

BPC, as we observed, claims a paradigm shift in biblical scholarship in the incorporation of performance criticism, the employment of a performance lens, and the inclusion of performance itself. EPA further implements this shift in paradigm, and offers ways for biblical scholarship in its many fields to more fully engage the whole human person in the interpretive process, rather than to relegate much of our human being to an acknowledgment of "bias." EPA, with BPC, may offer encouragement to scholars to integrate various methods in their exegetical work,[33] and bring more of their inherent embodied interpretive processes to that work.

Listening to Our Bodies

The simplest lesson to learn from this Embodied Performance approach may be that the body does indeed "speak" in response to biblical compositions. The more familiar a person is with the composition as known from within, the more helpful their insights will be regarding meaning.[34] It is only a matter of paying attention to the responses a receiver will inevitably have to the composition, and making the most of those responses as insightful teachers.

If a biblical interpreter is influenced by this study in no other way, I hope they will read each biblical portion or composition aloud. Listening to the natural emphasis, tone, and expression of their voice, and asking, what does that mean? What might expression indicate about the history of

---

33. Further, "it is problematic for a single method to make exclusive claims or to pronounce authoritative interpretations" (Porter, *Linguistic Analysis*, 95).

34. See Boomershine, *Story Journey*, 18; Ruge-Jones, "The Word Heard," 106.

interpretation with which a person has engaged through scholarship, classroom, or sermon? What might tone suggest of one's own questions or story in response to this composition, and is that story facilitating or impeding a meaningful reception of the composition for interpreter or audience?

If translating, it is helpful for the same reasons to read translations aloud. Read the Greek or Hebrew aloud, first, and feel the rhythm, letting it inform the translation as much as an understanding of what the words "mean." Language is more than symbols on a page. Putting the words on voice and breath, a translator or interpreter will *feel* the author's argument, the character's motivation, so as to understand from within.[35]

Standing up to read aloud, and letting the body move will highlight new features of the composition. If being brave and doing this, an interpreter can observe their gestures, facial expression, visualize their audience and notice to whom they instinctively "speak" certain portions, and how.

It may be helpful to record one's reading aloud and then listen back, or listen to others, and attend to intonation and expression. Notice what seems to make sense, or what feels incongruent with one's own understanding of the composition. There is meaning to discover through such questions. Watching performers live or on video is another excellent way to incorporate the breadth of human embodied epistemology into biblical interpretation, as we observed with Hearon's study of Rhoads and Ruge-Jones[36] in Chapter 2.

Listening to Our Feelings

As we read and listen, and our body moves, we also move internally. Scholars, readers, even preachers, perhaps need permission to feel, to come close to the composition, get inside it, and allow it to inhabit us. New insights will come from observing emotions in response to the composition. Scholars are more practiced at noticing the emotions within the composition, named or suggested by the author or narrator, even what is left unsaid: motivations, emotions, internal thoughts and feelings. Especially in a narrative, this is where the receiver participates with the author in the creation of the story. But there is little affirmation of allowing one's imagination to fill these gaps, and ask of oneself, what does *that* mean? Imaginations might be stirred, and new insights discovered, by writing something to fill the gaps, such as a monologue for one of the disciples, or a reply to a prophet from God or a

---

35. As Cousins experienced the Psalms becoming part of her ("Pilgrim Theology," 184).

36. Hearon, "From Narrative to Performance."

king, or the story of Phoebe carrying and delivering the letter from Paul to Rome (as can be seen in track 24).

Feelings and imagination may not, ultimately, be articulated in an article or commentary. However, by paying attention to them, we can discover questions that lead to valuable insights that are then discussed.

Listening to Our Audience

Much scholarship is directed at listening on behalf of an implied or real, original audience. But to what extent does a scholar really consider who is *my* audience? For whom am I writing this article or commentary? What is their context? What are the questions that context raises in response to this composition and not only as the "application" afterword to a commentary? Again, a scholar may be more practiced at considering what the real or implied author might have sought to say to their audience; but perhaps less so at giving attention to what we might want to say to our audience about this composition, and particularly in what ways our audience themselves shape that interpretation. Further, it is not only for reception historians to consider the many ways this composition has been interpreted through the years, and to what extent audiences today hear those interpretations when they receive the composition.

As for a physical response to the composition, listening with other listeners in a live, mutually embodied encounter with the composition can elicit new insight for audience-shaped interpretation. Noticing how neighbors respond will highlight specific features in the composition you may not otherwise see.

I hope that from the Embodied Performance approach, smaller elements might emerge that enable scholars working within any biblical interpretive method to attend to the fullness of their embodied responses to biblical works. Such engagement may transform biblical scholarship in subtle, hardly noticeable ways. It will transform the conversations we have by allowing the works themselves to speak more fully through the mutual inhabitation assumed by their composers and intrinsic to, but so often overlooked in, every encounter between human person and biblical composition.

Interpreting the Bible Aloud in Gathered Worship

The Bible may be read silently in libraries and offices in the academy, but it is heard aloud in gathered communities all over the world, every week, perhaps every day. In many of these encounters, potential for transformation and helpful meaning-making is lost because those who read aloud are not mindful of their reading aloud as *being* interpretation. But every voicing of the Bible *is* an interpretation.[37] Can EPA methods offer encouragement to the everyday reader of the Bible without expecting all to become "performers" or "scholars"?[38]

Preparing the portion to read aloud in gathered worship, a reader or preacher might read it aloud, listen to the words on their voice, and notice instinctive expression, tone, pace, and pauses. Attending to the questions that arise will elicit meaning in this portion for this time; doing so before the reading moment allows for unhelpful interpretations to be identified and overcome. In the same way that I engaged other methods and consulted scholars, a reader or preacher will also be helped by consulting commentaries to explore these questions.

Visualizing the "audience," or congregation, while reading aloud in preparation, will further elicit meaning in the portion for this time, and this community. It may be helpful to imagination oneself at the lectern or in the pulpit, to see in the imagination the children in their activity corner; the matriarchs in the pews in which they have sat for decades; the grieving widower who will duck out as the final hymn is sung; the minister who will preach a message she or he has discerned through this portion. Meaning will emerge as a reader or preacher imagines *how* to speak these words aloud when speaking them to *these* people.

As we observed in the letter to the Romans, Paul loved the gospel story he sought to tell, and loved the people with and to whom he told the story. And as with scholars in the academy, readers and perhaps less so preachers, are encouraged to leave their emotions aside when presenting the biblical compositions in worship. The Embodied Performance approach has been shown to utilize a performer-interpreter's interpretation and confession of faith as a strength in building a relationship of trust with a community of faith, and in communicating meaning faithfully from the Sacred writings of that community.

My hope is that through this examination of my practice, people might find encouragement to adopt behaviors and attitudes to the task of reading the Bible aloud that enrich those live, embodied encounters with their sacred compositions. Every time the Bible is heard on the voice of a reader, preacher, or performer, they *are* given meaning by that voice, body, person.

37. Childers, *Performing the Word*, 80.

38. A further practical guide for reading aloud effectively can be found in Agnew, "Ill-treated Traditions."

The task is to enable our embodied presentations to offer a faithful, careful, interpretation.

EMBODIED PERFORMANCE ANALYSIS: POTENTIAL YET TO REALIZE

Amending the Method

While I have shown there is much scope for application of the learning presented here, I have observed that some elements of the test case EPA were not as effective as hoped. In future, I anticipate making the following changes to my practice, and the process of implementing the method. The method itself remains as summarized in Chapter 4:

> Through preparation, performance, and reflection, the performer-interpreter employs tools of the body, emotion, and audience, integrated with a range of pertinent exegetical approaches, to discern meaning in a biblical composition, presented in an Analysis comprised of Performance Interpretation and Critical Reflection.

I indicated that the process for EPA comprises three stages of preparation, performance, and reflection. I noted that the first step in my process is to format the script. In future, I suggest that the process where possible begin with translation, and that translation include the voicing of the composition aloud in both the original and the performance languages. For example, I missed the emphasis of the Greek άυτος έγω (*autos ego*) at 7:25 by relying on the NRSV, which did not translate the reiterative, "I, myself." It would be helpful to make careful note of the reasons for choices in instances of nuanced meaning. Once a full translation has been undertaken, I would not necessarily re-translate for each return to the portion, but review the translation for each Performance Interpretation of the composition in light of particular audiences and contexts.

The Performance Interpretation employed for the Analysis of Romans did not include conversation with the audience. In future, I suggest that Performance Interpretations will ideally include conversation after the performance. Both Cousins and Perry have demonstrated the potential for meaningful insights with such engagement.

Considering embodied performance of Romans specifically, I would offer a Performance Interpretation of the letter in full and as it is (or abridged) only in an academic context. For a general audience, I am inclined to think that the performance of Phoebe's story and Rom 12–15 (track 24) is more appropriate for reception today. In either instance, I would include audience discussion, as noted. As discussion usually accompanies such reception in the form of a sermon, homily, or interactive "stations," performance of smaller portions for reception in gathered worship remains an effective mode of reception.

Extending the Method

A clear area for future development is the interpretive work of the audience for a Performance Interpretation. Greater incorporation of audience participation in performance events, will be helpful for both the reception of the composition for the audience, and the interpretive work of the performer-interpreter. Also, however, with performances of biblical compositions taking place, there is potential to better understand the ways in which audiences themselves are making meaning of the compositions in performance, the role of their own individual and communal reception history, the influence of performer and fellow audience members, and world and local events. As I have noted, interpretation is happening in churches every day, or at least every Sunday, whenever the Bible is read aloud. Not only will biblical scholarship be enriched by greater insight into the communal interpretation of listeners, but discipleship and Christian education practices may be enhanced by such research.

Future research with the EPA specifically will need to be carried out in order to test its applicability across performer-interpreters, reception contexts, and different biblical compositions and genres. Different forms of performance as the Performance Interpretation as I suggested would also yield rewarding insights into the compositions and the practice of biblical interpretation in our time. Using digital performance, or the ensemble performances described by Swanson are two examples I have mentioned. I hope my fellow performers and interpreters will engage with this method, help to improve it, and continue this work to bring the fullness of human interpretive process to the practice of biblical interpretation through Embodied Performance Analysis.

BRINGING THE STORY TO A CLOSE

A performer-interpreter stands before an audience and speaks; "Embrace one another with a holy kiss."

She has spoken Paul's letter to the Romans, and with her audience heard of the extension of Holy One's invitation into holiness beyond the previously chosen Israel, to all nations. She has spoken Paul's letter to the Romans and heard with her audience silence on the question *of* Israel; for, 2000 years on, Judaism is one of many faith traditions that the receivers of the letter in Adelaide recognize as life-giving for their neighbors. She has felt with her audience discomfort over the question of inappropriate sexual passion and the harmful history of interpretation that is present whenever these verses are voiced. She has heard with her audience that affirming vision of a body, diverse in its individual members, each of them necessary for the health of the community. She has wondered with her audience, what are the dividing lines in our community, how are we still divided?

This performer-interpreter has heard Phoebe introduced on her own voice as one who embodies the mutuality the performer and her audience have felt and seen through her embodied mediation of the letter. Together they have seen the extended arm of embrace for members of the community, across lines that would divide. Together, they have felt the love of Paul, disappointed, compassionate, full of care and encouragement for a community called to embrace one another in love. This performer-interpreter has been transformed, has come to appreciate a letter once made distasteful by unhelpful interpretations. Her audience have come to appreciate parts of the letter overshadowed by harmful consequences or the privileging of certain passages. All have felt loved, welcomed, embraced. All have been encouraged to embrace one another, as Holy One has embraced all, through the mutual indwelling of letter in performer, and in the embodied performance moment, audience and performer together.

This project began with the observation of embodied interpretation in practice, and proceeded to explore that practice in order to understand this mode of interpretation, and to search for a methodology that might allow the body, the emotions, and the relationships of the interpreter to speak in scholarly conversations about the Bible and its meaning. The question was not, *can* I interpret the Bible with the fullness of my embodied human being? I had experienced and observed a practice of oral storytelling that *was* a process of interpretation through the movement of the body, through felt emotion, through relationships of trust and transformative encounter with audiences. The question was, can we *learn* from this mode of interpretation, and can such interpretive work effectively speak in the scholarly conversation? I believe that EPA will help performer-interpreters realize the potential of embodied performance *as* interpretation. I know that this method has helped my audience and me to appreciate the potential of Romans as a call to embrace one another in love, physically, emotionally, in relationships of mutual indwelling.

Embodied Performance Analysis is a method of interpretation that is a living out of the enduring message of biblical compositions, that Holy One invites all into an embrace of mutual indwelling. Progressing beyond performance as test or communication medium for biblical interpretation by other methods, I hope I have demonstrated that performance itself is a method for interpretation. For embodied encounter with sacred compositions is a mutual indwelling that honors the whole human person, the composition, and the community: an encounter that thereby transforms performer and receiver alike. Through an embodied performance approach to interpretation, the Bible's receivers live out the mutual embrace to which the people of Holy One are called, as Paul's letter to the Romans has shown, in Embodied Performance Analysis.

Appendix A

Script for Performance Interpretation

ROMANS 1

[1] Paul, a servant of Jesus Wisdom,
    called to be an apostle, set apart for the gospel of Holy One,
[2] which they promised beforehand
    through their prophets in the holy scriptures,
    [3] the gospel concerning their Son,
        who was descended from David according to the flesh
[4] and was declared to be Son of Holy One
    with power according to the spirit of holiness
        by resurrection from the dead,
    Jesus Wisdom our Liberator,
[5] through whom we have received grace and apostleship
    to bring about the obedience of faith for the sake of his name
        among all the Gentiles—
[6] including yourselves who are called to belong to Jesus Wisdom,
[7] to all Holy One's beloved in Rome, who are called to be devotees:
    Grace to you and peace from Holy One our Creator
        and the Liberator Jesus Wisdom.

[8] First, I thank my Holy One through Jesus Wisdom for all of you,

because your faith is proclaimed throughout the world.
[9] For Holy One,
whom I serve with my spirit by announcing the gospel of their Son,
is my witness
that without ceasing I remember you always in my prayers,
[10] asking that by Holy One's will I may somehow
at last succeed in coming to you.
[11] For I am longing to see you
so that I may share with you some spiritual gift to strengthen you—
[12] or rather
so that we may be mutually encouraged by each other's faith,
both yours and mine.
[13] I want you to know, brothers and sisters,
that I have often intended to come to you
(but thus far have been prevented),
in order that I may reap some harvest among you
as I have among the rest of the Gentiles.
[14] I am a debtor to all Gentiles, both to Greeks and to non-Greeks,
both to the wise and to the foolish
[15] — hence my eagerness
to proclaim the gospel to you also, who are in Rome.
[16] For I am not ashamed of the gospel;
it is the power of Holy One for salvation to everyone who has faith,
to the Jew first and also to the Greek.
[17] For in it the holiness of Holy One is revealed
through faith for faith;
as it is written, "The one who is holy will live by faith."
[18] For the wrath of Holy One is revealed from heaven
against all ungodliness and wickedness of those
who by their wickedness suppress the truth.
[19] For what can be known about Holy One is plain to them,
because Holy One has shown it to them.

[20] Ever since the creation of the world
> Creator's eternal power and divine nature,

invisible though they are,
> have been understood and seen
>> through the things Creator has made.

So they are without excuse;
> [21] for though they knew Holy One,
>> they did not honor them as Holy One
>>> or give thanks to them,

but they became futile in their thinking,
> and their senseless minds were darkened.

[22] Claiming to be wise, they became fools;
> [23] and they exchanged the glory of the immortal Holy One
>> for images resembling a mortal human being or birds
>>> or four-footed animals or reptiles.

[24] Therefore Holy One gave them up in the lusts of their hearts
> to impurity,
>> to the degrading of their bodies among themselves,

[25] because they exchanged the truth about Holy One for a lie and worshipped and served the creature rather than Creator,
> who is blessed for ever! Amen.

[26] For this reason Holy One gave them up to degrading passions.
> Their women exchanged natural intercourse for unnatural,
>> [27] and in the same way also the men,
>>> giving up natural intercourse with women,

were consumed with passion—
> they committed shameless acts with one another

and received in their own persons the due penalty for their error.
> [28] And since they did not see fit to acknowledge Holy One,

Holy One gave them up to a debased mind
> and to things that should not be done.

[29] They were filled with every kind of wickedness,

      evil, covetousness, malice.
 full of envy, murder, strife, deceit, craftiness,
    they are gossips, [30] slanderers, Holy One-haters,
   insolent, haughty, boastful, inventors of evil,
 rebellious towards parents,
     [31] senseless, disloyal, unfeeling, without mercy.
  [32] They know Holy One's decree,
    that those who practice such things deserve to die—
     yet they not only do them
      but even applaud others who practice them.

2

[1] And so you have no excuse,
   whoever you are,
     when you judge others;
 for in passing judgment on another you condemn yourself,
because you, the judge,
   are doing the very same things.
[2] You say,
 "We know that Holy One's judgment on those who do such things
  is in accordance with truth."
[3] Do you imagine,
   whoever you are,
 that when you judge those who do such things
   and yet do them yourself,
    you will escape the judgment of Holy One?
[4] Or do you despise the riches of Holy One's kindness
   and forbearance
     and patience?
Do you not realize that Holy One's kindness is meant to lead you
     to turn towards holiness?
[5] But by your hard and impenitent heart

you are storing up wrath for yourself
on the day of wrath, when Holy One's holy judgment
will be revealed.
[6] For Holy One will repay according to each one's deeds:
[7] to those who by patiently doing good
seek for glory and honor and immortality,
Holy One will give eternal life;
[8] while for those who are self-seeking
and who obey not the truth but wickedness,
there will be wrath and fury.
[9] There will be anguish and distress for everyone who does evil,
the Jew first and also the Greek,
[10] but glory and honor and peace for everyone who does good,
the Jew first and also the Greek.
[11] For Holy One shows no partiality.
[12] all who have participated in tyranny apart from the law
will also perish apart from the law,
and all who have participated in tyranny under the law
will be judged by the law.
[13] For it is not the hearers of the law who are holy
in Holy One's sight,
but the doers of the law who will be welcomed into holiness.
[14] When Gentiles, who do not possess the law,
do instinctively what the law requires,
these, though not having the law,
are a law for themselves.
[15] They show that what the law requires is written on their hearts,
to which their own conscience also bears witness;
and their conflicting thoughts will accuse
or perhaps excuse them [16] on the day when,
according to my gospel, Holy One,
through Jesus Wisdom, will judge the secret thoughts of all.

[17] But if you call yourself a Jew and rely on the law
and boast of your relation to Holy One
[18] and know their will and determine what is best
because you are instructed in the law,
[19] and if you are sure that you are a guide to the blind,
a light to those who are in darkness,
[20] a corrector of the foolish,
a teacher of children,
having in the law the embodiment of knowledge and truth,
[21] you, then, that teach others,
will you not teach yourself?
While you preach against stealing, do you steal?
[22] You that forbid adultery, do you commit adultery?
You that abhor idols, do you rob temples?
[23] You that boast in the law,
do you dishonor Holy One by breaking the law?
[24] For, as it is written,
"The name of Holy One is blasphemed among the Gentiles
because of you."

[25] Circumcision indeed is of value if you obey the law;
but if you break the law,
your circumcision has become uncircumcision.
[26] So, if those who are uncircumcised
keep the requirements of the law,
will not their uncircumcision be regarded as circumcision?
[27] Then those who are physically uncircumcised but keep the law
will condemn you that have the written code and circumcision
but break the law.
[28] For a person is not a Jew who is one outwardly,
nor is true circumcision something external and physical.
[29] Rather, a person is a Jew who is one inwardly,

and real circumcision is a matter of the heart—

it is spiritual and not literal.

Such a person receives praise not from others

but from Holy One.

3

[1] Then what advantage does the Jew have?

Or what is the value of circumcision?

[2] Much, in every way.

For in the first place

the Jews were entrusted with the oracles of Holy One.

[3] What if some were unfaithful?

Will their faithlessness nullify the faithfulness of Holy One?

[4] By no means!

Although everyone is a liar,

let Holy One be proved true, as it is written in the Psalms,

"So that you may be made holy in your words,

and prevail in your judging."

[5] But if our injustice serves to confirm the justice of Holy One,

what should we say?

That Holy One is unjust to inflict wrath on us?

(speaking in a human way.)

[6] By no means!

For then how could Holy One judge the world?

[7] But if through my falsehood

Holy One's truthfulness abounds to their glory,

why am I still being condemned as a participant in tyranny?

[8] And why not say

(as some people slander us by saying that we say),

"Let us do evil so that good may come"?

Their condemnation is deserved!

[9] What then?

Are we any better off?

No, not at all;

for we have already charged that all,

both Jews and Greeks,

are under the power of Tyrant, [10] as it is written:

"There is no one who is holy, not even one;

[11] there is no one who has understanding,

there is no one who seeks Holy One.

[12] "All have turned aside, together they have become worthless;

there is no one who shows kindness,

no—not even one."

[16] Their paths are misery and ruin,

[17] the way of peace they have not known.

[18] "There is no awe before their eyes: no awe of Holy One."

[19] Now we know that whatever the law says,

it speaks to those who are under the law,

so that every mouth may be silenced,

and the whole world may be held accountable to Holy One.

[20] For "no human being

will be made holy in their sight" by works prescribed by the law,

for through the law comes knowledge of Tyrant.

[21] But now, notwithstanding the law,

the holiness of Holy One has been disclosed,

and is attested by the law and the prophets,

[22] the holiness of Holy One

through faith in Jesus Wisdom for all who believe.

For there is no distinction,

[23] since all have participated in tyranny

and fall short of the glory of Holy One;

[24] all are now welcomed into holiness by their grace as a gift,

through the redemption that is in Wisdom Jesus,

[25] whom Holy One put forward
> as a sacrifice of atonement by his blood,
>> effective through faith.

Holy One did this to show their holiness,
> because in their divine forbearance
>> they had passed over the tyranny previously committed;

[26] it was to prove at the present time
> that Holy One them self is holy

and that they make holy the one who has faith in Jesus.

[27] Then what becomes of boasting in pride of place?
> It is excluded.
>> By what law? By that of works?
>
> No, but by the law of faith.
>
> [28] For we hold that a person is made holy by faith
>> apart from works prescribed by the law.

[29] Or is Holy One the Holy One of Jews only?
> Are they not the Holy One of Gentiles also?

Yes, of Gentiles also, [30] since Holy One is one;
> and they will make holy the circumcised on the ground of faith
>> and the uncircumcised through that same faith.

[31] Do we then overthrow the law by this faith?
> By no means!
>> On the contrary, we uphold the law.

4

[1] What then are we to say was gained by Abraham,
> our ancestor according to the flesh?

[2] For if Abraham was made holy by works,
> he has a claim to glory,
>> but not before Holy One.

[3] For what does the scripture say?
> "Abraham believed Holy One,

and it was credited to him as holiness."
[4] Now to one who works,
 wages are not credited as a gift
  but as something due.
[5] But to one who without works
 trusts them who makes holy the unholy,
  such faith is credited as holiness.
[6] So also David speaks of the blessedness
 of those to whom Holy One credits holiness
 irrespective of works:
[7] "Blessed are those whose iniquities are forgiven,
 and whose participation in tyranny is covered;
[8] blessed is the one against whom the Liberator
  will not credit participation in tyranny."
[9] Is this blessedness, then,
 pronounced only on the circumcised,
  or also on the uncircumcised?
We are saying, "Faith was credited to Abraham as holiness."
  [10] And how was it credited to him?
 Was it before or after he had been circumcised?
It was not after, but before he was circumcised.
[11] He received the sign of circumcision
 as a seal of the holiness that he had by faith
  while he was still uncircumcised.
The purpose was to make him the ancestor of all who believe
 without being circumcised
 and who thus have holiness credited to them,
[12] and likewise the ancestor of the circumcised
 who are not only circumcised
  but who also follow the example of the faith
  that our ancestor Abraham had before he was circumcised.

5

[1] Therefore, since we are made holy by faith,
> we have peace with Holy One
>> through our Liberator Jesus Wisdom,

[2] through whom we have obtained access
>> to this grace in which we stand;

and we rejoice in our hope of participating in the glory of Holy One.

[3] And not only that, but we also rejoice in our sufferings,
> knowing that suffering produces endurance,

[4] and endurance produces character,
> and character produces hope,

[5] and hope does not disappoint us,
because Holy One's love has been poured into our hearts
> through the Holy Spirit that has been given to us.

[6] For while we were still weak,
>> at the right time Wisdom died for the unholy.

[7] Indeed, rarely will anyone die for a person made holy —
> though perhaps for a good person
>> someone might actually dare to die.

[8] But Holy One proves their love for us
> in that while we still were participants in tyranny
>> Wisdom died for us.

[9–11] So, if even while we were enemies
we have been reconciled to Holy One
> through the death of their Son,

much more surely
> will we be saved from the wrath of Holy One
>> through his life.

[12] This, just as Tyrant came into the world through one man,
> and Death came through Tyrant,

and so Death spread to all because all have participated in tyranny—

[15] But the free gift is not like the trespass.
> For if the many died through the one man's trespass,
>> much more surely have the grace of Holy One
>> and the free gift in the grace of the one man, Jesus Wisdom,
>>> abounded for the many.
> [16] And the free gift is not like
>> the effect of the one man's participation in tyranny.
For the judgment following one trespass brought condemnation,
> but the free gift following many trespasses
>> brings welcome into holiness.

[18] So just as the trespass of one man, Adam,
>> led to condemnation for all,
> so the act of holiness of one man, Jesus,
>> leads to welcome into holiness and life for all.
[19] For just as by the one man's disobedience
>> the many were made participants in tyranny,
so by the one man's obedience
>> the many will be made holy.
[20] Now law did come,
> with the result that the trespass multiplied;
>> but where Tyrant increased, Grace abounded all the more,
>> [21] so that, just as Tyrant exercised dominion in Death,
so Grace might also exercise dominion
>> through welcome into holiness leading to eternal life
>>> through Jesus Wisdom our Liberator.

6

[1] What then are we to say?
> Should we continue in Tyrant in order that Grace may abound?
[2] By no means!
> How can we who died to Tyrant go on living in it?

[3] Do you not know
> that all of us who have been baptized into Wisdom Jesus
>> were baptized into his death?

[4] Therefore we have been buried with him
> by baptism into death,

so that, just as Wisdom was raised from the dead
> by the glory of the Creator,
>> so we too might walk in newness of life.

[5] For if we have been united with him in a death like his,
> we will certainly be united with him in a resurrection like his.

[6] We know that our old self was crucified with him
> so that the body of Tyrant might be destroyed,
>> and we might no longer be enslaved to Tyrant.
>>> [7] For whoever has died is freed from Tyrant.

[8] But if we have died with Wisdom,
> we believe that we will also live with him.

[20] When you were slaves of Tyrant,
> you were free in regard to holiness.

[21] So what advantage did you then get
> from the things of which you are now ashamed?

The end of those things is death.

[22] But now that you have been freed from Tyrant
> and enslaved to Holy One,

the advantage you get is liberation from tyranny.
> The end is eternal life.

[23] For Tyrant's wage is death,
> but the free gift of Holy One
>> is eternal life
>>> in Wisdom Jesus our Liberator.

7

[15] Even so, I do not understand my own actions.

    For I do not do what I want, but I do the very thing I hate.

[18b] I can will what is right,

    but I cannot do it.

[19] For I do not do the good I want,

    but the evil I do not want is what I do.

[20] If I do what I do not want,

    it is not I that do it,

    but Tyrant dwelling within me.

[21] So I find it to be a kind of law,

    that when I want to do what is good,

        evil lies close at hand.

[22] For I do delight in the law of Holy One in my inmost self,

[23] but I see in my body

    another law at war with the law of my mind,

    making me captive to the law of Tyrant.

[24] Oh, I am a distressed human being.

    Who will rescue me from this body of death?

[25] Thanks be to Holy One

    through Jesus Wisdom our Liberator!

8

[1] For those who are in Wisdom Jesus

    know no condemnation.

[2] For the law of the Spirit of life in Wisdom Jesus

has set you free from the law of Tyrant and of Death.

[15] You have not received a spirit of slavery to fall back into fear –

    you have received a spirit of adoption.

When we cry, "Creator! Maker!"

[16] it is that very Spirit bearing witness with our spirit

SCRIPT FOR PERFORMANCE INTERPRETATION 225

               that we are children of Holy One,
    children—heirs,
        heirs of Holy One, joint heirs with Wisdom—
if, in fact,
      we suffer with him so that we may also
                participate in glory with him.
     [18] and I consider the sufferings of this present time
not worth comparing with that glory about to be revealed to us.
[22] The whole creation is groaning in labor pains
[23] and not only the creation,
      but we ourselves,
    have groaned inwardly, yearning for adoption,
            the redemption of our bodies.
[24] And, in hope, we are saved.
    Now, hope that is seen is not hope.
      for who hopes for what is seen?
        [25] But if we hope for what we do not see,
          we wait for it with patience.

[26] And the Spirit helps us in our weakness;
         for we do not know how to pray as we ought,
    but that very Spirit intercedes with sighs too deep for words.
[27] And Holy One, who searches the heart,
    knows the mind of the Spirit,
        because the Spirit intercedes for the devoted
      according to the will of Holy One.

[28] We know that all things work together for good
      for those who love Holy One,
         who are called according to their purpose.

[31] What then are we to say about these things?

If Holy One is for us, who is against us?

[35] Who will separate us from the love of Wisdom?

Will hardship, or distress,

or persecution, or famine,

or nakedness, or peril, or sword?

[36] As it is written,

"For your sake we are being killed all day long;

we are accounted as sheep to be slaughtered."

[37] No, in all these things we are more than conquerors

through Holy One who loved us.

[38] For I am convinced that neither death, nor life,

nor angels, nor rulers,

nor things present, nor things to come,

nor powers,

[39] nor height, nor depth,

nor anything else in all creation,

will be able to separate us from the love of Holy One

in Wisdom Jesus our Liberator.

11

[1] Yes, I do ask, has Holy One rejected their people, Israel?

By no means!

I myself am an Israelite,

a descendant of Abraham,

a member of the tribe of Benjamin.

[2] Holy One has not rejected their people whom they foreknew.

[33] But O—

the depth of the riches and wisdom and knowledge of Holy One!

How unsearchable are their judgments

and how inscrutable their ways!

[34] "For who has known the mind of Holy One?
>Or who has been their counsellor?"
[35] "Or who has given a gift to Holy One,
>to receive a gift in return?"
[36] For from Holy One and through them and to them are all things.
>To Holy One be the glory forever. Amen.

12

[1] I appeal to you therefore,
>brothers and sisters,
>>by the mercies of Holy One,
>to present your bodies as a living sacrifice,
>>sacred and acceptable to Holy One:
>this is your spiritual worship.
[2] Do not be conformed to this world,
>but be transformed by the renewing of your minds,
>>so that you may discern what is the will of Holy One—
>what is good and acceptable and perfect.
[3] For by the grace given to me
>I say to everyone among you
not to think of yourself more highly than you ought to think,
>>but to think with sober judgment,
each according to the measure of faith that Holy One has assigned.
[4] For as in one body we have many members,
>and not all the members have the same function,
[5] so we, who are many,
>>are one body in Wisdom,
>and individually we are members one of another.
[6] We have gifts that differ according to the grace given to us:
>prophecy, in proportion to faith;
>>[7] ministry, in ministering;
>>>the teacher, in teaching;

[8] the exhorter, in exhortation;

    the giver, in generosity;

  the leader, in diligence;

the compassionate, in cheerfulness.

[9] Offer genuine embrace;

  repel what is evil,

    hold fast to what is good;

      [10] love one another with mutual affection;

outdo one another in showing honor.

[11] Do not lag in zeal,

  be ardent in spirit,

    serve the Liberator.

      [12] Rejoice in hope,

        be patient in suffering,

          persevere in prayer.

[13] Contribute to the needs of the devoted;

  extend hospitality to strangers;

    [14] bless those who persecute you;

      bless and do not curse them.

  [15] Rejoice with those who rejoice,

weep with those who weep,

[16] live in harmony with one another.

    Do not be haughty, but associate with the marginalized.

    Do not claim to be wiser than you are.

  [17] Do not repay anyone evil for evil,

    but take thought for what is noble in the sight of all.

[18] If it is possible, so far as it depends on you,

    live peaceably with all.

[19] Beloved, never avenge yourselves,

  but leave room for the wrath of Holy One;

    for it is written,

      "Vengeance is mine,

>   I will repay, says the Liberator."

[20] No, "if your enemies are hungry, feed them;

>   if they are thirsty, give them something to drink;

for by doing this you will heap burning coals on their heads."

>   [21] Do not be overcome by evil, but overcome evil by good.

13

>   [1] Let every person be subject to the governing authorities;
>
>   for there is no authority except from Holy One,
>
> and those authorities that exist have been instituted by Holy One.
>
>   [2] Therefore whoever resists authority
>
>   resists what Holy One has appointed,
>
>   and those who resist will incur judgment.
>
> [3] For rulers are not a source of fear for those who do good;
>
>   but for those who do wrong—
>
>   Do you wish to have no fear of the authority?
>
>   Then do what is good,
>
>   and you will receive its approval;
>
>   [4] for it is Holy One's servant for your good.
>
>   But if you do what is wrong,
>
>   you should be afraid,
>
> For the authority does not bear the sword in vain!
>
>   It is the servant of Holy One
>
>   to execute wrath on the wrongdoer.
>
> [5] Therefore one must be subject,
>
>   not only because of wrath but also because of conscience.
>
> [6] For the same reason you also pay taxes,
>
>   for the authorities are Holy One's servants,
>
>   busy with this very thing.
>
> [7] Pay to all what is due to them—
>
>   taxes to whom taxes are due,
>
>   revenue to whom revenue is due,

respect to whom respect is due,
honor to whom honor is due.
[8] Owe no one anything,
except to love one another;
for the one who loves another has fulfilled the law.
[9] The commandments, "You shall not commit adultery;
You shall not murder; You shall not steal;
You shall not covet"; and any other commandment,
are summed up in this word,
"Love your neighbor as yourself."
[10] Love does no wrong to a neighbor;
therefore, love is the fulfilling of the law.

[11] Besides this,
you know what time it is,
how it is now the moment for you to wake from sleep.
For salvation is nearer to us now than when we became believers;
[12] the night is far gone, the day is near.
Let us then lay aside the works of darkness
and put on the armor of light;
[13] let us live honorably as in the day,
not in reveling and drunkenness,
not in debauchery and licentiousness,
not in quarrelling and jealousy.

14

[1] Welcome those who are uncertain in faith,
but not for the purpose of quarrelling over opinions.
[2] Some believe in eating anything,
while the uncertain eat only vegetables.
[3] Those who eat must not despise those who abstain,
and those who abstain must not pass judgment on those who eat;

for Holy One has welcomed them.
[4] Who are you to pass judgment on servants of another?
> It is before their own commander that they stand or fall.
And they will be upheld,
> for the Liberator is able to make them stand.
[5] Some judge one day to be better than another,
> while others judge all days to be alike.
>> Let all be fully convinced in their own minds.
[6] Those who observe the day,
> observe it in honor of the Liberator.
Also those who eat, they eat in honor of the Liberator,
> since they give thanks to Holy One;
while those who abstain, they abstain in honor of the Liberator
> and give thanks to Holy One.
[7] We do not live to ourselves,
> and we do not die to ourselves.
>> [8] If we live, we live to the Liberator,
>>> and if we die, we die to the Liberator;
so then, whether we live or whether we die,
> we are the Liberator's.
[9] For to this end Wisdom died and lived again,
> so that he might be Liberator of both the dead and the living.

[10] Why do you pass judgment on your brother or sister?
> Or indeed, why do you despise your brother or sister?
For we will all stand before the judgment seat of Holy One.
[11] For it is written,
> "As I live, says the Liberator, every knee shall bow to me,
>> and every tongue shall give praise to Holy One."
[12] So then, each of us will be accountable to Holy One.

[13] Let us therefore no longer pass judgment on one another,

>   but resolve instead never to put a stumbling-block
>   or hindrance in the way of another.
> [14] I know and am persuaded in the Liberator Jesus
>   that nothing is unclean in itself;
>   but it is unclean for anyone who thinks it unclean.
> [15] If your brother or sister is being injured by what you eat,
>   you are no longer walking in love.
> Do not let what you eat
>   cause the ruin of one for whom Wisdom died.
>   [16] So do not let your good be spoken of as evil.
>   [17] For the realm of Holy One is not food and drink
> but holiness and peace and joy in the Holy Spirit.
>   [18] The one who thus serves Wisdom is acceptable to Holy One
>   and has human approval.
> [19] Let us then pursue what makes for peace
>   and for mutual encouragement.
>   [20] Do not, for the sake of food,
>   destroy the work of Holy One.
>   Everything may be clean,
>   but it is wrong for you to make others fall by what you eat;
> [21] it is good not to eat meat or drink wine
>   or do anything that makes your brother or sister stumble.
> [22] The faith that you have,
>   have as your own conviction before Holy One.
> Blessed are those who have no reason to condemn themselves
>   because of what they approve.
> [23] But those who have doubts are condemned if they eat,
>   because they do not act from their conviction;
> and whatever does not proceed from faith is participation in tyranny.

15

> [1] We who are strong ought to bear with the frailty of the uncertain,

and not to accommodate ourselves.
[2] Each of us must accommodate our neighbor
for the good purpose of building up the neighbor.
[3] For Wisdom did not accommodate himself;
but, as it is written,
"The insults of those who insult you have fallen on me."
[4] And whatever was written in former days
was written for our instruction,
so that by steadfastness
and by the encouragement of the scriptures
we might have hope.
[5] May the Holy One of steadfastness and encouragement
grant us to live in harmony with one another,
in accordance with Wisdom Jesus,
[6] so that together we may with one voice love and honor
the Holy One and Creator of our Liberator Jesus Wisdom.

[7] Welcome one another, therefore,
just as Wisdom has welcomed you,
for the glory of Holy One.
[8] I tell you that Wisdom has become a servant of the circumcised
on behalf of the truth of Holy One
in order that they might confirm the promises given to the patriarchs,
[9] and in order that the Gentiles might praise Holy One for their mercy.
As it is written,
"Therefore I will confess you among the Gentiles,
and sing praises to your name";
[10] and again he says,
"Rejoice, O Gentiles, with Holy One's people";
[11] and again,
"Praise the Liberator, all you Gentiles,
and let all the peoples praise him";

[12] and again Isaiah says,

> "The root of Jesse shall come,
>> the one who rises to rule the Gentiles;
>>> in him the Gentiles shall hope."

[13] May the Holy One of hope fill you with all joy and peace in believing, so that you may abound in hope by the power of the Holy Spirit. [14] I myself feel confident about you,

> my brothers and sisters,
>> that you yourselves are full of goodness,
> filled with all knowledge,
>> and able to instruct one another.

[15] Nevertheless, on some points I have written to you rather boldly
> by way of reminder,
>> because of the grace given me by Holy One
>>> [16] to be a minister of Wisdom Jesus to the Gentiles
>>>> in the priestly service of the gospel of Holy One,
>> so that the offering of the Gentiles may be acceptable,
>>> sanctified by the Holy Spirit.

[17] In Wisdom Jesus, then,
>> I have reason to boast of my work for Holy One.

[18] For I will not venture to speak of anything
> except what Wisdom has accomplished through me
to win obedience from the Gentiles, by word and deed,

[19] by the power of signs and wonders,
> by the power of the Spirit of Holy One,
>> so that from Jerusalem and as far around as Illyricum
> I have fully proclaimed the gospel of Wisdom.

[20] Thus I make it my ambition to proclaim the good news,
> not where Wisdom has already been named,
>> so that I do not build on someone else's foundation,

[21] but as it is written,

"Those who have never been told of him shall see,

and those who have never heard of him shall understand."
[22] This is the reason
>that I have so often been hindered from coming to you.

[23] But now, with no further place for me in these regions,
>I desire, as I have for many years,
>>to come to you [24] when I go to Spain.

For I do hope to see you on my journey and to be sent on by you,
>once I have enjoyed your company for a little while.

[25] At present, however,
>I am going to Jerusalem in a ministry to the devoted;
>>[26] for Macedonia and Achaia
>>>have been pleased to share their resources
>with the poor among the devoted at Jerusalem.

[27] They were pleased to do this,
>>and indeed they owe it to them;

for if the Gentiles have come to share in their spiritual blessings,
>they ought also to be of service to them in material things.

[28] So, when I have completed this,
>and have delivered to them what has been collected,
>>I will set out by way of you to Spain;
>>>[29] and I know that when I come to you,
>>>>I will come in the fullness of the blessing of Wisdom.

[30] I appeal to you, brothers and sisters,
>by our Liberator Jesus Wisdom and by the love of the Spirit,
>>to join me in earnest prayer to Holy One on my behalf,
>[31] that I may be rescued from the unbelievers in Judea,

and that my ministry to Jerusalem may be acceptable to the devoted,
>[32] so that by Holy One's will I may come to you with joy
>>and be refreshed in your company.

[33] The Holy One of peace be with all of you. Amen.

16

[1] I commend to you our sister Phoebe,
> a servant of the church at Cenchreae,

[2] so that you may welcome her in the Liberator
>> as is fitting for the devoted,
>>> and help her in whatever she may require from you,
>> for she has been a benefactor of many—including me.

[3] Embrace Prisca and Aquila, who work with me in Wisdom Jesus,
> [4] and who risked their necks for my life,
>> to whom not only I give thanks,
>>> but also all the churches of the Gentiles.

[5] Embrace also the church in their house.
Embrace my beloved Epaenetus,
> who was the first convert in Asia for Wisdom.

[6] Embrace Mary, who has worked very hard among you.

[7] Embrace Andronicus and Junia,
> my relatives who were in prison with me;
>> they are prominent among the apostles,
>>> and they were in Wisdom before I was.

[8] Embrace Ampliatus, my beloved in the Liberator.

[9] Embrace Urbanus, our co-worker in Wisdom,
> and my beloved Stachys.

[10] Embrace Apelles, who is approved in Wisdom.
Embrace those who belong to the family of Aristobulus.

[11] Embrace my relative Herodion.
Embrace those in the Liberator
>> who belong to the family of Narcissus.

[12] Embrace those workers in the Liberator,
> Tryphaena and Tryphosa.

Embrace the beloved Persis,
> who has worked hard in the Liberator.

[13] Embrace Rufus, chosen in the Liberator;

and embrace his mother—a mother to me also.

[14] Embrace Asyncritus, Phlegon, Hermes, Patrobas, Hermas,
and the brothers and sisters who are with them.

[15] Embrace Philologus, Julia, Nereus and his sister, and Olympas,
and all the devoted who are with them.

[16] Embrace one another with a holy kiss.

All the churches of Jesus embrace you.

[17] I urge you, brothers and sisters,
to keep an eye on those who cause dissensions and offences,
in opposition to the teaching that you have learned.

Avoid them –

[18] for such people do not serve our Liberator Wisdom,
but their own appetites,

and by smooth talk and flattery
they deceive the hearts of the innocent.

[19] For while your obedience is known to all,
so that I rejoice over you,
I do want you to be wise in what is good,
and guileless in what is evil.

[20] The Holy One of peace will shortly crush Evil One under your feet.
The grace of our Liberator Jesus Wisdom be with you.

[21] Timothy, my co-worker, embraces you;
so do Lucius and Jason and Sosipater, my relatives.

[22] I Tertius, the writer of this letter, embrace you in the Liberator.

[23] Gaius, who is host to me and to the whole church, embraces you.
Erastus, the city treasurer, and our brother Quartus, embrace you.

[25] Now to Holy One who is able to strengthen you
according to my gospel and the proclamation of Jesus Wisdom,
according to the revelation of the mystery
that was kept secret for long ages [26] but is now disclosed,

and through the prophetic writings is made known to all the Gentiles,
    according to the command of the eternal Holy One,
        to bring about the obedience of faith—
[27] to the only wise Holy One,
    through Jesus Wisdom; to them be the glory forever!
        Amen.

Appendix B

Preparation and Rehearsal Notes

I do not expect that all Embodied Performance Analyses will include such full preparation and rehearsal notes as follow; should one attempt to compose an Embodied Performance Commentary, the Critical Reflection would include some of this further detail. This book does not attempt to present a full "commentary" on Romans through Embodied Performance Analysis, but I do include my notes here for a more complete picture of this new method I have introduced.

ROMANS 1

1:4 "by resurrection from the dead."

The gesture my body intuitively attached to these words was the raising of my right hand, palm up, indicating rising from the depths. It might even evoke for the audience the rising of one baptized from the water. I repeat this gesture at 2:4, and note there the resonating meaning.

Here at 1:4, the gesture then moves into the raised arms indicating the crucifix as I speak the words Jesus Wisdom, our Liberator—liberation coming through Jesus' death and resurrection. I do not repeat this gesture evoking the cross every time I name Jesus Wisdom Liberator, but there are multiple moments where the gesture is suggested, and in turn suggests this reminder of the crucifixion.

1:7 To all Holy One's beloved in Rome, who are called to be devotees:
grace to you and peace from Holy One our Creator
and the Liberator Jesus Wisdom.

As I gesture with arms open "to all," offering "grace and peace," I hold the gesture through to the words "Liberator Jesus Wisdom," and thus simultaneously evoke the crucifixion again, as at 1:4.

1:8 "your faith is proclaimed throughout the world."

The gesture I employ is arms pushing outwards as if to the all the world.

1:12 "that we may be mutually encouraged by one another's faith, yours and mine."

The first occurrence of the gesture for mutuality, discussed further in the Critical Reflection. Slow movement, and slowing down in the speaking of the words as I gesture from me to the audience and back to me. After inhabiting the letter through rehearsal, moving through the rhetorical ebbs and flows of the discussion and discovering through my embodied and emotional responses the theme of mutuality, the depth of love in these words, I came to understand the importance in this performed interpretation of the letter for this audience of introducing the gesture and the theme. Slowing down and taking the time to look at the breadth of the gathered audience, making eye contact as often as feels appropriate, I give the audience time to hear, see, and understand this mutuality as a foundation for understanding the letter.

1:13 "I want you to know"

I pause before 1:13, and take a breath, for I feel a shift in emotional, or at least rhetorical, tone here, from praise and celebration of the faithful in Rome, to the telling of his own story.

1:15 "to you also"

The emphasis here, as I felt the words in my voice, came to fall on both "you" and "also," as the meaning seemed to be in the perhaps unexpectedness of Paul wishing to proclaim the gospel in Rome, where another has already been. But he has described his sense of obligation to *all* Gentiles, as an apostle with a particular call from Holy One, and the Romans are among all the Gentiles; therefore, he *does* wish to proclaim the Gospel in Rome, at last.

1:16 "to everyone who has faith"

The rhythm of this verse leads me to slow down to speak "everyone who has faith"; doing so makes clear Paul's emphasis on *faith*, also clear in its repetition throughout.

The gesture is a quite quick opening of arms for "everyone," matching the emphatic "underlining" of the word as I speak it, and introduce another key theme to the letter. This gospel, this invitation from Holy One, is for all, Jew and Greek, contrary to the apparent questions both Jews and Greeks in Rome have regarding the other.

1:18 "suppress the truth"

The gesture here with hands down seemed an intuitive representation of "suppress." I repeated the gesture throughout the letter where similar themes of suppression of the truth or the way of Holy One were articulated.

1:20 "Creator's eternal power"

NRSV has "his eternal power" and "things he has made." I use Creator here as a way of avoiding the gendered pronoun. I might have used "Holy One," representing the Holy Three together, rather than "Creator," which represents One among the Trinity. Intuitively, it felt to me as though the particular movement of the Trinity that is identified here is the creative energy, sometimes named "Father," or "Maker."

The gesture I employ, with arms wide and gaze up, "heavenward," carries something of the elevated tone and posture I employ in the doxological moments.

1:21 "senseless minds"

The gesture for "minds" is tracing a shape like an inverted "L" across forehead and down towards the heart. In my understanding of the ancient world, "mind" is to some extent synonymous with "heart" or "soul," and I wished to convey my intuition that the senseless "mind" to which Paul refers is more than a twenty-first-century notion of "cognition," but more of the holistic interior self. (Such a holistic view of the human person being what I am actually seeking to employ in this embodied performance methodology.)

1:22 "Claiming to be wise"

At "wise" I gesture with my hands as if indicating a path before me to follow. My body picked up the sense of "wise" here as those who follow Holy One's Way, and the foolish as those who do not (cf. Ps 1:6). As noted below, there are instances of "foolish" that I have rendered "senseless" where this technical meaning seems not to be the intention of the author.

At "foolish," my hands fall away indicating loss, of way or wisdom, and as my hands fall, I feel a real sense of disappointment.

1:25c "who is blessed forever, Amen!"

This was omitted in most performances, and I am not sure why. Perhaps it simply felt out of place on my voice; perhaps I did not quite make sense of its purpose here.

As noted by Prof Timothy Lim at the New College Biblical Studies Seminar presentation (Feb 2017), an exploration of the meaning and impact of omissions in performance would prove an interesting line of inquiry. In some faith traditions, omission might be seen as a disrespect of the Sacred text. Following the method of the Network of Biblical Storytellers, which I do (and it is that practice under examination in this project), omissions and errors in the words are not considered disrespectful. We aim for 95% accuracy with the content, and 75% accuracy with the words. There is a fluidity inherent to oral storytelling that expects the words will change. What has not been studied, to my knowledge, is the expectations of a faith community, receiving the biblical compositions as they have been handed down: if they expect to hear them in the words as they would read them on the page, omissions from a storyteller performing by heart may be seen to detract from the presentation of the composition. It might be informative to explore this with other audience-related questions through further

1:26–27

I sought in my translation to represent Paul's choice of different words for different "passions" (πάθη, *pathe*, and ὀρέξις, *orexis*), and to stress the sense of strong desire in this second naming of "passion" (ὀρέξις).

Reading Lampe,[1] I was struck by the diversity in meaning for πάθος, from suffering, in particular of Christ and the martyrs and spiritual nature of that suffering, to the kind of "passion" that is particularly sexual, and negatively so, as found in the entry in BDAG,[2] which, noting a connotation to πάθος of strong sexual desire or passion, translates Rom 1:26 as "disgraceful passions." πάθος does have a passive sense about its range of meanings, though that passivity need not be negative. The range of meaning includes "what one has experienced," "emotion," "a state or condition," and the rhetorical "emotional style or treatment."

As I discuss in the Critical Reflection, I remain unconvinced to some extent on the translation; in particular, on how to render "shameless acts" between men.[3] I try to see this in the light of the understanding of sex as one active, one passive, partner, in an act that reinforces inequality and social hierarchy.[4] Several audience members who are part of the LGBTQ community suggested that these verses may not be appropriate for reception today without discussion and comment. I am inclined to agree.

1:31 NRSV: "foolish, faithless, heartless, ruthless"

I have chosen to render the Greek terms thus:

> ἀσυνέτους (*asunetous*)—"senseless." BDAG[5] notes meaning as "void of understanding, implying also a lack of high moral quality." Foolish is an appropriate translation into current English, but with the more technical use of "foolish" as referring to those not on the path

---

1. Lampe, *Patristic Greek Lexicon*, 995–98.
2. BDAG, 478.
3. Longenecker's "indecent acts" still seems to carry the sense of judgment I, and my audience, find to be not life-giving or affirming: Longenecker, *Epistle to the Romans*, 189.
4. Following, for example, Parker, "Teratogenic Grid."
5. BDAG, 146.

of wisdom as described in Torah and the prophets (cf. 1:14) I have chosen "senseless." This also then recalls the use of "senseless" in 1:21, "their senseless minds were darkened," providing aural links for the listeners between this list and Paul's earlier discussion.

ἀσυνθέτους (*asunthetous*)—"without loyalty." BDAG[6] prefers "undutiful," "pertaining to such as renege on their word." The meaning of the noun συνθήκη (*suntheke*) refers to "a formal agreement or compact," so an ἀσυνθέτος person "does not keep an agreement." Paul uses "faith" as a particular technical term within his discussions of salvation and human relationship with Holy One. For this reason, I choose to name the breaking of agreements as disloyalty rather than faithlessness, so that my audience does not make an aural link to the technical term "faith" (πιστις, *pistis*, in the Greek), which feels unnecessary and unintended at this point.

ἀστόργους (*astorgous*)—"without kindness." The Greek term describes "one who is lacking in good feelings for others, thereby jeopardizing the maintenance of relationships." In the Greek and, more, in the English, the meaning is close to the meaning of ἀνελεήμονας (*aneleemonas*), especially alongside "merciless." "Without kindness," I think, gives distinction to the terms, while still building towards "without mercy," which finishes off this list of "things that should not be done" (1:28).

ἀνελεήμονας (*aneleemenas*)—"without mercy." "Ruthless" of the NRSV translation felt in current English usage to be a more active verb, seeking to inflict harm. To act without mercy carries, for me, meaning of both causing harm, and also refusing to respond to those in need with the loving kindness required of Holy One. The sound pattern here differs from that of the Greek; Paul has three terms beginning with the "as" sound, then one with "an." Aurally, I have linked the final three judgments, and rely on my delivery to effect "without mercy" as the punch line.

2

2:1 "And so"

In the NRSV, this is "Therefore," but I find it difficult to commit to the direct reliance on what precedes, which "therefore" implies. As I build the

---

6. BDAG, 146.

argument, "and so" feels like it scaffolds this argument upon what has gone before with a sense of "likewise," not "because."

2:4 "turn towards holiness"

NRSV: "kindness is meant to lead you to *repentance*." I have rendered "repentance" as "turn towards holiness," as repentance is another of those terms that is loaded with baggage, much of it judgmental, from unhelpful eras and sections of Christian interpretation and application of the biblical writings.

The original Hebrew notion of what has been rendered in English as "repentance" is to turn back, to return, to Holy One. A Gentile audience may not be expected by Paul to *return*, as they are turning to the One Holy God (formerly specifically of Israel) for the first time.[7] However, if at this point Paul is addressing the Jewish portion of the churches in Rome, "return" to holiness would be appropriate. It may be that "return" is appropriate for my audiences as well, especially the Adelaide audience, expected to be more dominated by the presence of people of Christian faith, for whom the constant movement of return to Holy One is the pattern of life for flawed and fallible human beings. However, in recognition of the mixed nature of both Paul's Gentile / Jewish audience and my Christian / non-Christian audiences, I am choosing "turn" toward holiness.

A "turn toward holiness" moves us away from loaded language, enabling us to hear the letter anew with fresh ears, one of my hopes for this performance of the letter. It also picks up on the theme of "holiness," as discussed in the Critical Reflection.

2:5 "in the hardness of your heart"

The gesture here was a clenching of the fist, "hardness" seemingly understood by my body as "closed," tense, perhaps even a protection against the vulnerability required when one opens one's heart to Holy One.

2:7 "to those who by patiently doing good"

Here, I smile, as we move from the serious warning of 2:6 "Holy One will repay according to each one's deeds." The positive feeling in describing the outcome of "patiently doing good" and "seeking glory" contrasts with the negative feeling when describing "those who are self-seeking," for whom

---

7. Fredriksen, "Paul's Letter to the Romans," 806.

"there will be wrath and fury." Here, emotion is as important, if not more so, than the words themselves: if the audience believes more strongly what they feel than what they think,[8] communicating positive emotion and negative emotion effectively will leave the impression on my audience that the aim is to reach for participation in glory, not serve ourselves. If my audience feels this, they will understand and believe it much more strongly than if they hear the words dispassionately.

2:7 "seek for glory and honor and immortality"

I gesture upwards with the words "seek for glory and honor and immortality," as I do when naming Holy One. I had thought to change the English here, because in English today the seeking of glory and honor and immortality may refer to a self-serving reach for acclaim. But I think the language of glory is important throughout as another way of describing the redeeming work of Holy One as a welcome into the holiness of Holy One—the idea that all are now invited to participate in the glory of Holy One; so "glory" is worth retaining here.

"Honor" is worth retaining for the same reason: as I suggest elsewhere, Paul's discussion of the love and honor we are bound to show to Holy One and neighbor is commensurate with such participation in the glory of Holy One.[9]

Finally, "immortality" is worth retaining here for the link to Paul's use of "immortality" in the previous discussion of those who have not acknowledged Holy One in Rom 1. Therefore, my gesture seeks to counter the use of these English words in such a phrase today with an indication of the meaning they carry here, in this letter, translated from first-century Greek.

2:9, 10 "For the Jew first, and also the Greek"

Note the inflection for each articulation of "For the Jew first and also the Greek" in these two verses. As these lines sunk deeper into my being, and I envisaged Paul's audience, I felt him addressing the assumptions of the Jews, as he does throughout these chapters. Paul challenges again and again the boasting in pride of place of Jews who have been set apart as the holy people of the Holy One of Israel. Paul sees that in the death and resurrection of Jesus, *all* are now "welcomed into holiness" (3:24). Therefore my inflection

---

8. Shiner, *Proclaiming the Gospel*, 72.
9. Agnew, "Love and Honour as an Invitation to 'Glorify' God?"

for the first occurrence of "the Jew first and also the Greek" here conveys the expectation of surprise at judgment for the Jew; the second time, I convey knowledge of the Jewish addressee's expectation that the Jew will receive honor, glory and peace, and their surprise that this promise now extends to the non-Jew. It feels as though Paul is reminding his audience, with particular gaze upon the Jewish members of the audience, that the welcome of Holy One has been offered to the nations, not only Israel, through the death and resurrection of Jesus. This is Paul's emphasis, which I convey to my audience; I have no sense when performing this letter of addressing the audience or part thereof as "Jew" or "Gentile," but expect that individuals will make their own connections and interpretations.

Note also pace changes through these verses, slowing at the important points, the places a letter writer today might underline or capitalize for emphasis.

2:12 "All who have participated in tyranny"

It is important to repeat gesture and expression for each iteration of "All who have participated in tyranny," to again underline the point that *all have* participated in tyranny, though they may be held accountable in different ways.

2:15 "the secret thoughts of all"

Again, pace varies here in order to draw the listener's attention to the point: I slow down at "secret thoughts of all," with particular emphasis on *all*. This is the repeated point I hear and feel throughout this portion of the letter.

2:17–24

Embodying Paul's words here, I feel his disappointment, which helped me to find meaning here. First as a Jew himself, it seems Paul is disappointed by the ineffective application of the law by fellow Jews. Second, as an apostle called to ministry with Gentiles, he seems disappointed at the lack of understanding from Jews who do not see what he sees about how Holy One has opened up the welcome into holiness for *all*. As one in my tradition who sees new things to which we are called and am not always heard, understood, or supported in venturing out into that new territory, I understand this disappointment and frustration, and hear the letter resound across the generations to speak into my time.

2:21–23

I found it quite challenging to determine what Paul might have meant here. As I spoke these lines with different intonations and expressions, changing which words I emphasized, I gradually settled on expression that felt "right." The expression I use, then, conveys the sense of Paul incredulous that as his addressees are preaching against, forbidding, and abhorring these things, they are practicing them themselves. He is thus *accusing* his audience. The alternative was to express in such a way as to imply Paul is *asking* them if they do, or even would, practice these things, which felt inadequate as the argument built towards the accusation in 2:23 that they are dishonoring Holy One because they *are* breaking the law. Watching the performance interpretation it feels as though Paul's words are directed at those who are breaking the law, not expressing a general anti-Jewish sentiment.

2:24 "because of you"

I tried anger with "because of you," but it felt too harsh, too likely to alienate my audience. I felt that what was needed here was strength and challenge, but with disappointment that holds an invitation to change rather than anger that closes the door on redemption.

2:28 "a person is not a Jew who is one outwardly..."

As I—a female—embodied these words, it became apparent to me that this is one point where Phoebe being a woman delivering the words presents a layering of meaning in its original reception context.[10] I wondered if the presenting of these lines *as a woman*, with what my body intuitively did as a gesture, indicating towards the part of the body that would be circumcised, suggests not only that Gentiles are able to be within the bounds of holiness by spiritual "circumcision," but also women—*generations* of women—within

10. Storyteller Tracy Radosevic notes that her gender is something she brings to her performing, and that "Biblical Performance Criticism gives me the tools to play around with . . . possibilities, especially as a woman." Her experience as a woman has provided particular insight into the experience of the woman with the flow of blood, that the bending over might have been due to crippling pain, insight gained when her own experience came into contact with rehearsal of this story: Radosevic, "Carnal Knowledge."

the Jewish community, who are obviously not made holy by their own circumcision, so must be made holy by faith. Of course, the argument could be made that women may be made holy through the circumcision of the males to whom they are beholden; I would argue for a more empowered Jewishness for the women of ancient Israel—one which, by Paul's argument, comes through their own faith. I "saw" this meaning held between the lines of Paul's letter by observing my body moving in response to the words as I learnt them by heart; the knowledge our bodies hold.

As I prepared and rehearsed, I wrote this in my journal:

> Intuitively, I am coming to understand this portion of the letter as Paul calling out some complacency on the part of his fellow Jews, relying too heavily on their status as God's chosen people and forgetting the heart of the law and its command to love. They have forgotten, Paul seems to be saying, that their status has been not for the people of Israel alone, but for the nations—a light for the whole world. The gospel Paul is now proclaiming claims Jesus as the light for the world, not held by any one nation, but by people of any ethnic and cultural designation who choose to believe. This is an opening up of the invitation into the holiness of Holy One for all nations, no longer just the one.

3

3:1ff

As I embody the questions and responses, I feel myself moving from side to side, as if to physically represent the two sides of this conversation. Paul seems here to be giving voice to the questions of Jewish followers of Jesus wondering what the implications of this new Way of following God are for all that has gone before, all they have inherited from their Jewish spiritual ancestors. It feels to me as I inhabit and perform Rom 3 that the main question here concerns their relationship with Holy One (cf. 3:3). In Rom 4 that question becomes one concerning the stories they have inherited, represented by the major story of Abraham.

3:2 "For in the first place"

My intuition here, to place the emphasis on "in," highlighted that in this story of the revelation of Holy One, the oracles were entrusted to the ones in (occupying) the first place, i.e. the Jews. In the story of the revelation of Holy One, Jesus' followers come next. Novenson's perspective on Paul in relation to messiah thinking in the first century may resonate here:

> Paul was one of a number of Jews (some of whom were Christian, others not) for whom this particular messiah tradition provided an answer to the Gentile question: The Gentiles are to be neither converted nor destroyed; rather they share in the blessedness of the age to come by virtue of their obedience to the Davidic king of Israel. This is the view attested in Paul's reading of Isa 11:10 in Rom 15:12.[11]

The more I read as I learn and rehearse, the more the nuances shift, adjust, make deeper meaning.[12]

3:3 "Will their faithlessness nullify the faithfulness of Holy One?"

As I speak these words, I hear and feel not Paul posing a question for the sake of argument, but Jewish followers of Jesus genuinely uncertain about their relationship with Holy One now. I feel them concerned that Holy One might have abandoned the Jews in favor of the rest of the world. At this point, then, I am no longer taking on the persona of Paul the rhetorician, or Phoebe the orator, but the Jews themselves giving voice to their own question. This strips away all the oratorical and rhetorical technical skill to lay bare the emotion of the question, a question posed by generations of followers of Holy One who have wondered where Holy One is, whether Holy One has turned away. I hope this will invite connection for my audience with the story that lies between the lines of Paul's letter, the story of the first followers of Jesus working out what life following his Way meant for them.

3:4 "as it is written in the Psalms"

I therefore have a deep sense of Paul's encouragement and assurance for his audience in what follows, especially as he draws on their own tradition, their own sacred texts in his citation of the Psalms. This is why I have inserted "in the Psalms," which does not appear in the Greek. I don't assume the same

---

11. Novenson, "The Jewish Messiahs," 373.

12. As I was rehearsing, public conversations were exploring the implications of understanding "God" to be the one and / or the same for Muslim, Christian, and Jewish, faith traditions today. See, for example, Ralston, "The Same God, or the One God?" My own thoughts in response to this article: Agnew, "One, Three, You, Me".

sort of knowledge of scripture for my audiences as Paul could assume in a tradition of singing the Psalms, and better memory of texts for which we now have written copies for reference.[13]

3:10–18

In a late change, I condensed these verses, recasting them somewhat for rhythm in my performance poet voice. In the NRSV these verses are formatted as poetry, they are citations from various parts of scripture.

Specific translation choices:

> 3:11 there is no one showing wisdom, / no one seeking Holy One.

Here, decisions are made primarily for sound; the "m" and "n" sounds at the ends of lines an application of alliteration for holding these lines together as a unit.

> 3:12 They have all gone astray, are all alike corrupt;

Following Psalm 14:3 and 53:3, I have chosen "corrupt" rather than "worthless," as I think this will convey meaning more effectively for my audience. Alliteration is again in play with "alike," "corrupt" and "kindness."

> 3:16 Their paths are misery and ruin,
> 3:17 the way of peace they have not known;
> 3:18 "There is no awe before their eyes, no awe of Holy One."

Verse 17 remains as it appears in the NRSV translation, but verses 16 and 18 are changed for rhythm and sound.

3:19 "Now we know..."

I took some time in rehearsal to settle on expression and emphasis that conveyed meaning that made sense to me here. I speak quite quickly, this is about judgment, but the point seemed not to be judgment as much as the relationship of Jews with the nations and with Holy One. Paul seemed to be making sense of the tradition of Israel in light of the Jesus event. At this point I am aware of the implied or original audience being the Jewish component of the churches in Rome. I feel as though I speak these words to that audience, and here I do treat my audience as having taken on the

---

13. As observed of Swanson's adaptation of Mark for actors and choir: Swanson, "'This Is My...,'" 353.

persona of the Jewish audience for a moment. These words do not in themselves speak directly to a twenty-first-century audience in Adelaide. We are not Jews working out our relationship to Holy One having been the chosen elect holy people for the sake of the world. Christian audiences might find connections in the general situation of working out who Holy One is, how we relate to Holy One, in a changed context from the Christian West to the multi-faith global community. This may be a point in the letter in performance at which my audience, by taking the character of the original audience, and feeling what these words might have meant to that audience, are able to connect those feelings with their own in their own contexts, and thereby find meaning.

3:19d "the whole world may be held accountable"

The gesture of the hands making the shape of the earth is perhaps a gesture neither Paul nor Phoebe would have employed at this point. I find it helpful as an easily recognized gesture for my audiences today; it also helps me to know which words come next, as two subsequent pages of script end with "by works prescribed by the law" (3:20, 28), and I was getting confused as to which one came when. This gesture helps me to separate out the two occurrences of that phrase and know where I am in the flow of the argument.

3:20b "through the law comes knowledge of Tyrant"

I have in rehearsal gradually dropped the definite article found in the NRSV. The Greek reads διὰ γὰρ νόμου ἐπίγνωσις ἁμαρτίας (*dia gar nomou epignosis harmartias*).

It may not make a significant difference, but the important thing here is that I feel an awareness of all the things Paul is saying about the law, and find that "knowledge of Tyrant" means to me something like understanding of, or an ability to see and identify where we have gone astray (3:12) and that we need to turn back towards holiness (2:4b).

3:21 "notwithstanding"

The NRSV reads "irrespective of," which felt to me to be leaning towards the disrespect of the law some interpretations of this letter have applied, but which I do not feel Paul intends. χώρις (*choris*) has a meaning of "apart from, without making use of," so "notwithstanding" is within the semantic range while maintaining some respect for the law, I hope.

3:22 "the holiness of Holy One through faith in Jesus Wisdom"

The way I embody and speak these words was seeming to render "faith-in-Jesus-Wisdom" as an adjective of "holiness": the faith-in-Jesus-Wisdom kind of holiness. I am not speaking these words as if this kind of holiness is the only kind of holiness valued, correct, or leading to Holy One. In an age of ever-opening inter-faith conversation, when we are growing in respect for our different traditions, it seems important to articulate the revelation of Holy One in Jesus as *one particular* revelation of and path into holiness / right relationship with Holy One.

3:25a "as a sacrifice of atonement by his blood"

I am aware that I speak these lines quite quickly, and with a tone of intoning a formula. That is how I hear these words—formulaic, and almost code-like in an inherited understanding what Holy One is doing through Jesus. My personal theology recoils somewhat from the sacrificial atonement understanding of Jesus' crucifixion, for it can present a view of humanity that is inherently negative, and a view of Holy One as a hard-nosed accountant whose ledger must be perfect and so any amount of violence to the Holy Son is acceptable. It is inescapable that I bring this perspective into my speaking of the words of Paul. Many (though not all) in my audience—especially the Adelaide audience comprised predominantly of a liberal to progressive congregation—will also have let go of certain theologies of sacrificial atonement that have been espoused throughout the generations.

3:31 "we uphold the law."

Even after many weeks rehearsing this line, I was still unsure of its meaning. For a long time, I held in mind multiple possibilities of meaning:

> Paul affirms the law for his people, the Jews, as a rich and vibrant tradition
> Paul means the law of faith, not the law of works
> Paul is anticipating his reference to Jesus' great command—that the law is ultimately the law of love for God and for one another.

As I inhabited the later chapters of the letter, I discovered links with Rom 14 that illuminated meaning (on which I say more in the Critical Reflection).

4

4:2 "he has a claim to glory."

I am unsure exactly what this means. Embodying, rehearsing, is not offering any clarity on meaning here. I have settled on a tone that repeats the questioning of Jews from Rom 3, when Paul takes on the persona of the Jews. Thus, I speak verses one and two in the voice of the questioner, and verse three in the voice of the responder. I suspect this is more code-like formula for describing one's membership among the holy people of Holy One.

4:10 "And how was it credited to him."

The NRSV reads "How then." This is a minor adjustment for my own speaking voice, the way I naturally might progress the argument, my intonation, the rise and fall of my Australian-accented voice.

How, then was it credited to him, one might speak with intonation falling towards the end of the sentence. And how was it credited to him? Gives in my voice an inflection on how and him, in the manner of posing a question the answer to which I expect my audience to know.

4:9–12

Note the repetition of gestures to my left for circumcision / the circumcised, and to my right for uncircumcision / the uncircumcised.[14] The continuity is important if the audience is not to be confused. The holding of the two "sides" of divisions in Rome visually through my gestures is an important way I built and communicated the rhetorical development that Oestreich notes in Rom 14, from a church divided to a diverse church united.[15]

I omitted much of Rom 4. Considering the time constraints of the performance, I felt I could make Paul's point effectively enough in the first 12 verses, without the repetitive subsequent verses in this chapter.

---

14. It may be worth noting the disruption of inherited diminishing of Jews on the left, historically "wrong" side in theatre and oratory, by placing them on the audience's right.

15. Oestreich, *Performance Criticism of the Pauline Letters*, 157.

5

5:2 "through whom we have gained access to this grace in which we stand"

Again, I found myself speaking these words with a gentleness and openness, rather than a tone of exclusivism about the new understanding of relationship with the Divine for followers of Jesus.

There is a strong feeling of joy through this section; I cannot help but smile as I speak these words of delighted gratitude to Holy One for this welcome into holiness, this pouring out of love into our hearts (5:5). The joy feels like a key unlocking Paul's intent and purpose.

5:7 "a person made holy"

NRSV "righteous person": I discuss the translation choice in the Critical Reflection.

The flow of the argument shows me that "a person made holy" and "a good person" are being contrasted, and so there is something perhaps in ancient Greek culture about being a "good" person that I, in the twenty-first century do not fully comprehend. However, my body, my emotions, understand the contrast, understand intuitively that one might be made holy and not be deemed a "good" person.

5:9–11

I have condensed much of Rom 5 from verse 9 onwards, in the interest of simplifying what I was finding a convoluted argument. I needed to put this into words I could effectively speak to convey meaning. The decisions are difficult to explain, as they were intuitively made, from the feel and flow of the argument in my own body and voice imagining my audiences.

5:16 κατακριμα (*katakrima*): "condemnation"

Noting the word play in the Greek with *krima*—judgment.

"In this and the cognates that follow the use of the term 'condemnation' does not denote merely a pronouncement of guilt . . . but the adjudication of punishment."[16] Further meaning: "judicial pronouncement upon a guilty person, *condemnation, punishment, penalty.*"[17]

Although the translation had felt harsh at first, after exploring the Greek, I decided to leave "condemnation" and "judgment" as they are in NRSV—that is what is meant.

I noted also that the NRSV inserts "trespass" after "the one" in 16b. I could have chosen to speak just one occurrence of "trespass" at 16b rather than 16c, where it appears in the Greek, which would do the same thing as the Greek, but making more sense in contemporary English usage; however, I followed the NRSV.

5:18ff

I adopt a bit of a teacherly tone here, recapping the lesson of the day with pauses before "Adam" and "Jesus" in a light-hearted moment saying to the audience, I know you've got this, but just to be sure.

I am careful to place emphasis on "for all" in v. 18a and b, for I sense an important contrast of condemnation and welcome into holiness, and also an important reiteration of the point already made, that Jews and Greeks are all invited into this story.

5:19 "obedience"

The long "o" when speaking "obedience" feels somewhat odd, but felt necessary for illuminating the contrast being made.

5:20 "Now law did come"

I can feel the potential for exclusionary application of this section, or at least a negative portrayal of the law as inviting the multiplication of trespass. I speak these lines fairly quickly and lightly, as Paul comes back to his discussion of the law later.

I felt the suggestion that "Torah intended to give life . . . but because of sin all it could give was death"[18] was quite negative. Torah has continued to be life-giving for thousands of Jews still practicing Torah observance in various ways. Perhaps one could argue that Paul might have intended such

---

16. BDAG, 518.
17. BDAG, 518.
18. Wright, "Romans," 563.

a harsh judgment of the effects of Tyrant, but I did wonder if Jesus Wisdom fights *with* Torah against Sin / Tyrant? Both Jesus and Torah are on the side of Holy One; both fight fear with love; and the Great Commandment of Deut 6 is interpreted by Jesus (Mark 12) and Paul (Rom 3:31; 13:8–10) as the law of love. This is one insight into the consequences of immersion in the letter, engaging with the interpretations of others: it invigorates the imagination and evokes fascinating questions for rumination.

6

6:8 "if we have died with Wisdom"

I became aware, rehearsing this line, that when Paul says "died with Wisdom" here, one could easily say "been baptized with Wisdom." The point is not that if one dies with Wisdom this happens and if one doesn't this does not happen—well, in my reading of it, which is, as stated, intentionally one seeking openness to and respect for those of other faiths, especially Jews, this is not the point. The point seems to me to come to terms with what has happened for those who choose to believe, who have been baptized: what does this mean for *our* relationship with Holy One? In the first century, these questions of meaning and identity were necessarily with reference to and drawing a distinction from those of other faiths, ideas, and beliefs. Today, we have a more established identity as the Christian church and faith, and can afford to make claims about identity that lean less towards division, and more towards a celebration of difference.[19]

Again, a significant amount of Rom 6 has been excised in the interests of time. This was a rather intuitive, almost arbitrary omission, and does leave out some interesting ideas with which it might have been fun to play—6:14 and the idea of being "under law or under grace," and Paul's interchanging dualisms and juxtapositions of Tyrant, grace, law, holiness.

6:20 "When you were slaves of Tyrant..."

I am keeping a light tone here, letting the joy of the previous section overflow, rather than taking a condemnatory tone about "sin" or participation in tyranny—for that has been passed over, as Paul has said (3:25).

---

19. See also, Agnew, "One, Three, You, Me."

6:22 "liberation from tyranny"

NRSV: "sanctification," as discussed in the Critical Reflection.

6:22 "enslaved to Holy One"

In rehearsal, I spoke this line with an emphasis on "enslaved," but that did not feel right. If the point is not slavery, but to whom "your" allegiance is now, emphasizing "Holy One" conveys that meaning. On watching the recording, I noticed that in performance I employed a tone and expression that suggested I still had questions about the idea of being "enslaved" to Holy One. To some extent, that is unavoidable, the raising of new questions in performance, for I have noted that each performance is a new iteration of the composition, and each iteration will impact the performer as much as the audience, meeting you where you are in that moment.

6:22 "eternal life!"

Joy—the emotion here is joy. Could it be anything else for a person of faith presenting this composition to a community of faith, speaking of newness of life, liberation from tyranny? I note again that EPA is inherently confessional.

6:23 "For Tyrant's wage is death"

Change of word order from NRSV's very familiar "the wages of Tyrant (sin) is death" to "For Tyrant's wage is death." I wanted to foreground Tyrant, with whom Holy One and Jesus are contrasted, also emphasizing the way I am personifying Tyrant in this performance.

6:23 "our Liberator."

The day I began to learn these lines, I became suddenly aware of the importance of "our." Our liberator—the one through whom *we* have found liberation. In a performance that is seeking to move beyond exclusionary reading of Paul's writing, with its anti-Semitism and elitist view of Christianity as the only path to Holy One, this feels an important claim to make. *Our* liberator. Not *the* liberator, implying the only one. And taking into account my transposition of "liberator" for "lord" in this performance, we might thus hear the "our" as new as we hear "liberator" as new, and carry that awareness back to our reading of the more familiar NRSV and other English translations of the letter.

7

7:1–6

Omitted. Hefner observes that

> we need new metaphors for what it means to be church in the 21st century because we are seeking a more complex, deeper understanding of what it means to be human.[20]

In rehearsal, I discerned that the analogy of marriage in 7:1–6 might not function effectively for my audience, as it might have for Paul and his original audience. I imagined speaking these words to my audience, and looked back at me as performer from their perspective asking, "What does that mean?"[21] Notwithstanding the ways in which this analogy may have since been misapplied to become a proscription *for* marriage,[22] marriage itself is contested in our (Western, educated, middle-class) broader society.[23] With many Western nations now legalizing marriage in same-gender relationships, we can see that our culture is re-evaluating whether or not marriage is only legitimately for two people of opposite genders.[24]

In a different kind of performance I might *adapt* the letter, and search for a more pertinent analogy for my particular audience. An embodied performance approach responding to the lived experience of the audience by omitting these verses actually did feel consistent with Paul's own "process of negotiation that is always related . . . to the people, the context."[25]

---

20. Hefner, *Our Bodies Are Selves*, 164.

21. Recall discussion in Chapter 4 of the adaptation of *King Lear* for a young audience for whom the themes of family dynamics would hold more meaning than themes of aging and madness: Crouch, "Making Lear Accessible to Children."

22. Gaventa, "Romans," 408.

23. For example, Strasser, "Future of Marriage," 89–90.

24. An important consideration for the context of my audience of, predominantly, Uniting Church members, with this recent discussion in their tradition: "Discussion Paper on Marriage," Uniting Church in Australia Assembly. See also, Strasser, "Future of Marriage," 90–96.

25. Ehrensperger, *That We May Be Mutually Encouraged*, 188; Langton, *Apostle Paul in the Jewish Imagination*, 240.

7:7–14; 16–18a

Also omitted, for reasons concerning our view of the body, as discussed in the Critical Reflection.

7:15 "Even so"

As discussed in the Critical Reflection, I step forward here. This indicates stepping out of Paul's "I" to an "I" of an example human being. As I embodied these lines, the argument felt like the human condition, the human struggle between "good" and "evil."

7:22 "I delight in the law of Holy One in my inmost self"

From the script, it is evident that this is the way I intended to speak these lines; however, I ended up saying "inmost being": possibly reverting to a more natural word choice I might make if I was speaking my own words. This is the result of inhabiting the letter: giving voice to the words of Paul, I make them my own to some extent.

7:23 "dwelling in my members"

I had intended to omit "my members" here originally (as you can see in the script), but as I came to own the word and inhabit the script, the earlier phrase came to be repeated here after all.

7:24b "Who will rescue me from this body of death?"

Perhaps influenced by the history of reception of this passage that has turned it into a Reformation-inspired, individualistic, existential crisis,[26] I at first emphasized "body" in rehearsal, but this felt inadequate as an interpretation. My intuition was that such an interpretation, which implicitly diminished the value of the body, would be inappropriate for my audience, in a world that projects harmful images of the body.[27]

As I reflected with Gaventa on the cosmic battle of good and evil, Tyrant and Holy One (Sin and God for Gaventa), I was able to articulate

---

26. Paul is not writing in response to "Luther's pangs of conscience": Stendahl, *Paul among Jews and Gentiles*, 3. See also Gaventa, *Our Mother Saint Paul*, 132.

27. Hefner, *Our Bodies Are Selves*, 70.

what felt unsatisfactory about the emphasis on "body." Hearing Paul's argument here as part of a broader understanding of this cosmic battle, I placed the emphasis on "death"; for it seems we might receive meaning in these words by focusing on the consequences of Tyrant's grip on humanity, the human person, or "bodyself."[28] In so doing, perhaps we might not only hear meaning for today that more helpfully articulates the human condition, but may even point to a more helpful understanding of Paul's meaning in his context.

In Rom 1 it is not the creature that is the problem, but the worship of the creature for itself rather than worship of the Creator. It seems unlikely, on hearing the letter in its breadth, and the various ways in which Paul speaks of "body," that he would use the body as an image of the church that celebrates its diversity and vitality (12:4–8), if "body" was an inherently negative idea.[29] Surely the aural link in that case would be best avoided? Paul will go on to describe the yearning of creation for renewal (8:22–23); but do our bodies need redeeming if they are evil and of death? Rather, to present our bodies to Holy One is an act of—acceptable—spiritual worship (12:1), which seems not only to affirm the body, but to describe its integration with spirit.

7:25 "Thanks be to Holy One..."

I step backwards to speak these words from the main point on stage. Here, Paul's voice comes through again directing the recipients of the letter, the community of followers of Jesus, to remember they have entered into a new relationship, a relationship of hope that bursts the boundaries of life and death. A "yes, but" of his own.

7:25–8:1

(Note 25b omitted) As I scaffold each successive "chunk" and chapter onto the former, I feel the rhythm of the letter's discussion. I can feel the trust and joy in liberation with "our Liberator" in Rom 6, ebb into the struggle of Rom 7 as the cosmic battle continues though its outcome is understood to

---

28. As noted earlier, "bodyself asserts that my body is my very self, and that myself is a body": Hefner, *Our Bodies Are Selves*, 2.

29. Gundry argues that flesh is representative of the potential for sin to inhabit a person, rather than indicating an inherent sinfulness about the human body: Gundry, *Soma in Biblical Theology*, 138–39. Even so, there is a dualism that is almost gnostic at 7:24 with "this body destined to die through the domination of sin, which leads to death": Gundry, *Soma in Biblical Theology*, 138.

be in favor of Holy One, and now again, further reflections for those in the Liberator who continue to wrestle towards understanding how to live in the way of the Spirit rather than the way of evil.

8

8:1 "know no condemnation"

The NRSV's "There is no condemnation" becomes "know no condemnation." I like the poetry of it, and also I felt as though "there is" was more exclusive somehow. As I learnt these lines, I naturally spoke "know no condemnation" as an expression of the meaning I was finding there. I did not hear these words as an exclusionary, elitist and judgmental "Christ is the only way" statement, but as an observation of what the follower of Christ experiences.

I was getting the sense that, if Paul is shifting the pertinence of the letter from Torah-observers to non-Torah observers, this section is for all followers of Jesus. What I speak in Rom 7 is, too. And with the jump over chapters 9–11, you get a more direct flow from there to 12 with its message to *all*.

8:3–14

Omitted—for similar reasons as discussed pertaining to perspectives of "body."

8:15 "You have not received a spirit of slavery..."

Learning these lines, I felt once again the love of the sender for the recipients of the letter. If you look from inside this letter, inhabiting it, you see only the recipients, beloved of the sender. So the application of such lines as oppositional, condemning those who are not followers of Jesus, feels inappropriate. It feels, as I speak them, that these words are observing the experience of those who choose to follow Jesus, making sense of the transformation of their life in light of that choice and his teaching, his life and death and resurrection. Perhaps I am imposing too much of myself on the letter. But it *is* me who inhabits the letter for this performance; it *is* me who is allowing these words to become part of me by committing them to knowledge by heart. And this is what I find.

The gaze of the interpreter changes because you are looking through the letter, from the inside of the letter, with the eyes of the sender / author. This has to be an act of imagination. Looking through the letter to an actual audience today has to be an act of embodiment and presence together with that audience.

8:19–21

Omitted

8:23 "who have the first fruits of the Spirit"

In rehearsal, I consistently forgot this line. Eventually, I omitted it. I was probably influenced by the overall approach, which was to minimize the exclusionary overtones that have been exaggerated in the conversation surrounding this letter over 2000 years.

8:27 "according to the will of Holy One."

I struggled as I learned these words, to give expression in such a way as to represent the Spirit as one of the three persons of Holy One.

8:31 "If Holy One is for us..."

More and more I was feeling myself wanting to open up the letter for the context of my time and place, for the context of the whole human community in the midst of the struggle to connect with one another across boundaries.

"Holy One is for us" could be interpreted as Holy One is for "us" *and not* "them." But "Holy One is for us" could be interpreted as all creation, all humans. When I hear words like this, when I speak words like this, I hear a message that therefore no human is—or should be—against another.

8:32–34 omitted

The argument felt ratty, scatty, and difficult to give voice to for an audience today. I could not discern meaning, and when I was looking for places to abridge the letter for the time constraints, such staccato arguments were easy to cut.

8:37 "through Holy One who loved us."

I was leaving these words out in rehearsal, accidentally. When I did remember and spoke them, I spoke love with joy and a big smile!

8:38 "nor life"

Every time I say this, it strikes me as provocative somehow, the idea that life *could* get in the way, but even if it could, Paul is convinced that Wisdom can overcome that obstacle.

8:39 "nor anything else in all creation"

I feel a strong emphasis on *any*thing and *all* creation, with a gesture that spreads my arms as wide as possible, my knees bending in emphasis, my head moving to sweep my eyes over all the audience, as if to say, *are you listening, do you hear this, this is important.*

8:39 "love of Holy One in Wisdom Jesus our Liberator."

I am aware that within myself, this is almost the only point at which I speak such a phrase without a pause. Most times in speaking Holy One *in* Wisdom Jesus our Liberator, I pause, pulling back from the implications of the language for exclusionary understanding of salvation through Jesus only, which is entirely plausible as Paul's meaning and as an interpretation from any receiver of the letter. In this interpretation, I am exploring to what extent the letter can be spoken without leaning towards the dangerous exclusivity and arrogance of a Christianity that persecutes and condemns those of other faiths or none as outside the love and grace of Holy One (a purpose to which Pauline letters have been put through time). I do so trying not to dismiss the realm of possibility of such meaning in Paul's own words and theology. However, in an Embodied Performance interpretation, one meaning must be chosen for the moment, and I have erred on the side of received meaning rather than original meaning for this interpretation, I hope consistently and within the realms of possible meaning within the letter.

9:1—11:32 (EXCLUDING 11:1-2)

Omitted. See discussion in the Critical Reflection.

11

11:1 And yes, I do ask, has Holy One rejected their people, Israel?

As discussed in the Critical Reflection.

11:33-36

These verses are spoken with awe, joy, and trust. My gaze is up, the accepted and recognized gaze towards heaven and Holy One, towards the beyond. I say more on the doxological passages in the Critical Reflection.

12

12:1-2

Early in the rehearsal process, I noticed resonances here with Paul's earlier arguments concerning the mind and body, and thought to take care when making the abridgements for the implications of meaning lost here if omitting some of those earlier arguments.

12:1 "This is your spiritual worship."

In the NRSV—"which is your spiritual worship." As I rehearsed these words, it felt important to highlight this feature, that *this* is your spiritual worship. "Which" is your spiritual worship feels as though the whole sentence fades away without appropriate emphasis. Paul is about to go on to employ his body metaphor for the community of Jesus' followers. Body is important. "Present your bodies" is therefore, in the plural, your individual selves, embodied, all of life. It is important to highlight then that your whole self comes to the task of worship, and that worship goes with you into your whole life. Retrospectively, when the body / community metaphor is being articulated a few moments later, this presenting your body as spiritual worship is still hanging in the air, still processing in the listeners' ears and minds and hearts. This portion of the letter is profoundly about the embodiment of the love and grace that has been articulated in the first half of the letter; listening to the movement between individual and community, both as body, especially when mediated by a live body presenting the letter to a live audience, embodied—it is difficult to articulate the depth of knowing that resonates through this structure for his argument at this point, relying on the mutual embodiment of speaker and listeners to highlight the mutual embodiment of the love of Holy One within the Christian community, the focus of this latter half of the letter. Perhaps nowhere else in the letter, apart from Rom 16, is it clearer what embodied performance offers to the understanding of Paul's letter to the Romans.

As I speak these words—"present your bodies"—I point to my body by way of example—present yourselves, as you are, the gesture communicating meaning in the words.

As I speak the words "be transformed by the renewing of your minds," I use the gesture I have used for mind and soul/ spirit (Rom 1), which is to draw my left hand downwards past head and heart. Subtly, I hope, this communicates an ancient understanding of "mind/spirit," of being, that is whole and embodied, rather than the disembodied rationality idolized by the enlightenment and in times since.

As I speak the words "as in one body," I again point to my body; we have many members, I point to eye, head, hand, foot; so we—and I pause here while I gesture, slowly, arms extending across the whole gathered people—who are many are one body in wisdom—again I speak slowly as I gesture the movement for mutuality to accompany "and individually we are members one of another."

Embodied performance of this section puts the words into the body of the community, embodied in this time and place; puts the words into the bodies of those individual members of the community; invites such embodiment that the words themselves exhort through Rom 12–16 as an embodiment of Rom 1–11.

12:5b "Individually members one of another"

The gesture employed here is the repeated gesture for mutuality employed throughout, cf. 1:12, 12:10 etc.

As I prepare this section for the audience in Adelaide, I wonder if there will be some in the audience who will recall my performance of 1 Cor 12 for a state-wide meeting of the church some years ago, in which I employed similar gestures of sweeping arms across the whole room and identifying individuals among the gathered. Many in the Adelaide audience have experienced me telling the biblical stories before on various occasions; this comes with us into the room, into this embodied performance of Romans.

12:6 "We have gifts that differ"

I listened to myself giving voice to these words, and heard, in emphasizing "have" rather than "differ," and "grace" rather than "given" or "us," both the gifted nature of the gifts—generous, undeserved—and the collective reception of the gifts, the grace. Speaking "we have" with joy emphasizes gratitude as response. Speaking "gifts-that-differ" as a quality of the kind of gifts they are describes the need of difference for health within the community, and invites delight in difference, rather than a resigned tolerance of difference. That grace is given to "us," not to "each one" reminds us that grace is given to the community, a grace of varying colors that is manifest in individuals in unique ways. I was reminded of Wisdom delighting in creation, in the beautiful picture Proverbs paints, delighting in all the things created, and saw that grace permeates all creation which is infinitely varied, always changing, and necessarily diverse for the health of all, individually and collectively.

Giving voice to the list that follows, I do so with growing speed, as an orator would when listing an inexhaustive list of examples, and I let my voice tail off at "cheerfulness" as if to suggest, "I could go on." This is an intentional resistance to the kinds of interpretations and applications of Paul's lists of gifts as a guide book to the "spiritual" gifts sometimes privileged in some parts of the church.

12:9 "Offer genuine embrace"

This is a change from NRSV's "let love be genuine." As discussed above, this passage is feeling like an invitation to embody the message of Paul's letter, his theology, and it is appearing to be a theology of embrace, embracing difference, celebrating diversity.

In the context of the letter, these words follow Paul's exhortation to be the body of Jesus Wisdom, one body with different and diverse members all humbly and confidently taking their place and making space for one another.

I chose "embrace" for resonance with Rom 16, the climactic embodiment of embrace for members of the community across the main dividing line of Jew/Gentile.

It took some time to find the rhythm of the list that follows, a list of instructions. As I held the people in my imagination, it became easier to speak this guidance for living; I broke it into sets of four or three lines, and the structure became clear, meaning became clear, the rhythm settled—in a very fluid non-linear way. In some cases, finding the rhythm resolved what felt awkward in the structure; in others, the structure actually helped to find the rhythm for speaking aloud.

The mutuality gesture is repeated throughout at various places:

> 12:9 offer genuine embrace—as a way of indicating that each member should welcome the gifts of other members, offering their own gifts, and one of the gifts every member is to offer is genuine embrace of each other.
> 12:10 love one another with mutual affection
> 12:16 live in harmony with one another

It was like picking up the thread Paul showed at the beginning and saying, remember this? This is the beauty of the welcome of both Jew and Gentile we've been wrestling with.

12:16b "Do not claim to be wiser than you are"

A hint of humor, with a tip of the head and raised eyebrows suggesting that we know we are all inclined to claim to be wiser than we are; acknowledging that we are all in this together.

13

13:1 "Let every person be subject to the governing authorities;"

As I noted in the Critical Reflection, I placed the emphasis on "be," for as I built the performance, scaffolding Rom 13 onto Rom 12, I became aware of the progression from one argument to the next. "Overcome evil by good" leads into "let every person be subject to governing authorities," which seems to align the authorities with the evil we are called to overcome with good. But the argument progresses further even than that, to move away from equating the authorities with evil and instead aligning them with the very purposes of Holy One.

13:3a For rulers are not a source of fear for those who do good; but for those who do wrong—

Translation—"source of fear"—NRSV has "terror" (NIV "hold no terror"), but it felt inappropriate in contemporary English, as "terror" has a whole lot of social and political connotations in our time. So, returning to the Greek and the parameters of meaning, I determined on "source of fear" as a more appropriate rendering of the Greek in English to convey what "terror" might once have meant.

The more I rehearsed "but for those who do wrong," the more these words took on something of my own personality. I found myself not uttering it as a statement that rulers are a source of fear *for* those who do wrong, a sub-clause of the main sentence, but more as a follow-on statement that, in colloquial English of today leaves the consequences of doing wrong unspoken except for a tilt of my head, a shrug of the shoulders, trailing voice and particular expression of implied warning—like the ellipsis ... that trails a written sentence into implication.[30]

13:8 "except to love one another"

In the intonation of "except *to* love one another," I found I was implying backwards that the actions of paying taxes, giving revenue, respect and honor to whom it is due are also acts of love.

13:8 "the one who loves another has fulfilled the law"

Again, I naturally repeated the gesture of mutuality as I spoke "the one who loves another."

This is followed by the gesture of holding two hands upwards like the scales of justice, as at 4:31, at which point I gesture with my head and eyes to pay attention to the gesture, and do likewise here, explicitly inviting the connection between the two passages of the letter. This connection became evident to me in the embodying of the letter, the intuitive repetition of the gesture, and added an understanding of the connections between the two halves of the letter that I can only hint at in performance, but which comes with the embodiment for myself, and will invite further reflection through the gestured connection for the engaged and inquiring listeners in the

---

30. A further example is the shock that came into my expression speaking of the way Paul sees that someone's acting against their own convictions is a "participation in tyranny" at 14:23.

audience. This is something I did not have the capacity to explore in this project. Future research might engage with audiences for longer periods of time, to evoke responses not only in the live embodied moment, but days and perhaps even weeks after the performance, to explore the ways in which a performance goes with its recipient, as indicated in audience studies and the writing of professional storytellers.[31]

When I performed the second half of the letter only (Uniting College, 2016, track 24), I felt for myself in the performance moment that the impact of 13:8, 10, was lessened without the explicit link to the discussion in Rom 3. In this performance, the link to Torah was much more subtle, requiring the audience to make the connection to the traditions of Jesus for themselves through Paul's words, and through those traditions to Torah by way of Jesus' summary of the law in the law to love your neighbor. However, as there is still much in 12–15 that retains the context of the letter as addressing the complex relationships between Jewish and Gentile followers of Jesus, the impact on overall meaning of the letter was not diminished by the loss of the nuanced meaning of these verses. Further, the audience on that occasion were divinity students, of whom I could assume a deeper working memory—cultural capital—of the Bible and its themes.

13:9–10

The gesture of mutuality is repeated again at verse 9, and the gesture of upholding the law is repeated once more at verse 10.

I pause after verse 10, for there is a break in the flow of the letter, rather than flowing naturally to the next argument, it seems to jump to a new point entirely, with its consideration of apocalyptic consequences.

13:12 "works of darkness"

My instinct is to pull back from the possible intended association here with the law as demanding works—this is consistent with my reading throughout.[32]

---

31. I have noted that Perry suggests audiences are helped in their reception of biblical compositions in performance by experiencing multiple performances: *Insights*, 99.

32. And contrary to readings such as that of Esler in "Social Identity" (60), where he sees Paul presenting an anti-law perspective.

13:13 "let us live honorably..."

The pace of this verse is important in conveying meaning, and building the argument's flow towards Rom 14, which picks up the idea of quarrelling (14:1).

13:14 omitted

For the reasons discussed elsewhere that negative views of the flesh being unhelpful for an audience today, which is embracing the materiality and embodied nature of human being.

14

14:1 "welcome"

In hindsight, I wonder if using "embrace" for the Greek προσλαμβανεσθε (*proslambanesthe*)—with its range of meanings including "receive, accept, take along"—instead of "welcome," would have woven an aural thread of connection through this passage as I have with the translation of ἀσπάσασθε (*aspasasthe*) through Rom 16, and for ἀγάπη (*agape*) in 12:9.

14:1 "uncertain in faith"

Seeking to avoid a pejorative tone. For Oestreich, Paul is not demeaning in his use of "weak," but seeking to lift the vulnerable and their status in the community.[33]

Audience feedback from the preview performance at Uniting College 6 April 2016 indicated that some found the translation to "uncertain" to also change the meaning of strong. For these listeners, by not using "certain" in place of "strong," I seem to have allowed the strong to have the potential for doubt, which I had not anticipated.

However, others felt that "uncertain" for those following Torah was unsatisfactory, for they understood that Torah-observers would have been "certain" about their law keeping. This may be another example of the shorthand employed by Paul that may have been effective for his own audiences, but which for reception today needs further adaptation or explanation than a straightforward embodied performance of the letter we have inherited.

33. Oestreich, *Performance Criticism of the Pauline Letters*, 158.

14:2 "while the uncertain eat only vegetables."

Speaking this line with a judgmental or disdainful tone felt incongruent with the overall interpretation of this letter as welcoming of difference, this particular section as affirming the different traditions each group has for honoring Holy One through their practice. For Oestreich, for example, Paul's concern is the responsibilities of the "strong" to show sympathy and compassion for, to offer help to, the "weak."[34]

14:3 "Those who eat must not despise those who abstain..."

As noted in the Critical Reflection, the gestures here are a reflection of the gestures in earlier chapters that indicated the Jews / circumcised on my left, and the Gentiles / uncircumcised on my right. Then, I indicated to my sides, here, I indicate with those hands, but in front of me—drawing some link with Torah observers and Jews, and non-Torah observers and Gentiles, though some Jews had undoubtedly let go of Torah-observing practices, as Paul had, and would therefore here be on my right, when they might have been on my left in earlier passages.[35]

14:6

Again, giving voice to Paul's words gradually revealed meaning in them as I repeated them, sought to learn them, and came to speak them from my heart. I am finding it incredibly difficult to articulate this process in ways that might help the reader to understand what it feels like, how that meaning is revealed, but it is so embodied and organic, that it is proving near impossible. I hope my words are giving some sort of indication that helps in some way. As they appear on the page in English, Paul's words might be interpreted as a command—if you observe the day, do so in honor of the Liberator. However, as the Greek φρονει (*pronei*) is in the third person plural, it seemed to me to be describing what is happening, rather than commanding what *ought* to happen. This is so for the subsequent verbs in v. 6 also, ἐσθιει (*esthiei*), ἐθχαριστει (*ethcharistei*). And so my intuition in giving voice to these words with an expression indicating observation not command is supported when I return to the Greek for confirmation of the

---

34. Oestreich, *Performance Criticism of the Pauline Letters*, 159–60.
35. Oestreich, *Performance Criticism of the Pauline Letters*, 164.

language structure. "Paul does what he expects the Roman Christians to do: to not judge others and to not treat them with contempt."[36]

14:7–8 "we do not live to ourselves, die to ourselves..."

Embodying these verses I became aware that I was addressing in my mind a "we" who are this community, the followers of Christ. It could be a "we" that is universal, making claims for all the world, and thus passing an exclusionary judgment on those who do not live and die for the Liberator, but it feels at this point that Paul is charging the community of Christ in Rome to heal the divisions within, and this is therefore a reminder of the implications of following Jesus—that you do not live or die to yourself, but to Jesus Wisdom, and we are all saying we are followers of Jesus, so are the same in our living and dying to the Liberator. I found support from Oestreich who sees Paul addressing "all" the church here, leading them from seeing their differences, to acknowledging their commonalities.[37]

14:10, 12

The gestures I employed for indicating "we" here and in v. 10, and for "us" in v. 12, are gestures that resemble the "we" in "we are the body of Wisdom"— holding this gathered community within my open arms. This is about us, those who have chosen this Way, and how we are going to live that Way with integrity. That is the sense of the meaning I get when I stand and speak these words, having learnt them, inhabited the argument, and taken the words to heart.

This may be a particularly 21st-century progressive interpretation, for that is the point of view in which I stand. However, it does feel, as I articulate the argument in this way, to be an authentic reception of Paul's letter *for* the 21st century, whether or not Paul had in mind more of a sweeping statement made for all humanity.

14:14

I pause after "it is unclean," having placed stress on "is": in rehearsal I noticed I was emphasizing that something *is* unclean to the one who deems it unclean, and began to see that Paul might be affirming the beliefs of the

---

36. Oestreich, *Performance Criticism of the Pauline Letters*, 172.
37. Oestreich, *Performance Criticism of the Pauline Letters*, 173.

so-called "uncertain," acknowledging a kind of strength to those who appear weak on the conviction that *anything* is clean. It seemed to me that I was discerning meaning in these lines, this letter, that affirmed the different interpretations, the different traditions of those who follow Jesus, as bringing a richness into the community not to be resisted, but instead, to be welcomed and celebrated. Some have suggested that "weak" might mean the minority within the community, and in this case, it is the "strong," or majority, who have the power to ostracize or welcome those who are different.[38] Others have suggested that the "weak" might be those of Jewish ethnicity returning to Rome from Emperor-instigated exile, weak in the sense of being vulnerable in the city and the Roman Empire.[39] Those of strength are those more secure in their place within the broader culture, who have a duty to protect those more vulnerable. This latter interpretation also influences our understanding of the call to obey the authorities, for if the more secure Gentile members of the church resist from their position of strength, they may draw unwanted attention to the Jewish members of their community, and potentially put them in danger.

14:17

As I speak "the realm of Holy One is not food and drink," I adopt a lighter tone, inviting a little humor again, welcoming a laughing at ourselves for missing the point.

Speaking "but holiness and peace and joy. . ." I express joy, I smile, with my posture I invite the audience to feel and enter into the joy of the realm of Holy One in this moment. This is a real gift of the embodied performance moment, the sharing of the emotions of the composition together, feeling the joy of the realm of Holy One as a way of experiencing, and knowing by experience.

14:19 "mutual encouragement"

Note the repetition of the gesture of mutuality again here.

---

38. Cf. Wright, "Romans," 735. Oestreich sees that it is a responsibility of the strong to help the weak: Oestreich, *Performance Criticism of the Pauline Letters*, 160.

39. Witherington, *Paul's Letter to the Romans*, 8, 376.

14:23 "is participation in tyranny"

In rehearsal, I began to naturally speak the words "is participation in tyranny" not only accompanied by the gesture used throughout the first half of the letter, but with an expression almost of shock, certainly of concern for those who do not act from their own convictions about God. This emotional response is shaped by, and helps to flow into, the argument that follows in Rom 15, and the responsibilities of the "strong" (however that is defined in our interpretation) towards the "weak" in the community. Those who are strong, in the majority, or confident, have power, and they can use it to disempower, overpower, and disenfranchise those who are weak, or they can use it to empower, encourage, and "lift up." At no stage did it feel to me as though the lifting up of others was to bring them to "our level"; at no stage did it feel to me as though to accommodate our neighbor was to merely tolerate until they found their way to the correct point of view. In light of the arguments Paul has been offering, building, scaffolding on one another, I come to this section with the conviction that Paul is celebrating difference, that welcome is affirmation of the other as they are, for it is as they are that each person is loved and made welcome by Holy One. The embodying and performing of the letter from beginning to end (omissions notwithstanding) allows for this deep understanding of the letter in its scaffolded arguments, in the flow of one argument to another, and the holding in that live embodied space of all the arguments together, shedding light on one another for nuanced and fuller meaning.[40]

15

I repeat the mutuality gesture through Rom 15 at verses 2 (accommodate our neighbor, build up the neighbor), 5 (live in harmony with one another), and 7 (welcome one another). The repetition is increasing, growing the letter towards its climax in Rom 16.[41]

15:1–2 "bear with"... "accommodate our neighbor"

NRSV: "put up with the failings of the weak and not to please ourselves"

---

40. Oestreich draws attention to the "emotional influencing" of Paul's rhetoric here: *Performance Criticism of the Pauline Letters*, 183.

41. This is an example of Wilson's notion of the composition "growing" in performance: "Performance Critical Analysis," 161.

I translate this, rather, "to bear with the frailty of the uncertain, and not to accommodate ourselves." In contemporary English the phrase "to put up with" carries some connotation of begrudging tolerance. The mutuality of the Jesus-following community in this letter from Paul is much more positive, more open than that. BDAG's "to sustain a burden, to carry" as meaning for βαστάζω (*bastazo*) in 11:18, and to "bear patiently with" for 15:1[42] convey this more generous opening of space and giving of oneself for the other that I feel Paul to encourage in this letter. There may be a particular context of trying circumstances that yields this meaning, which the return from exile and/or the conflicting practices within the community may be. ἀρέσκω (*aresko*) has the meaning of acting in a manner seeking to please, flatter, win favor or approval. It may be that within the context of the formal reciprocity of Mediterranean relationships, such winning favor or approval is connected with carrying out obligations of reciprocal favors. Perhaps this is an instance of Paul using the language and customs of the culture with a twist, contextually adding more of the sacrifice of self-interest found in the example of Jesus than the documents stipulating honor and reciprocity.[43]

15:6 "love and honor"

Rather than "glorify."[44]

15:15 "I have written to you rather boldly..."

There is a hint of humor in the acknowledging that Paul has "written to you rather boldly on some points by way of reminder"—intuitively, how it felt to me to speak it on these occasions. Not at all an attempt to rediscover how Phoebe would have spoken the words, or what Paul intended. This is an example of the pure focus on reception—how do we receive this text, how do I mediate it through my body? It felt like humor to me, because that is how I would say it, how I *did* intuitively say it as *I* embodied the words.

15:19 "fully proclaimed the gospel"

I was intrigued by the change in the NRSV from v. 15's translation of εὐαγγελιον (*euangelion*) as "gospel" to translating it in v. 19 as "good news."

---

42. BDAG, 171.
43. BDAG, 129.
44. See discussion in Agnew, "Love and Honour as an Invitation to 'Glorify' God."

My voice was intuitively saying "gospel," even though I was originally learning it as "good news," so I went to the Greek to investigate, and discovered that it is the same word in the Greek. For an aural hearing, I find keeping the same translation for repeated Greek words in the English helpful where possible, to maintain the aural links inherent in the Greek text. Of course there are times when the Greek use of the same word is contextually carrying meaning more appropriately rendered by two different English words; and there are times when different Greek words are rendered by the same English word—see my use of the English "embrace" in Rom 12:9 and Rom 16, for example—in order to utilize aural connections for the listener to communicate meaning.

Here, it seems to me not necessary to change the translation from verse 15 to 19, the context does not appear to demand it, so I have rendered the Greek as "gospel" each time.

15:20 "good news"

I have, however, kept the English as "good news" at verse 20, as it is in the NRSV. εὐαγγελίζεσθαι (*euangelizesthai*)—to bring good news. In a rhetorical structure, the change here feels like a one-two-three punch, with the third occurrence bringing the change for emphasis and nuance in meaning. So the argument builds—in priestly service of the gospel of Holy One, proclaim the gospel of Wisdom, proclaim the good news, which now effectively operates as shorthand for "the gospel of Holy One and Wisdom" (God and Christ).

15:23 "with no further place for me in these regions"

Speaking this line aloud, I found it difficult to settle on the expression, intonation, and emphasis that felt right. With an emphasis on "place," it felt as though there was some threat to Paul, there was a withdrawal of welcome. When I shifted emphasis to "further" and evenly across "in these regions," it felt more as though Paul himself had finished what he felt called to do there, and was ready to move further afield. Following as this phrase does from Paul's explanation of his goal to proclaim the good news where it has not already been heard, I felt the latter interpretation more appropriate. Of course, there is threat to Paul named in the request for prayer, but that seems a specific threat he will face once *in* Jerusalem, not in the regions in which he has been travelling and proclaiming the gospel. This seems one of those occasions in which either interpretation / reading / expression could be "right," and the performer can only "play" it one way, so has to choose what sits best for her in that moment.

15:8–12, and 27b

Here I again repeat the gestures indicating Jews/circumcised on audience right and Gentiles/uncircumcised on audience left.

16

Of course, we have engaged in extensive discussion of Rom 16 in the Critical Reflection, but I will include some further notes here for completeness.

16:2 "welcome"

Throughout Rom 16 I have translated ἀσπάσασθε (*aspasasthe*) as "embrace." It is a different word here (προσδέξηασθε, *prosdexeasthe*). Although there would be some benefit to linguistically linking the welcome of Phoebe with the welcome of those named, by using either welcome or embrace throughout, if Paul has used a different word, perhaps Paul is singling Phoebe out for a different role within the church, a specific and particular role within the church at Rome, as bearer of the letter and example of the mutual relationships of care the people are to embody themselves. I have kept the words distinct in English.

16:2 "including me"

In the NRSV, "and of myself as well." I kept saying "including me" as I learned these lines, so eventually I changed the script to reflect the way I was giving voice to Paul's meaning here. Not strictly accurate in its translation of the Greek, I think it nevertheless conveys the meaning accurately, and is another example of the way a performer will tweak the language of a story / composition to render it appropriately in her voice, the way the text is mediated by this specific performer on this particular occasion.

16:5

On reflection, I realize I have in all the performances omitted "and embrace the church in their house also." A simple error.

16:16 "all"

Sweeping hands wide, wider than even this gathering—all the churches beyond here.

16:19 "do"

I insert "do." It seemed to help clarify the meaning, and render the phrasing more comfortably into contemporary English.

16:27 "to them be the glory"

Rather than, as in the NRSV, "to whom." This is to reflect throughout the theology of Trinity I have been portraying, which is admittedly a lower Christology than Paul has himself. Here especially, offering blessing, I feel like my voice takes over almost, as I pray using Paul's words, but from *my* heart. If Performance Interpretation is inherently confessional, it would seem to maintain integrity of performer and method for the performer-interpreter to enter that nature of the event fully, rather than resist. I therefore need to shape the words appropriately for my heart if I am to pray them authentically. If I was acting the part of Paul or Phoebe, I would, as I have indicated elsewhere, not change these words.

Appendix C

Performance Examples

TRACK LIST

Videos can be found at https://sarahagnew.com.au/embodied-performance/

1. 1:26–27
2. 1:20–27
3. 1:20–32 digital performance
4. 1:7
5. 1:12
6. Mutuality theme (1:12; 14:19; 12:5; 12:10; 13:9)
7. Interlocutor (3:1–4a)
8. 6:23–7:15
9. 7:24
10. 7:22–23
11. 12:20–13:1
12. 8:38–11:36
13. 14:1–3, 5–6
14. 3:29
15. Doxologies (6:22; 15:5–6)
16. 16:1–2 Uniting College preview performance

17. 16:1–2
18. 16:3–16
19. 16:17–20
20. Bookends (1:7 and 16:16)
21. 16:20–21
22. 16:20b–23
23. 16:25–27
24. Phoebe's story and Rom 12–15—Uniting College preview

Video Credits

WELCOME ONE ANOTHER IN LOVE, ADELAIDE, 17 APRIL 2016

Recorded at Blackwood Uniting Church, Adelaide, Australia

Videographers: Ray Bown and Tim Lee

Lighting and sound: Rowan Lee

Editing: Ray Bown

DIGITAL STORYTELLING, ROMANS 1:20-32

Recorded at 4H Youth Centre, Chevy Chase, MD, USA, August 2016

Videography and editing: Jason Chesnut, ANKOSFilms

PHOEBE'S STORY & THE LETTER TO THE ROMANS (12-16)

Recorded at Uniting College, Brooklyn Park, Adelaide Australia, 6 April 2016

Videography and editing: Adam Jessup

With thanks to Rev Dr Vicky Balabanski for the invitation

Bibliography

Adams, Fred. "Embodied Cognition." *Phenomonological Cognitive Science* 9 (2010) 619–28.

Agnew, Sarah. "Choice: Stories. Reception Theory and Storytelling: Choosing Stories to Tell and Ways to Tell Them." In *Perspectives on Storytelling: Framing Global and Personal Identities*. Edited by Lena Möller, Minerva Ahumada, and Laurinda Brown. Oxford: Inter-Disciplinary, 2014. http://www.inter-disciplinary.net/publishing/product/perspectives-on-storytelling-framing-global-and-personal-identities.

———. "Every Mistake We Make Is an Opportunity to Learn." In *sarah tells stories* (blog). Adelaide, 2010. http://sarahtellsstories.blogspot.co.uk/2010/03/every-mistake-we-make-is-opportunity-to.html.

———. "Ill-treated Traditions: Two Lecterns Lament, Then Offer Hope to Their Speakers." *Scottish Episcopal Institute Journal* 1.4 (2017) 20–31.

———. "Love and Honour as an Invitation to 'Glorify' God? Embodying and Performing the Great Command with the Letter to the Romans." In Exploring the Glory of God. Durham, 2016.

———. "The Mutuality of Esther and Mordecai: Narrative Analysis and Embodied Performance Preparation of Esther 4." Flinders University, 2013.

———. "One, Three, You, Me: On Worshipping the One / Same God." In *sarahtellsstories*, 2016. http://sarahtellsstories.blogspot.co.uk/2016/01/midweek-musing-one-three-you-me-on.html

———. "Romans 16: A Call to Embrace One Another in Love." Paper presented at British New Testament Conference, Chester, England, 2016.

———. "Romans 16: A Call to Embrace One Another in Love." *Oral History Journal of South Africa* 5.2 (2017) 1–9.

———. "Telling Mark 10:13–16—Jesus and the Little Children." In *sarah tells stories*, 2012. http://sarahtellsstories.blogspot.co.uk/2011/12/telling-mark-1013-16-jesus-little.html.

Agosto, Efrain. "Patronage and Commendation, Imperial and Anti-Imperial." In *Paul and the Roman Imperial Order*, edited by Richard A. Horsley, 103–24. Harrisburg, PA: Trinity, 2004.

Ahumada, Minerva, Lena Möller, and Laurinda Brown. "Introduction." In *Perspectives on Storytelling: Framing Global and Personal Identities*, edited by Lena Möller, Minerva Ahumada, and Laurinda Brown. Oxford: Inter-Disciplinary, 2014.

Alexander, Loveday. "Women as Leaders in the New Testament." *Modern Believing* 54.1 (2013) 14–22.

Assembly, Uniting Church in Australia. "Discussion Paper on Marriage." Uniting Church in Australia Assembly. https://assembly.uca.org.au/doctrine/ item/1536-discussion-paper-on-marriage.

Baniceru, Ana Christina. "Telling Academic Stories: A Different Method of Approaching Academic Writing." In *Perspectives on Storytelling: Framing Global and Personal Identities*, edited by Lena Möller, Minerva Ahumada, and Laurinda Brown, 11–20. Oxford: Inter-Disciplinary, 2014.

Banks, Robert J. *Paul's Idea of Community: The Early House Churches in Their Cultural Setting*. Peabody, PA: Hendrickson, 1994.

Bartow, Charles L. "Performance Study in Service to the Spoken Word in Worship." In *Performance in Preaching. Bringing the Sermon to Life*, edited by Jana Childers and Clayton J. Schmit, 211–23. Grand Rapids: Baker Academic, 2008.

Bassler, Jouette M. "1 Corinthians." In *Women's Bible Commentary*, edited by Carol A. Newsom, Sharon H. Ringe, and Jacqueline E. Lapsley, 411–19. Rev. ed. Louisville: Westminster John Knox, 2012.

Beckwith, Sarah. *Signifying God. Social Relation and Sybolic Act in the York Corpus Christi Plays*. Chicago: University of Chicago Press, 2001.

Berlin, Adele. *Poetics and Interpretation of Biblical Narrative*. Winona Lake, IN: Eisenbrauns, 1994.

Boomershine, Amelia Cooper. "Breath of Fresh Air: Spiritual Empowerment through Biblical Storytelling with Incarcerated Men and Women." United Theological Seminary, 2015.

Boomershine, Thomas E. "All Scholarship Is Personal: David Rhoads and Performance Criticism." *Currents in Theology and Mission* 37 (2010) 279–87.

———. "Audience Address and Purpose in the Performance of Mark." In *Mark as Story: Retrospect and Prospect*, edited by Kelly R. Iverson and Christopher W. Skinner, 115–42. Atlanta: Society of Biblical Literature, 2011.

———. "Mark, the Storyteller: A Rhetorical-Critical Investigation of Mark's Passion and Resurrection Narrative." Union Theological Seminary, 1974.

———. "Messiah of Peace." http://messiahofpeace.com.

———. *Messiah of Peace: A Performance Criticism Commentary on Mark 14–16*. Biblical Performance Criticism Series 12. Eugene, OR: Cascade Books, 2015.

———. *Story Journey: An Invitation to the Gospel as Storytelling*. Nashville: Abingdon, 1988.

———. "Teaching Mark as Performance Literature: Early Literate and Postliterate Pedagogies." In *Communication, Pedagogy, and the Gospel of Mark*, edited by Elizabeth E. Shively and Geert Van Oyen, 73–94. Resources for Biblical Study 83. Atlanta: SBL, 2016.

Bordieu, Pierre. *Distinction: A Social Critique of the Judgement of Taste*. Abingdon: Routledge, 2013.

Boyarin, Daniel. *A Radical Jew: Paul and the Politics of Identity*. Berkeley: University of California, 1994.

Bozarth, Alla Renee. *The Word's Body. An Incarnational Aesthetic of Interpretation.* Lanham, MD: University Press of America, 1997.

Brown, John Russell. "Learning Shakespeare's Secret Language: The Limits of Performance Studies." *New Theatre Quarterly* 24 (2008) 211–21.

Bryan, Victoria K. "Listening to the Audience: An Examination of the Audience's Experience of Theatre." Claremont Graduate University, 2011.

Buckley, Ray. *Dancing with Words. Storytelling as Legacy, Culture, and Faith.* Nashville: Discipleship Resources, 2003.

Buechner, Frederick. *Telling the Truth: The Gospel as Tragedy, Comedy, and Fairy Tale.* New York: HarperCollins, 1977.

Burns, Basil David. "St Thomas Aquinas's Philosophy of Love: A Commentary on *Mutua Inhaesio* (Mutual Indwelling) as the Most Proper Effect of Love in IA IIAE, QQ 26-28 of the 'Summa Theologicae.'" University of Dallas, 2013.

Byrskog, Samuel. "Co-Senders, Co-Authors and Paul's Use of the First Person Plural." *ZNW* 87 (1996) 230–50.

Cassidy, Tanya, and Conrad Brunström. "'Playing Is a Science': Eighteenth-Century Actors' Manuals and the Proto-Sociology of Emotion." *British Journal for Eighteenth-Century Studies* 25 (2002) 19–31.

Castelli, Elizabeth A. "Romans." In *Searching the Scriptures.* Vol. 1, *A Feminist Commentary*, edited by Elisabeth Schüssler Fiorenza, 272–300. New York: Crossroad, 1994.

Chesnut, Jason (dir.). "The Gospel of Mark: I Tell You, This Is the Way It Is." 104. Performer: Philip Ruge-Jones. Baltimore: ANKOSFilms, 2016.

Childers, Jana. *Performing the Word. Preaching as Theatre.* Nashville: Abingdon, 1998.

———. "The Preacher's Creative Process. Reaching the Well." In *Performance in Preaching: Bringing the Sermon to Life*, edited by Jana Childers and Clayton J. Schmit, 153–68. Engaging Worship. Grand Rapids: Baker Academia, 2008.

Christie, Douglas E. "What the Body Knows." *Spiritus: A Journal of Christian Spirituality* 13.2 (2013) ix–xi.

Clark, Margaret S., and Ian Brisette. "Relationship Beliefs and Emotion: Reciprocal Effects." In *Emotions and Beliefs. How Feelings Influence Thoughts*, edited by Nico H. Frijda, Antony S.R. Manstead, and Sacha Bem, 212–40. Cambridge: Cambridge University Press, 2000.

Collins, John N. "Georgi's 'Envoys' in 2 Cor 11:23." *Journal of Biblical Literature* 93 (1974) 9.

Conquergood, Dwight. "Performance Studies: Interventions and Radical Research." *The Drama Review* 46.2 (2002) 145–56.

Cooey, Paula M. *Religious Imagination and the Body: A Feminist Analysis.* New York: Oxford University Press, 1994.

Cook, Amy. "Interplay: The Method and Potential of a Cognitive Science Approach to Theatre." *Theatre Journal* 59 (2007) 579–94.

———. "Staging Nothing: *Hamlet* and Cognitive Science." *substance* 35.2 (2006) 83–99.

Cousins, Melinda. "Pilgrim Theology: Worldmaking through Enactment of the Psalms of Ascents (Psalms 120–134)." Charles Sturt University, 2016.

Crouch, Tim. "Making Lear Accessible to Children." In *Director Films*, edited by Royal Shakespeare Company: TES, 2013.

Cuddy, Amy. "Your Body Language Shapes Who You Are." In *TEDGlobal*: TED: Ideas Worth Spreading, 2012.

Cuddy, Amy J. C., Caroline A. Wilmuth, and Dana R. Carney. "The Benefit of Power Posing before a High-Stakes Social Evaluation." Working Paper, *Harvard Business School Working Paper* (2012). http://nrs.harvard.edu/urn-3:HUL.instrepos:9547823.

Cusack, Niamh. "Paulina Played by Niamh Cusack. Performances." In *Adopt an Actor*. Shakespeare's Globe, 2016.

Danker, Frederick W. et al. *A Greek-English Lexicon of the New Testament and Other Early Christian Literature*. 3rd ed. Chicago: University of Chicago Press, 2000.

Davies, Brian. *Thomas Aquinas's Summa Theologicae: A Guide and Commentary*. Oxford: Oxford University Press, 2014.

Dench, Judi. "Reflecting Nature: A Conversation with Dr Michael Parsons." *The Psychologist* (July 1990) 312–14.

Dewey, Arthur J. "A Re-Hearing of Romans 10:1–15." In *Semeia 65: Orality and Textuality in Early Christian Literature*, edited by Joanna Dewey, 109–27. Atlanta: SBL, 1995.

Dewey, Dennis. "Performing the Living Word: Learnings from a Storytelling Vocation." In *The Bible in Ancient and Modern Media*, edited by Holly E. Hearon and Philip Ruge-Jones, 142–55. Biblical Performance Criticism Series 1. Eugene, OR: Cascade Books, 2009.

Dewey, Joanna. *The Oral Ethos of the Early Church. Speaking, Writing, and the Gospel of Mark*. Biblical Performance Criticism. Edited by David Rhoads Eugene, OR: Cascade Books, 2008.

Dixon, Thomas. *From Passions to Emotions: The Creation of a Secular Psychological Category*. Cambridge: Cambridge University Press, 2003.

Donfried, Karl Paul. "A Short Note on Romans 16." In *The Romans Debate*, edited by Karl P. Donfried, 44–52. Edinburgh: T. & T. Clark, 1991.

Dox, Donnalee. *Reckoning with Spirit in the Paradigm of Performance*. Ann Arbor: University of Michigan Press, 2016.

Duffin, Aoife. "Katherine Played by Aoife Duffin: Interview with Rona Kelly." In *Adopt an Actor*. Shakespeare's Globe, 2016.

Dulwich Centre. "What Is Narrative Therapy?" The Dulwich Centre. http://dulwichcentre.com.au/what-is-narrative-therapy.

Dunn, James D.G. *Christology in the Making: A New Testament Inqiry into the Origins of the Doctrine of the Incarnation*. 2nd ed. London: SCM, 1989.

Dunnum, Eric. "'Not to Be Altered': Performance's Efficacy and Audience Reaction in *The Roman Actor*." *Comparative Drama* 46 (2012) 517–43.

Ehrensperger, Kathy. *Paul and the Dynamics of Power: Communication and Interaction in the Early Christ-Movement*. Library of New Testament Studies. Edited by Mark Goodacre London: T. & T. Clark, 2007.

———. *That We May Be Mutually Encouraged*. New York: T. & T. Clark, 2004.

Eisenbaum, Pamela Michelle. "Is Paul the Father of Mysogyny and Antisemitism?" *Cross Currents* 50 (2000) 506–24.

Ekman, Paul. "What Scientists Who Study Emotion Agree About." *Perspectives on Psychological Science* 11.1 (2016) 31–34.

Ekman, Paul, Eve Ekman, and The Dalai Lama. "Atlas of Emotion." http://atlasofemotions.com.

Elliott, Mark W. "Romans 7 in the Reformation Century." In *Reformation Readings of Romans*, edited by Kathy Ehrensperger and R. Ward Holder, 171–88. Romans through History and Cultures. New York: T. & T. Clark, 2008.

Erikson, Jorgen Weidemann. "Should Soldiers Think before They Shoot?" *Journal of Military Ethics* 9 (2010) 195–218.
Esler, Philip F. "Social Identity, the Virtues, and the Good Life: A New Approach to Romans 12:1—15:13." *Biblical Theology Bulletin* 33 (2003) 51–63.
Fairbairn, Susan, and Gavin Fairbairn. "Why Use Storytelling as a Research Approach?" In *Perspectives on Storytelling: Framing Global and Personal Identities*, edited by Lena Möller, Minerva Ahumada, and Laurinda Brown, 3–10. Oxford: Inter-Disciplinary, 2014.
Feldman Barrett, Lisa. "Constructing Emotion." *Psychological Topics* 20 (2011) 359–80.
Fischer-Lichte, Erika. *Ästhetik des Performativen*. Edition Suhrkamp. Frankfurt: Suhrkamp, 2004.
Foley, John Miles. "Man, Muse, and Story: Psychohistorical Patterns in Oral Epic Poetry." *Oral Tradition* 2 (1987) 91–107.
Fowler, Robert M. "In the Boat with Jesus: Imagining Ourselves in Mark's Story." In *Mark as Story: Retrospect and Prospect*, edited by Kelly R. Iverson and Christopher W. Skinner, 233–58. Resources for Biblical Study 65. Atlanta: Society of Biblical Literature, 2011.
Fredriksen, Paula. "Jewish Romans, Christian Romans, and the Post-Roman West: The Social Correlates of the *Contra Iudaeos* Tradition." In *Conflict and Religious Conversation in Latin Christendom: Studies in Honour of Ora Limor*, edited by Israel Jacob Yuval and Ram Ben-Shalom, 23–53. Cultural Encounters in Late Antiquity and the Middle Ages 17. Turnhout: Brepols, 2014.
———. "Paul's Letter to the Romans, the Ten Commandments, and Pagan 'Justification by Faith.'" *JBL* 133 (2014) 801–8.
Freshwater, Helen. *Theatre and Audience*. Basingstoke, UK: Palgrave Macmillan, 2009.
Friberg, Timothy, Barbara Friberg, and Neva F. Miller. *Analytical Lexicon of the Greek New Testament*. Grand Rapids: Baker, 2000.
Gale, Mariah. "Isabella Played by Mariah Gale: Early Rehearsal Part 1." In *Adopt an Actor*. Shakespeare's Globe, 2015.
———. "Isabella Played by Mariah Gale: Performance 1." In *Adopt an Actor*. Shakespeare's Globe, 2015.
Gallagher, Shawn. *How the Body Shapes the Mind*. Oxford: Oxford Scholarship Online, 2006.
Gamble, Harry. *The Textual History of the Letter to the Romans: A Study in Textual and Literary Criticism*. Studies and Documents. Edited by Irving Alan Sparks. Grand Rapids: Eerdmans, 1977.
Garrison, Roman. "Phoebe, the Servant-Benefactor and Gospel Traditions." In *Text and Artifact in the Religions of Mediterranean Antiquity*, edited by Stephen G. Wilson and Michel Desjardins, 63–73. Waterloo, ON: Wildrid Laurier University Press, 2000.
Garroway, Joshua. "The Circumcision of Christ: Romans 15:7–13." *JSNT* 34 (2012) 303–22.
Gaventa, Beverly Roberts. "The Cosmic Power of Sin in Paul's Letter to the Romans: Towards a Widescreen Edition." *Interpretation* 58 (2004) 229–40.
———. *Our Mother Saint Paul*. Louisville: Westminster John Knox, 2007.
———. "Romans." In *Women's Bible Commentary. Expanded Edition*, edited by Carol A. Newsom and Sharon H. Ringe 403–10. Louisville: Westminster John Knox, 1998.

———. "The Shape of the "I": The Psalter, the Gospel, and the Speaker in Romans 7." In *Apocalyptic Paul. Cosmos and Anthropos in Romans 5–8*, edited by Beverly Roberts Gaventa, 77–91. Waco, TX: Baylor University Press, 2013.

Gibbs Raymond W., Jr. *Embodiment and Cognitive Science*. Cambridge: Cambridge University Press, 2005.

———. "Walking the Walk While Thinking About the Talk: Embodied Interpretation of Metaphorical Narratives." *Journal of Psycholinguistic Research* 42 (2013) 363–78.

Giles, Terry, and William Doan. *The Naomi Story—the Book of Ruth: From Gender to Politics*. Eugene, OR: Cascade Books, 2016.

———. "Performance Criticism of the Hebrew Bible." *Religion Compass* 2 (2008) 273–86.

———. *Twice Used Songs. Performance Criticism of the Songs of Ancient Israel*. Peabody, MA: Hendrickson, 2009.

Gillan, Maria Mazziotti. "What the Body Knows." *Prairie Schooner* 81.4 (2007) 111–12.

Goodspeed, Edgar J. "Phoebe's Letter of Introduction." *Harvard Theological Reveiw* 44 (1951) 55–57.

Gorman, Michael J. *Becoming the Gospel: Paul, Participation, and Mission*. Grand Rapids: Eerdmans, 2015.

Graver, Viv. "Lucy Ellinson—Creating Puck, *A Midsummer Night's Dream*." In *RSC Blogs: Pathways to Shakespeare*. Royal Shakespeare Company.

———. "Paapa Essiedou." In *RSC Blogs. Pathways to Shakespeare*. Royal Shakespeare Company.

Gregg, Robert C. *Shared Stories, Rival Tellings: Early Encounters of Jews, Christians, and Muslims*. Oxford: Oxford University Press, 2015.

Gross, Jessica. "The Price of Being Single." *TED Explore Ideas Worth Spreading* (2015). Published electronically 21 October. http://ideas.ted.com/the-price-of-being-single/?Utm_campaign=social&utm_medium=referral &utm_source=facebook.com&utm_content=ideasblog&utm_term=global-social issues.

Gruber, June. "Human Emotion 1.2: Introduction." In *Human Emotion*. New Haven: Yale Broadcasting and Media Centre, yalecourses, 2013.

———. "Human Emotion 1.3: What Is an Emotion?" In *Human Emotion*. New Haven: Yale Broadcasting and Media Centre, yalecourses, 2013.

Gundry, Robert H. *Sōma in Biblical Theology: With Emphasis on Pauline Anthropology*. Society for New Testament Society Monograph Series 29. Cambridge: Cambridge University Press, 1976.

Gundry, Robert H. "The Moral Frustration of Paul before His Conversion: Sexual Lust in Romans 7:7–25." In *Pauline Studies: Essays Presented to Professor F.F. Bruce on His 70th Birthday*, edited by Donald A. Hagner and Murray J. Harris, 228–45. Grand Rapids: Eerdmans, 1980.

Gunn, David M. "Narrative Criticism." In *To Each Its Own Meaning*, edited by Steven L. McKenzie and Stephen R. Haynes, 201–29. Louisville: Westminster John Knox, 1999.

Habel, Norman C., ed. *Readings from the Perspective of Earth*. Earth Bible 1. Sheffield: Sheffield Academic, 2000.

Hearon, Holly E. "Characters in Text and Performance: The Gospel of John." In *From Text to Performance: Narrative and Performance Criticisms in Dialogue and Debate*, edited by Kelly R. Iverson, 53–79. Biblical Performance Criticism 10. Eugene, OR: Cascade Books, 2014.

———. "From Narrative to Performance: Methodological Considerations and Interpretive Moves." In *Mark as Story: Retrospect and Prospect*, edited by Kelly R. Iverson and Christopher W. Skinner, 211–32. Resources for Biblical Study 65. Atlanta: SBL, 2011.

———. "The Interplay between Written and Spoken Word in the Second Testament as a Background to the Emergence of Written Gospels." *Oral Tradition* 25 (2010) 57–74.

Hearon, Holly E., and Philip Ruge-Jones. "Preface." In *The Bible in Ancient and Modern Media: Story and Performance*, edited by Holly E. Hearon and Philip Ruge-Jones, xi–xii. Biblical Performance Criticism 1. Eugene, OR: Cascade Books, 2009.

Hefner, Philip, Ann Milliken Pederson, and Susan Barreto. *Our Bodies Are Selves*. Cambridge: Lutterworth, 2015.

Helms, Lorraine. "Playing the Woman's Part: Feminist Criticism and Shakespearean Performance." *Theatre Journal* 41 (1989) 190–200.

Henricks, Thomas S. *Selves, Societies and Emotions: Understanding the Pathways of Experience*. Boulder, CO: Paradigm, 2012.

Heschel, Susannah. *The Aryan Jesus: Christian Theologians and the Bible in Nazi Germany*. Princeton: Princeton University Press, 2008.

Hiebert, D. Edmond. "Behind the Word 'Deacon': A New Testament Study." *Bibliotheca Sacra* 140/558 (1983) 151–62.

Hill, Wesley. *Paul and the Trinity: Persons, Relations, and the Pauline Letters*. Grand Rapids: Eerdmans, 2015.

Horrell, David G. *Solidarity and Difference: A Contemporary Reading of Paul's Ethics*. London: T. & T. Clark, 2005.

Hristic, Jovan. "On the Interpretation of Drama." *New Literary History* 3 (1972) 345–54.

Hunt, Cheryl. "Be Ye Speakers of, and Listeners to, the Word: The Promotion of Biblical Engagement Through Encountering the Scriptures Read Aloud." *Expository Times* 129 (2018) 149–57.

Hurtado, Larry W. "Oral Fixation and New Testament Studies? 'Orality,' 'Performance' and Reading Texts in Early Christianity." *New Testament Studies* 60 (2014) 321–40.

Iverson, Kelly R. "Performance Criticism." In *The Oxford Encyclopedia of Biblical Interpretation*, edited by Stephen L. McKenzie. Oxford: Oxford University Press, 2014 (Online: accessed 24/01/2020).

———. "The Present Tense of Performance: Immediacy and Transformative Power in Luke's Passion." In *From Text to Performance. Narrative and Performance Criticisms in Dialogue and Debate*, edited by Kelly R. Iverson, 131–57. Biblical Performance Criticism 10. Eugene, OR: Cascade Books, 2014.

———. "'Wherever the Gospel Is Preached.' The Paradox of Secrecy in the Gospel of Mark." In *Mark as Story: Retrospect and Prospect*, edited by Kelly R. Iverson, and Christopher W. Skinner, 181–209. Resources for Biblical Study 65. Atlanta: Society of Biblical Literature, 2011.

Iverson, Kelly R., and Christopher W. Skinner, ed. *Mark as Story: Retrospect and Prospect*. Resources for Biblical Study 65. Atlanta: SBL, 2011.

Jacox, Francis. *Traits of Character and Notes of Incident in the Bible*. London: Hodder & Stoughton, 1873.

Jaggar, Alison. "Love and Knowledge: Emotion in Feminist Epistemology." In *Gender/Body/Knowledge*, edited by Alison Jaggar and Susan Bordo, 145–71. New Brunswick, NJ: Rutgers University Press, 1989.

Jervell, Jacob. "The Letter to Jerusalem." In *The Romans Debate*, edited by Karl P. Donfried, 53–64. Edinburgh: T. & T. Clark, 1991.

Jewett, Robert. "Paul, Phoebe, and the Spanish Mission." In *The Social World of Formative Christianity and Judaism: Essays in Tribute to Howard Clark Kee*, edited by Jacob Nesner et al., 142–61. Philadelphia: Fortress, 1988.

———. *Romans: A Commentary*. Hermeneia. Minneapolis: Fortress, 2007.

Johansson Falck, Marlene, and Raymond W. Gibbs Jr. "Embodied Motivations for Metaphorical Meanings." *Cognitive Linguistics* 23 (2012) 251–72.

Johnson, Lee. A. "Paul's Letters Reheard: A Performance-critical Examination of the Preparation, Transportation, and Delivery of Paul's Correspondence." *The Catholic Biblical Quarterly* 79 (2017) 60–76.

Johnson, Mark. *The Body in the Mind: The Bodily Basis of Meaning, Imagination and Reason*. Chicago: University of Chicago Press, 1987.

Joynes, Christine E. "Visualizing Salome's Dance of Death: The Contribution of Art to Biblical Exegesis." In *Between the Text and the Canvas: The Bible and Art in Dialogue*, edited by J. Cheryl Exum and Ela Nutu, 145–63. Bible in the Modern World 13. Sheffield: Sheffield Phoenix, 2007.

Keck, Leander E. *Romans*. Abingdon New Testament Commentaries. Nashville: Abingdon, 2005.

Kelber, Werner H. *The Oral and the Written Gospel: The Hermeneutics of Speaking and Writing in the Synoptic Tradition, Mark, Paul, and Q*. Philadelphia: Fortress, 1983.

Kemp, Rick. *Embodied Acting: What Neuro-Science Tells Us about Performance*. London: Routledge, 2012.

Kennedy, George A. *New Testament Interpretation through Rhetorical Criticism*. Studies in Religion. Chapel Hill: The University of North Carolina Press, 1984.

Khiok-Khng, Yeo. "Differentiation and Mutuality of Male-Female Relations in 1 Corinthians 112–16." *Biblical Research* 43 (1998) 15.

Kierkegaard, Søren. *Purity of Heart*. Translated by Douglas V. Steere. New York: Harper & Row, 1938.

Kreglinger, Gisela H. *Storied Revelations. Parables, Imagination and George MacDonald's Christian Fiction*. Cambridge: Lutterworth, 2014.

Lampe, G. W. H., ed. *A Patristic Greek Lexicon*. Oxford: Clarendon, 1961.

Lampe, Peter. "The Roman Christians of Romans 16." In *The Romans Debate*, edited by Karl P. Donfried, 216–30. Edinburgh: T. & T. Clark, 1991.

Langton, Daniel R. *The Apostle Paul in the Jewish Imagination: A Study in Modern Jewish-Christian Relations*. New York: Cambridge University Press, 2010.

Lawrence, Jeff. "The Spiritual Pilgrimage of a Biblical Storyteller: 'A' Guidebook for the Journey." Brisbane College of Theology, 2006.

Lee, Ahmi. *Preaching God's Grand Drama. A Biblical-Theological Approach*. Grand Rapids: Baker Academic, 2019.

Lee, Margaret Ellen, and Bernard Brandon Scott. *Sound Mapping the New Testament*. Salem, OR: Polebridge, 2009.

Levy, Shimon. *The Bible as Theatre*. Brighton: Sussex Academic, 2002.

Liddell, Henry George, Robert Scott, Henry Stuart Jones, and Roderick McKenzie. *A Greek-English Lexicon New Edition*. 2 vols. Oxford: Oxford University Press, 1940.

Livesey, Nina E. "Sounding out the Heirs of Abraham (Rom 4:9–12)." *Oral Tradition* 27 (2012) 273–90.

Long, Burke. O. "Recent Field Studies in Oral Literature and Their Bearing on OT Criticism." *Vetus Testamentum* 26 (1976) 187–198.
Longenecker, Bruce, ed. *Narrative Dynamics in Paul: A Critical Assessment*. Louisville: Westminster John Knox, 2002.
Longenecker, Richard N. *The Epistle to the Romans*. New International Greek Testament Commentary. Grand Rapids: Eerdmans, 2016.
MacGillivray, Erlend D. "Romans 16:2 *Prostatis/Prostates*, and the Application of Reciprocal Relationships to New Testament Texts." *Novum Testamentum* 53 (2011) 17.
Malbon, Elizabeth Struthers. "Characters in Mark's Story: Changing Perspectives on the Narrative Process." In *Mark as Story. Retrospect and Prospect*, edited by Kelly R. Iverson and Christopher W. Skinner, 45–69. Resources for Biblical Study 65. Atlanta: SBL, 2011.
Martin, Dale B. *Sex and the Single Savior: Gender and Sexuality in Biblical Interpretation*. Louisville: Westminster John Knox, 2006.
Mathew, Susan. "Women in the Greetings of Romans 16:1–16: A Study of Mutuality and Women's Ministry in the Letter to the Romans." PhD diss., Durham University, 2010.

———. *Women in the Greetings of Romans 16:1–16: A Study of Mutuality and Women's Ministry in the Letter to the Romans*. Library of New Testament Studies 471. London: Bloomsbury T. & T. Clark, 2013.
Mathews, Jeanette. *Performing Habakkuk: Faithful Re-Enactment in the Midst of Crisis*. Eugene: Pickwick, 2012.
Maxey, James A., and Ernst R. Wendland. *Translating Scripture for Sound and Performance: New Directions in Biblical Studies*. Biblical Performance Criticism Series 6. Eugene, OR: Cascade Books, 2012.
Maxwell, Kathy. "From Performance to Text to Performance: The New Testament's Use of the Hebrew Bible in a Rhetorical Culture." In *From Text to Performance: Narrative and Performance Criticisms in Dialogue and Debate*, edited by Kelly R. Iverson, 158–81. Biblical Performance Criticism Series 10. Eugene, OR: Cascade Books, 2014.
May, Melanie. "'A Body Knows': Writing Resurrection." *Cross Currents* 46 (1996) 343–51.
McKenna, Megan. *Keepers of the Story: Oral Traditions in Religion*. New York: Seabury, 2004.
McKenzie, Alyce M. "At the Intersection of *Actio Divina* and *Homo Performans*: Embodiment and Evocation." In *Performance in Preaching. Bringing the Sermon to Life*, edited by Jana Childers and Clayton J. Schmit, 53–66. Grand Rapids: Baker Academic, 2008.
McKnight, Edgar V. "Reader-Response Criticism." In *To Each Its Own Meaning: An Introduction to Biblical Criticism*, edited by Stephen R. Haynes and Steven L. McKenzie, 197–219. Louisville: Westminster John Knox, 1993.
Melters, Barbara, Alan Schwartz, and Ilana Ritov. "Emotion-Based Choice." *Journal of Experimental Psychology* 128 (1999) 332–45.
Merleau-Ponty, Maurice. *Phenomology of Perception*. Translated by Colin Smith. London: Routledge, 1996.
Miller, Marvin Lloyd. *Performances of Ancient Jewish Letters: From Elephantine to MMT*. Journal of Ancient Judaism Supplements. Göttingen: Vandenhoeck & Ruprecht, 2015.

Morgan, Alice. *What Is Narrative Therapy? An Easy-to-Read Introduction*. Adelaide: Dulwich Centre, 2000.

Muir, John. "A Shakespearean Actor on Acting. Interview with Simon Callow." 2012.

Nanos, Mark D. "Romans. Introduction and Annotations." In *The Jewish Annotated New Testament*, edited by Amy-Jill Levine and Marc Zvi Brettler, 253–86. New York: Oxford University Press, 2011.

"NBS Seminar." Network of Biblical Storytellers, http://nbsint.org/nbsseminar.

Ng, Esther Yue L. "Phoebe as Prostatis." *Trinity Journal* 25 (2004) 3–13.

Nicholls, Rachel. "Is Wirkungsgeschichte (or Reception History) a Kind of Intellectual Parkour (or Freerunning)?" In *British New Testament Conference*, 2005.

Novak, Julia. "Performing the Poet, Reading (to) the Audience: Some Thoughts on Live Poetry as Literary Communication." *Journal of Literary Theory* 6 (2012) 358–82.

Novenson, Matthew V. "The Jewish Messiahs, the Pauline Christ, and the Gentile Question." *JBL* 128 (2009) 357–73.

Nussbaum, Martha C. *Upheavals of Thought: The Intelligence of Emotions*. Cambridge: Cambridge University Press, 2001.

Oakes, Peter. "Made Holy by the Holy Spirit: Holiness and Ecclesiology in Romans." In *Holiness and Ecclesiology in the New Testament*, edited by Kent E. Brower and Andy Johnson, 167–83. Grand Rapids: Eerdmans, 2007.

Oestreich, Bernhard. *Performance Criticism of the Pauline Letters*. Translated by Lindsay Elias and Brent Blum. Biblical Performance Criticism Series 14. Eugene, OR: Cascade Books, 2016.

Ohira, Hideki. "Beneficial Roles of Emotion in Decision Making: Functional Association of Brain and Body." *Psychological Topics* 20 (2011) 381–92.

Osiek, Carolyn. "Diakonos and Prostatis: Women's Patronage in Early Christianity." *HTS Theological Studies* 61 (2005) 347–70.

———. "The Politics of Patronage and the Politics of Kinship: The Meeting of the Ways." *Biblical Theology Bulletin* 39 (2009) 143–52.

Otto, Tim. *Oriented to Faith: Transforming the Conflict over Gay Relationships*. Eugene, OR: Cascade Books, 2014.

"Oxford Dictionaries." Oxford University Press. https://en.oxforddictionaries.com.

Park, Eung Chun. *Either Jew or Gentile: Paul's Unfolding Theology of Inclusivity*. Louisville: Westminster John Knox, 2003.

Parker, Holt N. "The Teratogenic Grid." In *Roman Sexualities*, edited by Judith P. Hallett and Marilyn B. Skinner, 47–65. Princeton: Princeton University Press, 1997.

Pasquarello III, Michael. "Narrative Reading, Narrative Preaching: Inhabiting the Story." In *Narrative Reading, Narrative Preaching: Reuniting New Testament Interpretation and Proclamation*, edited by Joel B. Green and Michael Pasquarello III, 177–93. Grand Rapids: Baker Academic, 2003.

Pereira, Nancy Cardoso. "The Body as Hermeneutical Category: Guidelines for a Femenist Hermeneutics of Liberation." *Ecumenical Review* 54 (2002) 235–39.

Perry, Peter S. *Insights from Performance Criticism*. Insights. Minneapolis: Fortress, 2016.

Porter, Stanley E. *Linguistic Analysis of the Greek New Testament: Studies in Tools, Methods, and Practice*. Grand Rapids: Baker Academic, 2015.

Pryce, Jonathan. "Shylock Played by Jonathan Pryce. Pre and Early Rehearsal." In *Adopt an Actor*. Shakespeare's Globe, 2015.

Radbourne, Jennifer, Katya Johanson, Hilary Glow, and Tabitha White. "The Audience Experience: Measuring Quality in the Performing Arts." *International Journal of Arts Management* 11.3 (2009) 16–29.

Radosevic, Tracy. "Carnal Knowledge: How Performance Criticism Can Provide Insights into Biblical Women." *Oral History Journal of South Africa* 5.2 (2017) 1–7.

Raffel, Burton. "Who Heard the Rhymes, and How: Shakespeare's Dramaturgical Signals." *Oral Tradition* 11 (1996) 190–221.

Ralston, Joshua. "The Same God, or the One God? On the Limitations and the Implications of the Wheaton Affair." Australian Broadcasting Commission. http://www.abc.net.au/religion/articles/2016/01/12/4386793.htm.

Reid, Barbara E. *Wisdom's Feast: An Invitation to Feminist Interpretation of the Scriptures.* Grand Rapids: Eerdmans, 2016.

Rhoads, David. "Biblical Performance Criticism: Performance as Research." *Oral Tradition* 25 (2010) 157–98.

———. "Narrative Criticism and the Gospel of Mark." *Journal of the American Academy of Religion* 50 (1982) 411–34.

———. "The New Testament as Oral Performance." Moravian Seminary, 2016.

———. "Performance Criticism: An Emerging Methodology in Second Testament Studies—Part 1." *Biblical Theology Bulletin* 36 (2006) 118–33.

———. "Performance Criticism: An Emerging Methodology in Second Testament Studies—Part 2." *Biblical Theology Bulletin* 36 (2006) 164–84.

Rhoads, David, and Donald Michie. *Mark as Story: An Introduction to the Narrative of a Gospel.* 1st ed. Philadelphia: Fortress, 1982.

Rhoads, David, and Joanna Dewey. "Performance Criticism: A Paradigm Shift in New Testament Studies." In *From Text to Performance: Narrative and Performance Criticisms in Dialogue and Debate*, edited by Kelly R. Iverson, 1–26. Biblical Performance Criticism Series 10. Eugene, OR: Cascade Books, 2014.

Rhoads, David, Joanna Dewey, and Donald Michie. *Mark as Story: An Introduction to the Narrative of a Gospel.* 3rd ed. Minneapolis: Fortress, 2012.

———. "Reflections." In *Mark as Story: Retrospect and Prospect*, edited by Kelly R. Iverson and Christopher W. Skinner, 261–82. Society of Biblical Literature: Resources for Biblical Study. Atlanta: SBL, 2011.

Ricoeur, Paul. *The Rule of Metaphor: Multi-Disciplinary Studies in the Creation of Meaning in Language.* Translated by Kathleen McLaughlin et al. London: Routledge & Kegan Paul, 1978.

Rosenthal, Sheila. "Shakespeare as Biblical Performance Critic." *Oral History Journal of South Africa* 5.2 (2017) 1–16.

Rottman, John M. "Performative Language and the Limits of Performance in Preaching." In *Performance in Preaching: Bringing the Sermon to Life*, edited by Jana Childers and Clayton J. Schmit, 67–86. Grand Rapids: Baker Academic, 2008.

Ruether, Rosemary Radford. *Sexism and God-Talk: Towards a Feminist Theology.* Boston: Beacon, 1983.

Ruge-Jones, Philip. "Those Sitting around Jesus: Situating the Storyteller within Mark's Gospel." In *From Text to Performance: Narrative and Performance Criticisms in Dialogue and Debate*, edited by Kelly R. Iverson, 27–52. Bilbical Performance Criticism Series 10. Eugene, OR: Cascade Books, 2014.

———. "Omnipresent, Not Omniscient: How Literary Interpretation Confuses the Storyteller's Narrating." In *Between Author and Audience in Mark: Narration,*

Characterization, Interpretation, edited by Elizabeth Struthers Malbon, 29–43. New Testament Monographs 23. Sheffield: Sheffield Phoenix, 2009, 2013.

———. "The Word Heard: How Hearing a Text Differs from Reading One." In *The Bible in Ancient and Modern Media: Story and Performance*, edited by Holly E. Hearon and Philip Ruge-Jones, 101–13. Biblical Performance Criticism Series 1. Eugene, OR: Cascade Books, 2009.

Saunders, Stanley P. "Revelation and Resistance: Narrative and Worship in John's Apocalypse." In *Narrative Reading, Narrative Preaching: Reuniting New Testament Interpretation and Proclamation*, edited by Joel B. Green, and Michael Pasquarello III, 117–50. Grand Rapids: Baker Academic, 2003.

Schutte, P. J. W. "When *They, We,* and the Passive Become *I*: Introducing Autobiographical Biblical Criticism." *HTS Theological Studies* 61 (2005) 401–16.

Schwerdtfeger, Patrick. "Learned Intuition." In *TEDx Sacramento*: TEDx Talks, 2013.

"Scottish Storytelling Centre." Traditional Arts and Culture Scotland. http://www.tracscotland.org/scottish-storytelling-centre.

Seal, David, and Michael Partridge. *Performing Scripture*. Cambridge: Grove, 2019.

Seligman, Martin E. P., and Michael Kahana. "Unpacking Intuition: A Conjecture." *Perspectives on Psychological Science* 4 (2009) 399–402.

Seow, Choon Leong. "Consequences of Scripture: The Case of Job." In *Gunning Lecture Series*. Edinburgh: University of Edinburgh, 2015.

Shann, Steve. "Mating with the World: On the Mythopoetic Nature and Function of Storytelling." In *Perspectives on Storytelling: Framing Global and Personal Identities*, edited by Lena Möller, Minerva Ahumada, and Laurinda Brown, 21–32. Oxford: Inter-Disciplinary, 2014.

Shann, Steve, and Rachel Cunneen. "Mythopoetics and the English Classroom." *English in Australia* 46.2 (2011) 47–56.

Shapiro, Lawrence. *Embodied Cognition*. Abingdon: Routledge, 2011.

Shiell, William David. *Reading Acts: The Lector and the Early Christian Audience*. Biblical Interpretation Series 70. Leiden: Brill, 2004.

Shiner, Whitney. *Proclaiming the Gospel: First-Century Performance of Mark*. Harrisburg, PA: Trinity, 2003.

Shively, Elizabeth E., and Geert Van Oyen, eds. *Communication, Pedagogy, and the Gospel of Mark*. Resources for Biblical Study 83. Atlanta: SBL, 2016.

Skinner, Christopher W. "Telling the Story: The Appearance and Impact of *Mark as Story*." In *Mark as Story: Retrospect and Prospect*, edited by Kelly R. Iverson and Christopher W. Skinner, 1–16. Resources for Biblical Study 65. Atlanta: Society of Biblical Literature, 2011.

Slate Project Baltimore, The. "Slateprojectbaltimore." https://www.youtube.com/user/slateprojectbmore.

Smith, Tiffany Watt. *The Book of Human Emotions: An Encyclopedia of Feeling from Anger to Wanderlust*. London: Profile, 2015.

———. "Buzz Words." *New Scientist* 227/3039 (2016) 39–41.

Solomon, Robert C. *What Is an Emotion? Classic and Contemporary Readings*. 2nd ed. Oxford: Oxford University Press, 2003.

Stanislavski, Konstantin. *An Actor's Work: A Student's Diary*. Translated by Jean Bendetti. London: Routledge, 2008.

Stanislavski, Constantin. *An Actor Prepares*. Translated by Elizabeth Reynolds Hapgood. London: Bles, 1937.

Stendahl, Krister. *Paul among Jews and Gentiles, and Other Essays*. London: SCM, 1977.
Stott, John. *Between Two Worlds: The Challenge of Preaching Today*. Grand Rapids: Eerdmans, 1982.
Strasser, Mark. "The Future of Marriage (Family Law in the Twenty-First Century)." *Journal of the American Academy of Matrimonial Lawyers* 21 (2008) 87–119.
Swanson, Richard W. *Provoking the Gospel: Methods to Embody Biblical Storytelling through Drama*. Cleveland: Pilgrim, 2004.
———. *Provoking the Gospel of Matthew. A Storyteller's Commentary. Year A*. Cleveland: The Pilgrim, 2007.
———. "'This Is My . . .': Toward a Thick Performance of the Gospel of Mark." In *From Text to Performance: Narrative and Performance Criticisms in Dialogue and Debate*, edited by Kelly R. Iverson, 182–210. Biblical Performance Criticism Series 10. Eugene, OR: Cascade Books, 2014.
Sweet, Matthew. "The Luxury of Tears." *The Economist: 1843 magazine* April/May 2016, (2016). Published electronically March 2016. Https://http://www.1843magazine.com/features/the-luxury-of-tears.
Tait, Peta. "Bodies Perform Inner Emotions: Stanislavski's Legacy." *Australasian Drama Studies* 53 (2008) 84–102.
———. *Performing Emotions: Gender, Bodies, Spaces in Chekhov's Drama and Stanislavski's Theatre*. Aldershot, UK: Ashgate, 2002.
Thurston, Bonnie. *Women in the New Testament: Questions and Commentary*. New York: Crossroad, 1998.
Tillich, Paul. *The Courage to Be*. New Haven: Yale University Press, 1952.
Van Oyen, Geert. "No Performance Criticism without Narrative Criticism: Performance as a Test of Interpretation." In *Communication, Pedagogy, and the Gospel of Mark*, edited by Elizabeth E. Shively and Geert Van Oyen, 107–28. Resources for Biblical Study 83. Atlanta: SBL, 2016.
Walters, Jonathan. "Invading the Roman Body: Manliness and Impenetrability in Roman Thought." In *Roman Sexualities*, edited by Judith P. Hallett and Marilyn B. Skinner, 29–43. Princeton: Princeton University Press, 1997.
Walton, Heather. *Writing Methods in Theological Reflection*. London: SCM, 2014.
Ward, Richard F. "The End Is Performance: Performance Criticism and the Gospel of Mark." In *Preaching Mark's Unsettling Messiah*, edited by David Fleer and Dave Bland, 88–101. St Louis: Chalice, 2006.
———. "Pauline Voice and Presence as Strategic Communication." In *Semeia 65: Orality and Textuality in Early Christian Literature*, edited by Joanna Dewey, 95–107. Atlanta: SBL, 1995.
Ward, Richard F., and David J. Trobisch. *Bringing the Word to Life. Engaging the New Testament through Performing It*. Grand Rapids: Eerdmans, 2013.
Welton, Martin. *Feeling Theatre*. Basingstoke, UK: Palgrave Macmillan, 2012.
Whelan, Caroline F. "Amica Pauli: The Role of Phoebe in the Early Church." *JSNT* 49 (1993) 19.
White, Adam. "Visualising Paul's Appeal: A Performance-critical Analysis of the Letter to Philemon." *Oral History Journal of South Africa* 5.2 (2017) 1–16.
Whittle, Sarah. *Covenant Renewal and the Consecration of the Gentiles in Romans*. Society for New Testament Studies Monograph Series 161. New York: Cambridge University Press, 2015.

Wiebe, Rudy. "The Body Knows as Much as the Soul: On the Human Reality of Being a Writer." *Menonite Quarterly Review* 71 (1997) 189–200.

Wierzbicka, Anna. *Emotions across Languages and Cultures: Diversity and Universals*. Studies in Emotion and Social Interaction, sec. ser. Cambridge: Cambridge University Press, 1999.

Wilson, Glen D. *Psychology for Performing Artists: Butterflies and Bouquets*. London: Kingsley, 1994.

Wilson, Kelly Marie. "A Performance-critical Analysis of Lamentations." PhD diss., Catholic University of America, 2013.

Wire, Antoinette Clark. *The Case for Mark Composed in Performance*. Biblical Performance Criticism Series 3. Eugene, OR: Cascade Books, 2011.

———. *Holy Lives, Holy Deaths: A Close Hearing of Early Jewish Storytellers*. Studies in Biblical Literature 1. Atlanta: SBL, 2002.

———. "Performance, Politics, and Power: A Response." In *Semeia 65: Orality and Literacy in Early Christian Literature*, edited by Joanna Dewey, 129–35. Atlanta: SBL, 1995.

Witherington, Ben, III. *New Testament Rhetoric: An Introductory Guide to the Art of Persuasion in and of the New Testament*. Eugene, OR: Cascade Books, 2009.

———. *Paul's Letter to the Romans: A Socio-Rhetorical Commentary*. Grand Rapids: Eerdmans, 2004.

Wright, N. T. "The Letter to the Romans." In *The New Interpreter's Bible*, edited by Leanader E. Keck, 10:393–770. 12 vols. Nashville: Abingdon, 2002.

Wuellner, Wilhelm. "Paul's Rhetoric of Argumentation in Romans: An Alternative to the Donfried–Karris Debate over Romans." In *The Romans Debate*, edited by Karl P. Donfried, 128–46. Edinburgh: T. & T. Clark, 1991.

Zoubir-Shaw, Sadia. "Staging History: A Performative Experience." In *Embodied Performance: Design, Process and Narrative*, edited by Sadia Zoubir-Shaw, 5–26. Oxford: Inter-Disciplinary, 2016.

www.ingramcontent.com/pod-product-compliance
Lightning Source LLC
Chambersburg PA
CBHW050622300426
44112CB00012B/1615